The Peninsular War
1807–1814

The Peninsular War
1807-1814
A Concise Military History

Michael Glover

David & Charles
Newton Abbot   London

Archon Books
Hamden, Connecticut

1974

This edition first published 1974 in Great Britain by David & Charles (Holdings) Limited Newton Abbot Devon and in the United States of America by Archon Books 995 Sherman Avenue Hamden Connecticut 06514 USA

ISBN 0 7153 6387 5 (Great Britain)
ISBN 0 208 01426 8 (United States)

Set in 11 on 13pt Monotype Garamond
and printed in Great Britain
by Latimer Trend & Company Ltd Plymouth

Contents

List of Illustrations

PLATES

Preface

HISTORIES of the Peninsular War fall into two categories. There are the 'fully comprehensive', of which those of Napier and Oman are, deservedly, the best-known in English, and there are the 'crammer' type which are designed to assist the ambitious but unscholarly young officer to pass into the Staff College.* The 'crammers' give the skeleton of events during the war but do little to show that anything was involved but the movement of flags on a map. On the other hand, the 'fully comprehensive' type are immensely long. Oman's splendid *History of the Peninsular War* runs to 4,200 pages, $1\frac{1}{3}$ million words, apart from the appendices.

The aim of this book is to tell the story of the war in a comparatively concise form, less than one-twelfth of Oman's length, while relating it to the men who fought in Spain and Portugal, and to give some impression of what it was like to march and fight, to eat and be wounded, to command and be commanded at the beginning of the nineteenth century. Bound up with this must be some description of the technological limitations of warfare at this time, when the pace of battle was dictated by the rate at which a heavily laden infantryman could plod across country and the effect of fire power was limited by the capability of the principal weapon which was not notably accurate beyond the length of three cricket pitches.

If the human element is not to be sacrificed, the price of conciseness is massive omission. Deliberately this book concentrates on the

---

* In addition there are a large number of histories which do not set out to cover the whole course of the war. These include Jac Weller's *Wellington in the Peninsula*, Christopher Hibbert's *Corunna* and my own *Legacy of Glory* and *Britannia Sickens*.

struggle between the French and British armies. This was the decisive struggle. Busaco, Salamanca and Vitoria were the milestones to ultimate victory and defeat, but they are not the whole story. Behind the marches, countermarches, skirmishes, sieges and battles of Massena, Marmont, Moore, Soult and Wellington lies the vast, intricate sub-plot of the Spanish national effort to rid themselves of the invader. Spanish military history in this period veers between tragedy and farce. Their disasters were frequent and spectacular; their triumphs were myriad but, after July 1808, obscure. It was these obscure triumphs—a platoon shot down in an ambush, a courier and his message captured as he galloped across the plain—which made possible the orthodox victories of Wellington and his Anglo-Portuguese army and eventually the liberation of Portugal and Spain.

It is important to remember that behind all the manoeuvres and battles described in this book lies the Spanish contribution to victory, its all-pervasiveness and fragmentation making it impracticable to describe it in detail.

Whenever possible events are described in the words of those who took part in them. This method has its hazards. Memoirs written a decade or more after the war ended often contain embellishments which have crept in from frequent telling or from other men's accounts. What veteran of 1939–45 would care to take his oath on all his war reminiscences? Letters and diaries written at the time of the events they describe have their own perils. Usually the writer had only a partial knowledge of what was happening over the next ridge or even, in the thick black smoke of musketry, what was happening fifty yards away. Moreover, as Lord Alanbrooke pointed out when his own record of the Second World War was published, a diary 'is necessarily an impulsive and therefore somewhat unbalanced record of events'. The diary or letters of a junior officer, scrawled on his sabretache in a muddy bivouac or flea-ridden hovel, is unlikely to be a flawless record of events. First-hand accounts help to bring history to life, but the historian must cross-check them with other sources before using them as impeccable evidence.

With command decisions the situation is different. Hindsight is the curse of the historian, especially the military historian. A commander who has complete information about his enemy should have no difficulty in deciding a course of action, but Wellington, his colleagues and opponents never had more than a partial knowledge of what was happening 'on the other side of the hill'. In this case first-hand knowledge of the partial information available to commanders at the time they had to take their decisions is a vital element in the story.

The literature of the Peninsular War is vast. A not inconsiderable list of sources quoted in this book is given at the end, but this represents only a tiny proportion of the first-hand sources available. The reader who wishes to delve further into the subject may be glad to have some signposts to further reading. For the English-speaking student the largest and most fertile mine of information is the collection of Wellington's Despatches (abbreviated below as WD). There are eight volumes of these dealing with the Peninsula and five* more volumes in the Supplementary Despatches (SD) which contain also many letters written to Wellington. Only the committed enthusiast will wish to wade through this mass of information. It varies widely in interest and is very badly indexed. There is no better way of getting the flavour of it than to read Antony Brett James's *Wellington at War* (1961).

The French source most nearly comparable is the *Mémoires et Correspondance du Roi Joseph* (JN), of which volumes iv–ix refer to his time in Spain. Since the unfortunate king was never his own master, his published letters need to be supplemented from the *Correspondance de Napoléon 1er* (NC). Even the two together, supplemented by the published letters of Massena, Marmont and Jourdan (Soult's letters seem never to have been collected and published) do not add up to the same rounded picture as can be derived from the Wellington Despatches.

It is difficult to make a choice from the hundreds of volumes of reminiscences at a lower level in the armies. A personal selection from the books of British officers would include the Letters of

---

* To be precise, there are three volumes (SD vi, vii and viii) dealing wholly with the Peninsula, and substantial parts of two more (SD xiii and xiv) that also deal with it.

Simon Augustus Frazer, who commanded the Horse Artillery (1812–14), the Journal of Judge Advocate Larpent, covering roughly the same period, and the irresistibly gay *Adventures in the Rifle Brigade* by Johnny Kincaid. In the ranks *The Recollections of Rifleman Harris* are the best-known, but his Rifle comrades Surtees and Costello* wrote books which are more informative and almost as readable while, from the Fifty First, the *Letters of Private Wheeler* compare well with any of them. On the French side the autobiographies of Jourdan and Foy among the senior officers and those of Marbot and St-Chamans are the most illuminating. Marbot's memoirs, although very readable, are wildly unreliable. A most interesting civilian French source is the autobiography of Miot de Melito (MM), King Joseph's friend and confidant. Unfortunately the English translation, published in 1881, is abominable.

Two problems beset Peninsular historians. The first is the spelling of placenames. In the early eighteen-hundreds there was a good deal of fluidity in this matter in both Spain and Portugal and both French and English writers frequently had their own variations. Wherever possible the versions used in this book are those used on modern maps except where (eg Lisboa) they conflict with normal English practice.

The problem of the number of troops present at any one time is more complicated. French and Portuguese returns usually give the number of troops including both officers and soldiers. In the early stages of the war, however, Portuguese returns were works of imaginative fiction while French generals (although not their staff officers) were seldom averse to rigging a figure to prove a point. In particular it is never safe to trust any figure given by Marshal Soult in an official despatch.

British returns were trustworthy but confusing. Owing to the chaotic way in which the army was organised, gunners and engineers were returned separately from cavalry and infantry since they were

---

* It is not entirely regimental piety which gives the references to so many Greenjackets in this book. Statistics show that Riflemen were more literate (or at any rate more ready to go into print) than their red-coated comrades.

the responsibility of different cabinet ministers. Even then the usual return included only 'rank and file'.* In this book figures are given wherever possible as 'all ranks' but where they are shown as 'rank and file only' it is necessary to add approximately one-eighth for officers, sergeants and drummers, to reach a complete total.

Another complication in accounts of strength on both sides is the difference between the total number of troops in a force and the number of 'effectives' or *soldats présents sous armes*. There is a remarkable similarity between letters going from Spain to Paris and between Portugal and London in which harassed generals tried to explain to their governments that the number of troops sent to them was not the same as the number available for action. In June 1809 Wellesley, as he then was, wrote to the Secretary of State that, 'Nothing is more fallacious than the return you have sent me. It contains an enumeration of eleven battalions not arrived, of two gone to Gibraltar and of two ordered home. According to your account I have 35,000 men; according to my own I have only 18,000 [and] from all these returns a deduction of 10 in the 100 ought always to be made for the sick.'† Five months earlier Soult at Coruña had been patiently explaining to the Minister of War in Paris that although the strength of his corps was 44,395 only 23,000 were actually available for the invasion of Portugal, since he had more than 10,000 sick and even more who were strung out along the road back to Astorga either as garrisons or as stragglers. On this point generals in the field and historians have a problem in common.

MICHAEL GLOVER

---

* This figure was used because it represented the fire power of a battalion. Only corporals and privates carried muskets. Officers were armed with swords, and sergeants, except in light infantry and rifle regiments, carried halberds.

† The estimate of 10 per cent sick proved frequently to be too low. For example, according to the return for 29 Nov 1812 the total strength of the army was 53,648. Of these 19,540 were sick, 2,368 missing and 3,925 detached on various duties. The effective strength in rank and file was only 27,815.

His Majesty and the public have a right to expect from us that we should place a reasonable confidence in the gallantry and discipline of the troops under our command; and I have the satisfaction of reflecting that, having tried them frequently, they have never failed me.

WELLINGTON
20 September 1812

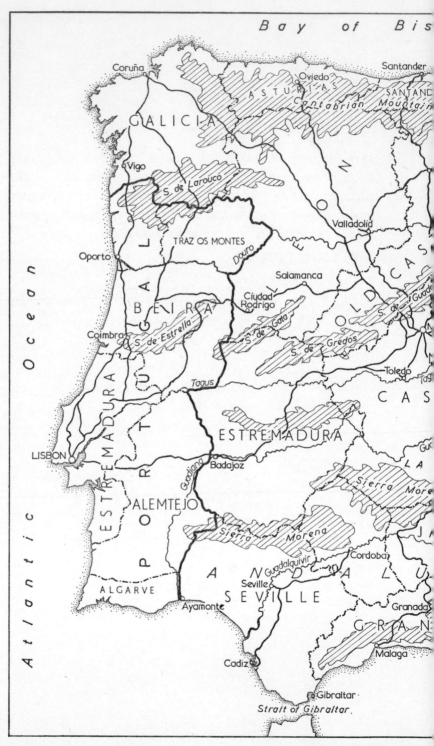

Spain and Portugal at t[...]

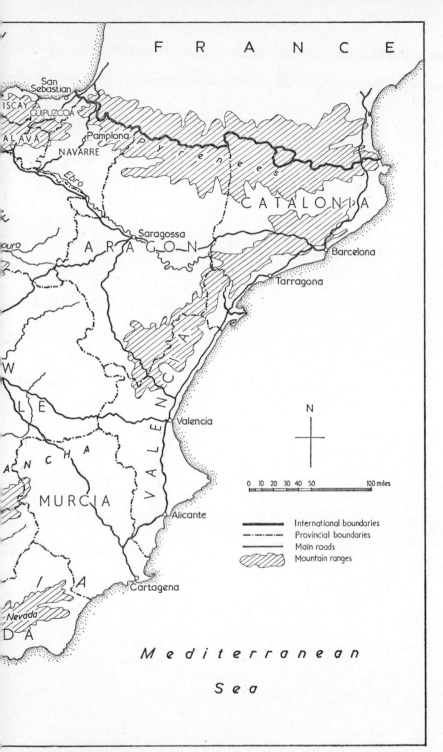

of the Peninsular War

PART ONE

Introduction

Note

The *Orders of Battle of the British Army* (Appendix 5) and the *Outlines of the Organisation of the French Army* (Appendix 6) are numbered individually and referred to in the text by these numbers, preceded by the appendix number. For example, the first Order of Battle is indicated in the text thus:[5/1]. No oblique strokes appear in the superior figures used to indicate reference notes.

CHAPTER I

Napoleon's Europe, 1807

NAPOLEON BONAPARTE attained power because France needed a strong man who could restore law, order and stability after the excesses of the Revolution. That upheaval had swept away the abuses and inefficiencies of the *ancien régime* and replaced them with the graft and incompetence of the Directory. The theorists, the idealists and the executioners had had their chance and produced only squalid chaos. In November 1799 France was prepared to accept a government far less liberal than that of the Bourbons provided it promised stability and paid lip-service to the ideals of the Revolution. The stage was set for absolute government and only one man seemed likely to be able to give the country internal tranquillity. General Bonaparte was only thirty but he was acknowledged as the first commander of his day. His 'whiff of grape shot' in 1795 had shown that he was able and willing to deal with civil tumult and, despite libels inspired by the Directory, he was recognised as a man who was not primarily interested in lining his own pockets. The *coup d'état* of 18th Brumaire whereby Bonaparte became one of three supposedly equal consuls was greeted with relief by all but a few discredited politicians. The proclaimed policy of the Consulate was 'Liberty, Victory and Peace'.

For nine years the promised diet of victory was forthcoming. Peace made only a pallid appearance for fourteen months in 1802–3. Liberty was an early casualty.

A month after Brumaire Bonaparte became First Consul; in 1801 Consul for life. In May 1804 he was proclaimed Emperor of the French. Democratic assemblies were reduced to consultative assemblies of decreasing influence, but Napoleon was doing the job for which the French had elevated him and he was doing it well. There was internal peace, a *modus vivendi* was reached with the church, a comprehensive code of laws was promulgated and, except where it conflicted with the interests of the state, it was enforced. New industries were established and captive markets conquered for them in Germany and Italy. Simultaneously power was concentrated in the Emperor's hands. His family and associates made fortunes but Napoleon was not interested in money. His lust was for power and glory.

A longing for *La Gloire* has been a characteristic of French rulers from Louis XIV to Charles de Gaulle. Napoleon, a Frenchman by adoption, embraced Glory with all the fervour of a convert. Endowed by nature with military genius and by the state with an apparently inexhaustible supply of conscripted soldiers, his longing for glory was disastrous. He became addicted to conquest. He was driven on by what a French historian has called 'the heroic urge to take risks, the magic lure of the dream, the irresistible impulse of his flashing temperament'.[1] 'My power,' he said, 'depends on my glory and my glory on the victories I have won. My power will fall if I do not feed it on new glories and new victories. Conquest has made me what I am and only conquest can enable me to hold my position.'[2]

The first three years of the Empire undoubtedly gave him victories. Ulm, Austerlitz, Jena and Friedland overthrew Austria and Prussia and humbled Russia. By July 1807 he was supreme in Europe. He was Emperor of the French and King of Italy. His brothers reigned in Holland, Naples and Westphalia. His troops occupied Prussia and her king was his abject client. Dalmatia and the Hanseatic towns were in his power. The princelings of the Rhine and the cantons of Switzerland acknowledged his protection. The Sultan of Turkey accepted his mediation. Bavaria and Saxony were his satraps. Russia, Austria and Spain were his allies. In all continental Europe only Sweden and distant Portugal were not subject to his direct influence. When he signed the Treaty of Tilsit with the Tsar in July 1807 and agreed to order the affairs of Europe to a scheme of his own devising his position seemed unassailable. His Foreign Minister commented, 'Now that he has made an agreement with

Russia, he is no longer afraid of any one.'³ So unafraid was he that
he immediately over-reached himself. 'The magic lure of the dream'
drove him too far.

Much of the Treaty of Tilsit dealt with measures to prevent
Britain trading with Europe. Britain remained Napoleon's implac-
able enemy. Whatever the vagaries of her foreign policy, Britain has
never been prepared to tolerate any single power dominating
Europe. Napoleon's France was doing just that and although the
British government was weak, ineffective and divided there was
never any serious question of making peace until French power had
been reduced to acceptable limits. The chances of achieving such a
reduction seemed remote in 1807. Britain's only allies were Portugal,
Sweden and Sicily. The sovereigns of the first two were mad. The
King of Sicily was feeble-minded and dominated by his termagant
queen. The British army was small and largely devoted to guarding
the home island and the overseas possessions. Such expeditionary
forces as had been sent to the continent since the French revolution
had shown themselves to be ill-organised, ill-supplied, ill-directed
and ill-led.

Britain's continuance as a belligerent depended on the Straits of
Dover and the dominance at sea of the Royal Navy. As long as the
fleet was in existence Britain could not be defeated. Conversely,
Britain could not win as long as the French army was in being. The
Royal Navy could not defeat the Grande Armée, nor could the
French Empire be brought to its knees by naval blockade. Europe
was self-supporting for food, and the blockade, apart from its
primary function of keeping the fleets of France and her allies in their
ports, was at least as much concerned with inserting British manu-
factures into the continent as with preventing Europe from import-
ing coffee and sugar.

The Royal Navy was a wasting asset. Its dominance depended on
the strength of its battle fleets. The battleships were unquestionably
the best-manned and the best-commanded in the world. Ship for
ship and squadron for squadron they were invincible, but their manpower was irreplaceable and the number of ships could not be
significantly increased. There were rather more than 100 battleships
and, excellent as they were, they could be overwhelmed by weight of

numbers. A French appreciation laid down that 'we shall be able to make peace safely when we have 150 ships of the line'.[4] Against a 50 per cent superiority in numbers the Royal Navy could not keep the sea-lanes open for long, especially as a proportion of the British strength must be on the far side of the Atlantic or in the Indian Ocean. After 1807 there was a constant danger that the United States, whose conduct in this situation closely foreshadowed that of Mussolini's Italy, would declare war on Britain in the hope of filching Canada as soon as French victory seemed certain. War with America could throw an intolerable strain on British naval resources.

Napoleon tried first to establish 50 per cent naval superiority by alliance and annexation. The combined French and Dutch fleets amounted, in 1807, to 75 ships of the line in various states of repair. The allied fleet of Spain could add 30 battleships and that of Russia 24 more. This would give a total of 129. Napoleon, a keen student of Steel's published lists of the strength of the Royal Navy, knew that the British strength was 104 battleships. He needed 27 more ships to gain a three-to-two superiority. The Danes had 17, the Portuguese 10. One of the secret clauses of the Treaty of Tilsit arranged that these two fleets should be acquired.

The British reacted to this threat with a speed and ruthlessness quite out of keeping with their previous conduct of the war. Details of the secret clauses of Tilsit reached London on 16 July.* Two days later orders were issued for a powerful fleet and 26,000 soldiers† to sail to Copenhagen and extract the Danish fleet by whatever means might be necessary. The Danes, who had been unfriendly neutrals ever since Nelson had destroyed their fleet in 1801, refused to hand over their ships until their capital had been bombarded for three days. Then they bowed to overwhelming force. Thirteen ships of the line and fourteen frigates, all that could be got ready for sea, were sailed to British ports. The remaining ships and the dockyards were burned.

---

* The information was not totally unexpected. In May 1807 the Prince Regent of Portugal had written to the Prince of Wales warning him that Napoleon intended to seize the Danish and Portuguese fleets.

† 8,000 of these men were already in the Baltic attempting to co-operate with the Swedes.

The British action at Copenhagen could scarcely have been more high-handed. Napoleon and the Whigs lost no opportunity of denouncing it as an act of piracy, an unprovoked act of aggression against a neutral state unable to defend itself. They were perfectly correct, although the Emperor weakened his moral case by announcing at the same time that, 'If Portugal does not do as I wish, the house of Braganca will no longer remain on the throne.'[5] The British government believed that it had no option. Unless Britain was prepared to become another of France's client states, she could not afford to let moral scruples prevent her from anticipating any French move to acquire ships of war. Nor could she afford to conclude a temporary peace. In it the British Parliament would insist on reducing all the armed forces while Napoleon would use any breathing space to press on with his naval building programme. With every dockyard from Cuxhaven to Trieste, saving only Lisbon, under his orders, an infinite supply of timber from the forests of Europe and a vast reservoir of trained manpower from the idle merchant fleets and fishing boats of Europe at his command, it needed only a short respite in the war to enable him to build and man a fleet which would swamp the Royal Navy.

A few men in the British government realised the seriousness of the situation, the inevitability of defeat if France could not be defeated within a comparatively short time. Those who did, and they included such under-rated figures as Spencer Perceval and Lord Liverpool, bore a burden of worry with a courage which is seldom realised. As Lord Melville, First Lord of the Admiralty, admitted in 1814, they knew that, given time, Napoleon would 'have sent forth such powerful fleets that our navy must eventually have been destroyed since we could never have kept pace with him in building ships or in equipping numbers sufficient to cope with the tremendous power he could have brought against us'.[6]

The seizure of the Danish fleet was only a negative success. It denied an asset to Napoleon but did nothing to help Britain win the war as she must do before very long. Somewhere, somehow a way must be found in which the British army could defeat the French. At the most optimistic calculation Britain could not commit more than 60,000 men to operations on the continent. The French army was more than a million strong and could call on support from France's allies, Austria, Prussia, Russia and Spain. In 1807 the British government had no idea how this problem could be solved. It was more than a year since French and British soldiers had exchanged shots. All that ministers could devise was a grandiose (and impracticable) scheme to seize the Spanish colonies in South America.

Napoleon solved the British problem for them. His loss of the Danish fleet made his acquisition of the Portuguese ships urgent. In his anxiety to secure it he sent a small army, unsupported, close to a coast where British seapower could land troops to crush it. To compound this error he made an irreconcilable enemy of his oldest ally across whose territory lay his communications with his isolated army. This combination of blunders added to his enemies two countries whose mountainous terrain went far to nullify the strength and efficiency of the Grande Armée. Into this inhospitable cul-de-sac he had to pour more than half a million French soldiers. He presented Britain with the support of two bitterly angry nations living in countries where a peasant with a knife was more than a match for a sentry with a musket, where a desperate band of roughly armed men could overpower a platoon of French veterans. The inveteracy of the Spanish and Portuguese peoples was so great that it compensated for the difference in size between the French and British armies. 'The magic lure of the dream' had led Napoleon to disaster.

CHAPTER 2

Arms and the Men

THE campaigns in the Peninsula can be understood only if the limitations under which armies operated are borne in mind. The first was the slowness with which troops moved and information travelled. An army's speed was controlled by the pace of the marching infantry. In battle this was little more than four miles an hour. In wide manoeuvring it was seldom more than fifteen miles a day. Forced marches could achieve remarkable distances. In Craufurd's famous march to Talavera the Light Brigade covered forty-two miles in twenty-six hours, mostly on sheep tracks under the heat of a Spanish July, but this was possible only with superb troops and for a limited period. After such a feat the soldiers would have to be rested and the steady fifteen miles a day would yield better results over long distances. Cavalry could cover longer distances but horses deteriorated more quickly than infantrymen under continuous long marching. Few roads in Spain and Portugal were better than cart tracks and, expecially in wet weather, an army would be constantly impeded by the difficulties of keeping the artillery and the supply train on the move.

The opening move of the war was Junot's march from the French frontier to Lisbon. He took forty-three days to cover 640 miles. For the first 300 miles he averaged twelve miles a day moving by main roads. He was then ordered to hurry but was directed to minor roads. His average rose to eighteen miles a day but he almost destroyed his army. He reached Lisbon with only a handful of picked infantry. His cavalry and artillery arrived ten days later having been forced to re-horse themselves on the road. More than five years later

Wellington achieved a remarkable administrative feat by marching an army of 80,000 men, three times the size of Junot's, from the Portuguese frontier to Vitoria at an average of more than fifteen miles a day without impairing the efficiency of any part of the force although the roads were no better than those Junot had used.*

Information also travelled slowly. Wellington's ADCs prided themselves on riding four miles in eighteen minutes or twelve in an hour,[1] but they were picked horsemen splendidly mounted. With a relay of horses a man could cover about 60 miles a day. From Ciudad Rodrigo to Badajoz is 174 miles. Military letters between them took from three to six days. Wellington rode the distance in seventy-six hours. His daily totals were 28, 51, 57 and 38 miles. On the last two days he left his baggage to follow and reached his destination at 2 pm on the fourth day.

For the French, long-distance riding usually took much longer. There were few parts of Spain and none of Portugal where a French horseman could travel unescorted. At every defile there was the danger of a guerrilla ambush. Early in 1813 the guerrillas of northern Spain were so effective that King Joseph did not receive a letter written in Paris on 18 December until 29 January. Wellington's communications with London were at the mercy of the winds in the Channel and the Atlantic. It was possible to get a letter from Plymouth to Freneda on the Portuguese frontier in seven-and-a-half days.[2] With foul winds the journey could take as many weeks.

A commander's freedom of action was circumscribed by the problems of feeding his army. As Wellington said, 'No troops can serve to any good purpose unless they are regularly fed. A starving army is actually worse than none.'[3] The French and British armies approached the problem in diametrically opposed ways. The French proceeded by requisition. Local magistrates were ordered to provide stated quantities of food at a stated time. They failed to comply at their peril. When fighting in a fertile countryside, as Napoleon was accustomed to do until 1812, this system worked well enough to provide not only sufficient for current needs but stocks for the lean

---

* It is fair to add that Junot performed his march in October-November with an improvised staff. Wellington's march was done at midsummer with a very experienced staff.

months. Even in peacetime, Spain was barely self-sufficient for food. Portugal relied on imports. The intrusion of a quarter of a million French troops and the dislocation which war caused to agriculture made it impossible for the Peninsula to provide rations for the French armies unless the inhabitants starved. This they were reluctant to do.

The continual requisitioning of irreplaceable food did more than any other factor to swell the ranks of the guerrillas. The longer the war continued, the less effective requisitioning became. The smaller the yield, the smaller the rations issued to the French. The smaller the rations, the more the French seized by force, thus driving more embittered and desperate men into the guerrillas. Napoleon harboured many misconceptions about Spain but none was more disastrous than the belief he acquired during his short stay in the country in 1808–9 that plenty of food was available in Spain.[4]

Even had Wellington wished to do so he could not have fed his army by requisition. The goodwill of the Spanish and Portuguese people was Britain's most valuable asset. His army had to be supplied by a system of magazines stocked with food which had to be paid for with cash or credit. A vast train of bullock carts and river boats brought supplies to the magazines, drawing food not only from the Peninsula but from Britain, Ireland, the United States and the southern shores of the Mediterranean. To move rations forward from the magazines to the troops a multitude of mules and their drivers were hired.

Each man in the army was entitled to a daily ration of 1lb of meat (which normally travelled on the hoof), 1lb of biscuit (or 1½lb of bread or rice), 1 pint of wine (or ⅓ pint spirits). Each horse needed 10lb oats, barley or Indian corn and 10lb of hay, or cut straw. In mid-1813 the daily consumption of the field army was 100,000lb of biscuit, 200,000lb of forage corn and 300 head of cattle.[5] All this had to be transported across long distances. Assuming that it took a loaded mule three days to get from the magazine to the troops, 'each mule should,' said Wellington, 'be made to carry 200 lbs, and besides this load, he should carry his own corn going from and returning to the magazine, which is 5 lb per diem, or 30 lbs for the six days. Upon this calculation a mule should carry biscuit for six days for 33 men;

rum for 6 days for 100; rice for six days for 20 men;* corn for 6 days
for 3 horses and 20 lbs over.'[6] A brigade of infantry required about
150 mules as did a single regiment of cavalry. A troop of horse
artillery had:

> including muleteers, 243 men requiring:
>
> | | |
> |---|---|
> | For bread | 71 mules |
> | For rum | 24 mules |
> | For rice | 12 mules |
> | And they have 206 horses requiring | 69 mules |
> | | 176 mules |
> | To which add spare mule for every six | 29 |
> | Total mules required | 205[7] |

These were only Commissariat mules. In addition every unit of the
army had its own beasts to carry camp-kettles, reserve ammunition,
pay chest, medical stores and, in the last year of the war, tents.†

Wellington's elaborately improvised supply system ensured that,
except in very unusual circumstances, his troops could count on
regular rations. It had the disadvantage that the army had to trail
behind it a vast and cumbersome horde of mules which slowed its
movements and curtailed its freedom of manoeuvre. In the summer
of 1812 Marmont forced Wellington back from the Douro to Salamanca with hardly a shot fired. He did this by threatening the allied
supply line. Wellington could not counter this move. 'It would
answer no purpose to attempt to retaliate on the enemy, even if it
were practicable. The French armies in Spain have never had any
secure communication beyond the ground which they occupy.'[8]

Requisitioning enabled the French to do without this enormous
administrative 'tail' but brought its own disadvantages. The French
army could not stand still. No district, however fertile, could support
an army of 50,000 men for more than a week or two. Rations could
not be brought from a distance because the French had no transport

---

* In the published Despatches this figure is misprinted as 200.
† This whole matter is dealt with in detail and with great clarity in S. G. P. Ward's
Wellington's Headquarters (1957).

to bring them. Therefore no French army could remain concentrated for more than a week or two: it had to disperse into quite small groups in search of food. Nor could it return to an area where it had recently been quartered. Manoeuvres which seemed obvious and simple on a map in Paris became impossible on the ground. In February 1812 Marmont was ordered to march from Salamanca against Ciudad Rodrigo, little more than fifty miles. He replied, 'His Majesty does not understand that in these parts even the smallest movement causes an enormous loss of means. It costs us as much as a major battle. If the army marches against Rodrigo now we should not be able to stay there for three days for lack of food. We should achieve nothing as the enemy knows we cannot stay there. It would cost us 500 horses and immobilize us for six weeks.'[9]

Napoleon's successes up to 1807 were made possible by his realisation that with the vast armies made possible by conscription victory could be achieved only by the sudden knock-out blow. Prolonged manoeuvring on the eighteenth-century model would entail starvation for the army. His battles were often expensive in French lives but they saved the greater number of lives which would have fallen to disease in a long campaign. Jena in 1806 was the last of the *blitzkriegen*. Thereafter his adversaries always managed to escape with their armies in being. Napoleon refused to believe that immediate, irreversible victory was no longer possible. He continued to strive for it.*

The difficulty in consummating a *blitzkrieg* lay in the ineffectiveness of contemporary weapons. Most battles were decided by the musket which threw a ball weighing about an ounce† and was inaccurate at more than eighty yards. Twenty drill movements were required to load and fire each shot and the practicable rate of fire was three or four rounds a minute. The musket was discharged by a flintlock which misfired once in seven rounds in dry weather. It was unlikely to fire at all in heavy rain. Only an exceptional flint would fire more than thirty rounds, after which it had to be changed.

---

* The next knock-out victory was Waterloo. Napoleon made its completeness possible by continuing to strive for a decisive victory after his chance of obtaining one had disappeared.
† The British ball weighed 14 to the pound, the French 20.

With such a weapon the only way of stopping an advancing enemy was to draw up the troops shoulder to shoulder and fire repeated volleys. In this way some of the musket balls were bound to find a mark among the enemy who, for the same reason, would also be shoulder to shoulder. Given equal discipline and morale, the advantage would go to the side which could bring the most muskets to bear and could fire the most volleys.

In such a lethal exchange, often conducted at a range of fifty yards, the British, and the Portuguese they had trained, had an in-built advantage. Although, like those of all European armies, their drillbooks called for a three-rank formation, they fought in a two-deep line. The fire of the third rank was never effective and could be dangerous to those in front. The object of the third rank was to fill gaps caused by casualties and give moral support to the front two ranks. By fighting in two ranks the British increased their fire power by 50 per cent and could often swing the wings of their longer line forward to enfilade the enemy's ranks.

The methods adopted by the French heightened this advantage. In their search for a decisive result the French had evolved a technique of hurling a column of men, screened by skirmishers and heralded by an artillery preparation, at their enemy's line. The results had been strikingly successful against opponents whose discipline and morale had been less than superb. A division of 5,000 men would assault on a front of 170 men, twenty-four ranks deep.* It was an awesome spectacle and many continental armies had crumpled before the column came to grips with them. Against confident, highly disciplined troops the technique was unsound. Only the two front ranks of the column could fire with effect. Out of 5,000 advancing men only 340 could shoot at the enemy. Their effective fire power was less than that of four companies of British infantry in line. Wellington wrote in 1811, 'I do not desire better sport than to meet one of their columns *en masse* with our line.'[10]

Rifles were carried by a small proportion of the Anglo-Portuguese infantry. They were accurate at more than 200 yards but they suffered from all the defects of the flintlock. Like the musket they were

---

* At least one-sixth of the strength of each French battalion would be in the skirmishing line, fighting in open order ahead of the column.

Page 33   (*above*) 'Battle of Coruña 16 January 1809', by H. Lecomte;
(*below*) detail: 'Bridge of Nodin May 1809', by Major T. St Clair

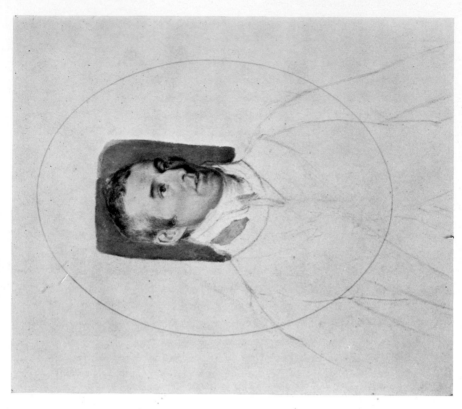

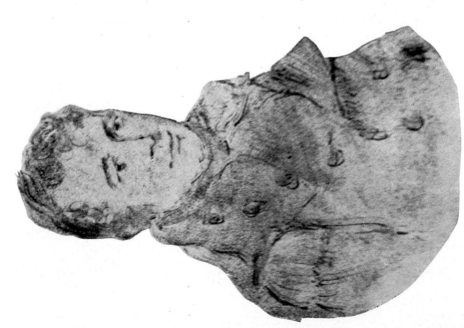

Page 34   (*left*) Sketch of Sir John Moore, by Thomas Lawrence; (*right*) Lord Wellington by

muzzle-loading and the need to force the ball down the rifling of the barrel made them very slow to load. Even a skilled rifleman could scarcely fire two rounds a minute. Because of this Napoleon had ordered all rifles to be withdrawn from the French army in 1807. In the allied army they were regarded as weapons for specialists only.

The chief defect of artillery was its flat trajectory. The principal discharge of artillery was roundshot. The largest field guns used were Napoleon's 12-pounders. These threw an iron ball 4·75 inches in diameter but they could throw it only in a straight line. It did not explode and could damage only those who stood directly in its path. Smaller guns threw smaller balls, but whatever the size of shot it could not harm a man if he was stationed behind a ridge or in a sunken road. One of the most remarkable features of the Napoleonic wars is the way in which continental commanders, including Napoleon himself, persisted in drawing up their troops in full view of the enemy and consequently within the danger zone of their roundshot.* At Ligny in 1815 Wellington suggested to Blücher that it was unwise to expose his army on a forward slope. The Prussian reply was, 'Our men like to see their enemy.' As the Duke rode away he remarked to his staff, 'If they fight there, they will be damnably mauled.'[11] They were, and two days later Napoleon's men, drawn up on a forward slope facing Waterloo, were also 'damnably mauled' before they reached the range of British musketry. Only Wellington seems to have grasped the simple truth that troops behind a ridge or bank were immune to roundshot. He never exposed a man sooner than was necessary and a French column advancing towards a British position would see only a thin chain of skirmishers, who presented no target, and the field guns which had to be posted on the forward slope because of their flat trajectory.

Explosive projectiles, known as 'common shell', could be burst in the air over the heads of troops and used for searching behind crests at ranges up to 1,000 yards. Especially on the French side the time fuses were very unreliable and the shell was unlikely to explode

---

* The maximum range of artillery was calculated to the point where a roundshot pitched when fired at maximum elevation. A 12-pounder (seldom used in the Peninsula) had a maximum range of almost 2,000 yards and a 4-pounder of 1,400. Effective range was rather more than half maximum range. Beyond the pitching point a shot would ricochet lethally for a mile or more if the ground was dry.

B

at the right moment. Far more effective was the British invention of
'spherical case shot' which came to be known as shrapnel, after its
inventor, Major Henry Shrapnell. This was a metal ball filled with
musket shot which exploded in mid-air. It had a longer range than
shell and more reliable fusing. Most effective of all was grape or
canister shot, a canvas or metal container which belched forth
musket balls from the muzzle. This was devastating but its effective
range was only 300 yards. It will be obvious that all these projectiles,
roundshot, shell, shrapnel or grape, would be more effective against
men packed in column than against those extended in line.

The British occasionally used rockets in the Peninsula. Wellington
had a low opinion of them, remarking, 'I do not want to set fire to
any town and I do not know of any other use for rockets.'[12] After
seeing some rockets tested, an unprejudiced observer wrote, 'I think
they would have hit Bayonne, for instance, somewhere or other; but
the part of the town you could not very well choose.'[13]

The Peninsula is not good cavalry country. Only the plain south
of the Douro and that around Badajoz gave scope for large-scale
cavalry actions. The main functions of mounted troops were reconnaissance and outpost duty. A few Franco-Polish units were armed
with the lance but the bulk of the cavalry on both sides was armed
with the sabre and a popgun of a carbine. Cavalry was useless against
steady infantry formed in square and ready to meet it.* Where infantry was caught dispersed or in line, as happened to Maucune's
division at Salamanca or to Colborne's brigade at Albuera, the results
were appalling. The French cavalry had several spectacular successes
in pursuing broken Spanish infantry but the British horse never
managed any long chase after the infantry had won a victory. At
Vitoria and Orthez the ground was too broken and at Salamanca the
pursuit, which in any case started as darkness was falling, went in
the wrong direction owing to the error of a Spanish subordinate.

If the weapons were, by twentieth-century standards, primitive,
the wounds they inflicted were ghastly and were made more terrible
by the state of contemporary medicine. Writing home after Vimeiro,
a doctor admitted that 'to several a simple inspection of their

---

* The exception was the charge of the German dragoons at Garçia Hernandez on 23
July 1812 which broke two French squares.

wounds, with a few words of consolation, or perhaps a little opium, was all that could be recommended. Of these brave men the balls had pierced organs connected with life; and in such cases, prudence equally forbids the rash interposition of unavailing art, and the useless indulgence of deceptive hope.'[14]

Surgical operations were almost as dangerous as the weapons of the enemy. So often did gangrene set in that the advice of a medical board to Harry Smith, who had a musket ball in his ankle joint, was 'to remain with a stiff leg of my own as better than a wooden one, for the wounds in Lisbon of late had sloughed so'. Smith insisted on the operation and 'it was five minutes most painful indeed, before the ball was extracted. It was jagged and the tendenous fibre had so grown into it, it was half dissected and half torn out with the most excruciating torture for a moment, the forceps breaking which held the ball.'[15] He was none the worse for the experience, but statistics compiled at the General Hospital in Toulouse in 1814 show that more than one in nine operations ended in death, the figure for amputations being $1:5\frac{1}{2}$ and for wounds to the joints $1:4$.[16]

Disease was a greater danger than either the enemy or the surgeons. During the Peninsular campaigns the British army lost 8,889 men from enemy action and 24,930 from disease. Malaria, the ague, was the worst killer. The doctors had no idea of how to treat it. One sufferer, a surgeon himself, recalled how he was bled and then 'they carried me into the yard, placed me erect and poured four or five and twenty buckets of cold well water over me from a third story window'.[17] Another patient recovered on 'a diet prescribed by an old Portuguese army doctor of "the best of living and at least two bottles of Maderia *per diem*" '.[18] Considering the conditions in the hospitals it is astonishing that anyone survived them. A sergeant, convalescent from malaria, noted that his hospital ward at Elvas was 'a long bomb-proof room; no ventilation except by the door and chimney; twenty patients of whom eighteen died'.[19]

It is impossible to generalise about the men who fought in the Peninsula. The French army was raised by conscription and so, in theory, was a cross-section of the population of France. The British army was raised by voluntary recruitment. Although it attracted a small proportion of men motivated by patriotic motives, the vast bulk of recruits were men forced into the ranks by economic, social or moral despair. The extreme meanness practised by Parliament to the army made service in the ranks the resort of the desperate and the shiftless. A man might enlist in the militia for home service only. If he did so his wife would receive an allowance. If he joined the regular army his wife got nothing. Wellington pointed out to the Secretary of State that 'when I was in Ireland, I had the opportunity of knowing that the women took the utmost pains to prevent the men from enlisting; naturally enough because from that moment they [the wives] went not upon the parish but upon the dung hill to starve. Indeed it is astonishing that any Irish militia soldier was ever found to volunteer; and they must be certainly the very worst members of society, who have left their families to starve for the inducement of a few guineas to get drunk.'[20]

As well as filling the ranks of the Irish regiments, the Irish provided a very high proportion of the recruits for the English and Scottish regiments. In May 1809 the 1st battalion Fifty Seventh Foot, known as the West Middlesex, was composed as follows:

	Sergeants	Corporals	Drummers	Privates
English	27	27	13	446
Scots	4	3	1	28
Irish	13	7	7	269
Foreigners	—	—	—	14
	44	37	21	757

Sergeant Cooper of the Seventh Fusiliers wrote that the 'army was composed of the lowest orders. Many if not most of them were ignorant, idle or drunken.'[21] This was inevitable as long as Parliament refused to provide money to make enlistment attractive or even tolerable. Wellington remarked that the 'French army is certainly a wonderful machine; but if we are to form such a one we must compose our army of soldiers drawn from all classes of the population; from the good and middling, as well in rank as education, and not, as we do, from the bad only.'[22] He knew that few but 'the scum of the earth' would join the army but it was always his way to 'do the best I can with the instruments which have been sent to assist me',[23] and 'it is really wonderful that we should have made them the fine fellows they are'.[24]

Whatever the differences in their backgrounds, the British and French soldiers were evenly matched in battle. In courage there was nothing to choose between them. They differed in their vices. The British vice was drink, a failing accentuated by the easy availability of wine in the Peninsula. 'No soldier,' said Wellington, 'can withstand the temptation of wine. This is constantly before their eyes in this country and they are constantly intoxicated when absent from their regiments.'[25] The French were no strangers to drunkenness. On one occasion a French pursuit was halted because an intelligent officer left full wine barrels across their road.[26]

Plunder was the besetting sin of the French army. The British were not averse to looting but they were not in the same class as their opponents. This was the consequence of the requisitioning system which was, in practice, legalised plunder. When requisitioning broke down the soldiers were forced to subsist on what they could steal and extort. They were encouraged to do so by their officers. Discipline suffered accordingly.

When the Anglo-Portuguese army invaded France in 1813 Wellington's chief concern was that the inhabitants would raise a guerrilla movement against him as the Spaniards had done against the French. The fear proved groundless. He was soon able to report that 'the natives of this part of the country are not only reconciled to the invasion, but wish us success, afford us all the supplies in their power and exert themselves to get us intelligence. In no part of Spain have we been better, I might say as well, received.'[27] The civilians of south-western France were not lacking in patriotism, but the habits of plunder which the French army had acquired in Spain were too deeply ingrained to be discarded when they returned on their native soil. They robbed their compatriots with all the savagery they had used against the Spaniards. Even Soult, a plunderer in the world class, was horrified by their depredations and tried ineffectively to restrain them. The civilians soon came to the conclusion that only a swift allied victory could save their countryside. 'It is a

curious circumstance,' wrote Wellington in January 1814, 'that we
are the protectors of the property of the inhabitants against the
plunder of their own armies; and their cattle, &c. are driven into
our lines for protection.'[28]

When the French marched into Spain in 1807 few would have
denied that their army was the finest in the world. By 1813 it was
clear that the British surpassed them in every department. By that
time the Russian campaign had destroyed the Grande Armée, and the
Army of Spain represented the cream of Napoleon's troops. Nevertheless Wellington was wholly justified in claiming that his army was
'the most complete machine for its numbers now existing in
Europe'.[29] This change was due very largely to the difference between the system of requisitioning on the French side and Wellington's careful husbanding of the magazine system of supply on the
other.

Little good could be said about the two native armies in the
Peninsula in 1807. The Portuguese army had little actual existence.
On paper it consisted of 30,000 men but not one of them could be
found to oppose Junot as his men straggled into Lisbon. An acute
observer writing at the turn of the century wrote that 'the officers
are ill-chosen, ill-paid and nevertheless are engaged entirely by
interest, without the least spark of military honour. The Portuguese
soldier is obedient, patient, robust, lively and dextrous; but he is at
the same time idle, filthy, and disposed to find fault with everything.'[30] Such military organisation as existed was dismantled by
Junot in 1807–8 and the Portuguese army which fought beside the
British with such distinction from Busaco to Toulouse was a completely new body, the creation of William Beresford. The extent of
his achievement is best illustrated by two quotations from Wellington. When he first reviewed Portuguese troops in May 1809 he said,
'the body of men very bad; the officers worse than anything I have
ever seen'.[31] In July 1813 he reported, 'No troops could behave
better; nothing could equal their forwardness now, and their ready
willing temper.'[32]

Wellington's eldest brother while ambassador at Seville remarked
to the Foreign Minister that he 'would not entrust the protection of
a favourite dog to the whole Spanish army'.[33] This was a tactless

remark for a diplomat, but it was no great exaggeration. The Spanish army had been the finest in the world in the sixteenth century and the Spaniards refused to believe that anything had changed. Wellington complained that their 'national disease' consisted of 'boasting the strength and power of the Spanish nation till they are seriously convinced they are in no danger and then sitting quietly and indulging their national indolence'.[34] For the first two years of the war they insisted on taking the offensive repeatedly with armies which were untrained, unpaid, ill-supplied, deplorably led and usually outnumbered. 'Nothing will answer excepting to fight great battles in the plains, in which their defeat is as certain as the commencement of the battle.'[35] By the beginning of 1810 the Spanish army scarcely existed.

It was not the Spaniard in the ranks who failed in the early years of the war. 'They make excellent soldiers. What spoils them is that they have no confidence in their officers—that would ruin any soldiers—and how should the Spaniards have confidence in such officers as theirs?'[36]

Wellington said many hard things about the Spanish government and their generals. He never forgot the debt he owed to the Spanish people whose determination to get rid of the French transcended the incompetence and corruption of their leaders.

From first to last Bonaparte sent 600,000 men into Spain, and I know that not more than 100,000 went out in the shape of an army. It is true that this result may in part be attributed to the operations of the allied army; but a greater proportion of it must be ascribed to the enmity of the people of Spain. I have known not less than 380,000 men of the French army in Spain at one moment and yet with no authority beyond the spot where they stood and their time passed and their force exhausted by the mere effort of obtaining subsistence.[37]

PART TWO

The French Initiative,
October 1807–May 1809

CHAPTER 3

Napoleonic Aggression

PORTUGAL was an obvious target for French imperialism. From a French point of view she was little different from a British colony. Britain was the largest customer for her exports and she was dependent on British manufactured goods to the extent that all the muskets and gunpowder for her army came from the British Board of Ordnance. There were large and flourishing coteries of British merchants in Lisbon and Oporto. She had a powerful fleet which Napoleon coveted. As soon as he published the Berlin Decrees forbidding trade with Britain, it could only be a question of time before France occupied the country. Foreseeing this, Britain arranged with Prince Regent John of Portugal to be allowed to occupy the island of Madeira.

By the Treaty of Fontainebleau (27 October 1807) Napoleon agreed with Spain that a joint expedition should invade Portugal and divide it into three parts, one of which should be an independent principality for Manuel de Godoy, the Spanish Prime Minister. Godoy had no scruples about concluding this squalid deal. Any move against Portugal was always sure of public support in Spain and Godoy was much in need of public support. The promise of a principality was an insurance against the inevitable day when he was driven from Spain. He was also anxious to curry favour with Napoleon who trusted him even less than the Spaniards did.

Before the treaty was signed a French corps of 28,000 men under General Junot crossed the Bidassoa into Spain. Knowing their destination, the Spanish people greeted them with enthusiasm. 'Our march,' wrote their chief of staff, 'was the occasion of a holiday for them and a triumph for us.'[1] On Napoleon's orders Junot entered Portugal along the Tagus valley on a road which existed only on a map. The Portuguese did not oppose him but the weather and the terrain almost wrecked his corps. He entered Lisbon on 30 November 1807 'without having in hand a single trooper, a single cannon, a single cartridge which would fire—with nothing but fifteen hundred grenadiers, the remnant of the four battalions of his advanced guard. The rest of the army straggled in over the next few days, some falling dead at the gates of the city.'[2] The two Spanish corps which had been ordered to support Junot had not been ready to march with him but occupied northern and southern Portugal before the end of the year. They were unopposed.

Napoleon had conquered Portugal. He had stopped her trade with Britain. But he failed to secure the Portuguese fleet. Prince John, the Regent, had been under diplomatic pressure for many months while the French and Spanish ambassadors urged him to declare war on his ally of many centuries. He was not a strong character and he was in an impossible position. He knew that his army could not withstand an invasion, but war with Britain meant a blockade of Portuguese ports. Deprived of overseas trade, Portugal must starve. He begged London to allow him to declare nominal war while continuing to trade. The British would not agree. Portugal must be friend or enemy. On 20 October he declared war, interned the British merchants and seized their goods. The British ambassador left Lisbon but established himself in the blockading squadron off the mouth of the Tagus. The Prince had left it too late. On 25 November the Ambassador sent ashore a copy of the *Moniteur Universel*, Napoleon's official newspaper, dated 13 October. In it the Prince read the Emperor's unequivocal words: 'The House of Braganca has ceased to reign.' Junot was only five days' march from Lisbon. Embarking his court and his treasury, Prince John sailed for the Brazils. With him went his fleet, the whole escorted by a British squadron. As the French staggered towards the capital they caught a glimpse of a host of sails heading out to sea.

The Portuguese people accepted the Franco-Spanish occupation with sullen resignation, punctuated with riots. Junot tried to rule them with moderation but this angered his master who wrote, 'You are in a conquered country, yet you carry on as if you were in Burgundy.'[3] Napoleon ordered Portugal to pay into the Imperial Treasury an extraordinary tax of 100,000,000 gold francs, fifty francs for every man, woman and child in the country. Meanwhile, grass grew on the quays of Lisbon and Oporto and off the coast the blockading men-of-war watched endlessly.

French control of Portugal could have continued indefinitely as long as Spain was France's ally. Junot's corps and the Spanish auxiliaries were more than sufficient to keep a dispirited population in subjection. To ensure that there was sufficient French strength to repel a British landing, Napoleon allocated another corps under General Dupont to the Army of Portugal. Dupont never set foot in Portugal but he was to play a key rôle in the future of the Peninsula.

Closing the Portuguese ports to British trade was a victory for France but it was only a step in Napoleon's greater plan. For years he had planned to bring Spain into his empire. In 1803 he had said that he must re-create the empire of Charlemagne, 'as much to consolidate the position of his own dynasty as for the security of France, repeating several times that a Bourbon on the throne of Spain was too dangerous a neighbour'.[4]

It would be hard to see the Spain of 1808 as a danger to anyone. King Charles IV, third cousin to the executed Louis XVI of France, was dangerous only to the animals he loved to hunt. The government was in the hands of Godoy who had risen from being a handsome young officer in the Royal Guards to the dual eminence of First Minister and lover to the queen. The king, who doted on him, had awarded him the title of Prince of the Peace. According to the French ambassador he was 'frightened, timid, exceedingly ill-informed, overwhelmingly covetous, insatiable. Money is his lode-stone and falseness his policy.'[5] He was loathed by all Spaniards outside the shrinking circle of his own adherents. The hopes of Spain were pinned to Ferdinand, Prince of the Asturias, heir to the throne. He had most of the characteristics of his deplorable parents but was redeemed in Spanish eyes by the running feud he conducted with Godoy.

Napoleon came to believe that the Spaniards would welcome a change of government. He assumed that they would prefer an en-

lightened regime, one more in line with the thinking of the early
nineteenth century. He was encouraged in this illusion by the reports
of his ambassador in Madrid, a rather stupid brother-in-law of the
Empress, who wrote: 'It is beyond understanding how this government can continue without governing, how it can support itself with
an empty treasury and without foreign credit. Everyone waits
patiently for the day when the Emperor turns his attention to this
country so that things may be set in order.'[6]

This was a gross misreading of the Spanish character. Many
Spaniards looked forward to better days. Only a handful of talented
idealists wanted any radical change, especially if imposed from
abroad. Hatred of foreigners was a strong national trait. In 1807 the
national hate was directed against Britain which had seized and continued to hold Gibraltar, had wrecked the Spanish navy at St Vincent
and Trafalgar and continued to tamper with the Spanish colonies.
This hatred could easily be switched to any other foreigner who
tried to interfere with Spain's internal arrangements. The king was
little respected and his minister was detested, but at least they were
Spaniards. Nor were the Spaniards in the least interested in enlightened ideas. Spain had slept throughout the eighteenth century
and was still set in the attitudes of the Wars of Religion. The anti-
clerical excesses of the French Revolution had left a searing mark on
priest-ridden Spain. Despite his Concordat with the Pope, Napoleon
was widely equated in Spain with Antichrist. He expected to be
hailed as a liberator. The Spanish people regarded liberation as an
impertinence.

The Treaty of Fontainebleau permitted France to march 40,000
men through Spain to reinforce Junot provided Madrid was consulted in advance. In the early months of 1808 75,000 Frenchmen
crossed the Pyrenees without consultation. They quietly occupied
all the frontier fortresses. One large corps quartered itself in Barcelona which was not on any recognised road to Lisbon. The
majority settled down between Bayonne and Burgos. Godoy had no
idea what to do. He toyed with the idea of following the Portuguese
example and removing the Royal Family to South America. As a
first step the court was moved to Aranjuez on the Tagus, south of
Madrid. The mob would not be deserted. A violent riot broke out

with Godoy as its target. To save the favourite's life King Charles abdicated in favour of Prince Ferdinand. It was 19 March 1808 and the advanced guard of a large French army was only four short marches from Madrid.

Marshal Murat, Grand Duke of Berg, commanded the French force. He was a dashing leader of cavalry and had married Napoleon's shrewish sister Caroline. He had the courage of a fighting cock and the brains of a chicken. In Napoleon's view, 'he is ambitious but ridiculously vain. He is under the delusion that he is gifted with political talents to a superior degree. In fact he is destitute of any such thing.'[7]

His military instructions were clear. He was to occupy Madrid. As a cover he was to 'give all possible assurances to the Prince of the Peace, to the king, to everybody. Say that your intentions are peaceable. Say that you are marching to Cadiz, to Gibraltar.'[8] He had no political instructions. Napoleon had promised to go to Madrid as soon as it was occupied and expressed the hope that 'there will be no war, that is what I most desire'.[9]

The revolution at Aranjuez changed the political situation out of all recognition. As long as Godoy was in power the Spanish government would obey French orders. With Godoy a prisoner and Ferdinand on the throne anything might happen. Napoleon was perplexed.

> This affair has complicated everything. Shall I go to Madrid? Shall I appear as the Great Protector and arbitrate between father and son? It would seem difficult to replace Charles IV on his throne. His government and his minister are so unpopular that they would not last three months. On the other hand, Ferdinand is the enemy of France. That is why they have made him king.[10]

With neither instructions nor acumen, Murat made every possible error. He entered Madrid in what was unmistakably a victory march. He refused to recognise Ferdinand, the public idol, and dealt only with Charles. He took Godoy under French protection when every Spaniard longed to see him tried for his life. As a crowning insult he filched the sword of Francis I* from the Royal Armoury

---

* Francis I (1494–1547), King of France. He was defeated and captured by the Spaniards at Pavia in 1526.

where for years it had been a treasured national trophy. His troops followed his example and looted freely.

There followed a stalemate with the old king recognised by the occupying army and the new king recognised by the people. Eventually both kings agreed to accept Napoleon's arbitration and set off to Bayonne to state their cases. Neither of them returned. With a mixture of threats and blandishments both were induced to renounce their claims and to retire to separate exiles in France. Joseph Bonaparte, King of Naples, was summoned to Bayonne to become King of Spain. He arrived on 7 June.

Joseph had been offered the Spanish crown and had accepted it six months earlier on 2 December 1807.[11] Since then Napoleon had had second thoughts and offered the throne to his younger brother Louis, the King of Holland, who had refused it. Joseph was forty years old and the antithesis of Napoleon. His military experience was minimal and he affected to believe that 'the art of war is charlatanism'.[12] He loved comfort, idleness and pretty women although he had married for money rather than beauty. In his younger days he had written a novel entitled *Moina, the nun of Mont Cenis*. He was a patron of the arts and a conversationalist of charm and sophistication. In politics he was a liberal and he set out for Spain full of enlightened ideas and devoid of a sense of what was practicable. A friend said of him, 'he was strongly opposed to all measures of severity. Of sanguine disposition, he flattered himself that he would be able to win all hearts by his speeches, by soft words and gracious manners.'[13] Napoleon considered that he 'has intelligence but hates work. He is ignorant of soldiering but pretends to knowledge. He knows nothing and he loves pleasure.'[14] 'If I love him, it is from habit and because he is my elder brother.'[15] Despite this unflattering opinion it was unthinkable that Napoleon should have awarded the Spanish throne to anyone else. He had a strong, Corsican, sense of family. Joseph was the head of the Bonaparte family and the best of a bad bunch. 'They are all,' said Napoleon, 'insanely ambitious, ruinously extravagant and devoid of talent.'[16]

While kings were being made and unmade at Bayonne, the Spanish people erupted in a protest against their oppressors. On 2 May, *Dos Mayo*, the Madrid mob heard that Murat was despatching the rest of the Royal Family to France. French soldiers were murdered in the streets and their barracks attacked. Murat reacted quickly and drastically to restore order. The riot cost the lives of thirty-one Frenchmen and about two hundred Spaniards. To teach Madrid a lesson Murat then executed a hundred ringleaders selected at random from the crowd.

Madrid was quietened for the time being, but the *Dos Mayo* riot sparked off resistance all over Spain. Everywhere, even in the areas occupied by the French, local juntas were set up dedicated to ejecting the invader. On the 25th the Asturias declared war on the French Empire. Their military force consisted of one regular regiment. In Andalusia five French warships which had sheltered in Cadiz since Trafalgar were bombarded until they surrendered. In Valencia the whole French merchant colony, 338 men, women and children, were massacred at the instigation of a fanatical priest. The Captains General of Galicia and Andalusia who advocated obeying orders from Madrid were murdered by mobs. On 18 May Murat reported that 'the country is tranquil, the state of the capital far happier than could have been expected. The native soldiery is showing an excellent disposition'.[17] Before the end of the month he took to his bed and soon left for France giving the impression to those he met that he 'thought himself lucky to have escaped'.[18]

At Bayonne Napoleon had his own junta. It was not the body for which he had hoped. He had given orders for 150 members to be chosen from all over Spain by a complicated series of indirect elections. Apart from a few intellectuals, delegates came only from areas where French troops were stationed and some of them escaped from their escorts on the road to Bayonne. By conscripting some grandees who had come to Bayonne with the Bourbon kings, ninety-one delegates were assembled. They were harangued by the Emperor and induced to proclaim Joseph as King of Spain and the Indies. They agreed to a constitution for Spain which had been prepared in the French Foreign Office.

On 7 July business was completed and Joseph took an oath 'to respect and enforce respect for our Holy Religion, to observe and enforce the observation of the constitution, to maintain the integrity and the independence of Spain and to govern with the sole aim of

establishing the welfare, happiness and glory of the Spanish nation'.
It was Joseph's tragedy that he took this oath in all sincerity.

Two days later he crossed the Bidassoa into his new kingdom. His
first impression was that 'there is much to be done to gain the good
opinion of this nation. However, with moderation and justice it will
be possible, especially once the rebels have been beaten.'[19] On 12
July he reached Vitoria, where the truth began to dawn on him. He
wrote to Napoleon, 'The townspeople are very hostile. People of
rank are intimidated by the mob. No one has told your Majesty the
truth. Apart from the handful who are travelling with me, not a
single Spaniard has declared for me.'[20] A week later he wrote,
'Opposition is everywhere. The task before us is enormous. It will
require enormous resources. We must have 50,000 men and
50,000,000 francs within three months.'[21]

A battle had to be fought to clear the king's road to his capital.
On 14 July Marshal Bessières routed the northern Spanish armies at
Medina de Rio Seco although he was outnumbered by three to two.
It was the prototype of many battles to come. The Spanish troops
were no match for the French. They were ill-equipped and sketchily
supplied. Their ranks were filled with untrained recruits. Their
generals bickered amongst themselves. They lost heavily but their
armies were not destroyed. Time and again Spanish armies lost their
artillery, their colours, their baggage. They suffered casualties on a
scale which would have crippled a French or a British army. They
never disintegrated. They would retire to some inaccessible fastness,
reorganise themselves and reappear to plague the French as they had
never been plagued before.

Joseph entered Madrid on 20 July. His chamberlain described it
as 'a melancholy occasion. The silence and scornful looks of the
townspeople contrasted sharply with the solemnity of the ritual.'[22]
The king thought that 'it was less bad than might have been
expected'.[23]

Napoleon had tried to take over Spain with a small army of
second-rate troops. 'I thought troops would only be needed to
maintain public order and to garrison the fortresses.'[24] He sent
91,000 men of whom only one in seven was a veteran. He dispersed
them recklessly. There was a corps in Barcelona, unable to com-

municate with France or Madrid; 8,000 men were sent to receive the surrender of Valencia. They were repulsed and hounded back to the Tagus. More than 20,000 men tried to keep open the road from Bayonne to Madrid. They were only intermittently successful; 13,000 were despatched from the capital to occupy Cordoba, Seville and Cadiz.

It is more than 400 miles from Madrid to Cadiz and the largest part of Spain's regular army was stationed near the latter city. The French corps was entrusted to Pierre Dupont, the man who had been designated to head the troops reinforcing Junot. He was forty-three, with a long and distinguished military career behind him. Napoleon personally appointed him to the Andalusian expedition, his first independent command.

He crossed the Sierra Morena, the chain of mountains which separates Andalusia from the rest of Spain, and reached Cordoba on 7 June. While his troops were sacking the city he heard that a large Spanish force was approaching. He retired to the Sierra and called for reinforcements. Another division was sent to him, giving him a total of 19,000 men. Except for a single battalion of Sailors of the Guard, his entire force consisted of foreign battalions or of units hastily assembled for the Spanish campaign. Nevertheless he felt strong enough to resume his advance although he knew that the Spaniards greatly outnumbered him and that their general was one of the few Spaniards of some talent, Xavier de Castaños. He sacked the town of Jaen and established a base for further operations at the little town of Bailen. Napoleon was unconcerned about Dupont's danger. 'Even if he suffers a setback, it will not matter much. He will just have to come back over the Sierra.'[25]

In Madrid Joseph was busy establishing a government, visiting hospitals and using his great charm to make a favourable impression on his new subjects. He also wrote a series of depressing letters to his brother. 'You are making a mistake, Sire. Your glory will not be enough to subjugate Spain. I shall fail and the limits of your power will be exposed. 50,000 more men and 50,000,000 francs are needed to set things right. Only this can save the country.'[26]

He had no news from Dupont, but rumour was rife in Madrid. On 26 July he reported that it was being whispered in the city that

'Dupont has been in action against 60,000 men; certainly the enemy are very strong'.[27] Next day, 'Very disturbing rumours are current about Dupont. I do not entirely believe them but we must be prepared for there to be some basis in truth. If they are true the rebels will be able to march on Madrid with 100,000 men. I can lead 20,000 from here to reinforce whatever is left of Dupont's corps.'[28]

Twenty-four hours later, on 28 July, an aide-de-camp from Dupont reached Madrid with despatches. Dupont had been surrounded by 32,000 Spaniards. He tried to break out of the ring but failed with heavy loss. Two of his Swiss regiments surrendered. Dupont was wounded in the hip and his men were desperate for water. He capitulated, including in his surrender a division which was outside the Spanish net and which could have escaped without difficulty; 17,635 unwounded men became prisoners of the Spaniards. It was the worst disaster suffered by the French army since the turn of the century.

The surrender at Bailen left Madrid uncomfortably exposed. Joseph sought the advice of the senior French officer in the city, General Savary, a man more distinguished as Minister of Police than as a field commander. He urged immediate retreat. On 1 August the last French soldier marched out of Madrid. Joseph had intended to go no further than Burgos but on the road he was joined by Marshals Moncey and Bessières and their troops. The marshals advised a longer retreat. By mid-August Joseph's headquarters were at Vitoria and his troops were deployed along the river Ebro, waiting for a Spanish attack which never came. He reported, 'I need not tell your Majesty that now it needs 100,000 more men to conquer Spain. I repeat that we have not a single Spanish supporter. The whole nation is exasperated and determined to fight.'[29]

Bailen came as a complete shock to Napoleon. He had been under the illusion that all that was needed in Spain was the mopping up of a few isolated pockets of resistance. He had written to Joseph, 'The rebels want nothing better than to be allowed to surrender.'[30] To the king's gloomy forecasts he kept repeating, 'Keep fit. Have courage and gaiety. Never doubt that we shall be completely successful.'[31] His attention was fixed on Austria which was arming against him. In July he had ordered his army in Germany to be reinforced. Dupont's surrender jerked his mind sharply back to Spain. 'Has there ever, since the world began, been such a stupid, cowardly, idiotic business as this? The loss of 20,000 picked men,* who have disappeared without even inflicting serious loss on the enemy, must have the worst possible effect on the Spaniards.'[32]

He ordered 100,000 men to be withdrawn from Germany and marched to the Pyrenees. He arranged for the Tsar to keep Austria in check. He put the blame for the disaster on the commanders in Spain. The army there, he wrote, 'seems to be commanded by postal inspectors rather than generals of experience'.[33] The great names of the Imperial army—Soult, Lannes, Ney, St Cyr and Victor—were put under orders for Spain. In mid-October he wrote, 'I shall be in Bayonne in less than a month. The war can be finished in a single properly concerted operation, and I must be there to concert it.'[34]

Bailen and the evacuation of Madrid changed the whole basis of Joseph's tenure of the Spanish throne. When he first entered his capital he had some claim to the kingdom. The previous incumbents had resigned in his favour. His accession had been ratified by the Council of Castile, the ancient substitute for a parliament, and the suspect junta at Bayonne. He could be replaced only by force. Napoleon had no illusions about the new situation. Reaching Vitoria on 6 November, he announced to the Spaniards of Joseph's entourage:

> I am here with the soldiers who conquered at Austerlitz, at Jena, at Eylau. Who can withstand *them*? Certainly not your wretched Spanish troops who do not know how to fight. I shall conquer Spain in two months and acquire the rights of a conqueror. Treaties, constitutions and all other agreements cease to exist. I am no longer bound by them.[35]

---

* Dupont's men were certainly not picked (élite) troops. Apart from the Sailors of the Guard and four Swiss regiments, the rest were battalions of the reserve and provisional cavalry units. This meant that they were young conscripts commanded by any officers who could be found in the depots.

CHAPTER 4

British Intervention

PUBLICLY the French attributed their early troubles in Spain to British intrigues. Murat announced that the *Dos Mayo* riot had been stirred up by 'agents of the English'. Napoleon proclaimed that the capitulation of Bailen was 'a machination paid for with English gold'. The British were both innocent and ignorant. Although they had been at war with Spain for four years, they had not a single secret agent in Spain. Their source of information about events in Madrid was the French newspapers, eked out by belated reports from Gibraltar where the Lieutenant-Governor was in 'direct and confidential communication' with the Spanish general who was besieging the Rock.

The government, headed by the ailing Duke of Portland, was weak and disunited. The two most prominent ministers were Canning and Castlereagh. Canning, the Foreign Secretary, was a born fighter. He had inspired the Copenhagen expedition and would support any offensive operation as long as it was demonstrably successful. His pugnacity, however, was that of the gadfly and many of his colleagues mistrusted his staying power and his devotion to any cause but his own. Castlereagh was Secretary for War and less of an opportunist than Canning. He had achieved marvels in the chaotic field of army organisation and had built up a disposable force of 30,000 men with sea transport permanently allocated to it. In the summer of 1808 the greater part of this force was in Baltic waters pursuing an abortive scheme devised by Canning. The Foreign Secretary and the Secretary for War were barely on speaking terms.

The idea of British support for the rising in Spain seems to have

originated with the third memorable member of Portland's government, the Chief Secretary for Ireland. At the end of May he sent a
memorandum to Castlereagh suggesting that 'this would appear to
be a crisis in which a great effort might be made with advantage.
That which I recommend is to send to Gibraltar all the disposable
force that can immediately be spared from England to be prepared
to act as circumstances would point out.'[1] Such a scheme would
seem to fall outside the normal scope of the Irish Secretary's duties
but it so happened that he was a soldier and had been appointed to
the command of the projected expedition to South America, a task
he viewed without enthusiasm. He was an old friend of Castlereagh
who was in the habit of taking his advice on military matters. He
was Lieutenant-General the Hon Sir Arthur Wellesley.

Wellesley was thirty-nine and had been in the army since he was
seventeen. He was not a tall man, about five foot ten, but slim and
wiry with a great natural presence. Shy to a fault with strangers, he
had an unmerited reputation for brusqueness which was accentuated
by a decisiveness in contrast to most of his colleagues, political and
military. His friends knew him as a kindly man, with a strong sense
of justice, great personal charm, a taste for music and a keen humour
which showed itself in a loud whinnying laugh. By contemporary
standards he was a temperate man, 'very abstemious with wine:
drank four or five glasses with people at dinner, and about a pint of
claret afterwards'.[2] This increased his reputation for unfriendliness.
He had made a serious study of his profession, a most unusual
undertaking among British officers in his day, and had distinguished
himself in the disastrous Flanders campaign of 1793–5, another rare
event for a British officer. In India he had shown his talent for command and had won two overwhelming victories at Assaye and
Argaum. Above all he had a strong sense of duty and believed that
all his energies and abilities must be at the disposition of his king and
his country.

He returned from India in poor health as a major-general in 1805.
Since the army could give him no active employment he entered
Parliament to defend the reputation of his eldest brother, whose
policy as Governor-General of India was under factious attack. Pitt
quickly recognised his qualities. 'He never makes a difficulty or

hides his ignorance in vague generalities. If I put a question to him he answers it distinctly; if I want an explanation, he gives it clearly; if I desire an opinion, I get from him one supported by reasons which are always sound. He is a very remarkable man.'[3] In 1807 he accepted office as Chief Secretary on the clear understanding that it would not prevent him from being appointed to any military command that might be offered. He commanded a division in the Copenhagen expedition without resigning his Irish office.

With all his ability and advantages, he was not without enemies. The Whig opposition hated him because he was a Wellesley, a member of a family which, under the leadership of his brilliant, arrogant brother, controlled twelve votes in the House of Commons. The place-hunters and favour-seekers in Dublin disliked him for the disdainful way he acknowledged their fawning requests, even when he granted them. The higher ranks of the army mistrusted him because he was a politician and because of his Indian victories. The Horse Guards, he remarked later, 'thought very little of anyone who had served in India. An Indian victory was not only no grounds for confidence, but it was actually grounds for suspicion.'[4] There were many men prominent if not distinguished in public life who would have been glad to see Arthur Wellesley come unstuck.

Delegates from the Asturias reached London on 8 June 1808. They asked for money and arms with which to carry on the war which their principality had declared against France. In the weeks that followed delegates from most of the other provinces of Spain arrived with similar requests. Press and politicians demanded prompt action to support the Spanish patriots. The government was anxious to oblige them and immediately decided to allocate the troops intended for the South American expedition, with Wellesley as their commander, to help the Spaniards. It even remembered, on 5 July, to announce in the *London Gazette* that His Majesty was no longer at war with Spain.

Having been so long ill-informed about events in Spain, the government was now swamped with information from the delegates. Much of it was contradictory and the confusion was worse confounded by reports from Gibraltar. On one point all the Spaniards agreed. They wanted no assistance from British troops. This was confirmed from Gibraltar from where a brigade was sent to Cadiz, only to be refused permission to land. In the Commons Richard Brinsley Sheridan was demanding that 'we should let Spain see that we were not inclined to stint the services we had in our power to render her'.[5] From the government's point of view the Spaniards were proving singularly obtuse.

Wellesley's expedition eventually set sail from Cork on 12 July. The orders were vague. Wellesley was to offer his services in the north of Spain and if they were not accepted he should try Portugal. Public opinion took not the slightest interest in Portugal but the navy had a deep interest in acquiring the use of the deep-water, all-weather harbour of Lisbon. To encourage the soldiers to take Lisbon, the admiral commanding the squadron off the Tagus reported that Junot had only 4,000 men in and around Lisbon. This information may have been given in good faith but even his own commander-in-chief commented that 'reports received in the way Sir Charles Cotton got his information should not have much confidence in the truth of them'.[6]

Wellesley sailed ahead of the transports in a frigate and landed first at Coruña. He was enthusiastically welcomed but assured that the Spaniards needed no assistance other than arms and money. To confirm the point the local junta regaled him with stories of imaginary Spanish victories. He went on to Oporto where he was regarded as a liberator. The French strength at Lisbon was, however, reported as being 12,000 and the small Portuguese force between Oporto and Lisbon had only one musket for every five men.

This was scarcely encouraging as his own force was only 10,000 strong, but worse news arrived two days later on 26 July. Major-General Spencer commanded a brigade of 5,500 men based at Gibraltar. He had been attempting to land his men at Cadiz but had been ordered to join Wellesley should his commitments at Cadiz permit. He wrote to say that he felt he ought to stay near Cadiz and that the French strength in Portugal was 20,500 of whom 12,500 were near Lisbon.

The prospects looked poor for Wellesley, but after consulting the admiral he decided to land his troops at Figueira da Foz, the port of Coimbra. The first men went ashore on 1 August and as they did so a devastating letter reached their commander from London. His corps was to be reinforced by 16,000 men and he was to be superseded by six senior generals.

This remarkable arrangement was fortuitous. Three days after Wellesley sailed from Cork Sir John Moore returned to England with the army which had been in the Baltic. It was agreed that the troops should sail at once for Portugal and nobody in the army would have disagreed with the appointment of Moore to command the combined force. Unfortunately the appointment of commanders-in-chief was a political responsibility, and Moore was anathema to Canning. On the Foreign Secretary's insistence, the cabinet appointed Sir Hew Dalrymple to the command in Portugal. He was four years senior to Moore and had been Lieutenant-Governor of Gibraltar since 1806. He could be expected to know more about affairs in the Peninsula than any other British general but his record showed that he knew less about fighting than most. In forty-five years of service he had seen only one campaign. Between 1793 and his appointment to Gibraltar he had served no further afield than Guernsey. In case Moore should reach the field of action before Dalrymple, ministers insisted that a second-in-command be appointed lest Moore should hold even temporary command. With a poor field available the Horse Guards nominated Sir Harry Burrard, who was ten months senior to Moore. They realised that he was only an amiable old buffer but he was known to be on friendly terms with Moore and would probably take his advice.

Wellesley had known that he must be superseded if the expedition was to be greatly reinforced. He was almost the most junior lieutenant-general in the army. He would gladly have served under Moore but he would have been less than human if he had not resented the chief command going to two elderly nonentities, to say nothing of three more generals senior to himself but junior to Moore. He wrote a dignified official reply saying that 'whether I am to command this army or not, or am to quit it, I shall do my best to ensure its success'.[7] In a private letter he said, 'I hope I shall have beaten Junot before any of them arrive, and then they may do as they please with me.'[8]

While he wrote these letters the landing of troops went forward hampered by heavy surf and a sandbar across the harbour mouth. The cavalry had to go ashore in flat-bottomed boats. 'We were directed to stand upright, bridle in hand and prepared, in case of accident, to spring into the saddle. One punt capsized upon the surf but no lives were lost because the horses, sometimes swimming, sometimes wading, carried their riders ashore.'[9] After five days, when all were landed, Spencer's brigade arrived from Cadiz and their disembarkation took three more days.

On the evening of 8 August Wellesley found himself at the head of 13,500 men. Most of them were infantry, 15½ battalions of them. There were 372 cavalrymen, but only 215 horses had been brought for them. Shortage of horse transports also meant that there were only enough horses to pull eighteen of the thirty guns available and although two companies of the Irish Corps of Waggoners had arrived, they had no waggons. Worst of all was the Commissariat, a Treasury responsibility. 'The people who manage it are incapable of managing anything outside a counting house.'[10] Although it was possible to hire some waggons and mules from the countryside, Wellesley had no alternative to marching the troops southward along the coast so that they could be supplied by the fleet.

So far there had been no sign of the French. Coimbra had been in the Spanish occupation zone, and when the juntas called home their troops Junot had refused to spread his own men so far north. His effective strength was 26,000 but many of them were tied down in garrisons. The French force nearest to Figueira was a division of 5,000 under General Delaborde at Alcobaça, fifty miles to the south. The British started to march towards them on 10 August and had their first brush with the enemy at Obidos five days later. The leading Riflemen unwisely tackled the French outposts. A Rifle officer admitted that they were 'rather too elevated with this, our first collision with the foe and dashed along like young soldiers'.[11] No great harm eventuated but the Rifles suffered twenty-nine needless casualties.

The first serious engagement took place, also by mistake, on 17 August near Roliça. Delaborde decided to take up a strong position to delay the British. Wellesley did not intend to attack him and sent forces round the French flanks so as to compel them to retire.

Lieutenant-Colonel Lake of the Twenty Ninth misunderstood his orders and launched his men up the steep front of the French position. His battalion advanced with enthusiasm and 'although obliged at times to climb on hands and knees, nothing could withstand their impetuosity'.[12] They were counter-attacked in great force and Wellesley was obliged to send forward his whole line to rescue them. Colonel Lake was killed and 190 of his men were casualties but at the end of the day the French were driven off in disorder, losing 600 men and six guns. The British lost 474. The battle proved nothing since the British greatly outnumbered their enemy who had every intention of retreating as soon as they were pressed. The unfortunate result of Roliça was that those who disliked Wellesley, and some others, got the impression that he had gone bull-headed at the ridge and incurred unnecessary casualties. It strengthened the impression, held by Dalrymple and Burrard amongst others, that he was a rash young general who would go at the French as he was reputed to have done to the Indians.

Next morning the British marched to Vimeiro.[5/1] Wellesley had heard that two brigades of reinforcements, not part of Moore's force, were off the coast. Behind Vimeiro was Maceira Bay where they could land. With this addition of 5,000 men Wellesley would be on equal terms with any corps Junot could bring against him. He reported to London that, 'I shall be able to give you a good account of the French army; but I am afraid that I shall not gain a complete victory: that is I shall not entirely destroy them from want of cavalry.'[13]

Junot was marching up from Lisbon with 13,000 men.[6/1] He could have brought more but he was worried about his base. News of the British landing had brought the capital to the edge of revolt and he felt it essential to leave a heavy garrison to overawe the population. His position was made no easier by the presence in the Tagus of a squadron of nine Russian battleships. Russia was at war with Britain but not with Portugal and the admiral announced that he and his 6,000 men were neutral. He refused to help the French in policing Lisbon but continued to demand rations. Junot was not greatly concerned at the smallness of his corps. He did not know that 5,000 men were joining Wellesley from the sea and expected the

two armies to be about equal in numbers. He had 2,000 cavalry
against 240 and 23 guns against 18.

The reinforcements had almost all landed by the evening of 20
August and Wellesley issued orders for an advance in the morning.
He knew Junot was in a strong position at Torres Vedras but did
not intend to attack him there. Instead he proposed to keep to the
coast, moving by Mafra so that he would be on Junot's flank and
closer to Lisbon than the French. Hardly were the orders despatched
than Sir Harry Burrard sailed into Maceira Bay accompanied only by
his personal staff. Wellesley was rowed out to see him and explained
his plans. Burrard was appalled at the younger man's rashness. 'I
gave the subject every consideration in my power, and decided that
the army should halt. Had our arms in the progress of advancing
received a check, it was impossible to calculate the disasters to which
it might have exposed them.'[14] No argument would induce him to
agree to an advance until Moore's corps had joined the army. He had
left them at sea, 200 miles to the north. Leaving Burrard on board,
Wellesley returned to the army and cancelled the order to advance.
'I came from the frigate about nine at night, and went to my own
quarters with the army, which, from the nearness of the enemy, I
kept on the alert.'[15] 'As I am the "Child of Fortune" and Sir Harry
did not chuse to march, the enemy came to us.'[16]

In the small hours of 21 August a sergeant of dragoons was sent
back from the outposts with a message that the French were advancing.

> I rode to the house where the general dwelt and found him, with a
> large staff, all seated on a long table in the hall, back to back,
> swinging their legs to and fro, like men on whose minds not a
> shadow of anxiety rested. The general himself closely examined me
> and then told me I had done my duty well. He then desired me to go
> below and get something to eat and drink from his servant, which I
> did, but not before I heard him give his orders in a calm, clear and
> cheerful voice. 'Now, gentlemen, go to your stations: but let there
> be no noise made, no sounding of bugles or beating of drums. Get
> your men quietly under arms, and desire all the outposts to be on
> the alert.'[17]

Junot was nicknamed 'the Hurricane' in the French army. He had
risen to his high rank through his personal bravery and his close

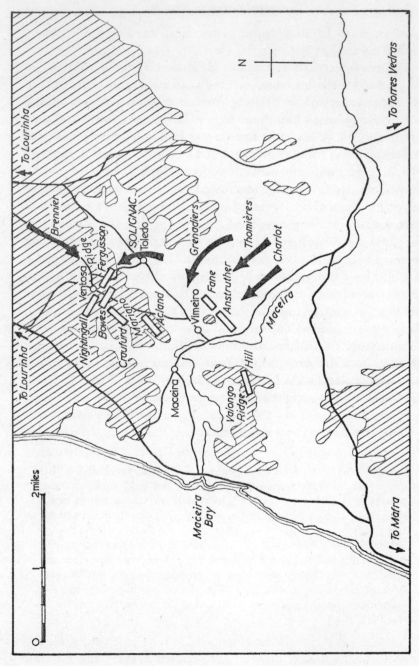

Vimeiro—shaded area indicates land over 260 feet above sea level

association with the Emperor, whose ADC he had been. His chief
of staff wrote that although 'blindly courageous as a soldier, he had
no comprehensive view, no foresight, no inspiration. In battle the
only thing he understood was shock action.'[18] Like most French
officers at this time he believed that if the British were attacked with
sufficient determination they would take to their ships. He planned
to launch three of his five infantry brigades at Vimeiro village while
sending another round Wellesley's left flank to cut off his retreat.

Wellesley had anticipated that Junot would attack his right in an
attempt to get between the army and the landing beach. The bulk of
the army was stationed so as to cover this approach. The village and
the little hill in front of it were held by two brigades as an advanced
post. Clouds of dust showed the way Junot's men were moving and
there was plenty of time to switch troops to the left before battle was
joined. Junot also had second thoughts. He decided to send another
brigade to his right but made no arrangement for the two on that
flank to work together. The first brigade having already started its
march, its commander remained in ignorance of being reinforced.

The main attack on Vimeiro village was thus reduced to two
brigades. Both suffered severely from Wellesley's screen of Riflemen
and from the artillery but they came on, said Wellesley, 'with more
confidence, and seemed to feel their way less than I always found
them to do afterwards'.[19] They made no progress. The steady British
volleys brought them to a standstill and they broke leaving seven
guns behind them. Undeterred, Junot threw in his reserve brigade,
2,000 picked grenadiers. Instead of attacking the hill, they swerved
round to the right and marched straight at the village, but battalions
had been sent down from the main position to strengthen it. There
was some hard fighting, especially in the cemetery, but the grenadiers
were outnumbered and outfought. They were driven away by two
brigades and Wellesley launched his handful of cavalry at them. The
Twentieth Light Dragoons wheeled up from behind the hill and
charged.

> In an instant we were in the heart of the French, cutting and hack-
> ing, and upsetting men and horses in the most extraordinary
> manner possible until they broke and fled in all directions. Though
> scattered, as always happens in a charge, we still kept laying about

us, till our white breeches, our hands, arms and swords were all besmeared with blood. As the enemy gave way we continued to advance, amid a cloud of dust so thick that to see beyond this distance of those immediately about yourself was impossible.[20]

The dragoons were out of hand and became an easy prey to the powerful French cavalry. They lost their colonel and one man in five, but Junot had used up all his available infantry and could not continue the attack on the village.

On the British left the attack did not start until the fighting near Vimeiro was over. The two French brigades attacked at different times and from different directions. The first advanced from in front of the British left. They came up a track which climbed the ridge and found themselves faced with a brigade waiting for them in line; 2,400 muskets opened on them at a range of 100 yards. Then, in complete silence, the line advanced towards them. 'The enemy retired before us. A part of them rallied but General Fergusson hussa'ed the Thirty Sixth, a very weak though fine regiment, to charge, which was done in great style three successive times.'[21] The French brigade was driven off leaving seven guns, but as they were being pursued the second of Junot's flanking brigades struck in behind the pursuers. They achieved surprise and had some initial success, but plenty of British reserves were on hand and after a short, bitter fight the last French attack was scattered.

This was the moment for which Wellesley had been waiting. His army had suffered only 720 casualties. They had captured 300 prisoners and all but nine of the French guns. The right could be wheeled up, led by three brigades which had yet to fire a shot, and the British could get between Lisbon and the French. Unfortunately, Wellesley was no longer in command. Burrard had landed from the sea in time to see the last shots fired. Wellesley rode up to him and said, 'Sir Harry, now is your time to advance, the enemy are completely beaten and we shall be in Lisbon in three days.' Sir Harry Burrard replied that he thought a great deal had been done very much to the credit of the troops, but that he did not think it advisable to move off the ground in pursuit of the enemy.[22] Wellesley pressed the case for following up the victory but Burrard 'saw no reason for altering my former resolution of not advancing'.[23] Wel-

Page 67 (*left*) Privates of the Toledo Regiment and Walloon Guards; (*above*) Fourth Regiment of the Portuguese Caçadores; both by Denis Dighton

Picquet of 45me Régiment by Denis Dighton

lesley 'turned his horse's head, and with a cold contemptuous bitterness, said aloud to his aide-de-camp, "You may think about dinner for there is nothing more for soldiers to do this day." '[24]

Next morning the army was still encamped round Vimeiro and Sir Hew Dalrymple arrived from Gibraltar to take the command. He was in conference with Burrard when a white flag was sent in from the French lines. Junot had held a council of war. All his generals agreed that their situation was impossible. General Kellermann was sent to negotiate. As he rode out through the French lines he remarked to a friend that he was 'going to see the English to try and find some way out of this mousetrap'.[25]

Dalrymple was happy to oblige him. Before dark an armistice was drafted and the new Commander-in-Chief asked Wellesley to sign it on his behalf. 'I read it over and at the table gave it to Sir Hew Dalrymple to read, with an observation that it was a very extraordinary paper. He answered that it did not contain anything that had not been settled, and I then signed it.'[26]

The armistice, which was later formalised into a convention, arranged that the French army should be taken back to France in British ships. They were to take with them their artillery, their horses and their baggage, which was stuffed with Portuguese loot. The terms were far more generous than Junot could have dared to hope. Wellesley wrote to Castlereagh next morning to explain his situation. 'Although my name is affixed to this instrument, I beg you will not believe that I negotiated it, that I approve of it, or that I had any hand in wording it. It was negotiated by the general himself in my presence and that of Sir Harry Burrard: and after it had been drawn out by Kellermann himself, Sir Hew Dalrymple desired me to sign it.'[27] In another letter he wrote, 'I have only to regret that I signed the agreement without having negotiated. I doubt whether good nature and a deference to the opinion of an officer appointed Commander in Chief on the day of his taking command, and to his orders, and the desire to avoid being considered the head of a party against his authority, will be deemed sufficient excuse for an act which, on other grounds, I cannot justify.'[28]

Dalrymple, on the other hand, was anxious to implicate Wellesley in the armistice. If the terms were to be queried in Britain, he could

c

say that a member of the government, as Wellesley still was, had 'borne that prominent part in the discussion which the situation he so lately filled, the victory he had just gained, and his own more perfect information, gave him a just right to assume'.[29] The armistice was signed on 22 August. Dalrymple neglected to write to London on this, or any other subject, until 3 September.

Vimeiro was the first significant victory which British troops had won on the continent for more than half a century. Wellesley's despatch reached London on 1 September. Government and press gave it a rapturous reception. The guns of the Tower of London were fired in jubilation. Newspapers assumed that the whole Peninsula was as good as liberated. The *Morning Chronicle* went so far as to write, 'We hope and trust that our army in Portugal, reinforced by a body now embarking, are intended to act in Italy . . . We might safely count on the emancipation of Italy—a thing most truly to be desired.'[30]

When Dalrymple's despatch eventually reached London, public opinion reacted violently and since Dalrymple had worded his letter carefully criticism centred on Wellesley.

> Who [demanded the *Chronicle*] will believe that Sir Arthur, a Minister of State, highly and powerfully connected, of a family certainly not distinguished for the meek submissiveness of their tempers, would involuntarily subscribe an instrument at once of his own and his country's dishonour? Had he not approved it, we are convinced that he would, rather than sign it, have cut off his right hand sooner than stoop to such ignominy.[31]

Dalrymple, Burrard and Wellesley were brought before a Court of Enquiry at Chelsea Hospital. The court produced a long report which exculpated everyone, paid a handsome compliment to Wellesley and attributed the fiasco to 'the very extraordinary circumstances under which two Commanders in Chief arrived from the ocean, the one during, the other immediately after a battle, and those successively superseding each other, and both the original commander within a space of twenty four hours'.[32]

This satisfied no one, least of all King George who publicly censured Dalrymple. A hundred and fifty-three members of Parliament voted against a motion approving the armistice and convention.

Many speakers in the debate blamed Wellesley for rashness and misjudgement. Before the storm died down more depressing news had come from the Peninsula. The British army had been driven to its ships.

CHAPTER 5

Napoleon and Sir John Moore

IN Paris the Emperor addressed the Corps Legislatif on 25 October. 'I leave in a few days to put myself at the head of my army and, with the help of God, I will crown the king of Spain in Madrid and plant my eagles on the ramparts of Lisbon.'[1] Eleven days later he reached Joseph's headquarters at Vitoria. His striking force consisted of 152,000 men organised in five corps and a reserve which included the Imperial Guard.* He intended to guard each flank with two corps used offensively against the Spanish concentrations while he blasted his way through to Madrid with Soult's corps and the reserve.

There was chaos on the Spanish side. The French seizure of the centre of Spain had driven the Spaniards back to their old provincial loyalties and the jealousies and rivalries that went with them. A national Junta had been assembled at Aranjuez but had contented itself with the delights of constitution-making. A conference of

---

* At the beginning of November the total strength of the Army of Spain was 314,612. Of these 70,000 were sick, detached or missing. 36,000 (VII Corps) were in Catalonia. 42,500 men (V and VIII Corps) were still north of the Pyrenees. The strength also included garrisons in Spain and on the French frontier.
The striking force consisted of:

I Corps (Marshal Victor)	3 divs
II Corps (Marshal Soult from 9 November)	3 divs
III Corps (Marshal Moncey)	4 divs
IV Corps (Marshal Lefebvre)	3 divs
VI Corps (Marshal Ney)	2 divs
Imperial Guard (Gen Walther)	14 bns infantry, 4¼ regts cavalry
King Joseph's Guard (Gen Saligny)	4 bns infantry, 1 regt cavalry
Reserve of Cavalry (Marshal Bessières)	25 regts
Dessolles's infantry division	

provincial Captains General had been an acrimonious affair. It had reached broad agreement on how to drive the French over the Pyrenees but its plan had little contact with reality. A holding force was to face the French across the Ebro while the enemy was to be assailed on both flanks. The details and timing of these attacks were left to the commanders on the spot since no commander was prepared to accept instructions from anyone else. They had 87,000 men available, less than the French had had before Napoleon arrived with the Grande Armée. The holding force on the French front consisted of only 12,000 men, most of them recruits. There should have been more but the Army of Estremadura was still besieging the French garrison of the Portuguese fortress of Elvas which had already surrendered to the British. Feeling that their centre was rather thinly held, the Spaniards swallowed their pride and suggested, without enthusiasm, that the British army in Portugal might care to strengthen them there by marching to Burgos.

After their own nominees, Dalrymple and Burrard, had proved futile the British cabinet could no longer refuse to appoint Moore to the command in Portugal. On 6 October he received orders to take 23,000 men from there and march into Spain where he was to be joined by 10,000 more who were to be landed at Coruña. 'There has,' he wrote, 'been no such command since Marlborough for a British officer.'[2] On the other hand, he had to point out that his army was 'without equipment of any kind, either for the carriage of the light baggage of regiments, artillery stores, commissariat stores, or other appendages of an army'.[3] *

John Moore was forty-seven years old in 1808. He had fought in America, Corsica, the West Indies, the Netherlands and Egypt and was the most respected soldier in the army. He was an excellent administrator and the finest trainer of troops the British army has ever known. As colonel of the Fifty Second he had set in train a revolution in the relationship between officers and men. He noted

---

* The government had deliberately sent the expedition abroad without equipment, explaining that 'the great delay and expense that would attend embarking and sending from hence all those means which would be requisite to render the army completely movable immediately on its landing, has determined HM Government to trust in great measure to the resources of the country for their supplies'. (WD iv 29, Castlereagh to W, 15 Jul 1808.)

with satisfaction that in his regiment 'it is evident that not only the officers, but that each individual soldier, knows perfectly what he has to do; the discipline is carried on without severity, the officers are attached to the men and the men to the officers'.[4] He had a knack of inspiring devotion in those who served under him. John Colborne, a future field-marshal, wrote that he was 'a most extraordinary man; the nearer you saw him the more he was admired; he had a magnificent mind. He was superior by many degrees to every one I have ever seen.'[5] His defects were few. Although a man of great charm he found it difficult to tolerate foolish politicians and diplomats, and sharp, if justified, comments in his despatches made him enemies in influential quarters. He had never held an independent command in face of the enemy and he was unduly sensitive to criticism both from London and from his own troops. Some accused him of indecisiveness, but Colborne said that he 'never met so decisive a character'.[6]

Before the end of the month the whole of the corps from Lisbon, with improvised transport, was on the march to the Spanish border. So ignorant were the Portuguese of the state of their own country that the only information Moore could obtain was that the direct road to the frontier at Ciudad Rodrigo was impassable for artillery. Seeing no alternative, Moore sent all but one of his batteries on a circuitous road by Badajoz, Talavera and El Escurial, which was almost on the outskirts of Madrid. They were escorted by two brigades of infantry and all the cavalry, two regiments. The main body of infantry marched by Coimbra and Celorico. It began to arrive at Salamanca on 23 November, having had no difficulty in moving the single battery that accompanied it. It was 4 December before the artillery column completed the longer march and reached Alba de Tormes, fifteen miles from Salamanca. The reinforcements coming from England suffered infuriating delays. The infantry reached Coruña on 13 October but the Galician junta refused them permission to land. A messenger had to be sent galloping to Aranjuez to consult the central junta who approved of the landing. The infantry began to go ashore on 4 November and the cavalry, who had been despatched late from England, were not disembarked until the 11th. There was great difficulty in finding transport for the regiments and Sir David Baird, who commanded the force, was induced by the junta to send his troops forward by small detachments. By 22 November Baird with his infantry had reached Astorga, 120 miles from Moore at Salamanca. Baird's three regiments of cavalry were several days' march behind him.

Moore, following his orders from London, had intended to march to Burgos so that he could take his place in line with the Spanish armies facing the Ebro. By the time two-thirds of his army was concentrated at Salamanca the whole situation had changed irrevocably. The French held Burgos and the two Spanish armies on their flanks had been defeated and driven away in disorder.

> This [wrote Moore] is a state of things quite different from that conceived by the British government when they determined to send troops to the assistance of Spain. It was not expected that they were to cope alone with the whole force of France; but as auxiliaries, to aid a people who were believed to be enthusiastic, determined and prepared for resistance. It becomes, therefore, a question whether the British army should remain to be attacked in its turn or retire from a country where the contest has become unequal.[7]

Moore's dilemma was acute. If he continued to advance, the French must overwhelm him. If he retreated the Spaniards would accuse him and his country of desertion. For a few days he waited at Salamanca for further news. It came on the night of 28 November and it was bad. Castaños, the victor of Bailen, had been routed at Tudela five days earlier. His course was clear.

> I have determined to give the thing up. It was my wish to have run great risks to fulfill what I conceive to be the wishes of the people of England, and to give every aid to the Spanish cause. But they have shown themselves equal to do so little for themselves, that it would only be sacrificing this army, without doing any good to Spain, to oppose such numbers as must now be brought against us.[8]

Baird was told to take his men back to Coruña and re-embark them. Moore prepared to take his corps back to Portugal, 'which I cannot long defend; but perhaps for a sufficient time to cover the embarkation of stores, &c., from Lisbon. Portugal must be evacuated if the French get Spain.'[9] The most he dared hope was that the army might sail to Cadiz so that a fresh effort could be made.

Moore's decision to leave Spain was unquestionably right but he was bombarded with appeals from the Spaniards and from the British minister to Spain to advance. Napoleon stormed the Somosierra pass over the Guadarrama mountains on 30 November. On 2 December the French were at the gates of Madrid. Only 3,000 Spanish regulars were in garrison. Their commander addressed a passionate appeal to Moore on the same day. Next day, before the appeal could have reached Moore, he surrendered without firing a shot. The Spaniards omitted to tell Moore of the surrender. He heard of it from one of his own officers six days later.

Despite the logic of his decision, Moore could not bring himself to retire. He continued to wait at Salamanca until 6 December when he made up his mind to advance. He could do no good at Madrid but he might make a valuable diversion by striking at Valladolid. 'I shall threaten the French communications and create a diversion, if the Spaniards can avail themselves of it.'[10] 'I shall be in Fortune's way; if she smiles, we may do some good; if not, we shall still, I hope, have the merit of having done all we could.'[11] 'I mean to proceed bridle in hand; for, if the bubble bursts, we shall have a run for it.'[12]

It was a chivalrous gesture, a determination to put loyalty to the Spanish alliance above military considerations. It was a gamble on a scale he had not realised. Moore estimated the French field army at 'from 80 to 90,000',[13] whereas the true figure was 150,000.

His boldness was rewarded by two strokes of good luck. On 12 December British hussars surprised a French cavalry patrol at Rueda, twenty miles from Valladolid. Thirty-five men were captured and from them it was learned that the enemy had no idea that any British troops were within a hundred miles of them. Two days later even more valuable information came in. Peasants murdered a French staff officer carrying a letter from Napoleon's Chief of Staff to Marshal Soult. They sold the letter to Moore's headquarters for twenty dollars. It showed the whole disposition of the French army in Spain and made it clear that Napoleon's intention was to drive on Lisbon from Madrid by way of Talavera and Badajoz. Napoleon believed that Moore and his army were already retreating to Lisbon. Most promising of all was the information that the only French troops in Moore's vicinity were two divisions* and four cavalry regiments, about 20,000 men, of Soult's corps holding the line of the river Carrion, well to the north of Valladolid. The nearest body of supporting French troops was Ney's corps at Madrid, 120 miles away.

At last Moore had a practicable operation in prospect. He had three men to every two of Soult's[5/2] and the marshal could be destroyed in isolation. On 20 December the British army, five divisions of infantry and two cavalry brigades, was concentrated at Mayorga, and next day the cavalry, led by Lord Paget, attacked one of Soult's cavalry brigades at Sahagun.

> The French, upon our coming in sight, made a flank movement, apparently with the intention of getting away; but the rapidity of our advance soon convinced them of the futility of such an attempt. They therefore halted and deployed. As soon as they were formed, they cheered in a very gallant manner and immediately began firing. The Fifteenth [Hussars] then halted, wheeled into line, huzza'ed and advanced. The interval betwixt us was perhaps 400 yards, but it was so quickly passed that they had only time to fire a few shots before we came among them, shouting 'Emsdorff† and Victory!' The shock was terrible; horses and men were overthrown, and a shriek of terror, intermixed with oaths, groans and prayers for mercy, issued from the whole extent of their front. Our men pressed forward until they had cut their way quite through the column. In many places the bodies of the fallen formed a complete mound of men and horses, but very few of our people were hurt.[14]

One of the two French regiments was all but destroyed and had to be disbanded.

Giving time for the infantry to come up and rest at Sahagun, Moore gave orders for the final advance to start on the morning of 23 December. That day one of his aides-de-camp wrote in his diary:

> Frost in the morning. Orders to march at 8 a.m. in two columns on Carrion. In the afternoon a despatch with the intelligence of the enemy marching [from Madrid] determined the general to abandon the attack on Soult's corps. A retreat on Astorga now becomes im-

---

* Soult's third infantry division had been detached as garrison of Santander.
† At the battle of Emsdorff (16 July 1760) the Fifteenth Light Dragoons had greatly distinguished themselves and subsequently wore the battle honour on their helmets and appointments.

periously necessary so as to prevent the enemy cutting in on the communication with Galicia. There is not a man in the army who will not feel mortified and disappointed at the counter orders just issued.[15]

Moore's bubble had burst. Napoleon was bringing up overwhelming strength. The only hope was to make for Coruña and the ships.

Napoleon was determined to destroy Moore's army. Nothing else, he believed, would stop the British government's meddling in the Peninsula. Although he had a very powerful force of cavalry with which to search for Moore, he preferred to rely on scraps of evidence and a preconceived idea that he would be to the west of Madrid. Some German dragoons* were captured near Talavera on 11 December. This convinced Napoleon that Moore was at Plasencia. In fact the Germans had been part of the escort to the British artillery on its circuitous march. They had lost touch with their regiment when they went off on an unofficial foraging expedition. He pressed on with his preparations for an advance through Badajoz and announced publicly that 'the enemy are in full flight towards Lisbon and if they do not make haste the French army may reach that capital before they do'.[16] In the next week news reached him that 14,000 British had been at Astorga and others at Salamanca. He continued to believe that Moore was at Plasencia.

Three German deserters were found at El Escurial on 18 December. They asserted that a large British force was at Salamanca and was about to march on Valladolid. Next afternoon a despatch arrived from Soult reporting the attack on his piquet at Rueda on 12 December. He estimated the British strength on that occasion at three squadrons of cavalry and 5,000 infantry. At last Napoleon was convinced that Moore was operating north of Madrid rather than to the west. Orders were issued immediately to crush him between two large French forces. From Madrid 35,000 men would march north to act as a hammer while Soult's corps would play the part of an anvil. Soult was to be reinforced by parts of Junot's VIII Corps which were now arriving from France.

---

* These were members of the King's German Legion. This body of all arms was part of the British army and was the successor to King George's Hanoverian army. It was originally recruited almost wholly of Hanoverians but was later diluted with less reliable Germans, some of whom had previously been in the French service.

Ney's corps marched out of Madrid at dawn on 20 December. Napoleon instructed King Joseph to 'put in your newspapers that 36,000 English are surrounded, that I am in their rear while Soult is in front of them'.[17] He also dashed off a note to the Empress. 'I am just setting off to deal with the English. They seem to have been reinforced and to want to try their luck. The weather is fine; my health is excellent. Do not worry.'[18] Then he rode out of Madrid at the head of the Imperial Guard, dismounting to march with them as they struggled through the snow drifts in the high Sierra de Guadarrama.

Even now Napoleon was wrong about Moore's whereabouts. He expected to find him at Valladolid and this belief was strengthened by one of his generals at Segovia who reported that his outposts had seen British cavalry ten miles south-east of Valladolid. In fact Moore was sixty miles north of Valladolid at Sahagun. Warned of Napoleon's march from Madrid, the British retreated rapidly and crossed the river Esla at Benavente on 27 December. Soult was acting sluggishly and Moore got clean away. His cavalry were ably commanded by Lord Paget and on the 29th fought an excellent rearguard action at Benavente in which the general commanding the cavalry of the Imperial Guard was captured.

From this time onwards more of Moore's difficulties were caused by the indiscipline of his own men than by the French pursuit. A highland soldier wrote, 'Our sufferings were so great that many of the men lost their natural activity and spirits, and became savage in their disposition. They began to seize food in the towns and villages, forced their way into houses and (the country being singularly destitute of wood) tore down sheds and doors to build up their bivouac fires.'[19] As yet the rigours of the retreat were only beginning. Moore had hoped to make a stand at Astorga but when he reached the town he found that the magazines there contained food for only two days. He ordered the retreat to be resumed. The troops were deeply resentful at not being allowed to fight.

On New Year's Eve the long columns began to wind up the passes of the Montes de Leon.

We pushed on all day without halting [remembered a Rifleman]. Night came down on us, without our having tasted food or halting

and all night long we continued this dreadful march. Men began to
look at each others faces and ask the question, 'Are we never to be
halted again?', and many of the weaker sort were now seen to
stagger, make a few desperate efforts, and then fall to rise no more.
Thus we staggered on for four days and nights before we could
discover the reason for this continued forced march. The discovery
was made in our company by a good tempered fellow named Patrick
Maclauchlin. He inquired of an officer marching directly in his front
the destination intended. I heard him say, 'By Jasus, Musther Hills,
where the divil is this you're taking us too?' 'To England, Maclauchlin,' returned the officer with a melancholy smile, 'If we can
get there'.[20]

Some men fell out from cold and fatigue. Many more left the
ranks in search of plunder or drink. At Bembibre 'the cellars were
unfortunately too well stored with a pernicious "black strap"
manufactured from the mountain vine that grew in the neighbourhood. The soldiers, not waiting to broach the barrels in the usual
way, stove them in, or picked the heads in with their bayonets; so
that they were wallowing in the liquor that flowed in black streams
around them. They floated in lakes of wine.'[21] In Villafranca,

> parties of drunken soldiers were committing all kinds of enormities;
> several houses were in flames. The gutters were flowing with rum,
> a number of puncheons having been staved in the street and a
> promiscuous rabble were drinking and filling bottles in the street.
> Numbers of the stragglers were so drunk that all our efforts to drive
> them on were fruitless, and we were obliged to leave them to their
> fate. They were soon overtaken by the French *chasseurs* who treated
> them most unmercifully, cutting to their left and right, and sparing
> none who came in reach of their swords. One of them who escaped
> and rejoined the army presented the most shocking sight I ever
> beheld. It was impossible to distinguish a single feature. The flesh
> of his cheeks and lips were hanging in collops; his nose was split and
> his ears were cut off.[22]

> Many regiments [noted a cavalryman] were nearly deserted; for
> miles the men were scouring the country and plundering every
> house. On one occasion I saw a regiment, if regiment it could be
> called, march into a town, consisting of two sergeants carrying the
> colours and not more than thirty men with them. The rest were
> scattered over the country.[23]

John Moore was the most humane commander of his time but he

was sickened by the excesses of his men. He executed a soldier for breaking into a rum store but this single example was ineffective. On 6 January he published a biting General Order.

> The Commander of the Forces is tired of giving orders which are never attended to: he therefore appeals to the honour and feelings of the army he commands; and if those are not sufficient to induce them to do their duty, he must despair of doing so by any other means. He was forced to order one soldier shot at Villafranca and he will order all others to be executed who are guilty of similar enormities: but he considers that there would be no occasion to proceed to such extremes if the officers did their duty; as it is chiefly from their negligence, and from the want of proper regulation in their regiments, that crimes and irregularities are committed in quarters and upon the march.[24]

His army was dissatisfied with a general who appeared determined not to let them fight. A surgeon wrote that

> many officers are inclined to blame our commander for the rapidity with which he has conducted our retreat over a country which, to the most unpractised military eye, appears so admirably calculated for defence. This conduct is defended on the plea of necessity, as it became impossible for the commissariat to procure supplies for the army. To this reasoning it has been answered that, for much of the way, the hills are covered with sheep: that we have killed between 5,000 and 6,000 horses with many draught bullocks, mules and asses —all of which might have afforded subsistence to the army for several weeks, had Sir John complied with the general sentiment of the army, and set himself to defend the passes of the mountains.[25]

The disorders and the grumbling were confined to the regiments who led the retreat. The rearguard, consisting of the Lord Paget's cavalry and the Reserve division, under his brother Edward Paget, never wavered in their discipline and were more than a match for the French who pressed them. The hard core of the Reserve were regiments Moore had trained five years earlier, the Fifty Second Light Infantry and the Ninety Fifth Rifles. They made a stand at every defile and riverline, buying time for the rest of the army to get away. Some of the stragglers also distinguished themselves. These were men whom only fatigue had forced from the ranks. One party under Sergeant William Newman of the Forty Third trudged on through the snow until they were overtaken by French dragoons. They formed a rallying square, fought off their attackers and then marched on to join their regiments.*

The first part of the pursuit had been directed by Napoleon. When he reached Astorga on 2 January he realised that Moore could not be caught. He handed the chase over to Soult and a reinforced corps and started his journey back to France. He wrote to Joseph, 'The Guard is returning to Benavente. I am returning to the centre of my army. Fire salutes to celebrate our victories over the English.'[26] He claimed to have 'nearly 4,500 English prisoners'† and assumed that 'the English army is reduced by a third; and if to this third is added the horses killed, thus making cavalrymen useless, I do not think that they can put in line more than 15,000 fit men and 1,500 cavalry. This is a long way from the 30,000 with whom they set out.'[27]

Moore had detached 4,500 men to Vigo but could still put 19,000 men in line at Lugo where he halted to offer battle and rest his exhausted men. Soult's men were as tired as Moore's and his divisions were strung out over miles of road. He saw the natural strength of Moore's position and declined to attack. After a halt of sixty hours the British continued their retreat and the army marched into Coruña on the night of 11 January. 'Our beards were long and ragged. Almost all were without shoes and stockings; many had their clothes and accoutrements in fragments, with their heads swathed in old rags, and our weapons were covered with rust; while not a few men had now, from toil and fatigue, become quite blind.'[28] The Reserve still kept the French at arm's length but among the main body of the army some regiments were little better than a rabble. Two battalions stood out. They swung into Coruña with their ranks dressed, their bands playing, their sergeants calling the step. 'Ah!' said Moore, 'those must be the Guards.'

Reaching the sea was not the end of their troubles. An easterly wind had held the troop transports off Vigo and they did not make Coruña until 15 January. Moore wrote:

---

* Newman was rewarded with an ensigncy in the West India Regiment and a cash grant of £50 from the Patriotic Fund. In 1811 he was promoted lieutenant in the Duke of York's Light Infantry.

† According to French figures, the total number of British prisoners taken in the whole of Moore's campaign was 2,189.

Had I found them on arrival the embarkation would easily have been effected, for I had gained several marches on the French. They have now come up with us. My position in front of this place is a very bad one; and Coruña, if I am forced to retire into it, is commanded by high ground within musket shot. In that case the harbour will be so commanded by cannon on the coast that no ship will be able to lay in it.[29]

As soon as the ships arrived a start was made with embarking stores, wounded and dismounted cavalrymen. By mid-day on 16 January all the non-essentials and most of the artillery were on board. Moore said, ' "Now, if there is no bungling, I hope we shall get away in a few hours." A few minutes after, Sir John Hope came with the news that the French were advancing in great force[6/2] and they soon opened a furious cannonade on us from the heights.'[30]

A naval officer who had gone ashore that morning was depressed to see that

The soldiers lay scattered about, wearied and dispirited, ragged in their dress and many of them sickly or rather broken down in appearance by the fatigue of the retreat. Most of their chins had been untouched by a razor for some days, perhaps weeks, while their hands and faces seemed rather less familiar with soap and water than with the smoke of their muskets and the charcoal of their cooking fires. The muskets were piled in pyramids along the ridge amongst the men who were stretched on the ground fast asleep, not in any precise order, but within a few yards of the summit of the ridge. Many were sitting on the grass which covered the ground and looking in silence, with very wistful eyes, towards the ships. I asked one of the officers whether he thought anything could rouse the men up. In reply he said, with a very expressive smile and a slight nod of his head, 'You'll see by and by, Sir, if the French choose to come over.'

The words were scarcely uttered when a movement along the whole enemy line became apparent and a furious cannonading was opened. At the first discharge the whole of the British troops, from one end of the line to the other, started to their feet, snatched up their arms and formed themselves with as much regularity as if they had been exercising themselves in Hyde Park. Before, a silence had reigned over the field—now there was a loud hum and occasionally a loud shout and many a burst of laughter, in the midst of which could be heard a peculiar click, click as the bayonets were fixed.[31]

Coruña

Soult slightly outnumbered the British. He made his main attack on the village of Elvina. Charles Napier, commanding the Fiftieth on the slope above the village, saw

a heavy French column coming on with great rapidity and shouting, 'En avant! Tue! En Avant! Tue!', while their cannon from above ploughed the ground and tore our ranks. Suddenly I heard the gallop of horses and, turning, saw Moore. He came at speed and pulled up so sharp and close that he seemed to have alighted from the air, man and horse looking at the approaching foe with an intentness that seemed to concentrate all feeling in their eyes. The sudden stop of the animal, a cream coloured one with black tail and mane, had cast the latter one streaming forward, its ears pushed out like horns, while its eyes flashed fire, and it snorted loudly with expanded nostrils. Thrown on its haunches the animal came, sliding and dashing the dirt up with its front feet, thus bending the general forward almost to its neck; but his head was thrown back and his look more keenly piercing than I ever saw it before. [A few minutes later], a round shot struck the ground between his horse's feet and mine. The horse leaped round, and I turned mechanically, but Moore forced the animal back and asked me if I was hurt. Meanwhile a second shot tore off the leg of a man who screamed horribly and rolled about so as to excite agitation and alarm in others. The general said, 'This is nothing, my lads; keep your ranks. Take that man away. My good fellow, don't make such a noise; we must bear these things better.' He spoke sharply but it had a good effect.[32]

At Elvina the fight swayed to and fro. The French seized the village but were driven out by the Black Watch and the Fiftieth. The French attacked again and there was momentary confusion in the British ranks. In the din of battle, an order to issue more ammunition was mistaken for one to retreat. The Black Watch fell back.

Seeing this, the general rode up to the regiment exclaiming, 'My brave Forty Second! If you have fired away all your ammunition, you still have your bayonets—more efficient. Recollect Egypt!* Think on Scotland! Come on, my gallant countrymen!' Thus directing the willing Forty Second to meet the renewed attack, he had the satisfaction to hear that the Guards were coming up and,

---

* The Black Watch had formed part of Moore's division at the battle of Alexandria (21 March 1801).

pleased, he sat proudly erect on his war-steed, calmly casting a satisfied glance at the raging war around.[33]

Henry Hardinge was beside Moore.

Our horses were touching at the very moment that a cannon ball
carried away his left shoulder and part of his collar bone, leaving the
arm hanging by the flesh. The violence of the stroke threw him off
his horse, on his back. Not a muscle of his face altered, nor did a
sigh betray the least sensation of pain. The blood flowed fast but
the attempt to stop it with my sash was useless from the size of the
wound. He assented to being removed in a blanket. In raising him
for this purpose, his sword, hanging on his wounded side, touched
his wound and became entangled between his legs. I was in the act
of unbuckling it when he said in his usual tone and manner and in a
very distinct voice, 'It is as well as it is. I had rather that it should
go out of the field with me.'[34]

The French were repulsed all along the line and next morning the
army embarked with little molestation. At eight o'clock in the morning Moore's body, wrapped in his cloak, was buried on the ramparts
of Coruña in a grave dug by the Ninth Foot. It was daylight and the
service had to be hurried as French shot was falling in the town.
Before he died he had said, 'I hope England will be satisfied. I hope
my country will do me justice.'

At first his country was far from satisfied. The largest British
army ever sent abroad, 'there had been no such command since
Marlborough for a British officer', had been hounded from the
continent, losing 6,000 men, a fifth of its strength. The plight of the
survivors horrified the people of the ports where they landed in
England. 'We were literally covered and almost eaten up with ver-
min, most of us suffering from ague and dysentry, every man a living
still active skeleton.'[35] The country believed that it had suffered a
major defeat and there were many, in Parliament, in the press and
even in his own army who were prepared to blame Moore for the
débâcle.

This was unjust. He had made mistakes. He had had his moments
of indecision but he had distorted Napoleon's grand strategy in such
a way that it never came right again. Just before his death he wrote
his own account of his achievement in a letter to Castlereagh.

Your lordship knows that had I followed my own opinion as a military man, I should have retired with the army from Salamanca. The Spaniards were then beaten; there was no Spanish force to which we could unite and I was satisfied that no efforts would be made to aid us. I was sensible, however, that the apathy and indifference of the Spaniards would never have been believed: that, had the British been withdrawn, the loss of the cause would have been imputed to their retreat: and it was necessary to risk the army to convince the people of England, as well as the rest of Europe, that the Spaniards had neither the power, nor the inclination, to make any efforts for themselves. It was for this reason that I marched to Sahagun. As a diversion it succeeded: I brought the whole disposable force of the French against this army.[36]

Moore bought time which the Spaniards, the Portuguese and the British desperately needed. Napoleon, with an Austrian war looming, could not afford to waste a week. Moore had drawn the French striking force to the coast of Galicia when it should have been marching on Lisbon. Wellington, who inherited the situation Moore left and turned it into overwhelming victory, remarked late in life, 'You know, we'd not have won, I think, without him.'

CHAPTER 6

The Second French Invasion of Portugal

'THE Spanish business is finished,' wrote Napoleon to his brother Jerome.[1] 'You can be assured that there is no longer a Spanish army,' he wrote to another correspondent. 'If the whole country has not yet been subjugated, it is because there is so much mud and because there has not been time; but everything will be finished.'[2] As he wrote these letters at Valladolid two Spanish armies were advancing on Madrid from the south. The French defeated them but could not destroy them.

The Emperor spent ten days at Valladolid giving orders for the completion of the conquest of Spain. Then he left Spain for ever, taking the Imperial Guard with him. His plan was simple, grandiose and utterly impracticable. It was based on three illusions. 'He kept repeating that the whole armed force of Spain could not resist 10,000 Frenchmen.'[3] He believed that Spain could easily provide rations for a large army. 'We have no need of supplies. There is plenty of everything.'[4] He was convinced that the British had taken such a beating that they would not return to the Peninsula. 'The English only escaped by one day's march. I doubt if half of them embarked. Those that did will be without horses, without equipment, very harassed, very demoralised, and, above all, covered with shame.'[5] 'He hoped that the British government would not dare to send another army to the Peninsula, or at least that they would not be able to do so until the country was conquered and quiet.'[6]

On all three points he was disastrously wrong. The Spanish armies were incompetent but indestructible. Unsuspected by Napoleon, the 'armed forces of Spain' were being supplemented day by day by guerrillas who were to impose an intolerable strain on the French army. The principal cause of their recruitment was the French attempt to extract from Spain food which did not exist. In the long run the most serious miscalculation was Napoleon's failure to realise that another British army was still in the Peninsula; 10,000 men held Lisbon and as long as Britain held that port the Peninsula could never be quiet.

In Spain 200,000 French troops 'present under arms' were available after the Guard had been withdrawn. They were organised in seven corps* of which one was isolated in Catalonia. The other six corps (112,000 men) were to be employed to conquer such parts of Spain as were not already occupied. Two corps were needed to prosecute the siege of Saragossa. The city put up an epic defence, setting an example to the rest of Spain. When it eventually surrendered on 20 February, 54,000 of its garrison and inhabitants were dead. So were 10,000 of the besiegers. Two more corps were needed to protect Madrid on the south and south-west. The available striking force had shrunk to two corps, those of Soult and Ney, which Moore had drawn up to Galicia. The first part of Napoleon's plan had, therefore, to be based on the north-west corner of Spain. Ney, with the smaller of the two corps, was to establish a firm base, give support to the main stroke and strike eastward to occupy the long mountainous principality of the Asturias. This was an ambitious programme for 16,500 men in bitterly hostile country, ideal for small defending forces.

---

* The seven corps, as reorganised in January 1809, were:

I Corps (Marshal Victor)	3 inf divs	23,000 men	(W and SW of Madrid)
II Corps (Marshal Soult)	4 inf divs	23,500 men	(Galicia)
III Corps (Gen Junot)	3 inf divs	16,000 men	(Saragossa)
IV Corps (Gen Sebastiani)	3 inf divs	15,000 men	(S of Madrid)
V Corps (Marshal Mortier)	2 inf divs	18,000 men	(Saragossa)
VI Corps (Marshal Ney)	2 inf divs	16,500 men	(Galicia)
VII Corps (Gen St Cyr)	7 inf divs	40,000 men	(Catalonia)

About 47,000 men comprised the Reserve of Cavalry (11,000), the Grand Park of Artillery, the garrison of Madrid (11,000) and other garrisons.

Soult's 23,500 fit men* were given a scarcely less formidable task. They were to march through the mountains from Coruña into northern Portugal. Oporto was to be occupied on 1 February, sixteen days after the battle of Coruña, and Lisbon nine days later.† This done, Soult was to detach one or two divisions to Badajoz where they were to join Marshal Victor for a triumphal march to Seville and Cadiz. King Joseph, who had reinstated himself in Madrid on 22 January, was advised to accompany Victor on the march to Seville. 'This operation will complete the Spanish business. I leave the glory of it to you.'[7]

Soult's opinion of his orders has not been recorded, but Joseph's chief of staff remarked mildly that the Emperor must have supposed that 'the roads were as freely passable as those from Paris to Lyons'.[8] The military opposition to Soult was small, ill-organised and fanatical. His first attempt to cross the river Minho into Portugal (16 February) ended in humiliating fiasco. He did not reach Oporto until 29 March when he stormed the town, against an incompetent defence, with great slaughter and a horrifying panic as the refugees broke the bridge of boats across the Douro under artillery fire from both banks. His army was exhausted and he could not contemplate a further move for several weeks. Portuguese irregulars closed round his rear, cutting his communication with Ney or any other French force.

While this was going on, the British government was havering. The cabinet was sharply divided and the Prime Minister's 'powers of attention were so weakened that he could neither read a paper nor listen for a while without becoming drowsy and falling asleep'.[9] The First Lord of the Admiralty was pressing for all available troops to be sent to the Scheldt to destroy a French naval squadron. Castlereagh favoured reinforcing the corps at Lisbon. Canning was determined to throw the main British weight behind the Spaniards in Andalusia. Canning had the best of the argument and troops were despatched to Cadiz. The Spaniards refused them permission to

---

* Soult's corps had 10,000 sick after the pursuit of Moore and 8,000 more had been detached in garrisons along the road. Of his 6,639 cavalry only 3,059 were available for operations. The rest were sick (572) or had lost their horses in the mountains.
† The dates were later put back one week.

land, affecting to believe that Britain intended to make Cadiz a second Gibraltar. With nowhere else to go, the troops went to Lisbon and the command there was entrusted once more to Arthur Wellesley on the unenthusiastic grounds that he was 'so young a lieutenant general that it will remain open to make a different arrangement if it shall appear proper to confide it to a general officer of higher rank'.[10] His task was specified as the defence of Portugal. He was not to enter Spain without specific authorisation from London. This time he resigned his office as Chief Secretary for Ireland before embarking.

The government had already taken one essential step towards making Portugal defensible. At the request of the Portuguese regency it had appointed a British general to be commander of the Portuguese army with the rank of marshal. It chose Major-General William Carr Beresford, largely on the ground that he was believed to speak the language and, although he later admitted that 'I was not then very much master of Portuguese',[11] no better selection could have been made. He faced a daunting task. The Portuguese army had been a useless body for fifty years and such organisation as existed had been deliberately disrupted by Junot in 1807–8. On arrival he commented to his half-sister, 'The confusion and chaos in which I found everything is not to be described, nor could I have believed that human ingenuity could so perfectly have confounded every-thing.'[12] He was a ferocious disciplinarian and needed to be. One of his British staff officers commented that 'the Portuguese is naturally indolent. He falls naturally into slouching and slovenly habits unless he is continually roused and forced to exert himself.'[13] 'The men,' said another, 'are well enough, very obedient, very willing and patient, but are naturally dirty and careless of their persons, dread-fully sickly and they have a natural softness, or want of fortitude, which makes them yield immediately to sickness or fatigue. The officers, for the most part, are detestable, mean, ignorant and self-sufficient.'[14] Out of this unpromising material Beresford and a small band of seconded British officers created a fine army which made the British force in the Peninsula large enough to take the field against the French.

Wellesley reached Lisbon on 22 April 1809. He was made Marshal

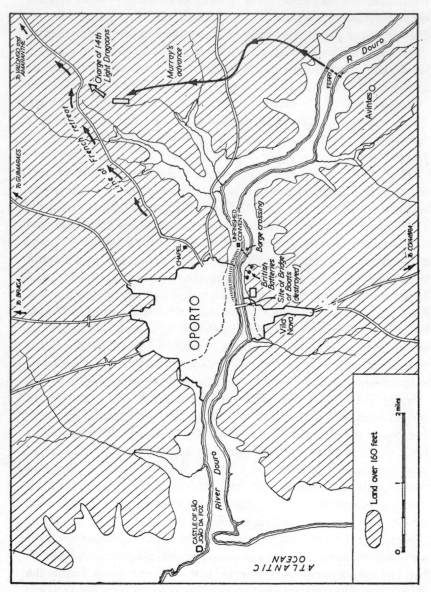

The forcing of the Douro

General of Portugal and thus received the overall command of both the British and Portuguese armies. He inspected a number of Portuguese units and reported 'the men very bad; the officers worse than anything I have ever seen'.[15] For the time being he would have to depend on his British troops, now reinforced up to 23,000 men.[5/3]

Two French corps appeared to threaten Portugal. In the north Soult was at Oporto with 20,000 men. To the east Victor, whom Wellesley believed to have 30,000, was at Merida, east of Badajoz. In March Victor had defeated a large Spanish army under General Cuesta at Medellin. Cuesta was busily reconstructing his shattered army but it would be some time before he could co-operate with the British in offensive operations. Soult posed the greatest threat to Lisbon and it was against him that Wellesley marched. Having detached troops to guard the eastern frontier and to garrison Lisbon, he concentrated 17,500 men at Coimbra in early May and, to make a show of numbers, brigaded with them 2,000 Portuguese. He knew that the Portuguese General Silveira was at Amaranthe holding the line of the Tamega which cut Soult's direct road to Spain. Silveira's corps could be invaluable in his projected operation, 'but I am not acquainted with its strength or its composition'.[16] He sent Beresford to support it with 5,000 Portuguese and two British battalions.

Knowing that Soult had a strong advanced guard on the south bank of the Douro, Wellesley tried to encircle it by landing two brigades from the sea at Ovar (10 May) but the French slipped away and on the evening of 11 May the two armies faced each other across the Douro, a river as broad as the Thames at Westminster. He had 18,000 men, including 2,000 Portuguese and 1,500 cavalry, and 24 guns. He had no plan for crossing the river but as a preliminary measure established three batteries of his heavier guns (6-pounders) on a height overlooking the river above the city.

Soult had decided to evacuate northern Portugal. Isolated from support and information, he realised that he could not hope to survive for long against a British strength which he overestimated. One of his divisions was probing Silveira's position on the Tamega hoping to find a short road back to Spain. Others were trying to open communication with Ney in Galicia. In Oporto he had 10,000 men

with which he guarded the waterfront of the city and the river between Oporto and the sea. He was confident that Wellesley would
not dare to attack him across the river and thought that any British
offensive would be undertaken in co-operation with the Royal Navy
landing troops behind his seaward flank. He kept no watch on the
river above the town although the stretch of river beyond the heights
on which the British guns were posted was invisible from his positions. The river there was 500 yards wide and he had given orders
that all boats should be brought across to the north bank. He
worked at his desk into the night of 11 May making arrangements
for his retreat. Next morning he slept late.

He was still asleep at ten o'clock when Colonel John Waters, one
of Beresford's British officers, reconnoitred the south bank of the
river east of the town. A Portuguese barber showed him a skiff
hidden in some bushes and pointed out four wine barges moored but
unguarded on the opposite bank about a mile and a half from
Oporto. Near the skiff 'were standing the prior of the convent and
three or four peasants. The latter, partly at Waters's entreaty, and
partly at the exhortations of the prior, were persuaded to leap with
him into the little skiff, and they made directly to the opposite bank,
where lay among the mud the barges, of which they made themselves masters. They returned with their prizes unobserved.'[17]

Waters reported the presence of the barges to Wellesley who
remarked quietly, 'Well, let the men cross.'

Each barge held thirty men. A company of the Buffs was immediately ferried across and took up a position in an unfinished convent on the north bank. The barges went back for a second lift and
the Buffs had time to build themselves a firestep within the convent
walls before they were molested. The barges had crossed four times
and General Edward Paget had almost a whole battalion ensconced
behind masonry on the north bank before the French realised what
had happened.

One of Soult's brigadiers, Maximilien Foy, happened during the
morning to climb the hill opposite Wellesley's batteries and looking
to his left saw 'barges full of men who had taken off their jackets, to
whom those already on the north bank were making signals. I was
convinced that these were Englishmen who, with unbelievable

impudence, were attempting to force a crossing by surprise.'[18] *
He sent an ADC to warn Soult and called up the nearest troops,
three battalions of 17me Léger. It was then about 11.30 am.

As Foy led the 17me to the attack they were swept by grapeshot
from the eighteen guns across the river and a French battery which
came up to support them lost a gun when a round of common shell
burst above it as it unlimbered. Foy was wounded and had a horse
shot under him. In half an hour the 17me lost one man in four but the
convent was perfectly secure and was being steadily reinforced.

The ADC woke Soult from his sleep. While dressing, the marshal
sent him back with orders to 'drive the English into the river'.
Three more French battalions reinforced the 17me. They made no
impression on the convent. Three British battalions were now in its
garrison. One of the few British casualties was Edward Paget whose
arm was shattered and had to be amputated. Desperate for reinforcements, Soult ordered the troops on the waterfront to abandon their
guard and march to their left to support Foy.

As soon as the quays were free of Frenchmen, the townspeople
rushed down to the waterside and launched everything that would
float. In an assortment of craft the Twenty Ninth Foot, with three
other battalions following, were ferried across the Douro and dashed
into the city. 'The people were mad with joy; every window, balcony
and door was crowded with people crying *Viva Ingleses! Viva
Ingleses!*, waving handkerchiefs, and scattering roses on the passing
troops.'[19]

Soult saw that Oporto was no longer tenable and ordered an
immediate retreat by the eastern road which led to Valongo and
Amaranthe. The French poured out of the town in disorder. An
officer of the Twenty Ninth recalled that 'They made no fight.
Every man seemed running for his life, throwing away their knap-
sacks and arms, so that we had only the trouble of making them
prisoners every instant, all begging for quarter and surrendering
with great good humour.'[20]

---

* According to some accounts, French patrols had seen redcoats around the unfinished convent but took them for Swiss troops in the French service who wore
scarlet. There were three Swiss battalions in Soult's corps, but Foy's account of men
crossing without jackets makes this story improbable.

Wellesley had only a fraction of his army across the river and a full-scale pursuit was impossible. Foreseeing this situation, he had sent his strongest brigade with two squadrons of cavalry across the river at Barca Avintas, a ferry five miles upstream. The appearance of this formed body across the escape route of the flying and disorganised French should have been decisive. Unfortunately it was commanded by Major-General John Murray, a stupid and irresolute officer who was to cause a great deal of trouble in Spain before the end of the war (see Chapter 18). Instead of attempting to block the road Murray held his men aside and only sent skirmishers to bicker with the French flanks. Castlereagh's brother Charles Stewart, who was Wellesley's Adjutant-General, did what he could to compensate for Murray's timidity and led forward the two squadrons of the Fourteenth Light Dragoons. Their colonel wrote:

> After going at full speed, enveloped in a cloud of dust, for nearly two miles we cleared our infantry and that of the French appeared. A strong body was drawn up in close column, with bayonets ready to receive us on their front. On each side of the road was a stone wall, bordered outwardly with trees. On our left in particular numbers of French were posted with their pieces resting on the wall which flanked the road, ready to give us a running fire as we passed. This could not but be effectual, as our men (in threes) were close to the muzzles, and barely out of reach of a *coup de sabre*. In a few seconds the ground was covered with our men and horses. Notwithstanding this we penetrated the battalion on the road, the men of which, relying on their bayonets, did not give way until we were close upon them when they fled in confusion. For some time the contest was kept up hand to hand. After some efforts we succeeded in cutting off 300, of whom most were secured as prisoners. But our loss was very considerable.[21]

The Fourteenth suffered 35 casualties out of 110 present.

That was the end of the pursuit on that day. Wellesley had to wait while his artillery and his supplies were laboriously ferried across the Douro. The French were going too fast for the weary infantry on the north bank to catch them. There were 1,800 prisoners, including men in hospital, to be secured. The British casualties were 125.

Soult had set out on the road to Amaranthe intending to join his detached division and batter his way through Silveira's men and return to Spain along the line of the Douro. Unfortunately Loison, who commanded the detached division, had suffered an unexpected repulse in trying to drive Silveira from a strong position and was falling back towards Soult. There was nothing for Soult to do but to abandon his artillery, baggage and plunder and set his army scrambling over the roadless Serra de Santa Catalina. He rejoined Loison at Guimaraes on 14 May and hoped to escape northward to Vigo but Wellesley moved up the main road so fast that he secured Braga before the French could reach it. Soult turned north-east but Beresford, acting on his own initiative, was marching there with his own force at great speed. He ordered Silveira to move across country to Salamonde. The Portuguese general took a wrong turning and lost a day's marching. There was a small gap for the French to escape and, after a scramble over the Serra da Louca, Soult reached Orense in Spain on 19 May.

Wellesley did not attempt to follow him over the mountains. His army was almost without rations and further pursuit would harm it more than it would the enemy. 'It is obvious that if an army throws away all its cannon, equipments, and everything that could strengthen it, and can enable it to act together as a body: and abandons all those who are entitled to its protection but add to its weight and impede its progress; it must be able to march by roads through which it cannot be followed with any prospect of being overtaken by an army which has not made the same sacrifices.'[22] 'Of this I am certain, that Soult will be very little formidable to any body of troops for some little time to come.'[23] In ten days Soult's corps had lost 4,500 men, all its guns, its baggage and its military chest.

Wellesley had liberated Portugal for the second time. Soult was disgracefully lax in guarding the riverline but Wellesley showed himself as a man of remarkable decision and determination. His only knowledge of the French dispositions came from an imperfect view of the far bank of the river which was scattered with trees amid broken ground. He formed his plan without hesitation and instantly put it into execution. He can have spent few more uncomfortable hours in his life than when he watched the unwieldy barges slowly ferrying the Buffs across the 500 yards of river. At any moment an overwhelming number of Frenchmen might appear and sweep the leading companies into the river. Curiously enough, the French continued to regard him as a cautious commander. His English detractors were confirmed in their opinion of his rashness.

The victory was belittled in England. It was not awarded as a battle honour to any of the battalions engaged and Captain Stanhope who carried the despatch to London was not given the promotion traditionally granted to bearers of the news of victories.* Wellesley clearly thought well of it and when he came to be raised to the peerage took Baron Douro as his second title.

---

* The news of Vimeiro, a much smaller affair, earned the bearer of the despatch, Capt Colin Campbell, a brevet majority. Stanhope was eventually compensated. He carried Graham's report of the action at Bergen-op-Zoom in 1814 and was promoted lieutenant-colonel by brevet. It is the only occasion when a despatch announcing a defeat has earned promotion for its bearer.

PART THREE

*The War in the Balance,
June 1809–December 1811*

CHAPTER 7

Talavera and Ocaña

THE expected war between Austria and France broke out in April 1809. Napoleon's attention was fixed eastward; 300,000 French troops were needed in Germany and Italy. There could be no reinforcements for the Army of Spain. The time seemed ripe for an allied offensive.

The French force in Spain was widely dispersed. King Joseph was in nominal charge of a field army of five corps, 100,000 men.* Two corps, those of Soult and Ney, were in Galicia. Mortier's was on the upper Ebro with orders not to move deeper into Spain in case it was needed in Austria. The king's immediate command consisted of only two corps near Madrid. South of the capital Sebastiani guarded the southern approaches beyond the Tagus. Victor watched the southwestern front. If Joseph brought to their support a brigade from the garrison of Madrid he could deploy a combined army of 46,000 men.

Two Spanish armies threatened Madrid from the south. Facing Sebastiani was the Army of La Mancha under Venegas who had his headquarters in the Sierra Morena, south of Ciudad Real. The Army of Estremadura was also in the Sierra around Llerena. Gregorio Cuesta commanded this army which was the one Victor had routed at Medellin in March. Before the summer it had been recruited and reorganised and by June it was 35,000 strong. Venegas had 22,000.

After driving Soult out of the north of the country Wellesley

---

* VII Corps was still in Catalonia and III Corps was in Aragon. There were also garrisons in all the main cities and in the towns along the roads from Madrid to France. The total strength of the French army in Spain was about 280,000.

D

could safely leave the defence of Portugal to the embryo Portuguese army, stiffened by a few newly landed British battalions. He could take his whole field strength, 22,000, to co-operate with the two Spanish armies.

The numerical comparison between 80,000 allies and 46,000 French was misleading. The French were of higher quality than their Spanish opponents. Most of them were veterans of the Grande Armée with experience of victory in Germany and Spain. The British did not have as much experience as the French, but Vimeiro and Oporto had given them confidence. Their training and steadiness in action were excellent but their supply system was an amateurish improvisation. Lack of supplies and pay played havoc with their discipline off the battlefield. At the end of May Wellesley wrote that, 'They have plundered this country which has given me great concern. They have plundered the people of bullocks, among other property, for what reason I am sure I do not know, except it be to sell it to the people again.'[1]

The Spanish troops were an uncertain quantity. Their regiments still had a cadre of highly trained regulars but their ranks were packed with recruits who scarcely knew how to load a musket. British officers who had been present at Medellin spoke highly of the steadiness of their infantry but were scathing about their cavalry. Their supply system was chaotic. There was little confidence in their generals and little more in their regimental officers. They would do best in strong defensive positions but their commanders favoured headlong offensives. Their real strength lay in their outraged patriotism. Rowland Hill commented, 'It is true that they are badly disciplined, but their inveteracy towards the French is so great that they are formidable.'[2]

Wellesley had written to Cuesta before leaving Oporto suggesting co-operation between their two armies. He sought permission from London to march into Spain. Cuesta replied with three proposals, two of which would inevitably have resulted in the destruction of both the British and the Spanish armies. Wellesley was prepared to consider the third plan whereupon Cuesta rejected it. All his plans had been based on the assumption that Victor's corps was between the Guadiana and the Tagus so that a British advance along the latter river would cut him off from Madrid. In June Victor, whose army was on the verge of starvation, withdrew to the north bank of the Tagus and established himself on the river Alberche, a few miles east of Talavera de la Reina.

Difficulties in communicating with Cuesta arose mainly from his pride and obstinacy. There was a physical problem in getting in touch with Venegas. Between the two Spanish headquarters lay two hundred miles of trackless mountains. Venegas was technically under Cuesta's command but disliked him and took little notice of his orders.

Wellesley had his own difficulties. It was not until 11 June that he received permission to enter Spain. His army was concentrated at Abrantes but he could not march until he received some money. The Spaniards had promised to provide rations but insisted on payment in cash. He knew that the troops would plunder intolerably unless they were regularly fed. There was not enough transport to bring food forward from Portugal and no credit could be obtained there. The army already owed £200,000 in that country.[3] It was a frustrating situation.

> The ball is now at my feet, and I hope I shall have the strength to give it a good kick. I should begin immediately, but I cannot venture to stir without money. The army is two months in arrears [of pay]; we are head over heels in debt everywhere; and I cannot venture into Spain without paying what we owe, at least in this neighbourhood, and without giving a little money to the troops.[4]

It was only on 25 June that some coin reached Abrantes and, with a promise of more to come, he could start to march with 'about £30,000 to begin with in Spain, leaving all our debts in Portugal unpaid'.[5] The army crossed the frontier at Zarza la Mayor on 2 July.

King Joseph was concentrating his energies on re-equipping Soult's corps and succeeded in making it an effective force by the end of June. He intended to use it to lead the third invasion of Portugal. The king was confident that Sebastiani and Victor could hold Venegas and Cuesta in check but had no information of Wellesley's intentions or whereabouts. On 9 July, a week after the British had entered Spain, he wrote, 'The English have not yet shown their hand. Will they advance into Galicia? Into Castile? Or will they stay in Lisbon? If they do the last should we advance by way of Ciudad Rodrigo to seek them out? This is the plan favoured by those who know the country best.'⁶ At his headquarters in Vienna Napoleon had decided that the British would confine themselves to the defence of Lisbon and, in an order which reached Joseph on 1 July, arranged for the corps of Soult, Ney and Mortier to form a single striking force under Soult. 'These three corps must manoeuvre as a single body, pursue the English relentlessly, defeat them and throw them into the sea. If they concentrate quickly the English must be destroyed and the whole Spanish business will be over.'⁷ This was written from the palace of Schönbrunn three weeks after Napoleon had failed to force the crossing of the Danube at Aspern and Essling, the most severe check an army under his personal command had ever suffered.

The armies of Wellesley and Cuesta joined at Oropesa on 20 July. The commanders agreed to make a joint attack on Victor near Talavera, and Cuesta sent orders to Venegas to push forward to the Tagus so as to hold the attention of Sebastiani. When the armies met, the effective strength of Cuesta's army was 33,000 and of Wellesley's 21,000. Victor was known to be about 22,000 strong. An intercepted letter which reached Wellesley on 13 July showed that Soult and Ney had concerted an operation in Galicia which should keep them from interfering with allied moves south of the Guadarrama for some weeks. The only corps which Wellesley thought might be able to intervene was Mortier's which had moved to Valladolid and was 15,000 strong.

King Joseph was ignorant of the allied approach until 22 July. On that day they were within seventy-five miles of Madrid but the king's information reached him from Soult who, having incontinently abandoned Ney in Galicia, had moved his headquarters to Zamora on the Douro. There he heard rumours that British were marching on Madrid. He sent General Foy to the king with a proposal that, should the rumours be true, Victor should hold the British in front while Soult and the three corps now under his command would march south through the Pass of Baños and get between Wellesley and Portugal. While Foy was expounding this plan to the king a report arrived from Victor saying that his outposts at Talavera had

been driven in by the main Anglo-Spanish army. Joseph immediately agreed to Soult's plan and sent him orders 'to concentrate
the three corps under your command, and march as rapidly as possible to Plasencia. General Foy assures me that you will be able to
reach Plasencia in four or five marches.'[8]

On 23 July Wellesley proposed to his ally that they should attack
Victor in his position on the east bank of the Alberche. Although the
allies would be 54,000 to Victor's 22,000, Cuesta refused on the
grounds that it was Sunday. Next day Victor retired. Cuesta insisted
on pursuing him. Wellesley had already made it clear that he would
not go further than the east bank of the Alberche until the Spaniards
fulfilled their promise to produce food for the British who had already been on half-rations for some days. The Spaniards advanced
on their own. 'I should certainly get the better of everything,' wrote
Wellesley, 'if I can manage General Cuesta; but his temper and disposition are so bad, that it is impossible.'[9]

Cuesta followed Victor for twenty-five miles to Torrijos where he
was confronted by King Joseph at the head of 46,000 men. Venegas
had neglected to obey his orders and Sebastiani had been able to
bring the bulk of his corps to join Victor. Only small garrisons had
been left on the Tagus crossings south of Madrid and the garrison
of that city had contributed 5,700 men to swell the combined force.
The Army of Estremadura retreated with great precipitation. On the
evening of 26 July it arrived at the Alberche in disorder. Cuesta in a
fit of what his ally described as 'whimsical perversity'[10] made his
men bivouac on the east (French) bank of the river. Fortunately
the French pursuit was slow and next morning Cuesta agreed to
bring his men back to a position Wellesley had chosen for them
with their right on the Tagus at Talavera.

This short retreat was covered by a British rearguard who were
themselves surprised by the French. Two brigadiers, thinking that
there was cavalry to their front, halted their men in a wood and
posted no sentries. In fact the cavalry had retired to a flank and, in
the words of the surgeon of the Eighty Seventh,

> the bloody business commenced much sooner than we expected.
> I myself sat eating under a tree without an idea the enemy could be
> less than three miles distant, when the most tremendous firing came

driving towards us. In an instant musket as well as cannon balls were flying about in every direction. The soldiers were surprised; some regiments had not loaded their firelocks. The [skirmishers] retreated upon us with the enemy after them. One British regiment fired into another. A slight confusion took place which gave advantage to the French and caused much bloodshed.[11]

The Eighty Seventh suffered 198 casualties and altogether the British loss was more than 400.

By dusk the whole allied army was in a strong position stretching three miles from Talavera town on the right to the Cerro de Medellin, a formidable hill rising three hundred feet above river level and presenting a steep face to the east where it fell into the dry gully of the Portina brook.[5/4] Knowing the Spaniards to be incapable of manoeuvring, Wellesley packed them into the southern third of the line where the ground was strong with buildings, olive groves, walls and a sunken road. The main British strength was on the Cerro, forming the left flank. Beyond it was a narrow plain filling the gap between the hill and the rough foothills of the Sierra de Segurilla. This plain was watched by a brigade of light cavalry. The weakest part of the British front was the mile-long stretch between the Cerro and the Spanish left. This was an open rolling slope where there was neither cover nor shade. It was entrusted to two battalions of Guards and two of the line.

Marshal Victor, whose men led the French advance,[6/3] had never encountered British troops before. When he surprised two British brigades on the afternoon of 27 July he thought he had frustrated an ambush and this gave him a low opinion of his enemy. Seeing that the Cerro de Medellin was the key to Wellesley's position he decided to seize it by a *coup-de-main*. He ordered Ruffin's division to attack it in silence as soon as it was dark.

Ruffin nearly succeeded. The brigades allocated to the forward edge had not taken up their position. 'We were,' wrote an ADC, 'by no means such good soldiers in those days as succeeding campaigns made us.'[12] Two French battalions reached the top before the alarm was given by the troops in the second line who found the French amongst them. Fortunately the general responsible, Rowland Hill, was nearby. Even he, 'not having an idea that the enemy were so

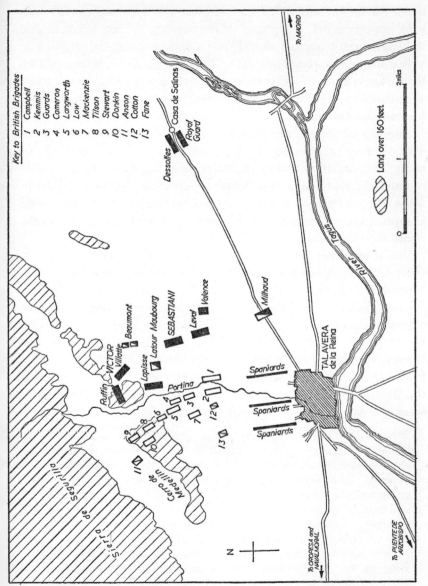

To MADRID

Dessolles

Casa de Salinas

Royal Guard

Beaumont

VICTOR

Villatte

Latour Maubourg

SEBASTIANI

Lapisse

Leval

Valence

Ruffin

Portina

Milhaud

Spaniards

Spaniards

Spaniards

TALAVERA de la Reina

River Tagus

Sierra de Segurilla

Cerro de Medellin

N

To OROPESA and NAVALMORAL

To PUENTE DE ARZOBISPO

Land over 160 feet

2 miles

Talavera

near, said at the moment, "I was sure it was the old Buffs, as usual, making some blunder." '[13] He put a reserve brigade under arms and led them up the hill. As he reached the summit, 'a French soldier got hold of my right arm and would have secured me if my horse had not at that moment sprung forward'.[14] There was a short, bitter fight in the darkness before the French were driven down the hill. They took with them 109 prisoners and had killed and wounded 275. Ruffin's loss was about 300.

The rest of the night passed uneasily. 'About midnight the stillness was suddenly interrupted by firing towards Talavera;—not the straggling, desultory, yet distinct reports of light troops, but a roll of musketry that illuminated the whole extent of the Spanish line. It was one discharge: but of such a nature that I never heard it equalled. It appeared not to be returned, nor was it repeated. All again became silent.'[15]

Victor had made his night attack on his own initiative. When it failed he sent a message to the king telling him that he would attack at dawn and capture the Cerro. Joseph and his chief of staff, Marshal Jourdan, both doubted the wisdom of such a course, but Victor had a great reputation and was a close friend of the Emperor. They did not forbid the attempt. At 5 am Ruffin's division again crossed the Portina brook and toiled up the steep face of the hill. Over their heads there was a cannonade by fifty-four guns. To avoid their fire the British line had been lying down behind the crest. The French were almost upon them when they were called to their feet.

> When the French had mounted the ascent, and were so near as to become endangered from the fire of their own artillery, a scene of great animation was exhibited. The summit, which had appeared deserted, now supported a regular line of infantry. Near the colours of the Twenty Ninth stood Sir Arthur Wellesley, directing and animating the troops.
> General Ruffin had nearly surmounted all the difficulties of the ground, when a fire burst forth that checked his advance. Sir Arthur ordered a charge. With one tremendous shout, the right wing of the Twenty Ninth, and the entire battalion of the Forty Eighth, rushed like a torrent down, bayoneting and sweeping back the enemy to the brink of the insignificant muddy stream.[16]

Hardly a shot was fired for the next two hours. Stretcher parties

from both sides removed the wounded from the forward slope of the
Cerro and French and British soldiers mingled to drink from the
muddy pools of the Portina. Joseph held a council of war with
Jourdan, Victor and Sebastiani. News had reached them that
Venegas was advancing to the Tagus. The small garrisons holding
the bridges and fords could not hold out for more than a day or two
and there was no defensive force between the river and Madrid.
Unless a quick victory could be won at Talavera troops would have
to be withdrawn to defend the capital. According to the estimate Foy
had given the king, Soult should be arriving in Wellesley's rear
either that day or the next. Jourdan and Sebastiani advised delay. As
soon as Soult's advance was known to the British they would retire
and they would be at their most vulnerable as they left their position.
Jourdan added his opinion that the Talavera ridge was 'impregnable
to frontal attack', and pointed out that since Wellesley had neglected
to occupy the plain on his left,

> his position could have been turned if, instead of drawing his
> attention to this point by attacking it twice, he could have been
> distracted by feints against his right while a large force was con-
> centrated on his left during the night. The left could then have
> been stormed at dawn. As things stood, Wellesley, warned by the
> earlier attacks, could be seen to be securing his left with a strong
> force of cavalry.
>
> When Marshal Victor was asked his opinion, he said that if the
> king would use Sebastiani's force to attack the British right and
> centre, he would undertake to seize the Cerro with his own three
> divisions. He added, 'If we cannot take that hill we ought to give
> up soldiering'.[17]

Joseph, anxious for a quick victory, agreed with Victor. At 2 pm
34,000 French infantry attacked Wellesley's 20,000 of all arms.
Three thousand French dragoons were allocated to screening Cuesta's
30,000 Spaniards.

Sebastiani came nearest to making a breakthrough. His left-hand
column attacked the extreme right of the British line. A sergeant in
the light company of the Fusiliers saw a column,

> threading its way among the trees and grape vines, directly in our
> front, and, while deploying, called out *Espanoles*, wishing us to

believe that they were Spaniards. Our captain thought they were
Spaniards and ordered us not to fire. But soon they convinced us
who they were with a rattling volley. We instantly retired upon
our regiment, which sprang up and met the enemy on the rising
ground, but our men, being all raw soldiers, staggered for a
moment under such a rolling fire. Our colonel, Sir William Myers,
seeing this, sprang from his horse and snatching one of the colours
cried, 'Come on, Fusiliers!' On rushed the Fusiliers and the Fifty
Third and delivered such a fire that in a few minutes the enemy
melted away, leaving six pieces of cannon behind, which they had
not had time to discharge.[18]

Sebastiani's right-hand column came even nearer to success. They
attacked the most exposed part of the ridge which was held by the
Guards brigade. Their divisional commander was General Sherbrooke whom Wellesley described as 'a very good officer, but the
most passionate man I think I ever knew'.[19] The Guards were also
hasty in their temper that day having been exposed since dawn to a
heavy bombardment and a beating sun. They were understandably
anxious to get at the French.

General Sherbrooke had cautioned his division to use the bayonet,
and when the enemy came to within about fifty yards of the Guards,
they advanced to meet them, but on attempting to close the enemy
by a charge, the latter broke and fled. The regiment on their left, the
Eighty Third, made a simultaneous movement, driving the enemy
with immense loss before them; but the impetuosity of the Guards
led to endangering the day. The flying enemy led them on till they
opened a battery on their flank, which occasioned so heavy a loss
that the ranks could not be formed after the pursuit, and on being
ordered to resume their ground produced confusion.

The enemy instantly rallied and followed them, and were so
confident of victory that their officers were heard to exclaim,
Allons, mes enfans, ils sont touts nos prisoniers. But Sir Arthur had seen
the probable difficulty into which the Guards were likely to become
entangled, and had ordered the Forty Eighth from the height to
their support. This gallant regiment arrived at the rear of the
Guards at the moment when they were coming back in confusion,
pressed by the enemy, on the line of the position. They allowed the
Guards to come through them, and then breaking in upon the
enemy, gave them a second repulse. The Guards quickly formed in
the rear, and moved up into the position, and spirit and appearance
and determination, after having lost in twenty minutes five

hundred men, were shown by their giving a hurrah, as they took their ground.[20]

Victor's third attack on the Cerro de Medellin was a fiasco. Ruffin's division was again sent to lead the attack and had no stomach for another assault. The two supporting divisions were also unenthusiastic. No progress was made. The only French success of the day was in the plain to the north. Wellesley had strengthened his position there with a Spanish division lent by Cuesta in an uncharacteristic burst of generosity. As Victor's right-hand division advanced to turn the Cerro, Wellesley saw that they were hesitant. He ordered Anson's light cavalry brigade to charge them. At the best of times it would have been a hazardous undertaking. In the event it was disastrous.

As the two regiments, Twenty Third Light Dragoons and First Hussars KGL, galloped forward they came unexpectedly on a wide, dry ditch concealed by long grass, a hundred and fifty yards from the French columns.

> Several lengths in front, mounted on a grey horse, consequently very conspicuous, rode Colonel Elley. Thus placed he first arrived at the brink of the ravine. No alternative was left to him. To have checked his horse and given timely warning was impossible. With some difficulty he cleared it at a bound and on gaining the opposite bank endeavoured by gesture to warn the Twenty Third of the dangerous ground they had to pass; but advancing with so much velocity, the line was on the verge of the stream before his signals could be either understood or attended to.[21]

> Too late to pull up, the foremost horsemen rode headlong at the hollow and a fearful scene ensued. Some tumbled in and over the ravine, while others leapt boldly across the chasm and gained the other side; but great disorder was the consequence. In front of the Hussars the ravine was from six to eight foot deep: while widening in front of the Twenty Third it was also more shallow.[22]

The remnants of the two regiments pressed on against the French, who had had time to form square. They were repulsed with heavy loss. As a major of the Twenty Third wrote home, 'We had a pleasing amusement of charging five solid squares with a ditch in their front. After losing 180 men and 222 horses, we found it not so agreeable, and that Frenchmen won't always run away when they see British cavalry, so off we went, and my horse never went so fast in his life.'[23]

Victor urged a fourth attack, asserting that the British were retiring. Joseph refused to allow it. The battle petered out in a desultory cannonade. During the night the French retreated behind the Alberche. They had lost 17 guns and 7,268 men—one man in six. This did not deter the king from claiming a victory. He denied the loss of the guns and claimed that 'the battlefield, on which we are encamped, is heaped with English dead'.[24]

The British were victorious but exhausted. In the two days' fighting they had lost 5,363 men, including 800 dead. Scarcely 15,000 fit men were in the ranks and Wellesley was greatly relieved when on the following morning 3,000 of Robert Craufurd's Light Brigade arrived on the field with their bugle horns playing 'merrily'. They had marched forty-two miles in twenty-six hours but they were the finest infantry in the world.* They were immediately put in charge of the outposts and 'were employed all that day in collecting the dead bodies and putting them in large heaps mixed with faggots and burning them. The stench from so many dead bodies was volatile and offensive beyond conception, as the heat of the weather was very great.'[25]

Although Joseph had failed to defeat the allies and had had to send Sebastiani's corps to protect Madrid, Wellesley's army could still be destroyed. According to Foy's calculation, Soult should already be in rear of the British and Wellesley was showing no signs of retreating. He was unconscious of the danger. Soult was much later than Joseph expected. It was not until 30 July, two days after the battle, that his leading troops reached the pass of Baños, sixty-five miles from the Tagus. The pass was a place where a small force of determined men could delay an army for days. Cuesta had assured Wellesley that he had stationed there an adequate garrison. The force he sent was two regiments who never arrived. A passing British staff officer found there only a single regiment of militia, who refused to fight.[26] Soult's men were in Plasencia on 31 July.

---

* 1st battalions of the Forty Third and Fifty Second Light Infantry and of the Ninety Fifth Rifles.

Soult could still have cut the British off from Portugal. Wellesley heard that French troops were approaching Plasencia on 30 July. Convinced that Soult and Ney were still entangled in Galicia he assumed that only Mortier's 15,000 men could be coming south. He knew he could deal with such a small force. After a prolonged haggle with Cuesta who was 'as obstinate as any gentleman at the head of an army ought to be',[27] it was agreed that the Spaniards would stay at Talavera to check Victor while the British marched against Mortier. They left Talavera on 3 August.

Next day three alarming pieces of news reached Wellesley. The first was that Cuesta had evacuated Talavera, leaving 1,500 British wounded to the French. Next he learned that the French corps coming from the north consisted not of 15,000 but of 30,000 men.* Most disturbing of all was a report that French cavalry already held Naval Moral, blocking the only main road to the bridge of Almaraz and Badajoz.

There was no time to be lost. If the French took Almaraz and crossed to the south bank of the Tagus in force the British would have to retreat on Cadiz. There would be no way of reaching Portugal and Soult would be able to occupy that country at his leisure. By the evening of 4 August the whole army had crossed the river at Arzobispo and was marching by side roads to regain the highway at Jaraicejo. The Light Brigade was sent on a desperate scramble over the hills, racing to reach the Almaraz bridge before Soult's advanced guard. They arrived there, with time to spare, on 6 August. That day they had marched for fifteen hours on a diet of 'boiled wheat and dried peas, without salt, bread or meat. I cannot,' wrote a Rifleman, 'call to my recollection having ever witnessed a day's march where so many men left the ranks from fatigue, to find their way to Almaraz at their leisure or, rather, as soon as exhausted nature had rallied.'[28]

Once his retreat to Portugal was secure, Wellesley halted for some weeks in the area north of Trujillo while he explored the possibilities of further co-operation with the Spaniards. Cuesta was as impossible as ever. Venegas was routed by Sebastiani at Almonacid de Toledo

---

* Even this was an understatement. Soult's three corps amounted to more than 50,000.

(11 August). No rations were forthcoming for the British. Spanish troops attacked British foraging parties and threatened to sack any village which provided their allies with bread.[29] With the comment that, 'No man can see his army perish by want,'[30] Wellesley withdrew to the area Badajoz–Merida, where the army could be fed from Portugal.

This was a turning-point in the war. Up to this point the British had seen themselves as auxiliaries to their allies. They had assumed that the Spaniards would take the lead in ejecting the invaders and the small British army would give such help as it could. By the end of August it was clear to Wellesley that only disaster could result from such co-operation. The allied strength was not enough for offensives. They must hold on to what they had until they were stronger. The Spaniards should guard Andalusia. The British must defend Portugal and, above all, their irreplaceable base at Lisbon. 'My plan now is to remain on the defensive, and not to enter into any plan of co-operation of any description (unless ordered from England) till I shall see defined objects and corresponding means to effect them.'[31]

The victory at Talavera had been hailed as a triumph in Britain. The Tower guns were fired and there were confident predictions in the press that the allies would soon liberate Madrid. Wellesley was created Viscount Wellington of Talavera and Baron Douro.* The news of a precipitate retreat aroused the same kind of public uproar as the Convention of Cintra had done in the previous year. The opposition in Parliament again accused Wellington of rashness and members asserted that he had only fought in order to gain a peerage. The City of London petitioned the king against making a grant of £2,000 a year to enable him to support his title. 'While admitting to the utmost extent the valour of Lord Wellington, we do not recognize in his military conduct any claim to this national remuneration.'

Wellington was not disturbed by Whig gibes.

> You see the dash which the Common Council of the city of London have made at me. I act with a sword hanging over me, which will fall upon me whatever may be the result of affairs here; but they

---

* He first signed his new title on 16 September 1809.

may do as they please, I shall not give up the game here as long as it can be played.[32]

I lament as much as any man can the necessity for separating from the Spaniards, but I was compelled to go and I believe there was not an officer in the army who did not think I stayed too long. The fault I committed consisted in trusting at all to Spaniards, who I have since found were entirely unworthy of confidence.[33]

The Spaniards believed themselves to have been deserted. The Junta at Seville was intent on launching a grand concentric attack on Madrid. They used every means to inveigle Wellington into taking part. He refused to be drawn, pointing out that there were 200,000 French troops in Spain and that the Junta commanded only 80,000 many of whom were unarmed; 25,000 British would not make up the difference. Spanish military thought was above logic. 'I am much afraid, from what I have seen of the proceedings of the Central Junta, that in the distribution of their forces they do not consider military defence and military operations, so much as they do political intrigue and the attainment of trifling military objects.'[34] In a less official letter he described the Spanish scheme as 'rank nonsense'.[35]

Undeterred, the Spaniards went on alone. Two armies drove at Madrid, one from the north, one from the south. In the north they had a momentary success and captured Salamanca. The southern army, 60,000 strong, almost managed to surprise the capital. On 9 November their cavalry were within thirty-five miles of the city and only 7,000 men stood between them and triumph. Then their commander, General Areizaga, lost his nerve and spent several days making eccentric marches and counter-marches. While he did so three French corps gathered to crush him. On 19 November Areizaga drew up his army for battle at Ocaña. There was no need for him to fight and his right flank was in the air. Joseph and Soult* did not wait for all their troops to come up. They rolled up the

---

* Soult succeeded Jourdan as Joseph's chief of staff during September. Jourdan had been sick for some months and, most unjustly, had been made the scapegoat for Talavera. Napoleon wrote to him on 21 August, 'When one attacks good troops, like the English, in good positions, without reconnaissance, and without being certain of success, one only condemns men to death uselessly.' The reproach would have been more fairly directed at Victor, and Napoleon would have done well to remember it himself six years later at Waterloo.

exposed Spanish flank with 3,500 cavalry while the infantry advanced against the Spanish line. Their opponents fled leaving the French with 14,000 prisoners and 50 guns. Nine days later the northern arm of the Spanish pincer movement was smashed at Alba de Tormes. The only unbroken Spanish army in western Spain was a corps of 10,000 men at Almaraz.

> I declare [wrote Wellington] that if they had preserved their two armies, or even one of them, the cause was safe. But no! Nothing will answer excepting to fight great battles in plains, in which their defeat is as certain as the commencement of the battle.[36]

> I don't yet despair, as it is impossible to say what will be the result of this defeat. If the troops collect again and if they will only manage them with prudence, I hope we may yet keep up the ball in the Peninsula sufficiently long to tire out Buonaparte.[37]

He, at least, was acting with prudence. 'The great object in Portugal is the possession of Lisbon and the Tagus, and all our measures must be directed to this object.'[38] On 20 October he had given his chief engineer orders to build a great series of fortifications to protect Lisbon—the Lines of Torres Vedras.

CHAPTER 8

Andalusia and the Siege of Cadiz

AT the New Year of 1810 King Joseph had half a kingdom, a large army and no substantial enemy to threaten him. Ocaña and Alba de Tormes had shattered the Spanish field armies. The British posed no danger. They had spent the autumn near Badajoz and French headquarters believed that they had retired into Portugal on 24 November.[1] (In fact the British withdrawal into Portugal did not start until two weeks later.) Reinforcements from France were again available. Napoleon had defeated the Austrians at Wagram (5–6 July) and had dictated peace to them in October. A British expedition sent to the Scheldt had petered out from 'Walcheren fever'.

Joseph and Soult, now his chief of staff, were certain that the next step must be the conquest of Andalusia. Napoleon had assured the king that 'the invasion of Andalusia will finish the Spanish business'.[2] Joseph was anxious to complete his kingdom and to acquire more taxable subjects to swell his meagre revenue. Soult, who should have known better, looked for an easy triumph and a rich haul of loot. The Emperor was asked to sanction the operation but evaded giving a reply. The king and the marshal decided to go ahead without waiting for sanction. By 11 January an army of 60,000 men*

---

* The army for the Andalusian expedition was as follows, according to return of 15 Jan 1810.

	All ranks (effective)
I Corps (Marshal Victor)	22,664
IV Corps (Gen Sebastiani) (less 2 divisions)	10,078
V Corps (Marshal Mortier)	16,009
Dessolles's Division (Madrid garrison)	8,354
Royal Guard	2,500 approx
Enlisted Spaniards	2,000 approx

was concentrated along the Sierra Morena and Soult wrote to Paris that 'it is to be hoped that the war in Spain will be finished in a single day'.[3]

The Spaniards could deploy only 25,000 dispirited men on a front of 160 miles. Contemptuously Soult sent forward the French in four disconnected columns and was superior at every point of attack. The passes over the Sierra were seized by 20 January. Next day the standards lost by Dupont were triumphantly recaptured from the cathedral at Bailen. Jaen fell on 22 January and two days later Victor entered Cordoba. Sebastiani was detached to occupy Granada. On the 29th only the river Guadalquivir separated the advanced guard from Seville.

Joseph reported, 'Andalusia will soon be pacified. The towns are sending in delegations. Seville is doing the same. The Supreme Junta has fled. I hope to enter Cadiz without a shot being fired. Public feeling is good.'[4]

A disastrous decision was taken at King Joseph's dinner table on the evening of 29 January. Seville had already offered to surrender. Two corps were available to carry through the offensive. The discussion turned on whether Seville should be occupied in strength or whether troops should immediately be sent to secure Cadiz, Spain's greatest seaport and the new seat of the Supreme Junta. Several voices were raised in favour of pressing on to the coast since a single corps would be more than enough to secure Seville. Soult overruled everyone. 'Give me Seville,' he said, 'and I will answer for Cadiz.'[5]

On 1 February King Joseph had the greatest triumph of his career. He entered Seville on horseback, surrounded by his Guard, and took up residence in the ancient palace of the Alcazar. His Master of the Household wrote, 'He was received and followed by an immense crowd, who filled the streets and public places. Cries of *Viva el Rey* arose on every side. No doubt, curiosity and fear had a greater share in that triumphant reception than any other sentiment but, whatever its true cause, it seemed at the time to justify the occupation of Seville.'[6] Joseph, at last, could believe that he was king of Spain. 'I entered this city yesterday to the cheers of the whole populace. Andalusia has been pacified; order has been restored; the

Junta has dissolved itself. The First Corps [Victor] passed the night here. It will march on Cadiz tomorrow.'[7]

The First Corps was too late. Had Soult not forbidden it to march on 29 January it could have seized Cadiz with ease. The only garrison was four battalions of hastily raised Volunteers. Few cities are stronger by nature against a land-bound enemy, but 2,400 recruits could not have defended it. While Joseph was celebrating the capture of Seville a rare phenomenon came on the scene—an intelligent Spanish general. The Duke of Albuquerque had been stationed near Merida with 8,000 men. The French advance had passed to the east of him. The disintegrating Junta ordered him to attack the flank of the nearest enemy corps, Victor's, which was nearly three times his own strength. He refused to obey and marched south skirmishing with French detachments and picking up stray Spanish units on his march. He was too late to help with the defence of Seville. Being without orders he made for Cadiz, arriving on 3 February with 10,000 men; 3,000 more Spaniards reached Cadiz by sea from Ayamonte at about the same time. Two days later Victor's advanced guard found the defences fully manned. He summoned the city to surrender and received the defiant answer, 'Cadiz, faithful to its word, recognizes no king but Ferdinand VII.'

Inside Cadiz the members of the Supreme Junta found themselves exposed to mob violence and troops had to be spared to protect them. They were glad to be allowed to resign and their place was taken by a three-man regency led by General Castaños, the victor of Bailen. As a government the Regency was only marginally more efficient than the Junta but, unlike the Junta, it recognised that Spain could be saved only by adhering to the British alliance. It immediately asked Wellington to send troops to Cadiz. In the second week in February three British and two Portuguese battalions landed there, bringing the regular garrison up to 17,000.

There was now no serious chance that the French could take Cadiz by military means. To reach it by land the attacker must first cross the San Petri river which is at least 200 yards wide and was flanked with marshes. Then he must fight his way across the triangular island of Leon, which was liberally equipped with forts and earthworks. This was only the beginning of his troubles. From the island to the city ran a sandy spit of land, four miles long, with the inner harbour on one side and the sea on the other. In places the spit is only 200 yards across and at one place it was cut by a wide ditch covering the stone-built battery of San Fernando which runs from shore to shore. At the offshore end the spit widens to 400 yards and is sealed by the ramparts of the city. In the waters around the city were twelve Spanish and four British battleships with a swarm of gunboats. It was an unattractive prospect to the French, and Joseph could only suggest that 'it would be opportune if your Majesty could send us the Toulon squadron'.[8] The Emperor did not reply to this appeal. He remembered that between Toulon and Cadiz lay Lord Collingwood and the British Mediterranean Fleet.

Soult's negligence in failing to secure Cadiz was the greatest disaster which had yet occurred to the French in Spain. The city gave the Spanish government an inviolable refuge on Spanish soil, a rallying-point for the spirit of the Spanish people. French strategy was distorted for the next thirty months. Twenty thousand men were the fewest who could man the abortive siege lines. As many more were needed to guard the communications back to the Sierra Morena and the eastern frontier with Murcia. The French army in Andalusia continued to have an effective strength of not less than 60,000 until the middle of 1812. In that time they made few and indecisive forays north of the Sierra where the fate of Spain was being decided.

The French siege of Cadiz was largely illusory. There was no real hope that they would ever take the place. Far more real was the siege of the French army in Andalusia. Spanish forces from the mountains of Murcia constantly harried the eastern part of the province. They were frequently defeated but always reformed. A ragged army under General Ballasteros usually operated within Andalusia itself. Soult repeatedly sent columns against it. It always escaped. Sometimes it hid in the mountains, sometimes it escaped by sea. At times it slipped into Portuguese Algarve. At others it sheltered under the guns of Gibraltar. French dominion was secure only in the plains of the Guadalquivir and in Seville where Soult reigned with more splendour than Joseph ever achieved in Madrid. A French officer wrote:

No monarch ever surrounded himself with more majesty: no court was ever so deferential. Like Homer's Jupiter, Olympus trembled at his nod. The marshal was always surrounded by a glittering guard. Every Sunday picked troops lined the route between his palace and the cathedral while he went in procession to the Mass, followed by the municipal authorities and a resplendent staff.[9]

Spanish armies were not Soult's only problem. Andalusia has a long coastline which was open to British seapower. The British contingent at Cadiz was expanded. More troops were available at Gibraltar. Their first attempt was not a success. In October 1810 two battalions from Gibraltar and a Spanish regiment were landed at Fuengirola in a bid to seize Malaga. Their commander, Major-General Lord Blayney, was short-sighted and incompetent. He was surprised and captured on the beach with half a battalion of the Eighty Ninth.

The next expedition was more formidable. Early in 1811 it was known in Cadiz that Soult had marched north over the Sierra towards Badajoz with 20,000 men. To gather this field force he had cut the troops investing Cadiz to the bare minimum. The garrison decided to land a force behind the French lines and attack them in the rear. The moving spirit behind the plan was the commander of the British contingent, Lieutenant-General Graham.

Thomas Graham of Balgowan was a Scottish laird who had no military ambitions until the French Revolution when a drunken mob in Toulouse insulted the body of his newly dead wife. Incensed, he raised a regiment, the Ninetieth Foot, at his own expense, becoming its first colonel. He was then aged forty-five. He had been on Moore's staff at Coruña and it was at Moore's dying request that his temporary commission as colonel was converted into a regular commission.* In 1811 he was sixty-two and the soldiers of all ranks were devoted to him. The only criticism levelled at him came from a young gunner officer who rode with him on a reconnaissance. 'Whether the general is mad or blind I have not decided; it required

---

* His colonelcy was given him as a reward for raising the Ninetieth, but owing to the Duke of York's reforms he could not qualify for promotion since he had not served in the lower commissioned ranks. In 1809, as an exceptional reward for merit, his promotion to major-general was backdated to 1803, the date at which he would have been promoted had his colonelcy been a permanent commission.

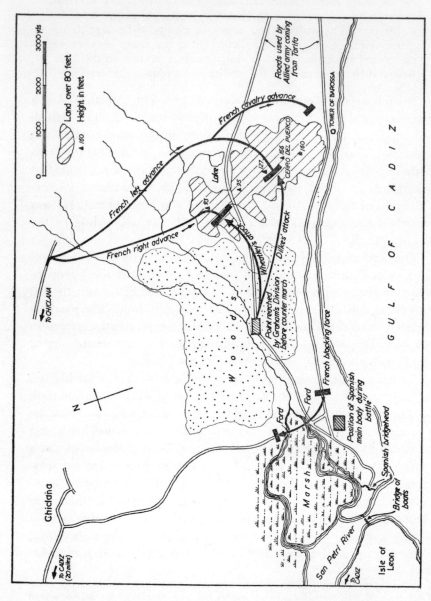

To CADIZ
(20 miles)

Chiclana

To CHICLANA

N

WOODS

French left advance

French right advance

Lake

French cavalry advance

Roads used by
Allied army coming
from Tarifa

TOWER OF BAROSSA

CERRO DEL PUERCO

160

155

127

95

93

Wheatley's

Dilkes' attack

Point reached
by Graham's Division
before counter march

French blocking force

Position of Spanish
main body during
battle

Ford

Ford

Ford

Marsh

San Petri River

Spanish bridgehead

Bridge of
boats

Isle of
Leon

To CADIZ

G U L F   O F   C A D I Z

0   1000   2000   3000 yds

Land over 80 feet.
▲ 160   Height in feet.

Barossa

one of those imperfections to carry him in cold blood over those rocks and precipices. I should as soon have thought of riding from Dover to Calais.'[10] It was most unfortunate that Graham did not command the expedition. Since the Spaniards provided twice as many troops as the British,* he agreed to serve under Manuel La Peña although he knew him to be 'weak and timid'.[11]

At the end of February the whole force, 15,000 men, was assembled at Tarifa, the southerly tip of Spain. They began to march north on the last day of the month. They met only light opposition but the march was harassing since La Peña constantly changed his mind and filled the nights with counter-marching. The climax came on 5 March when the army came within sight of Cadiz.

A small French force barred the road to the San Petri river crossings. Immediately La Peña abandoned all thought of attacking the rear of the siege lines. His only thought was to hustle the army back on to the island of Leon. He asked Graham to cover the retreat. A small hill, the Cerro del Puerco, was to be held by an ultimate rearguard of one British and five Spanish battalions with the support of the exiguous cavalry of both nations. Graham allocated to this duty a battalion composed of the flank companies of the Gibraltar garrison under Brevet Lieutenant-Colonel John Frederick Brown of the Twenty Eighth.

Brown took up his post on the Cerro but no Spanish infantry appeared. Between the hill and the sea near the Torre de Barossa were two squadrons of German hussars. Three squadrons of Spanish cavalry rode up but only to announce their departure. Soon Brown saw two French divisions, 7,000 men, converging on him. Sending a brief message to Graham, he withdrew his men, firing as they retired. The French advanced to the Cerro.

Graham was with his main body, retreating through pine woods. A French roundshot and Brown's message reached his staff almost simultaneously. He turned the column about and rode to the edge of the wood. There he met Brown and snapped:

'Did I not give you orders to defend Barossa hill?'

---

* Graham took 4,900 British (including 1,000 from Gibraltar) and 332 Portuguese.[5/6] The Spanish contingent was 9,600.

'Yes, sir. But you would not have me fight the whole French army with 470 men.'

'Had you not five Spanish battalions together with artillery and cavalry?'

'Oh, they all ran away long before the enemy came within cannon shot.'

'It's a bad business, Brown. You must instantly turn round and attack.'

'Very well.'[12]

Riding to his men, Brown took off his hat and shouted, 'Gentlemen, I am happy to be the bearer of good news. General Graham has done you the honour of being the first to attack these fellows. Now, follow me, you rascals!' He led them up the hill, singing 'Hearts of Oak', a song to which he was much addicted in moments of elation. The flank battalion suffered 236 casualties but it won time for the rest of the force to return to the battle and deploy along the edge of the wood.

'Form as you can' was Graham's order to his two brigades. Every man present was dog tired, having 'undergone a long and harassing night march, and had been about twenty hours under arms with their packs on'.[13] On the right Dilkes' brigade, two battalions of Guards, advanced in a ragged, unguardsmanlike line with two companies of the Rifles on their open flank. Twice the French sent columns down the hill against them. Twice the Guards' musketry drove them off. Joined by the remnants of Brown's battalion, they reached the summit and held it. They lost one man in three. The French division which tried to resist them lost two in seven, 900 in all.

Wheatley's brigade on the left attacked a French division which was trying to cut between the British and the Spaniards. Wheatley had 2,600 men and was supported by all Graham's ten guns. Laval, commanding the French division, had 4,000 men and sent them against Wheatley in four battalion columns, each with a front of seventy men, nine deep. The columns drove away a thick screen of Riflemen and *caçadores** but they were helpless against the three red-coat battalions in line. In the centre, where this part of the engagement started, the French 8me met the Eighty Seventh, an Irish

---

* *Caçadores* = Portuguese light infantry, about half of whom were armed with rifles.

battalion led by Hugh Gough, a future field-marshal. Locked in their column, only 140 Frenchmen in the front two ranks could fire out of a battalion 800 strong. The 600 Irishmen in line could all bring their muskets to bear. Both battalions held their fire until they were within fifty yards of each other. Then they exchanged volleys, both sides advancing. The result was inevitable.

> The French waited until we came within 25 paces of them, before they broke, and as they were in column when they did, they could not get away. It was therefore a scene of most dreadful carnage. They made while we were amongst them, (about a quarter of an hour), little or no opposition. We could have taken or destroyed the whole regiment but at this moment the French 45me regiment came down on our right and General Graham, who during the whole of the action was in the midst of it, pointed them out and begged I would call off my men. With the greatest difficulty, by almost cutting them down, I got the right wing collected, with which we charged the 45me, but after firing until we got to within about 50 paces of them, they (for us, fortunately) broke and fled, for had they done their duty, fatigued as my men were, they must have cut us to pieces.[14]

Ensign Edward Keogh seized the eagle of the 8me but was immediately bayoneted and fell dead. Sergeant Masterman then ran the eagle-bearer through with his pike* and secured the eagle, the first to be captured by the British in the Peninsula.† The Eighty Seventh lost 173 men but they inflicted twice that number on the two battalions they broke.

All along the line Wheatley's brigade, brilliantly supported by the artillery, drove back their opponents and 'after two and a half hours' roar of cannon and musketry', the action ended with a gallant charge by a single squadron of the German hussars. Had they been supported by the Spanish cavalry, the French defeat would have been a disaster.

Barossa cost the British 1,200 casualties and secured the allied

---

* Sergeants in British infantry regiments (other than light infantry and Rifles) carried a pike or halberd seven feet long.

† The Eighty Seventh were permitted to wear an eagle on their colours and appointments and received the title of 'Prince of Wales' Own Irish Regiment'. Masterman received an ensigncy in the Duke of York's Light Infantry Volunteers from which he exchanged back to the Eighty Seventh, becoming a lieutenant in 1813.

retreat over the San Petri. That it achieved no more was the fault of
La Peña. Throughout the action he stood by watching his ally com-
peting with more than double numbers. When his divisional commanders proposed going to Graham's assistance, he forbade them to
advance. Even a limited advance by the Spaniards could have ensured the rout of Victor's corps and the destruction of much of the
siege works round Cadiz.

Graham was bitterly angry. As soon as the French retired the
British collected their wounded and retired to the island. Just as his
exhausted infantry had crossed the bridge of boats across the San
Petri, La Peña proposed that they should counter-march and attack
again. Graham would have nothing to do with him.

When Wellington wrote to congratulate Graham on his victory,
he said:

> The conduct of the Spaniards throughout this expedition is
> precisely the same as I have ever observed it to be. They march the
> troops night and day, without provisions or rest and abusing every-
> body who proposes a moment's delay to afford either to the famished
> and fatigued soldiers. They reach the enemy in such a state as to be
> unable to make any exertion or execute any plan, even if any plan
> had been formed; and then, when the moment of action arrives, they
> are totally incapable of movement and they stand by to see their
> allies destroyed, and afterwards abuse them because they do not con-
> tinue, unsupported, exertions to which human nature is not equal.[15]

The description of Fuengirola and Barossa has carried the narrative
far in advance of events on the Spanish-Portuguese border. The
campaigns there stagnated after the collapse of the Spanish autumn
offensive at Ocaña in 1809. Wellington waited near Badajoz until
December. The sickness rate in the valley of the Guadiana was high
and it was unlikely that the inevitable French offensive against
Portugal would come by way of Badajoz. Over Christmas and the
New Year the bulk of the army was redeployed to guard the Ciudad
Rodrigo–Lisbon road. A corps of 12,000 men under Rowland Hill*

---

* Hill's corps consisted of Second British Division (three brigades), Hamilton's
Portuguese Division (two brigades) and two British and two Portuguese cavalry
regiments.

was stationed in central Portugal to block any secondary French thrust.

The experience of Junot in 1807 and Soult in 1809 had shown that the roads to Lisbon along the Tagus valley and from Galicia were not practicable as invasion routes. Two roads only were usable, those which crossed the frontier at Ciudad Rodrigo and Badajoz respectively. It was most probable that the French would use the Rodrigo road as that shortened the communications with France and led directly to Lisbon whereas the Badajoz road led only to the wrong side of the broad Tagus estuary.

Wellington stationed four of his five divisions on the road from Ciudad Rodrigo and set about building up his defensive strength behind them. From October 1809 thousands of Portuguese labourers, militiamen and civilians, toiled under the direction of British Engineers at the construction of the Lines of Torres Vedras. These were not continuous lines of entrenchments but an interlocking series of fortifications and earthworks all mutually supporting. In front of them fields of fire had been cleared, low ground flooded and hillsides scarped. Two front lines stretched from the Tagus to the Atlantic and barred the approaches to Lisbon. A third, an insurance against unforeseeable disaster, covered the little port of St Julian where the army could re-embark at the end of the Lisbon peninsula.

Simultaneously Beresford was training the Portuguese army. It was given regular pay and rations. The Portuguese officers were pressed to attend to their men by the example of their seconded British colleagues. Beresford's discipline was ferocious but it was scrupulously just. The British drill books were translated and British bugle calls introduced. In February 1810 Portuguese brigades were incorporated into British divisions* and Wellington's field army which had been only 22,000 at Talavera became 45,000 strong.

While Wellington made his preparations and tried to instil his own confidence into the government in London and into his own

---

* The standard arrangement was to put one Portuguese brigade of five battalions with two British brigades, each of three battalions. This was originally done only in the Third and Fourth Divisions but the practice was followed with the Fifth, Sixth and Seventh Divisions as they were formed. In the Light Division there was one Portuguese battalion in each of the two brigades.

generals, King Joseph was far from happy. He toured Andalusia to the plaudits of enthusiastic crowds but his euphoria was soon shattered by a decree from Paris. All Spain north of a line from Burgos to Tarragona was removed from his control and handed over to military governors responsible to Paris. Soult made it clear that he had outstayed his welcome in the south. He returned to Madrid to find that another imperial decree had removed Old Castile and Leon from his authority. A little later his nominal control over Soult in Andalusia was revoked. His kingdom stretched only from the Sierra de Guadarrama to the Sierra Morena and even this little realm was not immune from incursions from the independent French generals who surrounded it. He complained that he was 'no more than a watchman for the military hospitals in Madrid, the guardian of the army's stores, the commandant of a prisoner of war camp'.[16] Not for the first time, he threatened to abdicate. In the presence of the French ambassador and several generals he declared in a rage that he would call the Spaniards to arms against the French.[17] Napoleon ignored him.

Between December 1809 and August 1810 Napoleon sent 138,000 more French troops into Spain. He was determined to complete the conquest of the country but many of these reinforcements had to be used to hold ground already won, especially in Aragon and Catalonia. The Emperor was in no doubt where the main blow must be struck. 'The English are the only danger in Spain. The rest are no more than a rabble who can never stand against us.'[18]

It was Napoleon's well-publicised intention to lead the final attack on Lisbon in person. The Old Guard marched to Bayonne. The imperial carriages were ordered to Spain. On 3 December 1809 he told the Corps Legislatif that 'When I show myself beyond the Pyrenees the terrorstruck leopard* will take to the ocean to avoid shame, terror and defeat.'[19]

He never again showed himself beyond the Pyrenees. In mid-December his attention was diverted by the more domestic concerns of his divorce and remarriage. In his place he appointed André

---

* Napoleon habitually referred to the British as the leopards in public speeches. He referred to the lions passant regardant in the royal arms of England. According to some pedantic heralds, lions looking towards you are leopards.

Massena, Prince of Essling, the greatest of his marshals. He was given a striking force of three corps, 65,000 men, designated the Army of Portugal. He was promised a further corps of 20,000 when they were ready.

Wellington had long before maintained that the French could not 'overrun Portugal with a smaller force than 100,000 men'.[20] Napoleon disagreed. In May 1810 he ordered, 'Write to the Prince of Essling and tell him that it appears from the returns extracted from the English newspapers that Wellington's army consists of 23,000 English and Germans and of 22,000 Portuguese. Thus the Prince should have more troops than he needs.'[21]

CHAPTER 9

The Third French Invasion of Portugal

MASSENA was fifty-three, eleven years older than Napoleon and Wellington. He was born in Nice and in his youth had been a cabin boy, a grocer, a smuggler and a sergeant-major in the royal army. He had commanded a division in Bonaparte's memorable Italian campaign of 1795. His great military virtue was stubborn tenacity. His defence of Switzerland against Suvarov in 1799 was a classic. His defence of Genoa in the following year had made possible Bonaparte's victory at Marengo. His performance in the Austrian campaign of 1809 had earned him the title of prince, only the third such title awarded to a marshal for military rather than marital reasons.* No one could doubt his talents as a general. Personally he was detestable—avaricious, lecherous, dishonest and suspicious. He had never been handsome and his looks had not been improved when Napoleon destroyed one of his eyes in a shooting accident. Characteristically the Emperor handed his gun to Berthier and blamed him for the unlucky shot.

The Prince of Essling took up his new command at Salamanca in May 1810. Those who knew him from previous campaigns were distressed to see how he had aged. He aggravated this impression by saying to his assembled staff, 'Gentlemen, I am here against my

---

* The other princely marshals in 1810 were Berthier, Prince of Neufchâtel, and Davout, Prince of Eckmühl, for military reasons. Bernadotte was Prince of Ponte Corvo since he had married King Joseph Bonaparte's sister-in-law. Murat became a king as he was married to the Emperor's sister. Ney was created Prince of the Moskowa in 1812 for his epic rearguard action in the retreat from Moscow.

wishes. I feel too old and too tired to go to war again. The emperor has ordered me here and when I told him why I wished to decline he replied that my reputation alone would be sufficient to end the war. That was gratifying to me but no man has two lives to live, a soldier least of all.'[1]

Napoleon was relying greatly on Massena's reputation. So certain was he that the Army of Portugal could drive straight through to Lisbon that he gave no orders to the other French commanders in western Spain to co-operate with him. Wellington was thus left to concentrate against the single French thrust down the Ciudad Rodrigo–Lisbon road. Despite his reluctance to go campaigning, Massena seems to have had no qualms about his task. Both his actions and his omissions show that he thought it a comparatively easy task to drive the small British army back to its ships as Soult had done at Coruña. Of the Portuguese troops he had no opinion at all.

He was almost equally ill-informed about the topography of Portugal. Like all French commanders of his time, he relied on the maps produced in the second half of the eighteenth century by the Spaniard, Tomàs Lopez. While Lopez' maps of Spain give a fair representation of his own country, he had drawn Portugal largely from his imagination, marking in roads where he thought they ought to exist. It was by one of these putative roads that Napoleon had ordered Junot to advance along the Tagus valley in 1807. The attempt to advance along a line on the map had crippled Junot's army. Lopez was to contribute to Massena's ill-success.

Napoleon and Massena had considerable grounds for their confidence. The British army was small, though not as small as they imagined. The Portuguese were untried. The Army of Portugal outnumbered both together and was composed of veterans led by generals of experience and reputation. It was unfortunate that two of the three corps commanders were among the select band of French generals who had been defeated by the British—Junot at Vimeiro, Reynier at Alexandria (1801) and Maida (1806).

French calculations had overlooked the ancient laws and customs of Portugal. The country had so often been invaded from Spain that drastic powers were available to the government in such an event.

There was universal military service for all able-bodied males except priests. Those who did not join the regular army were drafted into a militia which, if it had not the training for field operations, was fully capable of defending fixed fortifications like those being built at Torres Vedras. Those too old or too young for the militia were liable to serve in the *ordenanza*, a local levy admirably suited to guerrilla warfare. In the path of an invader the government could order the country to be evacuated by the population and stripped bare of provisions and stores which might be of use to the enemy.

It was on these factors and on his lines protecting Lisbon that Wellington relied. He had no intention of fighting battles unless victory was certain. He commanded Britain's only field army and he knew that if he suffered heavy casualties, even in winning a victory, his political masters would insist on withdrawing from the Peninsula. His greatest problem was to convince the British government that, if the worst came to the worst, the army could be withdrawn without disastrous loss. In his own estimation, evacuation was not even a remote possibility but, 'I should be able to effect my object with greater ease if I was not under the necessity of effecting everything not only without loss but without risk, or even the appearance of risk, to please the good people who make themselves judges of these matters in England.'[2]

He planned to draw the French into an artificial desert. The supply service of the French army was notoriously sketchy. Massena could not live off the country when it had been stripped bare. When the French had committed themselves irretrievably they were to be faced by an impregnable barrier. If they were foolhardy enough to attempt to assault it they would be bloodily repulsed. If they decided against assault, starvation would cause them more loss than several pitched battles. The *ordenanza*, supported by the militia, would close round their rear, circumscribing their foraging area and cutting them off from Spain. The Anglo-Portuguese field army would remain intact.

During April French troops started to appear round Ciudad Rodrigo in strength. The town commanded the road over the frontier and no invasion could be attempted until it was in French hands. Rodrigo was not a first-class fortress but it had a governor of exceptional determination, Andreas Herrasti, and a Spanish garrison of 5,500 men. The French did not invest the town until 25 June. Massena was in no hurry. His orders were to proceed methodically. Napoleon had said, 'I do not wish an immediate entry into Lisbon, as I could not feed the city [before the harvest] with its immense population accustomed to live on food brought from the sea.'[3]

Wellington's forward troops, the Light Division, were at Gallegos within twelve miles of Rodrigo. Despite Herrasti's appeals, Wellington would not attempt to save the fortress. 'With an army one fourth inferior in numbers, a part of it being of a doubtful description, at all events but just made, and not more than one third the numbers of the enemy cavalry, it would be an operation of some risk to leave our mountains and bring on a general action in the plains.'[4] As one of his generals put it, 'If we attempt to relieve the place, the French will drive us out of Portugal; while, if they get possession of Ciudad Rodrigo, they will lose time, which is more important to them; but they will have to find this out.'[5] Rodrigo surrendered on 9 July after a gallant, hopeless defence.

The next obstacle in Massena's path was the small Portuguese fortress of Almeida, less formidable than Rodrigo and standing on the eastern, Spanish, bank of the river Coa, a fast flowing stream running in a steep rocky gorge. To reach it the French must drive in Craufurd's five battalions.

Ney advanced with 24,000 men on 24 July. Since January Craufurd had conducted an outpost war of unrivalled brilliance, keeping at bay a greatly superior force. On 24 July his judgement failed him. He decided to fight a rearguard action against odds of six to one with an unfordable river, crossed by a narrow bridge, at his rear. Too late he decided to withdraw his cavalry, his battery and his two Portuguese battalions. A tumbril overturned at the hairpin bend by the bridge, blocking the road just at the time that Ney launched his main attack. It was met by 2,900 light infantry and Riflemen. That they extricated themselves, with the guns, limbers and tumbrils, from the imbroglio is the highest tribute to the way in which Moore had trained them and Craufurd had perfected them. The steep slope down which they had to retreat was intersected with stone walls. 'The fire was hot, and the ground very difficult for us but much

E

easier for the enemy because we made passages for ourselves and thus made them for the French.'[6] At one point a company of the Forty Third was trapped by a ten-foot wall at their rear and escaped only by pushing it over by main force. Twice the three battalions had to counter-attack to recapture a small knoll which dominated the bridge. They suffered 333 casualties but they got across and established themselves strongly on the west bank. Ney, who was as rash as Craufurd, tried to storm across the bridge with packed columns of grenadiers. They failed and suffered more than 500 casualties.

Almeida did not put up the defence Wellington had hoped. When the French bombardment opened on 26 August a chance shell exploded the main magazine, devastating much of the town and destroying all the store of powder.

Despite this piece of good fortune Massena continued to move methodically. It took him a long time to collect fifteen days' rations for the army which now had all three corps concentrated in a relatively small area. When he resumed his advance on 15 September[6/4] he took the Viseu road. Wellington broke contact and fell back towards Coimbra by the Gouvea–Moita road. From the atlas of Tomàs Lopez the Viseu road is the obvious route to take from Almeida to Coimbra. On the ground it was, as Wellington gleefully remarked, 'the worst in the whole kingdom'.[7] Massena found it 'affreux'. He reported that 'worse roads could not be found. They bristle with rocks. The artillery and waggons have suffered severely.'[8] The field park was to suffer even more when Portuguese militia under Nicholas Trant ambushed them in a narrow defile and were beaten off only with difficulty. Worst of all, the road leads to the finest defensive position in Europe.* On 21 September Wellington wrote from the Convent of Busaco, 'We have an excellent position here in which I am strongly tempted to give battle.'[9]

An officer who asked a friend on the staff for a map of the Busaco position was told, 'You have only to draw a damned long hill, and that will be sufficiently explanatory.'[10] It is a ridge ten miles long with its southern end dropping sharply into the river Mondego. It is steep-fronted for its whole length except at the extreme northern end

---

* With the weapons of 1810 it would have been at least as difficult to attack Busaco frontally as it was to attack Cassino with the weapons of 1944.

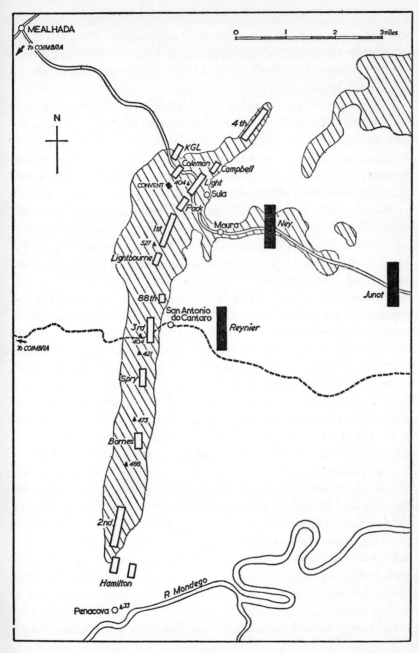

MEALHADA

To COIMBRA

N

0   1   2   3miles

4th

KGL

Coleman

Campbell

CONVENT 404

Light

Sula

Pack

Moura

Ney

1st

527

Lightbourne

Junot

88th

San Antonio
do Cantaro

Reynier

3rd

To COIMBRA

404

421

Spry

473

Barnes

488

2nd

Hamilton

R Mondego

Penacova   33

Busaco

and rises 1,000 feet in places from the valley below.* The crest is 400 yards wide and undulates gently, bearing a passable track from end to end. Today the forward slope is thickly afforested but in 1810 it was bare of cover.

Two roads crossed the ridge from east to west. Three miles from the northern end the main road to Coimbra wound up a spur. At the summit it passed the walls of the solidly built convent. At the centre of the ridge there was a cart track which rose from the hamlet of San Antonio do Cantaro in the valley. It is extraordinary that a general of Massena's calibre should have attempted to seize such a position by frontal attack. Had he taken the trouble to reconnoitre he would have discovered a side road which, with a substantial detour, avoided the ridge. Wellington knew of this road and sent orders for Trant to block it. This message miscarried and the French would have found it unguarded.

The advanced guard under Ney came in sight of the ridge just before dusk on 25 September. Next morning Ney and Reynier made cursory reconnaissances and reported that the position was strong but was held only by a rearguard. Ney sent back to Massena a recommendation for immediate attack. The prince was travelling with a Mme Henriette Leberton and, according to one account, Ney's ADC had to shout his message through the bedroom door. Certainly he had to wait two hours before Massena would see him. Late in the afternoon Massena rode to the front, glanced at the ground and gave orders for an attack on the following morning.

These orders called for an attack in two phases. Reynier's corps was to move first, ascending the ridge by the San Antonio track. Massena and his corps commanders believed that Wellington had only a rearguard at Busaco and it was assumed that Reynier would reach the crest beyond the allied right. As soon as Reynier was seen to be *maître des hauteurs* Ney's corps was to advance astride the main road and attack Wellington's centre. Junot's corps and the cavalry were to remain in reserve ready to assist Reynier or Ney and to exploit success.

The fallacy behind these orders was that Busaco was held not by a

---

* The Malvern Hills are not dissimilar but on a smaller scale.

rearguard but by the whole of Wellington's infantry, 50,000 men, sixty guns and two squadrons of dragoons.[5/5] Reynier's attack was aiming at the allied centre rather than beyond their right flank and Ney's corps was marching towards the point where Wellington had stationed his reserves.

It was misty on the morning of 27 September. This could have been serious for Wellington since he had insufficient men to guard the whole length of the ridge but needed to see the direction in which the French attacks were heading so that troops could be moved to meet them. In the event Reynier suffered more from the mist. Some of his formations lost direction as they climbed the shrouded slope and co-ordination of their attacks was impossible. His attacks fell piecemeal and some columns reached wrong objectives.

Reynier's two divisional columns moved off at 6 am. From the beginning they were assailed by allied skirmishers. On the left Heudelet's division followed the San Antonio track. They had a heavy screen of *voltigeurs* and advanced on a front of one company. The track enabled them to keep their direction but brought them to a point on the crest which was well guarded. They were stopped by the fire of the Seventy Fourth supported by two Portuguese battalions and twelve guns. Heudelet's men did not give way. They clung to their position near the crest and exchanged fire with their opponents until the failure of the other French attacks.

Reynier's other division, Merle's, reached the crest a mile to the north of Heudelet having veered to their right in the mist. Their march would have taken them to one of the gaps in the allied deployment but the Eighty Eighth with a wing of the Forty Fifth raced to their left to receive them. Alexander Wallace, commanding the Eighty Eighth, called to his men, 'Now, Connaught Rangers! Mind what you are going to do. Pay attention to what I have so often told you. Don't give the false touch, but push home to the muzzle!'[11] Jumping from his horse Wallace led his men to the charge. 'All was now confusion and uproar, smoke, fire, bullets, officers and soldiers, French drummers and drums knocked down in every direction; British, Portuguese and French mixed together. Never was a defeat more complete—for Wallace never slackened his fire while a Frenchman was within reach.' Then he reformed his line and waited for further orders. 'Wallace,' said Wellington as he rode up, 'I have never witnessed a more gallant charge.'[12]

Reynier's final attempt was made by Foy's brigade from the rear of Heudelet's column. Inclining to the right, Foy led them to the crest at a point strewn with rocks which had no defenders. He had no time to consolidate his position. The mist had lifted and the generals on the allied right could see that no troops threatened them. James Leith, commanding the newly formed Fifth Division, led his nearest brigade across the rear of the Seventy Fourth and attacked with the Ninth leading. Foy recalled that, 'Despite all my efforts, the head of my column fell away to the right. I could not get the troops to deploy; disorder set in. At this moment a ball went through my left arm, breaking it. I was swept away in the flight.'[13] Reynier's corps had failed. Twenty-three of its twenty-seven battalions had been engaged. They had suffered 2,000 casualties.

From Ney's position in the valley it seemed that Reynier had reached the crest and the marshal ordered his corps to advance. Loison's division with its left on the main road suffered much from two troops of horse artillery and from a heavy screen of Riflemen around the village of Sula. The *tirailleurs* had to be reinforced before the bugle horns were sounded to call the greenjackets in and the column toiled uphill. In front of them they could see no one but the solitary figure of Robert Craufurd standing by a windmill. Behind him, lying in a sunken road, were 2,000 men of the Forty Third and Fifty Second. When the French came close to him 'he turned round, came up to the Fifty Second and called out, "Now, Fifty Second! Revenge the death of Sir John Moore!" '[14]* An artillery officer standing near by wrote home that the French column

> had reached to within nine or ten yards of the summit of the hill: I had watched it advance and was attentively observing it, when the shout of our troops astonished me. I never experienced a sensation like that produced by that '*huzza!*' and instant charge. I cannot describe the exhilaration of the feeling. The enemy scarcely stood a moment, but the massive column, so formidable in appearance, flew like lightning down the descent. The French locked up in columns could not act; it was a carnage, not a conflict.[15]

---

* Moore had been colonel of the Fifty Second.

Ney's second division had been halted by a brigade of Portuguese but Loison's repulse decided Massena to order a retreat. Four thousand five hundred casualties, including five generals, convinced him that Busaco could not be stormed out of hand. He sent out scouting parties who found the flanking road. On the evening of 29 September the French army began to file away to its right. Wellington, whose army had lost only 1,250 men, continued his retreat by easy marches. He had stood at Busaco only because it offered such opportunities for checking the French and for giving his untried Portuguese confidence under fire. Both aims had been fulfilled. Although a Portuguese militia regiment had taken to its heels at the mere sight of the French, the regular troops had fought steadily and well. 'It has given them a taste for an amusement to which they were not before accustomed, and which they would not have acquired if I had not put them in a very strong position.'[16]

The retreat was uneventful apart from a few cavalry skirmishes. Ahead of the army went a flood of refugees.

> Old people, lame and sick people, women just risen from childbed, children, and whole families with all their belongings packed either on bullock carts, mules, horses or donkeys, were to be seen mixed up with all kind of beasts, among which pigs, owing to their unruliness and horrible cries, were the most conspicuous. Now and again the cry would arise that the French were coming, and then the young girls would implore all those who were riding to help them upon the saddle with them. Ladies who, according to the custom of the country, had never perhaps left their homes except to go to Mass, could be seen walking along, three in a row, wearing silk shoes and their heads and shoulders covered only with thin scarves.[17]

> [At Coimbra] the civil authorities, in making their own hurried escape, had totally forgotten that they had left a gaol full of rogues unprovided for, and who made the most hideous screaming for relief. Our quartermaster general very humanely took some men, who broke open the doors, and the whole of them were soon seen howling along the bridge, in the most delightful delirium, with the French dragoons at their heels.[18]

Coimbra delayed the French for three days. There was no opposition but the city was given over to sack. Massena set a bad example

The Lines of Torres Vedras

by purloining a collection of scientific instruments from the university. One telescope he presented to Ney, who returned it with the comment that he was not a receiver of stolen goods. Relations between the two marshals, never warm, deteriorated sharply. When Massena marched out of Coimbra on 4 October he left his sick and wounded there with an inadequate guard. They and the city were captured by Trant and his militia three days later.

French cavalry patrols came in sight of the Lines of Torres Vedras on the morning of 11 October. There was some skirmishing around the village of Sobral and, on the 14th, Massena came to see the Lines for himself. He realised at once that he could not break through and said that 'he would compromise the army if he were to attack lines so formidable'.[19] He could not advance. His pride would not allow him to retreat. He sat down in front of the lines and waited for something to turn up.

Three events might enable him to complete his task. First, the British government might lose its nerve and withdraw its army. Napoleon thought there was a good chance of this happening. The Prince of Wales was acting as Regent but Parliament had limited his powers until February. Many people in England believed that when the Regency became unrestricted he would dismiss the Tory government and call in his life-long friends the Whigs, who favoured appeasement. When it came to the crunch the Regent retained Spencer Perceval and his ministers.

Second, Wellington might emerge from the Lines and give Massena the chance of defeating him in a battle. As the French army dwindled from hardship and starvation the temptation to attack them was very strong but, said Wellington, 'They won't draw me from my cautious system.'[20] To fight a 'general action in the plains' outside Lisbon would expose the allied cause to the same risks as a battle for Ciudad Rodrigo. Wellington looked at the French through his telescope and wistfully remarked, 'I could lick those fellows any day, but it would cost me 10,000 men and, as this is the last army England has, we must take care of it.'[21]

Finally, there remained the possibility of help from Soult. As has been seen, Napoleon issued no orders for Soult to co-operate with Massena. To do so Soult would have first to capture Badajoz and

'Elvas, an even stronger fortress. Once the English have been beaten and re-embarked, Badajoz and Elvas will fall without further ado.'[22] Two days after Busaco the Emperor changed his mind. Soult was to send Mortier's corps into Estremadura with the limited aim of stopping the Spaniards there co-operating with Wellington. On 14 November, when Massena had already been a month before the Lines, Soult was told that Mortier ought to have gone deep into Portugal to threaten Lisbon from the south bank of the Tagus.[23] This order reached Soult in mid-December and he refused to obey it. He pointed out that Mortier had only 10,000 men and that between him and his goal there were 20,000 allied troops, to say nothing of two large and four smaller fortresses. 'The corps could never reach its destination. It would be surrounded before I could come to its aid.'[24] Instead he collected a force of 20,000 men and marched north to capture Badajoz. This scheme appealed to him since the acquisition of a major fortress would redound to his own credit and, while it might help Massena, there could be no question of sharing the glory. He started the siege of Badajoz at the end of January 1811. Not a single Anglo-Portuguese soldier was detached from the army facing Massena.

As the orders to sweep the country had been executed with insufficient thoroughness, the Army of Portugal gleaned enough to remain close to the Lines for four weeks, twice as long as Wellington had estimated. Then it retreated twenty-five miles to a strong position anchored on Santarem with the Tagus on its left flank and the Rio Maior covering its front. This brought it into new foraging grounds but did not help Massena to solve his problem of how to capture Lisbon.

One of the worst of his difficulties was his total isolation. He had no communication with Spain. The militia and *ordenanza* had drawn an invisible net round his rear. They murdered his stragglers, harried his foraging parties and intercepted his despatches. The two ends of the net were secured on the fortresses of Peniche and Abrantes. Only a powerful force could break through. The marshal's first report to Paris was carried by General Foy in November. He had a close escort of a battalion of infantry and a squadron of cavalry. Three brigades mounted diversionary operations. Foy returned to

Santarem on 5 February with an escort of 1,800 men. He brought the Emperor's orders to hold on and decide the war by attrition. This did nothing to feed the Army of Portugal which was steadily fading away from want. Sixty-five thousand had entered Portugal in September. Only 46,500 were with the eagles by New Year's Day. A reinforcement division fought its way through early in January but this meant only that there were 7,600 more mouths to feed without giving Massena the strength to attempt a breakthrough.

While Massena's army dwindled, Wellington's grew. He was close to his supply base. His sick and wounded could rejoin the army quickly. There was time to continue the training of the Portuguese. When the army entered the Lines in October there were 34,000 British troops in six divisions. By March there were 43,000 in seven divisions with an eighth forming.*

Only Massena's iron determination kept the French close to Lisbon for five months. No other commander in Europe would have stayed for half the time. Nor was his situation made easier by the disloyalty of Ney and Junot who openly criticised him and let it be known that, in their opinion, the army should return to Spain as soon as possible. By mid-February even Massena acknowledged the inevitable and called a council of his corps commanders. Ney, Junot and Reynier all knew retreat to be inevitable but none of them had the courage to propose it. Each put forward a scheme for taking the offensive which they knew to be impracticable. Massena issued warning orders for retreat a few days later and, early on 6 March, a peasant came into the British outposts opposite Santarem with the news that the French had decamped during the night, leaving their watchfires burning.

Ironically, Badajoz was betrayed to Soult by the acting governor four days later. In theory the way was open for co-operation between the Armies of Portugal and the South. In practice no co-operation was possible. There was no communication between them. A message from one to the other would have to travel under heavy escort by way of Madrid, a month's journey. In any case Soult

---

* Sixth Division was formed on 6 October 1810. Seventh Division came into being on 5 March 1811 but was not complete until May.

heard of Graham's victory at Barossa just as the fortress fell. He had to take much of his field force back to Cadiz by forced marches.

Massena's retreat caught Wellington on the wrong foot and the French gained a twenty-four-hour start. It was not until 11 March that the allied advanced guard came up with Ney's rearguard at Pombal. For five days there were repeated actions between Ney's men and the Light Division who had to contend not only with the French but with the fumbling direction of Sir William Erskine who commanded them in the absence of Craufurd.

The fate of the campaign, and probably of the Peninsula, was decided in those five days. It was not the Light Division which decided it but Colonel Nicholas Trant. Massena did not intend to retreat into Spain but to cross the Mondego and wait, on the unravaged foraging grounds north of Coimbra, until help reached him. Wellington had no regular troops north of the Mondego but Coimbra was held by Trant with six weak battalions of militia and six guns. At Penacova, the southern end of the Busaco ridge, were four more battalions of militia. In all there were 5,000 partially trained men to defend the riverline. Trant had orders to retire as soon as he was seriously threatened, and as early as 8 March Wellington 'concluded' that he had done so. He was, however, a literal-minded officer and determined to stay until the last possible moment.

French cavalry approached the long bridge at Coimbra on 10 March and found two arches blown out of it. On the north bank could be seen artillery and an impressive number of infantrymen. Montbrun, commanding the French advanced guard, sent his cavalry upstream to search for fords. The river was running strongly and at each possible crossing-place they were greeted by lively, if inaccurate, musketry. Montbrun decided that the crossing could be made only if he was lent a brigade of infantry. He was joined by a single battalion on 12 March and used it to endeavour to persuade the defenders of the broken bridge to surrender. Trant had withdrawn all his troops except a single battalion and two guns, but they put up a defiant front. Montbrun had no time to do more. On 13 March Wellington manoeuvred Ney's rearguard out of Condeixa, ten miles south of the bridge. Massena could not mount a river crossing with

Wellington pressing so close to his rear. The Army of Portugal swung its line of retreat eastward and set out for Ciudad Rodrigo.

The last of the rearguard actions was fought on 15 March. Ney had conducted his retreat with great skill but on this day he made a serious mistake. Probably he was overtired. He left three brigades on the allied side of the river Ceira and did not ensure that they posted adequate guards. Behind them was the bridge of Foz do Arouce, a hundred yards long and fourteen feet wide. The French sense of false security was increased when the Light Division came in sight. Erskine refused to attack. Just before dusk Wellington came up and ordered an immediate advance. Rifle companies infiltrated behind the French along a sunken road. The Light Division attacked in front. The Third Division came up on the French left. Appalled to find Riflemen behind them, the French centre panicked. Fugitives jammed the bridge. Men were drowned trying to ford the Ceira. Ney restored the situation with a counter-attack, but the French lost 250 men. The eagle of the 39me was thrown into the river and recovered by the British.

Massena then accelerated his retreat. He abandoned all inessential waggons and hamstrung most of his emaciated draught and pack animals. Then he hurried the army on by forced marches. By 22 March the Army of Portugal was concentrated in the area Guarda–Celorico and in touch with Ciudad Rodrigo. Wellington did not press the pursuit. He had outrun his supplies and the line of Massena's retreat was full of excellent defensive positions. 'Our Chief,' wrote an officer, 'had the option of disorganising his army by a close pursuit without supplies, which while it lasted must have been brilliant, or a temporary halt, forgoing the opportunity, not to return, but retaining his army in discipline, supply and efficiency. He chose the latter alternative without a hesitation.'[25]

Massena was still not prepared to admit complete failure. From Guarda he ordered a march south-east to the Tagus. Ney refused to obey and was dismissed from his command. Junot and Reynier went through the motions of obedience but within a week the whole misconceived operation collapsed from lack of food. By the beginning of April the French hold on Portugal was reduced to the fortress of Almeida and a narrow strip between the frontier and the river Coa.

Reynier with 10,000 men held the French left at Sabugal. Seven miles separated his right from the nearest part of Ney's corps.* Junot was ten miles behind him. Reynier was isolated and Wellington planned to destroy him. His open left flank was to be turned by Erskine with two cavalry brigades and the Light Division. Simultaneously his front would be attacked by four divisions. The allied superiority would be three to one.

Reynier was saved by mist and Sir William Erskine. The mist was so thick that the commanders of the frontal attack halted their divisions before they became hopelessly confused. Erskine saw no reason to halt. He had acquired a baronetcy and a reputation for bravery as a young cavalry officer in 1793. He suffered from two defects. He was 'very blind'[26] and, in the intervals of being a Member of Parliament, he had been confined as insane.†

Sydney Beckwith had halted the leading brigade of the Light Brigade in the mist when an ADC from Erskine rode up and 'in a hasty and petulant manner asked Colonel Beckwith why he had not marched to the ford?'[27] Beckwith immediately led his brigade to the river and crossed although the ford was chest-deep. Owing to the mist he used a ford half a mile to the left of the one intended. As a result he advanced against the French flank instead of behind their rear. A piquet fired a few shots at them and retired. A screen of Riflemen pushed up the hill. The Forty Third followed and with great difficulty two horse artillery guns were dragged across the river to support them.

Having rashly launched Beckwith, Erskine became cautious. He forbade Drummond's brigade to cross the river in support and himself vanished with the cavalry into the mist. He crossed the Coa far to the right and took no part in the battle except to capture the baggage of two French generals.

Meanwhile Beckwith with 1,500 men found himself opposed by

---

* Since Ney's dismissal on 22 March VI Corps had been commanded by the senior divisional commander, General Louis Henri Loison.

† When Wellington heard that Erskine was being posted to Portugal he remonstrated that he had 'generally understood him to be a madman'. The Horse Guards replied that, 'No doubt he is sometimes a little mad, but in his lucid intervals he is an uncommonly clever fellow; and I trust he will have no fit during the campaign, though he looked a little wild as he embarked.'

two French divisions. Fortunately the mist prevented the French from realising how few men were attacking them. Their first counter-attack was beaten off, a howitzer being abandoned as the French fell back. Then Beckwith found himself being assailed by seven battalions and realised that he must give ground.

> 'Now, my lads,' he called, 'we'll go back a little if you please.' On hearing which, every man began to run, when he shouted again, 'No, no, I don't mean that—we are in no hurry—we'll just walk quietly back, and you can give them a shot as you go along.' This was quite enough—the retiring force kept up a destructive fire and regulated their movements by his as he rode quietly back in the midst of them, conversing in a cheerful encouraging manner.[28]

As they retired a musket ball grazed his forehead, covering his face with blood. From the ranks a soldier 'called out, "Old Sydney is wounded." Beckwith heard the remark and instantly replied, "But he won't leave you; fight on my brave lads; we shall beat them".'[29]

The brigade must have been driven back to the river and destroyed but Drummond heard firing coming nearer and decided to ignore his orders and march to Beckwith's support. Supported by the guns 'which had the opportunity of doing considerable execution',[30] and a stray squadron of light dragoons which had become detached from Erskine in the mist, it was time to advance again. Beckwith 'called out, "Now, my men, this will do—let us show them our teeth again!" This was obeyed as steadily as if the words halt, front, had been given on parade, and our line was instantly in battle array, while Beckwith, shaking his fist in the faces of the advancing foe, called out to them, "Now, you rascals, come on here if you dare".'[31] The Light Division surged up the hill and re-captured the howitzer, in the limber of which was found 'a couple of fine hams and a keg of concentrated *eau-de-vie*'.

At that moment the mist lifted and Reynier saw four divisions sweeping across the river and up the ridge. At the head of the leading division was Thomas Picton 'with his stick over his shoulder. "Steady, my lads, steady," said he; "don't throw away your fire until I give you the word of command." '[32]

The French had been so concerned about the flank attack that only 3,000 men were left facing to the front. Outnumbered nine to one, these men fought a splendid rearguard action. One of their attackers wrote, 'They never fought better. So rapidly did they fire that instead of returning their ramrods, they stuck them in the ground and continued to fight until overpowered by our men.'[33] Their comrades hastily retreated into Spain. By nightfall the only legacy of Massena's invasion of Portugal was a trail of devastation from Ciudad Rodrigo to the Tagus and the fortress of Almeida which was invested the following day. Sabugal cost Reynier 760 men, including 180 prisoners. The British lost 161. Wellington wrote that he considered 'the action that was fought by the Light Division to be one of the most glorious that British troops were ever engaged in'.[34]

Wellington had liberated Portugal for the third time. He did not have to repeat the process. The French had suffered terrible loss. From September to April they had lost 25,000 men, of whom a quarter were prisoners of war. Deaths in battle amounted to only 1,500. The remainder, about 15,000, fell victims to disease, starvation or the vengeance of the *ordenanza*. Almost 6,000 horses were lost and there were only thirty-six waggons left with the army.

Massena had failed, but he had failed with honour. His only serious mistake was the frontal attack at Busaco. No general could have shown more determination and courage. As he came to realise, he was faced with an impossible task. It is just possible that Napoleon might have captured Lisbon if he could have co-ordinated several of the French armies in Spain instead of leaving the job to Massena and 65,000 men.* Wellington had estimated that the French would need 100,000 men for the task. He had added that if they brought that number deep into Portugal they would starve.

---

* The three corps had a combined strength of 65,050 all ranks and arms on 15 September 1810. On 15 March 1811 they totalled 44,417. In between these two dates drafts of 3,255 had joined the army. In addition d'Erlon's IX Corps had entered Portugal with a strength on 1 January 1811 of 17,889 *présents sous armes*. They contributed about 4,000 more casualties although, since much of the corps did not go deep into Portugal, they were able to evacuate a higher proportion of their sick.

CHAPTER 10

The Watershed

MASSENA later declared that Wellington 'had not left him one black hair on his body, he had turned grey all over'.[1] He had not lost the iron determination which had made his reputation. His army was weary and dispirited. It had lost faith in its commander and was very short of transport but, having fallen back on its depots, it could put 50,000 men into the field. Massena had left a pledge inside the Portuguese frontier, the garrison of Almeida, and he was intent on redeeming it.

Almeida was one of the four fortresses around which the war was to revolve for a year after the action at Sabugal. Situated in pairs astride the frontier, they controlled movement between Portugal and Spain. In the north Almeida and Ciudad Rodrigo blocked the road from Portugal to Salamanca and Valladolid. In the south Elvas and Badajoz, both more formidable than the northern pair, blocked the road to Talavera and Madrid. If Wellington was to turn from defence to attack he must hold all four. One pair would give him an open doorway into Spain. The other would be a door locked to prevent the French striking into Portugal while he was in Spain. Soult's capture of Badajoz meant that the allied army must be divided. As soon as he had been certain that Massena was headed for Spain, Wellington had detached Beresford* with 20,000 men to drive Soult away and, if possible, re-capture Badajoz. He was left with 35,000 to blockade Almeida† and guard against Massena and the Army of Portugal.

---

* Rowland Hill, the usual commander of the southern corps, was sick in England.
† Almeida could only be blockaded, ie starved into surrender, since there were no heavy guns available with which to undertake a siege.

Before the end of April Massena's army was massing around
Ciudad Rodrigo and feeling forward at the allied outposts. This was
sooner than Wellington had expected but he was convinced that the
French object would be limited to trying to relieve Almeida and 'I
do not intend to allow them to relieve this place unless I shall be
convinced that they have such a superiority of force as to render the
result of a contest for this place doubtful. The enemy may be
stronger than they were when they were obliged to evacuate Portugal, and they may have been reinforced by detachments of troops
under the command of Marshal Bessières; but I still feel confident
that they have it not in their power to defeat the allied army in a
general action.'²

Bessières commanded the French Army of the North which had
been formed in January to protect the communications with
Bayonne. Massena had asked him for the loan of 8,000 infantry and
some gun teams. Bessières had offered to bring 10,000 men but, in
the event, arrived with 30 gun teams, one battery and 1,700 cavalry.
Massena commented that 'he might have done more good if he had
sent me some more troops and stayed at his own headquarters, instead of coming here to ask questions and criticize everything I do'.³
The combined army was 48,000 men, including 4,500 cavalry, and 46
guns.

Knowing that Massena was in no state to undertake a major
incursion into Portugal, Wellington could afford to run risks in
choosing his position. He could concentrate on the single object of
stopping the French reaching Almeida. The best position for doing
this was the ridge running north from Fuentes de Oñoro and it was
unimportant that the river Coa ran in its deep ravine five miles in
rear of the position. If the allied army had been forced to retire into
Portugal only the narrow bridge of Castello Bom would have been
available. Such an eventuality was so improbable that the risk was
acceptable.

The Fuentes ridge is a well-marked feature with the Dos Casas
stream in front. The northern end of the ridge is steep-faced and the
stream runs among rocks. At the point where the direct road from
Rodrigo to Almeida crosses the ridge there were the ruins of a
substantial fort blown up the previous year. It was morally certain

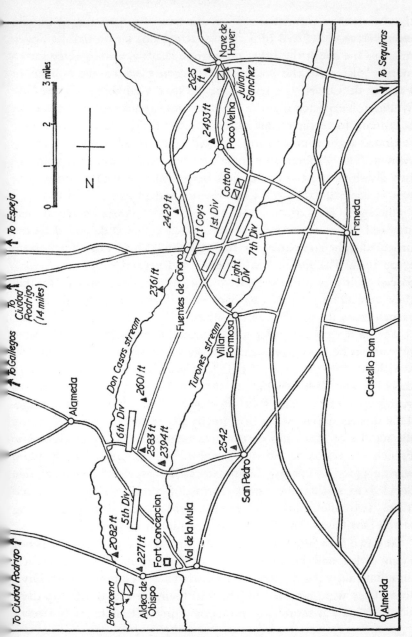

Fuentes de Oñoro—position of Allied troops on 3 May 1811

that Massena would not attack on this line. His memories of Busaco
would have convinced him that it would not be profitable. Seven
miles to the south the ridge ends quite sharply, falling away into a
marshy plain. At the south-eastern corner stands the village of
Fuentes de Oñoro, a small maze of streets climbing up the hill.
Wellington expected that the French would attack the ridge from the
south and force their way along it. Four of his six divisions were
stationed at the southern end, flanked by his two brigades of British
cavalry. The northern five miles of the position were entrusted to
two divisions and 300 Portuguese dragoons. The whole force in line
was 37,000 men including 1,800 cavalry and 48 guns.[5/7]

Massena's first attack came on 3 May.[6/5] Fourteen battalions*
attacked the village frontally from the east. It was defended by the
brigaded light companies of the First and Third Divisions, about
2,500 men. The fighting was heavy and several times the French
forced their way into the heart of the little village, but by nightfall
they were all back on the east bank of the stream having suffered 650
casualties, twice as many as the allies.

The next day was quiet and Massena made a reconnaissance, a
precaution he does not seem to have taken before his first attack.
Watching from the ridge, Wellington saw French troops moving to
their left and deduced that on the 5th Massena would attempt to
swing wide of his flank so as to attack the south end of the ridge.
This was the move he had originally expected but, encouraged by
the repulse of Massena's first attack, he decided to try to check the
French advance as far away as possible. The only troops in the plain
were a party of Spanish irregular cavalry at Nave de Haver. He
decided to station the newly formed Seventh Division at Poco
Velha, two miles south of Fuentes, where it could deny the crossing
of the Dos Casas. The British cavalry supported it.

At dawn on 5 May the bulk of the French cavalry swung wide of
Poco Velha and hounded the Spaniards from Nave de Haver.
Simultaneously the cavalry of the Guard attacked the Seventh Division. They were repulsed but behind them were two infantry divisions.† This was more than Houston's nine battalions, only two of

---

* The whole of Ferey's division and four battalions from Marchand's.
† Those of Marchand and Mermet. Solignac's division was in reserve behind them.

them British, could hope to withstand. He ordered a retreat although it would be a difficult operation as they were beset by more than 4,000 French cavalry.

Wellington realised that he had made a mistake in extending his flank too far.[4] To put matters right he despatched the Light Division to cover Houston's retreat. Robert Craufurd had returned to the command of the Light a few days earlier and no one could be more suited to this task. He marched his men to a wood on the low watershed south-west of Poco Velha and lined the forward edge with Riflemen. 'French sharpshooters kept up a fire, but did not attempt to drive us out.'[5]

While Craufurd drew the French infantry and some of the cavalry away from Houston, the Seventh Division retreated steadily in close columns, protected by the British horsemen and Bull's troop of horse artillery. Heavily outnumbered, the light dragoons and German hussars repeatedly charged, were checked, reformed and charged again.

> Our men *evidently* had the advantage as individuals. Their broad-swords, ably wielded, flashed over the Frenchmen's heads, and obliged them to cower to their saddle bows. Many turned their horses and our men shouted in the pursuit but it was quite clear that, go which way they might, we were but scattered drops amidst their host, and could not possibly arrest their progress.[6]

Once the Seventh were in safety, Craufurd formed his men in battalion columns 'at quarter-distance ready to form square at any moment if charged by cavalry',[7] and marched back to the ridge. 'The French horsemen continually outflanked but never dared to assail him. Many times Montbrun* feigned to charge Craufurd's squares but always he found them too dangerous to meddle with, and this crisis passed without a disaster, yet there was not during the whole war a more perilous hour.'[8] To those looking down from the ridge it seemed a miracle that the Light Division could survive but a second lieutenant in the division regretted that 'for the first time we were not heavily engaged'.[9] Meanwhile Wellington had swung back his main

---

* Montbrun commanded all the French cavalry on 5 May but his task was made more difficult because Gen Lepic (from the Army of the North) insisted on referring his orders to Marshal Bessières for confirmation.

defensive line so that it faced south with Fuentes village on its left and the Seventh Division on the right holding the banks of the Turones stream in front of Freneda. When the French came face to face with this position they decided it was too strong to assault and contented themselves with a cannonade at long range.

The heaviest fighting again took place in the village of Fuentes where Massena renewed the attack from the east with three divisions.* The defenders suffered heavily and their commander, Lieutenant-Colonel Philips Cameron, son of the man who raised the Cameron Highlanders, was killed. At one time the French drove them from the houses at the top of the village. Close above stood the Connaught Rangers in reserve. Edward Pakenham, Wellington's brother in law,† galloped up to their colonel, the hero of Busaco, and said,

> 'Do you see that, Wallace?'
> 'I do,' replied the colonel, 'and I would rather drive the French out of the town than cover a retreat over the Coa.'
> 'Perhaps,' said Sir Edward, 'his lordship don't think it tenable.'
> 'I shall take it with my regiment and keep it too.'
> 'Will you?' was the reply; 'I'll go and tell Lord Wellington so.'
> In a moment or two Pakenham returned at a gallop and, waving his hat, called out, 'He says you may go—come along, Wallace.'[10]

Followed by the Seventy Fourth, the Rangers plunged into the village 'with bayonets fixed, in column of sections,‡ left in front, in double quick time, their firelocks at the trail. There was no noise or talking in the ranks; the men stepped together at a brisk trot, as if on parade.'[11] The French were swept back over the stream.

In the streets of Fuentes there was 'a shocking sight; our highlanders lay dead in heaps, while the other regiments, though less remarkable in dress, were scarcely so in the numbers of their slain. The French grenadiers, with their immense caps and gaudy plumes, lay in piles of twenty and thirty together—some dead, others wounded with barely strength to move.'[12] Massena did not order another attack. His reserve of ammunition was down to four rounds per man. The defence of Fuentes was taken over by the Light Division.

---

* Those of Ferey, Claparede and Conroux.
† At this time Pakenham was Deputy Adjutant General.
‡ A section was half a company, the nearest contemporary equivalent to a platoon.

The opposing lines of sentries were very close to each other: the French sentries being divided from us only by a narrow plank thrown across the stream. A blacksmith of ours by the name of Tidy, who had erected his forge in the old mill, was at work close by shoeing the officers' horses. The French sentry had crossed the plank to light his pipe and was standing carelessly chatting with me, when who should I see approaching but General Craufurd, inquiring if Tidy had shod his horse. The Frenchman's red wings* soon attracted the general's notice, and he suddenly, with his well known stern glance, inquired 'Who the devil's that you're talking to, Rifleman?' I informed him the French sentry who had come over for a light to his pipe. 'Indeed,' replied Craufurd. 'Let him go about his business, he has no right here—nor we either,' said he in a low whisper to his aide-de-camp, and away he walked.[13]

Wellington was not pleased with the battle of Fuentes de Oñoro. He did not count it as one of his victories. He did not nominate an ADC to carry the despatch† and wrote that the Secretary of State 'was quite right not to move [a vote of] thanks [in Parliament] for the battle, though it was the most difficult I was ever concerned in. If Boney had been there, we should have been beat.'[14] He said that 'he committed a fault by extending his right too much to Poco Velha; and that, if the French had taken advantage of it, there might have been bad consequences, but that they permitted him to recover himself and change his front before their face'.[15]

Massena had no reason to be pleased with the battle. He had a limited objective and superior numbers of infantry and cavalry. He dissipated his infantry strength by keeping Reynier's 10,000 men on the main Almeida road where they achieved nothing. His three-to-one superiority in cavalry was thwarted by four British regiments and by the steadiness of the infantry, British and Portuguese, of the Seventh and Light Divisions. He had trouble with Bessières who interfered with his handling of the battle, but the real reason for the French defeat was that the divisions which had been in Portugal were tired and dispirited. Napoleon's order to recall Massena arrived a week later.‡

---

* Wings were the large epaulettes worn by flank companies. In both armies they were red for grenadiers and green for light or *voltigeur* companies.
† See p 98 above.
‡ The order was dated 20 April and had, of course, no connection with Fuentes de Oñoro. It reached Massena on 10 May.

As it happened, it had been an unnecessary battle. Massena did not relieve Almeida but Wellington did not capture the garrison. On the night of 10–11 May the garrison, led by General Brennier escaped. They blew up the fortifications and, threading their way through the investing force, crossed the Agueda to rejoin the Army of Portugal. On the British side everything went wrong. There was carelessness, stupidity and plenty of straightforward bad luck. Brennier behaved with extraordinary skill and bravery. Wellington was extremely angry. 'I have never been so much distressed by any military event as by the escape of even a man of them.'[16] 'They had about 13,000 men to watch 1,400. There they were all sleeping in their spurs even; but the French got off. I begin to be of opinion that there is nothing on earth so stupid as a gallant officer.'[17]

Eleven days after Fuentes de Oñoro the southern corps of the allied army was in action near Badajoz. Beresford had had every difficulty in besieging the city. He had driven the French covering force away without much trouble but everything else had gone wrong. The Spaniards had contrived to lose the only available bridging equipment and he was forced to depend for the crossing of the Guadiana on three flying bridges* and a bridge improvised out of empty wine barrels which was promptly washed away by a sharp rise in the river. His siege train was a collection of Portuguese antiques culled from the walls of Elvas. The plan of attack, devised by his engineers and reluctantly approved by Wellington, was faulty. Work on the trenches started on the night of 8 May and continued, uselessly, for four days at a cost of 733 casualties.

At midnight on 12–13 May he heard that Soult with a relieving army was marching up from Seville and had reached Monasterio, seventy-five miles from Badajoz. His engineers pleaded with him to continue the siege and assured him that the town must fall in two more days. Wisely rejecting their advice, Beresford left only a small screening force round Badajoz and concentrated his corps at Albuera which Wellington had selected as 'the most central and advantageous

---

* A flying bridge consisted of one or two pontoons tied together, pulled to and fro across the river by ropes.

place' to fight a covering action. The corps[5/8] amounted to 20,358 all ranks of whom half were untried Portuguese. He also had 2,500 Spaniards and had been promised the support of 12,000 more who were in the mountains to the south-west under General Blake. Wellington's orders were that he was to fight to protect his siege works if he thought he would be successful 'according to a view of the relative numbers of both armies, and making a reasonable allowance for the number of Spanish troops which shall cooperate with him. I authorise him to fight the action if he should think proper, or to retreat if he should not.'[18]

Beresford's information was that Soult had between 23,000 and 25,000 men with a marked superiority in cavalry.[6/6] His problem should have been whether 24,000 Portuguese and Spaniards were equivalent to the 12,000 men by which the French outnumbered his British troops. The decision was taken out of his hands by his ally and the weather. Blake had agreed to serve under Beresford but when the two met for the first time on 13 May he made it clear that he was going to fight whatever the British did. Beresford was faced with the choice of fighting a battle he suspected was unnecessary or abandoning his ally in the face of a superior enemy. Even this choice was denied him as the rain again swept away his bridge across the Guadiana, making retreat impossible. He wrote to Wellington:

> We are now placed in that position that has always made me uneasy and from which I have not been able to extricate myself, as General Blake would not listen to crossing the Guadiana and stated that, whether the position was good or bad, you had pointed it out. I agreed with him that our numbers gave us every prospect of advantage, and that we had not much to fear. I yet could not agree with him on the propriety of anything so circumstanced. However, the weather has decided the business and we have only now to meet the enemy, if he desires it, to the best advantage we can.[19]

For Beresford the battle of Albuera was a succession of disastrous misfortunes caused by the incompetence and worse of his subordinates. He overcame every one of them with pertinacity and courage but has been pilloried by historians ever since. The first setback happened on the afternoon of 15 May when his cavalry screen made no attempt to delay the French advance. His chief of staff wrote:

Our cavalry, instead of retiring leisurely, fell back (indeed I may say *fled*) rapidly before the advanced guard of the enemy. The left bank of the Albuera [stream] was given up without the slightest attempt at dispute. This error on the part of the officer commanding the cavalry [Brig-Gen Robert Ballard Long] was so completely of a piece with his conduct upon more than one occasion that it became imperatively necessary to relieve him.[20]

Throughout the 15th Beresford had been waiting anxiously for the arrival of Blake's Spaniards. They had only eight miles to march along a good road but they did not start to arrive until 3 am on the morning of the 16th. They were in such confusion that they were told to bivouac where they were and to sort themselves out in the morning. Since they came from the south they were allocated to occupying the right-hand end of the low, gentle ridge which forms the position. The left was assigned to the Portuguese. In the centre, where the Seville–Badajoz road crosses the ridge, Beresford stationed his main strength, the three British brigades of Second Division. In reserve behind them were the only two brigades available of Fourth Division, one British and one Portuguese. Two light battalions of the German Legion under Charles Alten were in advance holding Albuera village and the bridge over the stream.

Beresford expected that Soult would attempt to break his centre. British experience at Vimeiro, Coruña, Talavera and Busaco strongly suggested that this was normal French practice. In fact Soult, despite what he wrote subsequently in his report to Paris, greatly underestimated the allied strength. He believed that Beresford had only 17,500 men of whom 3,000 were Spanish and 6,000 Portuguese.[21] His own army was 24,246 strong including 4,000 cavalry and 48 guns. Convinced that Blake could not join Beresford before 17 May, Soult 'decided to anticipate [his] arrival and attack the enemy's right so as to put myself across his communications. I never doubted that I should be successful.'[22]

Soon after 8 am on the morning of 16 May Soult sent one of his four brigades* to demonstrate against the bridge in the centre while the other three made a long march to their left, screened by trees.

---

* The French army at Albuera was organised as two divisions and two brigades, but since one of the brigades was larger than either of the divisions it seems simpler to refer to each of the four formations as a brigade.

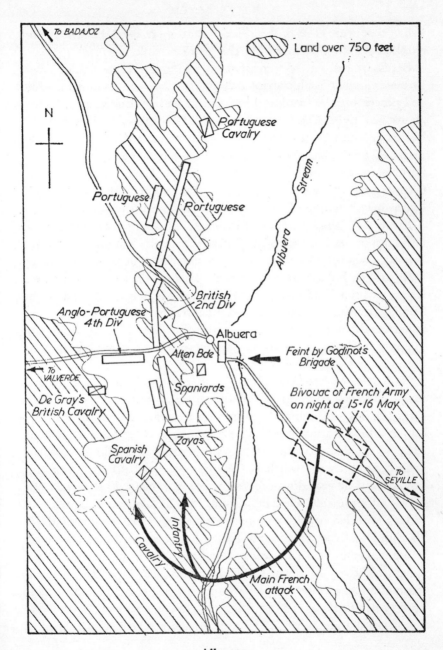

Albuera

When they were clear of the allied right they crossed the stream and climbed the ridge well beyond the Spanish flank.

Beresford had started to reinforce the Germans at the bridge when he realised what Soult was intending. He 'observed them for a while and perceiving the [flanking] movement was continued said, "They attack our right. Call General Blake!" This officer was in front of his troops and at no great distance and immediately joined the marshal, who observed to him, "You see, general, the enemy's movement; he is going to attack our right. Have the goodness to form your front line without delay, and as much of your second* line as may be required, at a right angle to our present line." '23

Blake was being asked to pivot his line so that his main front faced south astride the ridge. There are gentle undulations in the summit line of the ridge and his new position would be covered by a dip and each flank by a re-entrant. This would have been quite a strong position, and to support the Spaniards Beresford ordered the Second Division to march to its right and form line in their rear. The allied cavalry was moved to the Spanish right flank and the Portuguese were brought in to the centre on the ground vacated by Second Division.

Had these orders been obeyed Albuera would not have been a memorable day's fighting. Probably there would have been only a skirmish. Two foolish and headstrong generals succeeded in bringing on a bloodbath. General Blake, courageous survivor of a dozen defeats, decided that Beresford was wrong in thinking that the French were about to attack his right. He did not mention this opinion but he issued no orders for redeployment. Fortunately one of his subordinates, General Zayas, saw the danger and, without orders, wheeled four battalions to the right. Beresford sent Major Hardinge to Blake to reiterate the order. 'General Blake positively refused; saying the attack was evidently on the front by the village. When told the village was sufficiently occupied, he persisted in his refusal.'24 Meanwhile 14,000 Frenchmen were marching straight at the Spanish flank.

Beresford rode across and supervised the wheel of the Spanish

---

* The Spanish infantry normally fought in two lines each three deep.

line. It was an agonisingly slow manoeuvre. Many of the soldiers were raw recruits ignorant of the drill movements needed to pivot their cumbersome, three-deep lines. Before it was complete forty French guns opened on their disordered ranks. Girard's division followed by Gazan's, more than 8,000 men, started to cross the dip towards them in column. Only Zayas' four battalions, 2,000 strong, opposed them. The Spaniards fought magnificently, firing volley after volley into the French mass at a range of a hundred yards. Step by step, Zayas was forced back.

William Stewart had been ordered to bring the three brigades of Second Division to a position behind Zayas. Seeing that the Spaniards were giving ground, he decided to act on his own initiative. As a battalion commander Stewart was surpassed only by Moore; as a general he was a menace. As Wellington said, 'with the utmost zeal and good intention and abilities, he cannot obey an order'.[25] When three of the four battalions of his leading brigade arrived behind Zayas' position, Stewart deployed them each into line and led them to the right so as to attack the flank of the French column. He would not wait until the battalions were aligned with each other but rushed them forward in a ragged echelon. A heavy shower fell and visibility became short. The British musketry shattered the French flank and Stewart ordered a charge. As he did so he looked round and saw two regiments of cavalry, one of them Polish lancers, galloping in on the rear of the brigade. It was too late to form square. 'Our men,' wrote a survivor, 'ran into small groups of six or eight to do the best they could. The officers snatched up muskets and joined them, determined to sell their lives dearly. Quarter was not asked or given.'[26]

The three battalions were destroyed. They had gone into action 1,650 strong. One thousand, two hundred and fifty were casualties, almost half of them prisoners of war. The Buffs lost 643 out of 755.

Blake and Stewart had created an appalling situation. The remainder of the Spanish infantry, shaken by the fate of the British brigade, would not advance to support Zayas. Beresford, who had just unhorsed a lancer with his bare hands, tried to bring them up into line. He seized a Spanish ensign by the collar and carried him, colour and all, up the slope. Not a man followed. As soon as the

marshal relaxed his grip the terrified ensign ran to the rear. Zayas'
men, crippled by casualties and out of ammunition, fell back although they still retained their order and discipline.

The brunt of the French onslaught now fell on four battalions
under Daniel Hoghton.* 'A most dreadful fire of artillery was
opened upon us. There we unflinchingly stood, and there we fell;
our ranks were at some places swept away by sections.'[27] Worst hit
were the Fifty Seventh. Their King's Colour was shot through
seventeen times and had its staff broken. The Regimental Colour had
twenty-two gashes. Their colonel, William Inglis, urging his men to
'Die hard!', 'was struck down by a grape shot which penetrated his
left breast and lodged in his back. He lay on the ground, close to the
regiment, refusing all offers to be carried to the rear, and determined
to share the fate of his "die-hards", whom he continued to cheer to
steadiness and exertion.'[28] 'Our line at length became so reduced
that it resembled a chain of skirmishers in extended order.'[29]

While Hoghton's brigade was suffering, Soult realised the odds
against him. He had ridden up to the ridge behind his troops and 'I
was surprised to see so many troops. Shortly after I learned from a
Spanish prisoner that Blake had joined the enemy with 9,000 men at
three o'clock in the morning. The affair was no longer on equal
terms.'[30] He was faced with an urgent choice. He must either withdraw from the unequal fight or throw in all his reserves to make a
breakthrough while the allies were still in disorder. He had a great
local superiority in infantry and guns. His overwhelming cavalry
could sweep round the allied rear and turn defeat into rout. Soult
was at his worst in such a situation. As Wellington remarked,
'though a great strategist, he never seemed to me to know how to
handle his troops after the battle had begun'.[31] He took no decision.
'I judged it inopportune to proceed with my plan and gave orders
that we should defend the ground we had gained.'[32] The ground he
had gained amounted to no more than a stretch of ridge which had
previously been occupied by a vedette of Spanish cavalry. Unless he
was prepared to continue his advance he could hope for nothing

---

* Hoghton's brigade (29th, 1/48th, 1/57th) was joined by the 2/31st which had not
arrived in time to take part in Stewart's disastrous attack with Colborne's brigade.
Abercromby's brigade on the left was not so fiercely engaged.

more than a drawn battle. This would not help him to relieve Badajoz.

By contrast Beresford was acting with decision. Hoghton's brigade, its commander now dead, must be reinforced. Alten was ordered to evacuate Albuera village, which could be re-taken by Portuguese as soon as they could arrive, and move up the ridge to reinforce the dwindling line. The order was carried by a Portuguese ADC and Alten, a good and conscientious Hanoverian soldier, believed that it must have been distorted in transmission. He refused to move until relieved by the Portuguese. Beresford's ill luck was still holding. Before the order could be repeated the battle had been won.

Behind the allied centre were the two brigades of Fourth Division* under Lowry Cole. Cole had been anxious to join the battle and had sent an ADC to Beresford to ask for orders. The marshal was convinced that the Fourth should stay where it was. To the south of them were 3,000 French cavalry against whom the allies could oppose only two British regiments and a rabble of Spanish horsemen. If Cole's division became involved on top of the ridge there was little to stop the French cavalry sweeping round the allied rear. As the agony of Hoghton's brigade continued on the crest, Cole, urged on by two of Beresford's staff officers, decided to advance diagonally up the ridge. The division moved forward with the three British battalions on the left, four Portuguese units in line on the right, and a battalion in square on either flank.

> Having arrived at the bottom of the hill, we began to climb its slope with panting breath, while the roll and thunder of furious battle increased. Under the tremendous fire of the enemy our thin line staggers, men are knocked about like skittles; but not a backward step is taken. Here our colonel is killed, and all the field officers of the brigade fell killed or wounded but no confusion ensued. The orders were 'Close up! Close up! Fire away! Forward!'[33]

The Portuguese brigade, all inexperienced troops, beat off an

---

* The third brigade of the division, that commanded by Kemmis, had been isolated on the north bank of the Guadiana by the bridge being washed away. The light companies of the brigade, which were on the south bank, fought with Cole.

attack by French cavalry with the steadiness of veterans. The advance of the British brigade has passed into literature in William Napier's words.

> The Fuzileer battalions, struck by an iron tempest, reeled and staggered like sinking ships; but suddenly and sternly recovering, they closed on their terrible enemies, and then was seen with what strength and majesty the British soldier fights. In vain did Soult with voice and gesture animate his Frenchmen; in vain did the hardiest veterans break from the crowded columns and sacrifice their lives to gain time for the mass to open up on such a fair field; in vain did the mass itself bear up, and fiercely striving, fire indiscriminately upon friend and foe, while horsemen hovering on the flank threatened the advancing line. Nothing could stop that astonishing infantry.[34]

One of the Fusilier colonels wrote:

> The men behaved most gloriously, never losing their ranks, and closing to the centre as casualties occurred. The French faced us at a distance of about thirty or forty paces. During the closest part of the action I saw their officers endeavouring to deploy their columns, but all to no purpose. For as soon as a third of a company got out, they would immediately run back, to be covered by the front of their column.[35]

'The closest part of the action', the exchange of volleys at short range between the Fusiliers and the French, lasted about twenty minutes. Both sides suffered dreadful casualties. More than one Fusilier in two fell. The French, locked in their columns, suffered even more severely and at last 'the mighty mass, breaking off like a loosened cliff, went headlong down the steep: the rain flowed after in streams discoloured with blood'.[36] 'We followed down the slope, firing and huzzaing, till recalled by the bugle.'[37] 'The wreck of the Fifty Seventh, cheered on by their prostrate and almost exhausted chief, was on the point of joining in the charge, when Marshal Beresford exclaimed, "Stop! Stop the Fifty Seventh; it would be a sin to let them go on!" '[38]

Beresford, despite his subordinates, had defeated Soult. The French were in no state to renew the attack and retreated across the Sierra Morena as soon as their huge convoy of wounded and prisoners got two days start. Soult claimed to have inflicted 9,000

Page 165   'Joseph Bonaparte, King of Naples and Spain', by Wicar

Page 166   (*left*) 'General Sir Thomas Graham, Lord Lyndoch', by Thomas Lawrence
(*below*) 'André Massena, Duke of Rivoli', by F. S. Delpech

casualties, that his cavalry 'entirely destroyed' three British brigades and that at the end of the battle 'the enemy left us in the position we had won and did not dare to attack us'.[39] He estimated his own casualties as 2,800 but later increased this to 5,936.[40] The actual total was between 7,000 and 8,000.

The allied loss was not as heavy as Soult had asserted, but it was desperately serious. The total loss was 6,000, but of these 4,159 were British. In four infantry brigades 184 out of 392 officers were casualties. The senior unwounded officer in Hoghton's brigade was a captain. As Wellington remarked, 'another such battle would ruin us'.[41]

On the day Albuera was fought King Joseph was at Rambouillet pleading with his imperial brother. His repeated threats to abdicate had resulted in a sharp admonition that he would be treated as a deserter if he left Spain without permission from Paris. Napoleon had told him that he intended to invite him to the christening of his son, the King of Rome. Taking the will for the deed, Joseph sneaked out of Madrid on 23 April and reached Paris on 15 May. He brought with him a memorandum cataloguing his grievances and asking for authority over the generals in Spain and for loans from France until Spain was pacified.

It was more than time that someone had authority over the generals. It was serious enough that their depredations in search of rations and loot destroyed any hope that the Spaniards could be brought to accept Joseph's government. Far worse was the lack of military co-ordination. The French armies in Spain were being steadily reinforced until by the autumn they totalled 368,000 men. The regular armies of their opponents, Spanish, Portuguese and British, could not put half this number into the field yet the French hold was secure only in the immediate neighbourhoods of Madrid and Seville. More than a quarter of the French were in Catalonia and Aragon, yet the security of Barcelona was a constant source of concern to the commanders in the east. In January 1811 the Spanish Army of Catalonia almost destroyed a French division at Pla, north of Tarragona. The Catalan army was often defeated but always

F

managed to survive. Even more troublesome to the French were the *somatenes*, the Catalan peasantry summoned by the church bells, the heirs to a tradition of irregular warfare centuries old. In April 1811 they captured the fortress of Figueras which dominated the main road from Barcelona to France. It took the French four months and 4,000 dead to recapture the place. Almost 100,000 Frenchmen were allocated to Bessières' Army of the North which had the task of keeping open the communications from Bayonne to Salamanca and Ciudad Rodrigo. They were insufficient to the task. Their hold on the Asturias was confined to Oviedo and, occasionally, Gijon, and in the mountains of Navarre the guerrillas, though constantly pursued, went almost unchecked.

Two armies shared the task of containing Wellington on the Portuguese border. The Army of Portugal, now under Marshal Marmont, although 40,000 strong, was largely a spent force. Even the shortest move exhausted its exiguous transport and the men were demoralised by their failure in Portugal. The Army of the South, Soult's army, had 70,000 fit men on its rolls but was constantly torn in two by the need to take Cadiz in the south of its area and retain Badajoz in the north. Bessières, crying out for reinforcements for his own area, put his finger on the great French weakness. 'We are occupying too much ground. Our resources are spread too thinly. Cadiz and Badajoz swallow up everything we have; Cadiz because we cannot take it; Badajoz because it needs an army to support it. We should destroy Badajoz and, for the moment, give up hope of taking Cadiz.'[42]

Napoleon made many promises to Joseph when he saw him in May 1811. Most of them were not kept, but one point he would not pretend to yield.

> I cannot give the supreme command of my armies in Spain as I can see no man capable of leading them, although the command ought to be unified. It is in the nature of things that a marshal stationed in Madrid and directing operations would expect to have the glory to go with his responsibility. The commanders of the Armies of the South and of Portugal would consider themselves under the command of the King's Chief of Staff rather than of the King himself. Consequently they would not obey orders.[43]

Joseph started to ride back to Madrid on 16 June. On the same day his brother made a speech about the Peninsula to the Corps Legislatif.

> Since 1809 most of the fortified towns in Spain have been taken by memorable sieges; the rebels have repeatedly been beaten in battle. England understands that the war is coming into its final phase. She has found that her position has changed. Money and intrigue will no longer keep the war going. From being no more than an auxiliary, she has had to take a leading role. All her regular troops are in the Peninsula. England, Scotland and Ireland are stripped of troops.* Rivers of English blood have flowed in battles which have proved glorious for the French army. Our struggle against Carthage, which they thought could be decided on the seas or beyond them, will now be settled on the plains of Spain. A clap of thunder will put an end to the Spanish business. It will finish the English army. It will avenge Europe and Asia by ending this second Punic war.[44]

The king's Spanish adherents had never expected to see his return. They feared he had deserted them. They gave him a tumultuous reception when he reached Madrid on 16 July.

> A large concourse of people was waiting for him on the road. A kind of triumphal arch had been erected a short distance from the town and the magistrates were assembled there to greet him. Numbers of carriages belonging to the principal inhabitants were drawn up on either side of the road. The satisfaction visible on the faces of the people and their frequent acclamations made this a happy day for the king.[45]

Meanwhile the military situation was deadlocked. Soon after Albuera Wellington brought his main army south to renew the siege of Badajoz. His siege train was still the venerable collection which Beresford had used. The engineers modified their plan but did not improve it. Wellington had not been hopeful. 'If we do not succeed in a few days, we shall not succeed at all.'[46] There was a slight chance that the fortress could be seized before the French armies could combine to drive him away. It was not to be. Marmont brought the Army of Portugal south to join Soult's field force. They had 60,000

---

* There were 63,500 regular troops in the United Kingdom at this date (apart from 84,000 militia). In the Peninsula (or on passage there) were 58,600. 89,000 were in other overseas stations.

men against Wellington's '50,000, including every Portuguese I can get together'.[47] The siege had to be raised, but the allies took up a strong position near Elvas and the two marshals refused to attack them.

Neither side wanted to stay in the unhealthy valley of the Guadiana. Soult had to withdraw to secure Andalusia. Marmont fell back to the valley of the Tagus around Talavera. Wellington took the bulk of his troops to the Ciudad Rodrigo front. The chance of taking Badajoz had gone for the time being. 'The only chance is to watch for opportunities of undertaking important operations of short duration with the means at our own disposal, till the Spanish armies shall be in a better state.'[48]

PART FOUR

The British Initiative, 1812

CHAPTER 11

The Fortresses

'THE next operation which presents itself,' wrote Wellington in July 1811, 'is the siege of Ciudad Rodrigo. I am tempted to try this enterprise but I beg you to observe that I may be obliged to abandon it.'[1] To take Rodrigo would be the first of the two essential preliminaries to invading Spain. Only when Rodrigo and Badajoz were both in allied hands could the prevailing deadlock be broken. An immediate siege was out of the question. The allied army north of the Tagus was only 46,000 strong with many sick. Across the frontier Marmont had 40,000 men and could call on up to 30,000 reinforcements from the Army of the North. No reinforcements could be drawn from the allied corps in Estremadura where Hill with 16,000 men watched Badajoz which was supported by d'Erlon with an equal force and the ability to call up 20,000 men from Andalusia. Wellington could not find enough men to lay siege to Rodrigo and ward off Marmont. What he could do was to throw a loose blockade round the fortress so that the French could re-victual it only by making a major effort. Meanwhile the siege train which was lying on board ship in the Tagus could be landed and brought forward to the shelter of Almeida so that it could be ready when an opportunity offered.

Moving the siege train was a massive operation. Wellington calculated that it would take sixty-two days and in fact it took longer. First the transports had to sail from Lisbon to Oporto where the equipment was loaded into 160 boats. These carried it up the Douro as far as Lamego, the limit of navigation. 'At Lamego they must be landed and the ordnance removed at once by 384 pairs of oxen. The stores, that is to say, 350 rounds for each 18 pounder and 24 pounder gun, and 160 rounds for each 10-inch mortar, to be removed on 892 country carts. The engineer's stores to be removed on 200 country carts.'[2]

Meanwhile the blockade continued. Rodrigo was known to be provisioned until early October and if the French wished to put more supplies into the town they 'must bring 50,000 men to oblige us to raise [the blockade] and they can undertake nothing else this year'.[3] It was no surprise to Wellington to hear in mid-September that a heavily escorted convoy was being marshalled at Salamanca. His plan was 'to take up a position on the left of the Agueda, if I should find the enemy in such strength as that it is not advisable that I should attack them, and leave it to them to attack us if they should think it proper'.[4]

This was a sound plan but Wellington did not implement it. He convinced himself that Marmont would be content with putting supplies into Rodrigo and that he would then retire. Consequently when the French entered the town without opposition on 23 September Wellington omitted to take up a position and left his army widely dispersed.

Wellington's nonchalance was more dangerous because the French escort was much stronger than he had anticipated, giving them a superiority of 14,000 men* over the allied army. At their head was Marmont who still had his reputation as an independent commander to make. Unlike his older colleagues, he was prepared to embark on enterprises beyond the strict demands of his duty.

Having reached Rodrigo without incident Marmont decided to make reconnaissances to discover whether Wellington was planning a siege. At dawn on 24 September two strong forces of cavalry were sent out to the west and south-west of the city. The right-hand thrust was easily halted at Carpio. On the left Montbrun with 2,500 French horsemen found the Third Division strung out over a six-mile front. Montbrun summoned help from the French infantry and

---

* Marmont had 58,000 men including 4,500 cavalry. The Army of the North had sent 27,500 men. One French division was detached on an abortive diversion further south. Wellington had 44,000 of whom 17,000 were Portuguese. His cavalry were 3,100 strong (including 900 Portuguese).

without waiting for their arrival tried to break through Picton's
front at El Bodon. He nearly succeeded. Only five squadrons of
British cavalry* were available to oppose him. They charged repeatedly but they could not prevent the French from capturing a
Portuguese battery although the gunners fought their guns until the
dragoons reached the muzzles. The French success was checked by
the Fifth Foot. Against all the conventions of war their commander,
Major Henry Ridge, led his battalion uphill in line against the
cavalry. Three volleys drove the dragoons away in disorder. The
guns were recovered and opened fire once more.

This check to Montbrun gave time for Picton to concentrate his
scattered battalions and begin an orderly retreat. They fell back in
column of companies at quarter distance, the easiest marching
formation from which to form a square.

> For six miles across a perfect flat, without the slightest protection
> from any incident of ground, without artillery, and I might say
> without cavalry (for what are four or five squadrons to twenty or
> thirty) did the division continue its march. During the whole time
> the enemy's cavalry never quitted them; a park of six guns advanced
> with the cavalry, and taking us in flank and rear, poured in a most
> frightful fire of roundshot, grape and cannister. Many men fell in
> this way, and those whose wounds rendered them unable to march
> were obliged to be abandoned to the enemy. General Picton re-
> mained on the left flank of the column and repeatedly cautioned the
> different battalions to mind the quarter distance and the 'tellings
> off'. 'Your safety,' he added, 'my credit and the honour of the army
> is at stake: all rests with you at this moment.'[5]

The Third Division escaped with only eighty casualties, the
cavalry suffering sixty, but since the rest of the army was still scattered the retreat had to be continued. It was not until 28 September
when the whole of Wellington's army was concentrated in a strong
position at Quadrazias, thirty-two miles from Rodrigo, that Marmont decided to withdraw to the fortress and beyond. His advance
had largely nullified his original aim. By keeping his army in the
neighbourhood of Rodrigo he had been forced to issue to them
two-thirds of the rations he had brought forward for the fortress.

---

* 11th Light Dragoons (2 sqns) and 1st Hussars KGL (3 sqns).

This week of manoeuvring was the least satisfactory of all Wellington's field operations. He left himself open to defeat in detail by under-rating his opponent's strength and determination. Disaster was averted only by his own confident handling of the units which were available and by the steadiness and discipline of the troops. As Graham, now Wellington's second-in-command, remarked, 'It was very pretty, but spun rather fine.'[6]

The blockade was immediately resumed and Wellington continued to watch for his opportunity. 'As long as the enemy remain in their present situation it is impossible for me to do anything except keep them in a state of inactivity. Indeed our army is so sickly that I can scarcely venture to wish that an opportunity should offer of doing anything.'[7] One opportunity did occur and was not missed. News arrived that a division of d'Erlon's corps was isolated on the north bank of the Tagus. Rowland Hill was sent against them with 10,000 men, British, Portuguese and Spanish. A complete brigade was surprised at Arroyo dos Molinos on 28 October. Hill returned with 1,300 prisoners and three guns.

Napoleon himself gave Wellington the chance for which he had waited. The Emperor was anxious to break the deadlock in Spain before he embarked on the Russian campaign he now knew to be inevitable. In September he sent Marmont orders to capture the great Portuguese fortress of Elvas as the only move which 'can bring back honour to our arms, free us from the defensive posture into which we have fallen, strike terror into the English and bring us nearer to the end of the war'.[8] Before the marshal had time to write his objections to this scheme Napoleon changed his mind. Priority was to be given to the conquest of Valencia. The main attack was to be made by Suchet and the Army of Aragon, but to ensure success large detachments were to be made from the Armies of the North, the Centre and of Portugal. On 13 December Marmont received orders to detach 10,000 men to support Suchet and 4,000 more to replace men sent from the king's central army for the same purpose. Thus Marmont was deprived of a third of his strength. The Army of the North was even more depleted.

Wellington knew on Christmas Eve that parts of the Army of Portugal were moving eastwards. Their intentions were not immediately clear. 'There are various reports about their ultimate destination; some that they are going to Valencia.'[9] Four days later he knew that the French were moving towards Valencia and gave orders for the siege of Rodrigo to begin. 'By these measures we shall bring Marmont back and probably oblige the Army of the North to reassemble.'[10]

The fortress was invested on 8 January in appalling weather.

We were under arms at five. The rain fell in torrents; the snow on the surrounding hills drifted down with the flood and nearly choked up the roads. At half past six the brigade was in motion for a march of nine leagues. I scarcely remember a more disagreeable day; the rain which had fallen in the morning was succeeded by snow and sleet, and some soldiers, who sank from cold and fatigue, fell down exhausted, soon became insensible and perished; yet strange to say an Irishwoman of my regiment was delivered of a child on the road and continued the march with her infant in her arms.[11]

Ciudad Rodrigo was only a second-class fortress. It stands on the east, or French bank of the Agueda on rising ground. The main wall was 'of an old construction, of a height of 32 feet, and [was] generally of bad masonry, without flanks, and with weak parapets and narrow ramparts'.[12] Some modern improvements had been made to the works, but the fortress's chief defect was that it was overlooked at a range of 600 yards by a low hill, the Grand Teson. Massena had erected his breaching batteries on the Teson for the siege of 1810. To guard against Wellington doing the same the French had erected a redoubt on the crest. There was a garrison for the town of 2,000 men but one in ten of them were sick. Within the walls were 153 heavy guns, only 14 fewer than the number of gunners in the garrison. The allied blockade had not succeeded in keeping supplies from reaching the fortress but it had made it impossible to remove the siege train of the Army of Portugal which had been stored within the walls.

No time was wasted. On the night of the investment the redoubt on the Teson was stormed by detachments of the Light Division. Immediately men got to work with picks and shovels opening approach trenches in the rocky soil and marking out sites for breaching batteries.

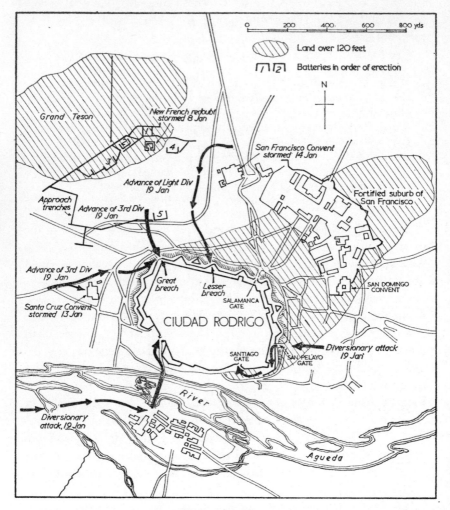

Ciudad Rodrigo

The investment of Rodrigo could not have come at a more in-convenient time for Marmont. Two divisions and most of his cavalry were on a wild goose chase to Valencia. He had just received orders from Paris to leave two divisions in the Tagus valley and march with the remainder to Valladolid. It was Napoleon's opinion that Wellington might take the offensive in February 'but such a move is improbable. The English have suffered heavy losses lately and are having great difficulty in recruiting their army. This leads us to believe that they will confine themselves to the defence of Portugal.'[13]

With three divisions following him, the marshal was marching to Valladolid where he was to meet General Dorsenne, now com-manding the Army of the North. On the road he received a letter from Dorsenne saying that the governor of Salamanca reported Wellington to be moving against Rodrigo. 'But,' added Dorsenne, 'I am not convinced by such reports as I have been receiving similar stories from the same source for the last six months.'[14]

On 12 January, four days after the Teson had been stormed, Marmont and Dorsenne met in Valladolid and discussed ways of revictualling Rodrigo. Two days later, when the two were at dinner, a despatch arrived from Salamanca telling them that the town had been invested and that Wellington had at least five divisions around the walls. This was bad news but not disastrously bad. Marmont had only 20,000 men in hand and believed that he would need 40,000 to force Wellington to abandon the siege. This number could be avail-able by 1 February. In 1810 it had taken Ney twenty-four days of intensive siege work to take Rodrigo from a Spanish garrison. Marmont calculated that the new redoubt on the Teson would cause another 8–10 days' delay.[15] A concentration of his force at Sala-manca on 1 February should give him plenty of time. On 21 January, while he was riding up to Salamanca, he heard that Rodrigo had fallen on the night of 19–20 January.

Work on the trenches and batteries had been difficult. 'In some instances the soil had been so unfavourable it was next to impossible to make head against it. Instead of clay or gravel, we frequently met a strain of rock and invariably when this occurred our losses were severe for the pickaxes, coming in contact with the stone, caused a [spark] to issue that plainly told the enemy where we were.'[16] The weather was bitterly cold and working parties when being relieved had to ford the Agueda. 'Pieces of ice that were constantly carried down this rapid stream bruised our men so much that to obviate it cavalry were ordered to form four deep across the ford, under the lee of whom we crossed comparatively unharmed, although by the time we reached our quarters our clothes were frozen in a mass of ice.'[17]

On the afternoon of 14 January the batteries opened on the walls. Twenty-three 24-pounders and four 18-pounders aimed at the breach the French had made the previous year where the masonry was weak. For five days they battered the wall, firing 9,515 rounds and using 834 barrels of powder.* They opened two practical breaches. Wellington's orders for 19 January began: 'The attack upon Ciudad Rodrigo must be made this evening at 7 o'clock.' The larger breach was allocated to the Third Division, the smaller, left-hand breach to the Light. Each was to be preceded by a storming party of 300 men and each storming party was led by a Forlorn Hope† of an officer and 25 men.

Major George Napier led the storming party of the Light Division.

> When it was nearly dark in the evening the Light Division was formed behind an old convent on the outside of the town, nearly opposite the small breach. While waiting here for orders I told a friend of mine, the assistant surgeon of the 52nd, Mr Walker, that I had an idea I should lose my arm and, if so, I hoped he would perform the operation of taking it off. A few minutes later Lord Wellington sent for Colonel Colborne‡ and myself and, pointing out as well as the light would permit, the spot where the foot of the breach was, he said to me, 'Now, do you clearly understand the way you are to lead, so as to arrive at the breach without noise or confusion?' I answered and we then went back to the regiment. Just before I moved on, some staff officer present said, 'Why, your men are not loaded. Why do you not make them load?' I replied, 'Because if we do not do the business with the bayonet, without firing,

---

* Each barrel held 90lb of powder.
† The command of the Forlorn Hope was eagerly sought since the lieutenant commanding would receive a captaincy if the storm succeeded and if the officer survived.
‡ Commanding Napier's regiment, the Fifty Second.

we shall not be able to do it at all, so I shall not load.' I heard Lord Wellington, who was close by, say, 'Let him alone; let him go his own way.'

The signal for the attack being made, I gave the order to move forward, cautioning the officers and men to be silent, and having once gained the breach to wheel right and left to clear the ramparts. Lieutenant Gurwood was in advance a few yards with the Forlorn Hope. We soon came to the ditch and, immediately jumping in, we rushed forward. We all mounted the breach together, the enemy pouring a heavy fire on us. When about two-thirds up, I received a grape shot which smashed my elbow and great part of my arm; and on falling the men, who thought I was killed, checked for a few moments and, forgetting they were not loaded, commenced snapping their muskets. I immediately called out, 'Recollect you are not loaded; push on with the bayonet!' Upon this the whole gave a loud 'Hurrah!', and driving all before them, carried the breach and wheeling, as I had given orders, soon drove off the enemy.[18]

Simultaneously the Third Division broke in at the larger breach and although they suffered heavily from the explosion of a mine, the defenders were driven from the walls. The governor and his staff shut themselves up in the citadel but they did not have enough troops to defend themselves and surrendered at the first opportunity. Wellington had captured the northern gateway to Spain for the loss of less than six hundred men. Two major-generals were among the 125 dead. One of them was Robert Craufurd, the invaluable commander of the outposts.

There followed some plunder and much drunkenness. Next morning General Picton rode past some men of the Connaught Rangers 'who were more than usually elevated in spirits and called out, "Well, General! We gave you a cheer last night; its your turn now!" The General, smiling, took off his hat and said, "Here then, you drunken set of brave rascals, hurrah! We'll soon be at Badajoz!" '[19]

It was as clear to Marmont as it was to Picton that Wellington would next turn his attention to Badajoz. Military necessity dictated that the allies must hold both the gateways before taking the offensive. The marshal proposed moving some of his divisions south to help in the

fortress's defence. He was sharply rebuffed from Paris. Badajoz, he
was reminded, was Soult's responsibility.

> The best way for you to help the Army of the South is to establish
> your headquarters at Salamanca and concentrate your army there.
> You will thus oblige the enemy to stay around Almeida for fear of
> an invasion. You can drive in his outposts. Since your honour is
> involved, you could march on Ciudad Rodrigo and, if you have the
> necessary siege artillery, you might take the place. This will engage
> the enemy's attention. You must think the English to be mad if you
> suppose they are capable of marching on Badajoz while you are at
> Salamanca from where you could reach Lisbon before they could.[20]

Marmont replied that it was impossible to keep the army concentrated at Salamanca. 'It could not subsist there for a fortnight. None
of our magazines hold food for as much as four days. We are without
transport. To make requisitions on even the poorest village we have
to send a foraging party two hundred strong.'[21] He was answered
that 'Badajoz is a very strong fortress. Marshal Soult has 80,000 men
and can call on Marshal Suchet for more.* If Lord Wellington were
to move against Badajoz you could bring him back instantly by
marching against Ciudad Rodrigo.'[22] Badajoz, therefore, was left to
the sole care of Soult, who was convinced that it was secure. 'The
garrison lacked for nothing. There were rations for more than two
months and plenty of ammunition. The 5,000 men in garrison, having beaten off three assaults in the previous year, were confident that
the enemy could not break in, whatever strength he brought.'[23]

Wellington, who knew the state of Marmont's supplies almost as
well as the marshal did himself, realised that it was impossible for the
French to make a serious attack on Portugal on the Rodrigo front.
As soon as his siege train had almost completed its wearisome
journey to Elvas, all the allied divisions followed. By 16 March they
were all close to Badajoz. Marmont had no opponents but some
Portuguese militia and a single regiment of German hussars.

Badajoz was a much more powerful fortress than Rodrigo. Along
the northern front of the town ran the river Guadiana, nowhere less

---

* Suchet had occupied the main towns of Valencia, but unconquered Murcia still lay
between him and Soult. Soult's army had only 64,000 men *présents sous armes* on 1 March
1812.

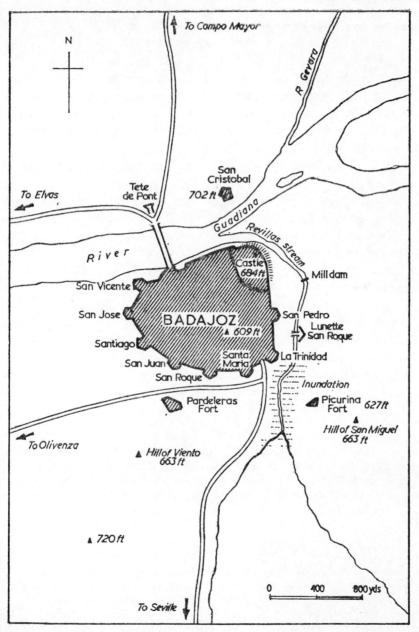

Badajoz

than 300 yards wide. The town was surrounded by a curtain wall 23–26 feet high in which were eight bastions, each 30 feet high, which had been rebuilt sixty years earlier. A castle stands at the north-eastern corner of the walls. It is flanked on the north by the river and on the east by the flooded Revillas stream. The castle stands on a hill rising sharply a hundred feet from river level. The slope is precipitous, only to be climbed with hands as well as feet. Badajoz has only one defect. Across the Guadiana is another hill, higher than the castle hill. A battery on this height could make the castle untenable. To guard against such an eventuality the height had been crowned with a stone-built work, Fort San Cristobal. It had been this transpontine fort that both Beresford and Wellington had attempted to take in their sieges in 1811. Both men had made up their minds that, whatever their engineers might think, Fort San Cristobal was impregnable.

After the failures in the previous year Wellington had been heard to mutter that 'he will be his own engineer'.[24] In 1812 he decided to attack from the south-east. An outwork, the Picurina fort, was bombarded and, on 25 March, stormed. Breaching batteries were then established against the town wall and by 6 April three breaches had been opened between the Trinidad and Santa Maria bastions. The Fourth and Light Divisions were to assault the breaches. The Third Division was to attempt the escalade* of the castle and the Fifth that of the bastion of San Vicente at the north-west corner of the town.

> [The Light Division] drew up in the most profound silence in a large quarry three hundred yards from the breaches. A small stream separated us from the Fourth Division. Suddenly a loud voice was heard from that direction giving orders about ladders so loud that it might be heard by the enemy on the ramparts. It was the only voice that broke the stillness of the moment. It was about half past nine that this happened but at a quarter before ten the ill-timed noise ceased and nothing could be heard but the loud croaking of the frogs. Soon after ten o'clock a little whispering announced that the Forlorn Hope was stealing forward, followed by the storming parties, composed of three hundred men; in two minutes the divi-

---

* To escalade = to climb over the wall with scaling ladders without previous bombardment.

sion followed. One musket shot, no more, was fired from the breaches by a French soldier who was on the look-out. We gained ground leisurely but silently. There were no obstacles. All was hushed and the town lay buried in gloom. The ladders were placed on the edge of the ditch, when suddenly an explosion took place at the foot of the breaches and a burst of light disclosed the whole scene—the earth seemed to rock under us. It was a volcano. What a scene. The ramparts crowded with the enemy—the French soldiers standing on the parapets—the Fourth Division advancing rapidly on our right, while the short lived glare from the barrels of powder and combustibles flying through the air, gave to friend and foe alike a look as if both sides were laughing at each other.[25]

We moved on under a most dreadful fire of grape and musketry that mowed down our men like grass. The French cannon were sweeping the ditch with a most destructive fire. Lights that burned brilliantly were thrown amongst us and made us easier to be shot at.[26]

We flew down the ladders and rushed at the breach, but we were broken and carried no weight with us, although every soldier was a hero. The breach was covered by a breastwork from behind, and ably defended by *chevaux de frise*, chained to the ground and each containing thirty-six sword blades, each sharp as a razor. The ascent to the top of the breach was covered with planks, hung from the top and resting on the slope. These planks were thickly studded with iron spikes six inches long.[27]

The ditch now, from the place where we entered to the top of the breaches, was covered with dead and dying soldiers. If a man fell wounded, ten to one he never rose again, for the volleys of musketry and grape that were incessantly poured amongst us made our situation too horrid for description.[28]

The five succeeding hours were passed in the most gallant and hopeless attempts, on the part of individual officers, forming up fifty or a hundred men at a time at the foot of the breach, and endeavouring to carry it by desperate bravery; and, fatal as it proved to each gallant band in succession yet, as one dissolved, another was formed. About two o'clock in the morning the order was reluctantly given and we fell back about three hundred yards and reformed all that remained of us.[29]

The chief medical officer was beside Wellington when he received the news that the main assault had failed.

At that moment I cast my eyes on the countenance of Lord
Wellington, lit by the glare of a torch held by Lord March; I shall
never forget it to the last moment of my existence, and I could even
sketch it now. The jaw had fallen, and the face was of unusual
length, while the torchlight gave his countenance a lurid aspect; but
still the expression of the face was firm. He ordered the troops back
behind the ditch and began to give orders for another attack. As he
was doing so, a staff officer rode up calling, 'My Lord! The castle is
yours!'

'Are you certain of the information, sir?'

'I entered the castle with the troops and I have but just left it, and
General Picton in possession.'

'With how many men?'

'With his division, my Lord.'

'Return, sir, and desire General Picton to maintain his position at
all hazards—do you understand?—at all hazards.'[30]

Picton had seized the castle against all probabilities. To approach
the foot of the castle hill the Third Division had had to file across the
flooded Revillas stream on a mill dam. Then they struggled up the
steep, rocky slope encumbered by their muskets and their unwieldy,
thirty-foot scaling ladders. The assistant engineer who guided them
wrote:

The whole face of the wall was so swept by discharges of round shot,
broken shells, bundles of cartridges and other missiles that it was
almost impossible to twinkle an eye on any man before he was
knocked down. In such an extremity, four of my ladders with troops
on them, and an officer on top of each, were broken. On the remaining ladder was no officer; but a private soldier at the top, in
attempting to get over the wall, was shot in the head, as soon as he
appeared over the parapet, and tumbled backwards to the ground;
when the next man (45th regiment) to him upon the ladder instantly
sprung over. I instantly cheered, 'Huzza! There is one man up!'[31]

Picton was in the castle but the French had barricaded all the
gateways and it would have required another assault to break out
into the town. Meanwhile Leith and the Fifth Division were over the
wall at the bastion of San Vicente. The French had had to reinforce
the breaches with so many of their men that there was little opposition to Leith.

Having succeeded in penetrating and dispersing all his opponents,

General Leith sent an officer to report to Lord Wellington that the 5th division was in the town. His bugles sounded the advance in all directions, distracting the enemy's attention, and inducing him to believe that he was to be assailed in all directions. The Fourth and Light Divisions again advanced and marched into the town by the breaches.[32]

In the main breach there lay a frightful heap of thirteen or fifteen hundred British soldiers, many dead but still warm, mixed with the desperately wounded, to whom no assistance could yet be given. There lay the burned and blackened corpses of those who had perished by the explosions, mixed with those that were torn to pieces by round shot or grape, and killed by musketry, stiffening in the gore, body piled on body, involved and intertwined into one mass of carnage. The smell of burning flesh was shockingly strong and disgusting.[33]

[Inside the town], the officers lost all command of their men; those who got drunk and satisfied themselves with plunder congregated in small parties and fired down the streets. I saw an English soldier pass down the middle of the street with a French knapsack on his back; he received a shot through the hand from some drunkards at the top of the street; he merely turned round and said, 'Damn them, I suppose they take me for a Frenchman.'[34]

If the men were not all drunk, there were none of them quite sober, but very able to get on with the plunder. One fellow might be seen with a bag of dollars; another would take him to a wine house, make him stupidly drunk, and carry off the dollars; two more, working in concert, would knock this chap down and rob him of his dollars.[35]

Badajoz cost Wellington 5,000 men. 'When the extent of the night's havoc was made known to him the firmness of his nature gave way for a moment, and the pride of his conquest yielded to a storm of grief for the loss of his gallant soldiers.'[36] He wrote to London:

The capture of Badajoz affords as strong an instance of the gallantry of our troops as has ever been displayed, but I anxiously hope that I shall never again be the instrument of putting them to such a test as that to which they were put last night.[37]

CHAPTER 12

Salamanca

THE initiative passed to Wellington with the capture of Rodrigo and Badajoz. The French no longer had it in their power to drive him out of Portugal. Three years earlier he had calculated that they could not drive him from Lisbon 'with a smaller force than 100,000 men'. Massena's experience had shown that this calculation was correct. In 1812 the French could not bring this number of men to the frontier. They lacked another requirement for success. The frontier fortresses would have to be retaken. A siege train would be essential and none was available. Soult had a siege train but it was fully engaged at Cadiz. Marmont had lost his in Rodrigo.

The allied army was much stronger than in 1810. The Portuguese infantry and artillery had had battle experience and could be relied upon. Their cavalry was still of dubious quality but the British cavalry had been strongly reinforced. In May 1811 Fuentes de Oñoro and Albuera had been fought with the French having more than a two-to-one superiority in cavalry. Since then seven British and KGL regiments had landed at Lisbon and Wellington, at last, had a sizeable force of heavy horsemen.* Despite the heavy losses at Albuera, Rodrigo and Badajoz, the British infantry was 3,000 stronger on 1 May 1812 than it had been a year earlier.

With a field army more than 60,000 strong, exclusive of any support the Spaniards might be able to provide, Wellington could

---

* Since 1809 the army had had only two heavy regiments, 3rd Dragoon Guards and 4th Dragoons. 1st (Royal) Dragoons, which was technically a heavy regiment, had been present since 1809 but was trained as a light dragoon regiment. The distinction between Dragoon Guard and Dragoon regiments was imperceptible.

consider invading Spain. His freedom of action was, however, limited. He was strong enough to defeat any of the French armies singly but the total French force in Spain was still overwhelming and in the event of a disaster the French forces must inevitably combine and oppose him in numbers he could not hope to defeat. No advantage he might gain could be pressed too far. He could not plan for the liberation of Spain. The more successful he was the greater the likelihood that he would be forced back behind the border fortresses. From England the news was disturbing. Before he could start any offensive a letter reached him, on 27 May, from Falmouth saying that the Prime Minister, Spencer Perceval, 'was shot through the heart when coming out of the House of Commons on Monday 11th inst., by a broken Liverpool merchant, who it is said by some was mad, by others not, but much exasperated against Perceval for having refused him compensation under the Orders in Council.* I have no letters of so late a date from London.'[1] Perceval's government had never been strong but it was hard to predict a Tory alternative and if the Whigs came to power they would probably withdraw the army from the Peninsula. Wellington was deep into Spain before he heard that another government had been formed under Lord Liverpool.

The uncertainty caused by Perceval's death was offset by fresh dissensions on the French side although they were known only imperfectly at allied headquarters. Napoleon lost interest in Spain. All his energies were devoted to organising the army of half a million men which was to invade Russia. Responsibility in Paris for the Spanish war was made over to the Minister for War, General Clarke, whom the Emperor described as 'a man of no talents—he is only conceited'.[2] Simultaneously Napoleon instructed his Chief of Staff to 'Let the King of Spain know, by special messenger who must leave tonight, that I confide to him the command of all my armies in Spain and that Marshal Jourdan will act as his Chief of Staff.'[3]

This long overdue centralisation of command in Spain was bungled in Paris and ignored in Spain. No orders to act under the king's command were sent to Dorsenne, commanding the Army of

---

* The Orders in Council were the regulations by which the blockade of the French Empire was enforced.

the North,* who consequently continued to act independently. The
orders sent to Marshal Suchet on the east coast of Spain were so
worded that he was able to ignore them. Marmont paid lip service
to Joseph's orders but Soult moved closer and closer to open
mutiny, bitterly resenting Jourdan's appointment as Chief of Staff
in preference to himself.

Napoleon's orders to Joseph were to

> keep the conquests already made and extend them successively. Do
> not take the offensive against Portugal unless circumstances are
> wholly favourable. Above all keep the communications with France
> open. Special attention must be paid to the north of Spain as it is
> essential that the enemy do not establish themselves there. In
> present circumstances you should maintain a defensive posture
> against the English but you must keep up an imposing attitude so
> that they cannot take advantage of our situation. The forces put
> under your command will be sufficient to do what is necessary in
> that direction.[4]

The day this order was despatched Napoleon rode eastward out
of Paris and put Spain out of his mind. He spared it a thought a
month later at Danzig. At dinner he had been silent for a long
time. Turning to an ADC he 'suddenly asked me how far it was
from Danzic to Cadiz. "Too far, Sire." "It will soon be much
further." '[5]

Despite the Emperor's bland assertion, the forces under Joseph's
command were not 'sufficient to do what is necessary'. There were
230,000 effectives† in Spain in May 1812. Half of these were occupation troops in the parts of Spain east of Madrid and could play no
part in resisting Wellington's advance unless vast tracts of eastern
Spain were abandoned to the guerrillas. Soult's Army of the South
had a corps besieging Cadiz and another watching Badajoz. The
remainder were fully occupied in pacifying the space of more than
200 miles between the two corps. Only the corps watching Badajoz,
d'Erlon with 12,000 men, affected the campaign against Wellington.

---

* This seems to have been intentional on Napoleon's part. His instructions to Berthier
only called for the orders to be sent to Suchet, Soult and Marmont (NC xxiii 18583).
† Six months earlier the number of French effectives had been 310,000. Napoleon had
withdrawn 27,000 men of the Young Guard and Polish regiments for the Russian
campaign. The deficit of 50,000 men represents the wastage due to battle and disease.

In an emergency Soult could reinforce them up to 20,000 for a limited period.

In and around Madrid Joseph commanded the Army of the Centre. This had 18,000 on its muster rolls but a third of them were enlisted Spaniards of dubious reliability. Unless the king was prepared to abandon his capital he could give little help on the western front.

Marmont must carry the main burden of resisting Wellington. The Army of Portugal had been reinforced to a strength of 52,000 men but its sphere of responsibility had also been extended. This now stretched from the Tagus at Talavera to the Bay of Biscay at Gijon, 250 miles as the crow flies. One of Marmont's divisions could not be moved out of the Asturias without the Emperor's permission. The equivalent of another was required for garrisons between Astorga and Palencia. Marmont's field force was only 35,000 and it had to be stationed over a wide area so that it could find food.

Summing up their situation, Joseph and Jourdan came to the gloomy conclusion that 'It is clear that if Lord Wellington, who has 60,000 men, apart from the Spanish armies and the guerrillas, moves against either the Army of the South or that of Portugal, whichever he attacks will not be able to resist him. As things stand, only a disaster can be expected.'[6]

To avoid that disaster a central reserve must be created. No further divisions could be expected from France and the king and the marshal sought Napoleon's permission to evacuate Andalusia. Their letter went unanswered. As a stopgap orders were sent to Marmont and Soult instructing them to reinforce whichever was not attacked. Marmont reluctantly consented to obey. Soult flatly refused. The king sent an ADC to Soult with orders that if Wellington attacked Marmont, the Army of the South was to detach d'Erlon's corps to the north. The ADC reported:

I should warn you that the orders appointing Your Majesty to the supreme command of the army have not been published to the troops. People around him say that the marshal is dissatisfied that he was not appointed Your Majesty's Chief of Staff. I asked the marshal whether, if the English advanced in the north, he would order Count d'Erlon to cross the Tagus. The answer was a positive 'No!'[7]

To make co-ordination of the two armies more difficult, an allied
force under Hill made a brilliant raid to Almaraz and destroyed the
bridge there. In future the only main road linking Soult with Marmont crossed the Tagus at Toledo. In the same month the British
Colonel Sturgeon repaired the broken arch, seventy-five feet wide,
in the Roman bridge at Alcantara which had been blown three years
earlier. This meant that allied troops could be switched from the
Rodrigo to the Badajoz front at least two weeks quicker than the
French could carry out the same manoeuvre.

After the fall of Badajoz Wellington had toyed with the notion of
marching straight into Andalusia and relieving Cadiz. He quickly
discarded the idea since it would lay his flank open to the Army of
Portugal and 'enable the enemy to bring the largest body of men to
act together at one point [which] would be a false move'.[8] The
alternative was to strike at Marmont. If Marmont could be defeated
Soult must evacuate Andalusia or be cut off. Rowland Hill was left
round Badajoz with 18,000 men,* and the main Anglo-Portuguese
army, 48,000 strong, was assembled near Rodrigo where it was
joined by a small Spanish division. Wellington had 'reason to believe that Marmont has 45,000 men under his command', and was
cautiously optimistic. 'I think I can make this move with safety,
excepting always the risk of a general action. I am of opinion also
that I shall have the advantage in the action and that this is the period
of all others in which such a measure should be tried.'[9]

To make sure that Marmont was not reinforced, Wellington had
arranged for diversions to be staged against the other French
armies. Soult was to be harried by the irrepressible Ballasteros; an
Anglo-Sicilian expedition was to land on the east coast of Spain† to
divert Suchet; the Army of the North was assailed by the powerful
guerrillas from the mountains north of the Ebro, supported by a
naval squadron under Commodore Home Popham with two battalions of Royal Marines. This last diversion was spectacularly successful. For short periods ports as important as Santander and Bilbao

---

* Hill's corps consisted of the Second Division, Hamilton's Portuguese Division, 2nd
Cavalry Division (6 regts under Erskine) and an improvised Portuguese infantry
brigade. Of the 18,000 men about 7,500 were British.
† The fortunes of this expedition are referred to in Chapter 18.

were in allied hands and the Army of the North, now commanded by General Caffarelli, exhausted itself in fruitless attempts to march as fast as Popham's battleships could sail.

The allied army started its advance from Ciudad Rodrigo on 13 June. That night Wellington heard that Marmont's army was larger than he had been informed and outnumbered his own, even including the Spaniards. 'The [French] effective for duty are 51,492 and there are besides about 1,500 infantry and 1,000 cavalry returned on command which ought to be added. Notwithstanding that the enemy is considerably stronger than I believed he was, I propose to continue our movement.'[10]

Marmont's army was still widely dispersed. His magazines held so few rations that he dare not concentrate his divisions until he was certain where Wellington would strike. Only two divisions were immediately available to defend Salamanca. Wisely the marshal withdrew them, leaving 800 men in three fortified convents which commanded the town bridge across the Tormes. He gave the remaining divisions a rallying point at Fuente Sauco, midway between Salamanca and the Douro. By 27 June he had 40,000 men assembled there but had still to be joined by Bonet's division from the Asturias which he called in despite the Emperor's prohibition.

Wellington spent ten days taking the convents. All this time he was hoping that Marmont would attack him on the strong covering position he had taken up on the heights of San Cristobal, north of the city. For a week there was skirmishing and cannonading but neither commander was prepared to commit himself. When the convents fell Marmont withdrew to the line of the Douro with his right at Toro, his left at Tordesillas. He was confirmed in a belief he had held since the previous September that Wellington was a very cautious commander who would fight only on a strong defensive position.

Three thousand miles away President Madison declared that the United States were at war with Britain on 20 June. Like Mussolini in 1940, the President saw the chance of easy territorial gains while the enemy's strength was involved elsewhere. There were only four

British battalions in Canada. Any reinforcement for this tiny force must consist of battalions which might have gone to the Peninsula.

Wellington followed Marmont up to the Douro but made no attempt to force a crossing.

> It is obvious that we could not cross without sustaining great loss, and could not fight a general action under circumstances of greater disadvantage than those which would attend the attack of the enemy's position on the Douro. The enemy's numbers are equal if not superior to ours; they have in their position twice the amount of artillery which we have, and we are superior in cavalry alone, which arm, it is probable, could not be used in the attack we should make.[11]

He knew that Marmont could not stay on the north bank for long.

Bonet's division joined Marmont on 4 July and, having scraped together some more cavalry from the depots in Valladolid mounted on spare horses requisitioned from his officers, Marmont now had his army complete, with a strength of 50,000.[6/7] His position on the Douro was uncomfortable. A Portuguese cavalry brigade patrolled his rear and circumscribed his foraging parties. Soon the army would be starving. His troops were grumbling that he was unwilling to lead them against the enemy. Communications with other French commanders were erratic and uncertain.

Caffarelli had told him that he could help him only with a brigade of cavalry and a battery, although he had earlier promised 8,000 men and 24 guns. The latest letter from Madrid was dated 30 June and took sixteen days to reach Marmont. This informed him that Wellington's army contained only 18,000 British troops and reproved him for not having taken the offensive. He was asked to explain his reasons for not doing so 'by express messenger. His Majesty thinks you are strong enough to win a victory and wishes you to take advantage of present circumstances to fight Wellington while he has not got his full strength in hand.'[12]

Goaded on all sides, Marmont took the offensive on 15 July. Feinting with his right at Toro, he struck with his left at Tordesillas, catching Wellington off balance. It was a brilliantly conceived and executed manoeuvre, but Wellington recovered himself with equal skill and ordered a retreat on Salamanca, the nearest good defensive position in his rear. Next day a letter written by the king to Marmont on 9 July was delivered to Wellington. Joseph had decided that no help could be expected from Soult, Suchet or Caffarelli. He had resolved to reduce his commitments in the centre of Spain to a few vital garrisons and to march with every available man, about 13,000, to Marmont's assistance.

This information altered the whole aspect of Wellington's campaign. Once Marmont and the king joined forces the French would be too strong for him. He would have to fall back on Ciudad Rodrigo. What he could not know was whether Marmont knew of the king's intention. He had acquired one copy of Joseph's letter but bitter experience had taught the French to send all letters in two or three copies by different routes. One might have got through.

For five days the two armies marched parallel to each other a few hundred yards apart.

> The air was extremely sultry, the dust rose in clouds and the close order of the troops rendered it oppressive, but the military spectacle was strange and grand. For then were seen the hostile columns of infantry, at only half musket shot from each other, marching impetuously towards a common goal, the officers on each side pointing forwards with their swords, touching their caps and waving their hands in courtesy. At times the loud tones of command to hasten the march were heard passing from the front to the rear, and now and then the rushing sound of bullets came sweeping over the columns.[13]

On the 21st the allied army reached Salamanca and the leading divisions forded the Tormes at Santa Marta. 'Everyone got wet up to near their shoulders in crossing.'[14] The French crossed at Huerta a few miles upstream. Wellington had decided to avoid unnecessary risks. 'I have determined not to give up our communication with Ciudad Rodrigo; and not to fight an action unless under very advantageous circumstances.'[15] Next day the 'very advantageous circumstances' arose.

Marmont did not want a general action. The armies were too evenly matched for him to risk a full-scale attack. The allies had a defensive position at least as strong as those at Talavera, Fuentes de Oñoro and Albuera. He knew that Caffarelli's trifling reinforcement

would reach him within twenty-four hours, but he had not heard of
the king's march to join him. His instinct told him that a major
battle would certainly be expensive and might be disastrous. On the
other hand, he was young and ambitious. He had never won an
independent victory. He had commanded the Army of Portugal for
more than a year and had very little to show for it. He was smarting
under the king's implication of timidity and sensitive to the grumbling of his own troops. All these factors made him anxious to
achieve some concrete success.

He thought he saw an opportunity on 22 July. He assumed that
Wellington would put the maintenance of his communications above
all other considerations. That morning he had seen a great cloud of
dust moving westward behind the allied position. He concluded that
Wellington was continuing his retreat, thinning out his forward
troops and leaving only a rearguard to cover Salamanca. He believed that his chance had come. 'It seemed likely that there would
not be a battle but a rearguard action could be fought late in the day
when only a portion of the English army was left in front of me while
I would have every chance of scoring a point by employing my
whole army.'[16]

He was right in thinking that Wellington was preparing to retreat.
The dust cloud was raised by the allied baggage moving off on the
road to Rodrigo. He was wrong in believing that any large part of
the allied army was moving with it. The escort consisted of a single
regiment of Portuguese dragoons. Wellington had, as usual, concealed most of his troops[5/9] and Marmont's view was too restricted
to form a basis for considered judgement. He could see only 'an
English division in open woodland astride the road to Salamanca
and, far to the rear, a small column climbing the heights of Tejares;
the rest of the English army was hidden from us by a line of hills
which ran from north to south ending in the south in high, steep-
faced peaks. Lord Wellington could be seen on the hills, quite close
to us, surrounded by his staff.'[17]

Marmont made his observations from near the hamlet of Calvarrasa
de Arriba on the eastern slope of the valley of the Algabete stream
which ran north to the Tormes. Facing him, on the western slope of
the valley, was the main allied line with its left on the Salamanca

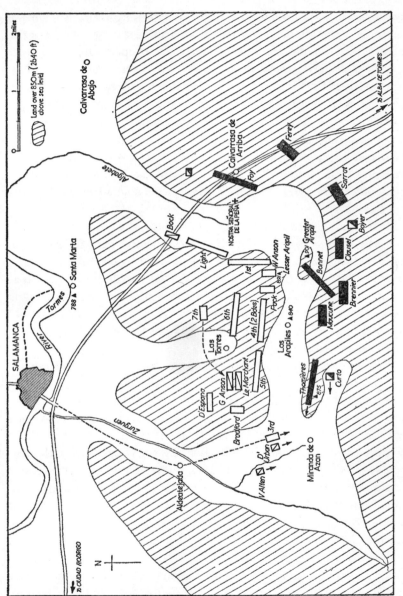

Salamanca

road. A few hundred yards in front of him was the chapel of Nostra Señora de la Peña, an allied outpost. Skirmishing round the chapel continued throughout the morning. The hills on the west side of the valley ended on the south in a steep, flat-topped hill, the Lesser Arapil. Nine hundred yards to the south there is another hill of similar shape but thirty feet higher, the Greater Arapil, which is free-standing. Between the two Arapils runs a low ridge which is the watershed between the Algabete stream, running north, and another minute stream, dry in summer, which runs in a smooth-sided valley from east to west. The ground here is two L-shaped ridges, one lying inside the other. The Lesser Arapil marks the angle of the inner ridge. The Greater Arapil stands alone inside the angle of the outer ridge.

Marmont believed that Wellington had only two divisions on the east-facing ridge and that the other six divisions were enveloped in the dustcloud visible to the west. He planned to hold the two divisions in place with half his army while the remainder turned their left by marching along the most southerly ridge towards Miranda de Azan. This entailed a long march for his rear divisions and it would be afternoon before they would be in a position to isolate the supposed rearguard.

On the previous evening Wellington had written: 'I have invariably been of opinion that unless forced to fight a battle it is better that one should not be fought by the allied army, unless under such favourable circumstances as that there would be reason to hope that the allied army would be able to maintain the field while those of the enemy would not.'[18] The last day on which such a clearcut victory might be won was 22 July. Next day Caffarelli's cavalry would join Marmont. Soon afterwards King Joseph would give the French an indisputable superiority. There was just a chance that Marmont might give him an opening on the 22nd and Wellington was prepared to wait and watch for it. He had 50,000 men on and behind the inner ridge.

Early in the morning he had sent a battalion of *caçadores* to seize the Greater Arapil. They had been forestalled by a French division. He had toyed with the idea of attacking the hill with two divisions but had been dissuaded by Beresford. As the day wore on the equi-

Page 199 (*above*) 'Passage of the Tagus at Villa Velha 1811', artist unknown; (*below*) detail: 'The Battle of Fuentes de Oñoro', painted by Major T. St Clair, engraved by C. Turner

Page 200   (*above*) 'Artillery on a March'; (*below*) 'Soldiers Drilling';
both by J. A. Atkinson 1807

valent of five divisions had been switched from the east-facing ridge
to that facing south. They were out of sight except for a garrison of
Guardsmen who were established in the village of Los Arapiles.
Only two divisions now faced east and the remaining division, the
Third, was marching from Santa Marta through the city of Sala-
manca to the extreme right flank.

All morning Wellington had seemed 'a little nervous'.

> [He] had not thought of breakfast and the staff had grown very
> hungry; at last, however, there was a pause (about two o'clock)
> near a farmyard enclosed by a wall, where a kind of breakfast was
> spread on the ground, and the staff alighted and fell to; while they
> were eating Wellington rode into the enclosure; he refused to
> alight, and advised them to make haste; he seemed anxious and on
> the look out. At last they persuaded him to take a piece of bread and
> the leg of a cold chicken, which he was eating without a knife from
> his fingers, when suddenly they saw him throw the leg of the fowl
> far away over his shoulder, and gallop out of the yard, calling to
> them to follow him.[19]

With his food in one hand, his telescope in the other, Wellington
had seen the opening for which he had waited. Marmont had sent
three divisions along the southern ridge. These three divisions,
14,000 infantry with 1,700 cavalry, were marching straight across the
front of Wellington's main striking force. They were badly strung
out and had their cavalry on the south, safe, flank. Turning to his
Spanish liaison officer, Wellington remarked, 'Mon cher Alava,
Marmont est perdu.' He put spurs to his horse and galloped the two
miles to his extreme right where the Third Division, commanded by
his brother in law,* was marching up from Salamanca accompanied
by D'Urban's Portuguese dragoons. Riding up to Pakenham, he
tapped him on the shoulder and said, 'Edward, move on with your
division—take the heights in your front—and drive everything
before you.'[20]

Pakenham's infantry had two miles to advance, most of this distance out of sight of the French. While they marched Wellington
galloped to the left to set his main attack in motion. Pakenham's task

---

* Pakenham was commanding the division in place of Picton who had been wounded
at Badajoz.

G

was to block the leading French troops and drive them back on the succeeding divisions. Wellington next launched the Fifth and Fourth Divisions, supported by the Sixth and Seventh and flanked by two Portuguese brigades, against the French flank. At the Fifth Division, 'Lord Wellington arrived from the right and communicated to General Leith his intentions of immediately attacking the enemy. On this, as on all other occasions, he gave his orders in a clear, consise and spirited manner; there was no appearance of contemplating a doubtful result; all he directed was as to time and formation, and his instructions concluded with commands that the enemy should be overthrown and driven from the field.'[21]

The battle started when D'Urban's dragoons charged in on the outside flank of Thomières' division, leading the French advance. A few minutes later the Third Division came up to the head of Thomières' column.

> The entire French division, with drums beating and uttering loud shouts, ran forward to meet them and belching forth a torrent of bullets from five thousand muskets. Wallace* looking full in the face of his soldiers, pointed to the French column and, leading them up the hill, brought them face to face with the French. Thomières' division wavered; nevertheless they opened a heavy discharge of musketry, but it was irregular and ill-directed. At last their fire ceased altogether, and the three regiments, for the first time, cheered. The effect was electric; Thomières' troops were infected with panic.[22]

Half a mile on Pakenham's left the Fifth Division advanced in two lines, each two deep and 1,500 yards long. They came up to Maucune's division which had ill-advisedly advanced down the slope and was far from any support. Fearing British cavalry, Maucune had formed them into square.

> All was quiet in those squares;—not a musket was discharged until the whole opened. Nearly at the same moment General Leith ordered the line to charge. In an instant every individual was enveloped in smoke and obscurity. No struggle for ascendancy took place: the French squares were penetrated, broken and discom-

---

* Lieut-Col Alexander Wallace, Connaught Rangers, was commanding the first brigade of Third Division in place of Maj-Gen Mackinnon, killed at Ciudad Rodrigo.

fited; the victorious division pressed forward, not against troops opposed, but a mass of disorganised men, flying in all directions.[23]

At that moment Stapleton Cotton led Le Marchant's heavy cavalry brigade obliquely into the angle between Pakenham's left and Leith's right. A thousand dragoons charged into Maucune's broken division 'at full speed, and the next moment twelve hundred French infantry were trampled down with a terrible clamour and disturbance. Bewildered and blinded they cast away their arms and crowded between the intervals of the squadrons, stooping and crying for quarter, while the dragoons, big men on big horses, rode onwards smiting with their long glittering swords in uncontrollable power.'[24]

Unfortunately the dragoons, encouraged by Le Marchant, pressed their advantage too far. The regiments became inextricably mixed, 'it being impossible to see for dust and smoak'.[25] They broke a brigade of the next French division, Brennier's, but they were brought up and their brigadier killed, trying to break a French square.

With the divisions of Maucune and Thomières in flight and Brennier's severely mauled, the French army needed resolute and immediate direction. None was forthcoming. Marmont had been disabled by a cannon ball as the action started and his successor, Bonet, was wounded before he could give any orders. The army was without a commander for more than an hour before the next senior general, Clausel, could be found and could take over.

Bertrand Clausel did everything that could be done to restore the situation. Wellington's Fourth Division, forming the left of his attacking force, had its left unguarded as it advanced. Pack's Portuguese brigade tried to remedy this by attacking the Greater Arapil only to be repulsed in disorder. Profiting from this, Clausel launched Bonet's division against the exposed flank of the Fourth. For a moment it seemed that the allied line might be rolled up from the flank. Fortunately Beresford was on the spot. He requisitioned Spry's Portuguese brigade from the second line of Fifth Division and led them against the exposed flank of Bonet's division. Beresford was wounded but his Portuguese stopped the French counterattack in its tracks.

At this moment the second wave of British divisions came sweeping forward and Bonet's halted and disordered men found themselves in the Sixth Division's line of advance.

It was about half past six. The ground over which we had to pass was a remarkably clear slope, most favourable for the defensive fire of the enemy. The division advanced with perfect steadiness and confidence. A craggy ridge, on which the French were drawn up, rose so abruptly that they could fire four or five deep. An uninterrupted blaze was maintained, so that the crest of the hill seemed to be one long streak of flame. Our men came down to the charging position and commenced firing, at the same time keeping touch to the right so that the gaps opened by the enemy's fire were instantly filled up. At the very first volley that we received about eighty men in the right wing of my regiment [32nd] fell to the rear in one group. The commanding officer immediately rode up to know the cause and found that they were all wounded. The success of the attack was complete; for as soon as the Sixth Division got near enough they dashed forward with the bayonet, and another portion of our troops acting on Clausel's right flank,* his army was quickly driven to the rear; but before this, night had come on.[26]

Foy's division on the extreme right was still intact and covered the French retreat to the south-east. The Light Division led the pursuit and William Napier, commanding the Forty Third, wrote that:

After dusk, Wellington rode up *alone* behind my regiment and I joined him. The flush of victory was on his brow and his eyes were eager and watchful, but his voice was calm and even gentle. He was giving me some orders when a ball passed through his left holster and struck his thigh; he put his hand to the place, and his countenance changed for an instant; and to my eager inquiry if he was hurt, he replied sharply, 'No!' and went on with his orders.[27]

'We continued the pursuit until past twelve at night',[28] but the French got away. Wellington had planned to destroy the whole Army of Portugal but he was frustrated by the action of a Spanish subordinate. The French were flying into a bend of the river Tormes. There were only two places where they could cross, the fords at Huerta and the bridge at Alba de Tormes. The bridge was dominated by a castle held by a Spanish battalion. Knowing that the

---

* The First Division seized the Greater Arapil against light opposition.

French would not have time to eject the garrison, Wellington led
the pursuit to Huerta.

> I had desired the Spaniards to continue to occupy the castle of Alba.
> Don Carlos de España had evacuated it, I believe, before he knew
> my wishes; and he was afraid to let me know that he had done so;
> and I did not know it till I found no enemy at the fords. When I lost
> sight of them in the dark I marched upon Huerta, they went by
> Alba. If I had known there had been no garrison in Alba, I should
> have marched there, and should probably have had the whole.[29]

Even without that final triumph, the battle of Salamanca changed
the whole course of the campaign. The allies captured 20 guns, 2
eagles and 7,000 prisoners. Another 7,000 Frenchmen were killed or
wounded. There were so many stragglers that Clausel, who was
wounded in the foot, reported that he had only 20,000 men in the
ranks. The allies lost 5,000 men, half the total being in the Sixth and
Fourth Divisions.

Wellington attained a moral ascendancy over the French which he
never subsequently lost. In Britain all parties were convinced at last
that the war in the Peninsula could be won. The Prime Minister
wrote:

> I have never in my life seen anything equal to the enthusiasm which
> the knowledge of this event has excited throughout this town, and
> throughout every part of the country from which accounts of its
> reception have yet been obtained. In addition to all the other advan-
> tages, it must be gratifying to you to reflect that you have made the
> army as popular as the navy has hitherto been.[30]

Wellington, who had been created an earl after the storm of
Ciudad Rodrigo, was given another step in the peerage. Charac-
teristically, he remarked: 'What the devil's the use of making me a
Marquess?'[31]

CHAPTER 13

Madrid and Burgos

THE allied army entered Madrid on 12 August, deafened by the cheers of the inhabitants. 'If Lord Wellington would have let them, they would have knelt down and prayed to him,' wrote his escort commander.[1] Another officer told his sister, 'If I live a thousand years I shall never pass such a day as yesterday, so full of delirium that the only assurance that it was not all a dream is that every one I meet has dreamed the same dream with myself.'[2] Wellington reported that, 'I am among a people mad with joy at their deliverance,'[3] but added, 'I do not expect much from the exertions of the Spaniards, notwithstanding all we have done for them. They cry *viva*, and are very fond of us, and hate the French; but they are in general the most incapable of useful exertion of all nations that I have known; the most vain, and at the same time the most ignorant, particularly of military affairs, and above all of the military affairs of their own country.'[4]

The march to Madrid had been largely a political gesture made for lack of any profitable military employment for the army. There had been little point in pursuing the Army of Portugal beyond Valladolid. The damage done to it at Salamanca had been consummated by a brilliant cavalry action on the following day at Garçia Hernandez. The German dragoons had wrecked the only one of Marmont's divisions which had escaped unscathed from 22 July. Clausel reported that although 'armies usually suffer in morale after a setback, it is hard to understand the extent of discouragement existing in this one. I cannot conceal that a very bad spirit prevails. Disorders and the most revolting excesses mark every stage of our retreat. Deplorable outrages are committed every day under the very eyes of the officers, who do nothing to prevent them.'[5]

Wellington shepherded them back across the Douro and liberated Valladolid on 30 July. To chase them further would do more harm to his own army than to the French. His supply lines were already dangerously stretched and he was short of generals.* There was a mounting threat to his southern flank. Marmont's defeat must force Soult to evacuate Andalusia and he and the king could mass 75,000 men and place them between the allied army and Portugal. The allied occupation of Madrid, apart from being a sharp blow to Napoleon's prestige, would deprive Soult and Joseph of their most convenient point for joining their armies. Nothing could prevent the junction but, with Madrid held against them, geography and the road system would dictate that they joined near the coast in Valencia. Wellington left a covering force near Valladolid and marched on Madrid.

King Joseph was near despair. On the day Salamanca was fought he and his corps had been at the northern end of the Guadarrama pass. He heard from peasants that Wellington and Marmont were moving towards Salamanca and marched westward reaching Blascosanchez, less than fifty miles from the battlefield, on 24 July. There a message brought by a Spaniard told him that the Army of Portugal had been defeated and was retreating east towards Arevalo. Next day he received a letter from the wounded Marmont minimising his defeat. 'Our loss is about 5,000 men. That of the English infinitely greater.'[6] This left the king with the hope that co-operation between the two forces might still be practicable. A letter from Clausel soon disillusioned him. The general wrote that he had only 20,000 men with the eagles and announced his intention of going to all lengths 'to avoid engagements and the risk of another useless battle'.[7] Joseph had to retreat rapidly to Madrid to save what he could from the débâcle. He was clear that the disaster had occurred through Soult's refusal to help Marmont. The situation could be

---

* Even before Salamanca he had been without two divisional commanders, Graham (sick) and Picton (wounded). Five of his British infantry brigades were commanded by lieutenant-colonels. At Salamanca Le Marchant was killed and Beresford, Cotton, Cole and Leith were wounded as were two commanders of Portuguese brigades.

restored only by bringing the whole of the Army of the South up to the centre of Spain. He wrote to Soult, 'I lose no time in ordering you formally to evacuate Andalusia and march with all speed to Toledo.'[8]

Soult received this order on 12 August, the day Wellington entered Madrid making it impossible for Soult to march to Toledo. It did not occur to Soult to obey the order, 'which strikes me as very extraordinary. I am far from believing that Your Majesty is really determined upon it. The loss of a battle by the Army of Portugal is a thing which can easily be remedied, but the loss of Andalusia and the raising of the siege of Cadiz are events which will be felt throughout Europe and even in the New World.' Instead he proposed that Joseph and his army should join him in Seville. 'As soon as we have 70 or 80,000 concentrated in the south of Spain, the theatre of war will change and the Army of Portugal will find itself disengaged.'[9]

By the time the king received this insubordinate reply he was in Valencia. He could not hope to hold Madrid and contented himself with a cavalry skirmish at Majalahonda where a division of French dragoons routed a Portuguese cavalry brigade and temporarily captured three British guns. Meanwhile he sent off a convoy of 2,000 vehicles under a heavy escort. With them went a swarm of Spaniards, men, women and children who had committed themselves to the French and dared not face the wrath of their compatriots. Joseph left Madrid on 11 August and set off for Valencia.

It was a dreadful march. *Guerrilleros* haunted the flanks and rear of the column, massacring stragglers and foragers. The country people laid waste the land in front of the French advance. They drove off the animals and destroyed mills and ovens. No rations were issued; there were none to be had.

Many of the soldiers died of thirst. They could be seen by the roadside, stretched on their backs, dying in terrible convulsions under the eyes of their comrades. The thirst was made worse by the cloud of dust raised by the convoy, a cloud half a league wide and several leagues long. This formless corrosive dust penetrated everywhere. Nothing could keep it out. It blinded infantry and cavalry alike, clogging the palate, drying the tongue, choking the lungs and causing a violent, racking cough.[10]

The king reached Valencia on 31 August and was received by Suchet.

Wellington knew that the king had ordered Soult to leave Andalusia and that Soult was raising objections. He could not know when the marshal would consent to obey. Until he did the allies had the freedom of central Spain. There was an outside chance that this area could be held even after Soult and Joseph joined forces but it depended on a very fortunate combination of circumstances. The Army of Portugal, which would soon be recreated as a fighting force, must be held back in the valley of the Ebro. The combined armies of the South and the Centre must be held south of the Tagus. Both French forces would outnumber the allied troops containing them, but they could be contained if three conditions were met. Burgos, which controls the road from the Ebro valley to that of the Douro, must be captured and held. The rains must swell the Tagus so that the number of crossing-places was limited. Spanish forces must harry the western flank of a French advance from Valencia to Madrid.

None of these conditions was impossible of fulfilment. Burgos was not a strong fortress. The Tagus was usually high in the autumn and the Cortes had voted to give Wellington the supreme command of all their forces so that he should be able to co-ordinate the flank attacks. It was 'a game that might succeed (the only one that could succeed)',[11] and he decided to play it as long as it was reasonably safe to do so.

He left his three best divisions, those which had borne the brunt at Ciudad Rodrigo and Badajoz, at Madrid to watch the line of the Tagus. He set out with the remainder at the beginning of September and reached Burgos on the 18th, driving the Army of Portugal in front of him.

Clausel put up no resistance but left a garrison of 2,000 men in the castle of Burgos which 'stands on a knoll above the town and is separated from the remaining part of the height by a deep valley and there is a hornwork, unfinished, on the height which seems the only approach'.[12] The governor was an enterprising and determined soldier, General Dubreton.

Wellington later admitted that he underestimated the difficulty of taking Burgos. 'It was not unlike a hill fort in India and I had got into a good many of them.'[13] The facilities he needed were not available. There were only eight Engineer officers and eight other ranks. His siege train consisted of three 18-pounders with 1,306 rounds between them. He might have got more guns, but moving them was a slow business and he did not know how much time would be allowed him.

Burgos was Wellington's only serious failure in the Peninsula. Both he and the troops were tired. He hoped to get into the castle quickly but, sickened by the slaughter at Rodrigo and Badajoz, he could not bring himself to commit enough troops to ensure success. He was not convinced that Burgos was worth a large butcher's bill. He used men in inadequate driblets and suffered 2,000 casualties in achieving nothing. The troops were inexperienced in siege work. 'If I had here some of the troops who have stormed so often I should not have lost a fourth of the number.'[14]

He had to conduct the siege looking over his shoulder; 150 miles and the Sierra de Guadarrama separated the two halves of his army. If Suchet could be prevailed upon to reinforce the king and Soult, the detached allied corps could be attacked by 100,000 men. He had counted on Ballasteros acting against Soult and on the Anglo-Sicilian expedition which had landed at Alicante causing the French to divide their strength. Neither hope was fulfilled. Ballasteros mutinied in protest against the offer of the Spanish supreme command to Wellington. Before he could be exiled and replaced it was too late for his army to affect Soult. The force at Alicante preserved a timorous immobility. Meanwhile the siege went badly. 'This is altogether the most difficult job I ever had in hand with such trifling means. God send that they may give me a little more time.'[15]

He was not given time. Soult started to leave Andalusia in late August. By the 24th he had completed the destruction of the siege lines round Cadiz. His rearguard was driven out of Seville three days later. He paused at Granada until d'Erlon joined him from Estremadura and reached Suchet's outposts in Valencia at the end of September. On 3 October he met Joseph with Jourdan and Suchet at Fuente de Higuera, fifty miles from Valencia city.

It was an uncomfortable meeting. Eight weeks earlier Soult had written a letter to the Minister of War in Paris suggesting that Joseph had ordered him to evacuate Andalusia so that some 'profitable arrangement' could be reached between the king and the Cortes at Cadiz. His evidence for this assertion was circumstantial and tenuous. He added:

> I draw no conclusion from these facts. However, I have felt obliged to reveal my fears to six generals of this army, having put them under oath never to disclose what I have told them except to the Emperor himself, or to persons specially authorised by the Emperor to receive this testimony if, meanwhile, I am no longer able to give evidence myself.[16]

He entrusted this letter to the captain of a French coasting vessel who was attempting to run the blockade along the Mediterranean coast. When British cruisers drove him into Grao, the port of Valencia, the captain, ignorant of its contents, handed the letter to Suchet who gave it to the king. Joseph was justifiably angry and sent an ADC to Napoleon in Moscow to demand 'justice from Your Majesty. Let Marshal Soult be recalled, tried and punished. I can stay here no longer with such a man.'[17] *

On 3 October Joseph first saw Soult alone. 'One can imagine,' wrote Jourdan who was waiting outside the room, 'that their first interview brought out some sharp words. However, the king, always a generous man, controlled himself and offered to forget the past. He called in Marshals Jourdan and Suchet and they settled down to immediate business.'[18] Soult remained unco-operative and before a plan of campaign could be agreed Joseph had to threaten to deprive him of his command. Eventually it was decided that the combined force, 61,000 men with 84 guns, should advance on Madrid in two columns commanded respectively by Soult and d'Erlon. Their aim was to cut Wellington off from Portugal. On the left Soult's column marched on the Albacete road. D'Erlon moved on the Cuenca road. They started to march on 15 October and met

---

* The ADC reached Moscow on the day before the French army left the city. Napoleon's reaction was that Soult's letter was 'not important. The marshal was mistaken but he, the Emperor, could not bother with such trifles at that moment. He added that Soult was the only military brain in Spain and that he could not withdraw him without risking the safety of the army' (JN ix 176. Deprez to JN, 3 January 1813).

with no opposition until the 25th when the advanced guard exchanged shots with British vedettes near Ocaña.

The allied corps at Madrid had been increased by the addition of Hill's corps from Badajoz and a British brigade from Cadiz. Hill was in command and had 31,000 Anglo-Portuguese and 12,000 Spaniards. There had been no rain on the headwaters of the Tagus although the siege trenches around Burgos had been inundated. The great river was fordable in many places and useless as a defensive line.

Wellington's gamble had failed. 'If this game had been well played, it would have served my purpose. Had I any reason to expect it would be well played? Certainly not. I have never yet known the Spaniards do anything, much less do anything well.'[19] 'It was,' he confessed, 'all my fault.'[20]

His third assault on the castle of Burgos had already failed when, on 21 October, the reorganised and reinforced Army of Portugal started to press in on his covering force. He decided to retreat at once. That night the siege guns, their wheels muffled in straw, were dragged over the bridge of Burgos unheard by the garrison of the castle. Two days earlier, on 19 October, the Grande Armée, with its booty and its hangers-on, left the ruins of Moscow on its long, disastrous march westward. Before he left Napoleon dictated a letter to General Clarke in Paris. 'Being so far away there is nothing I can do for my armies in Spain. Tell the king and Marshal Soult how necessary it is that they should work together and, as far as possible, minimize the effects of a bad system.'[21]

CHAPTER 14

Retreat to Portugal

ON 21 October 1812 Wellington found himself in 'the worst military situation I was ever in'.[1] That morning he heard from Rowland Hill that Joseph and Soult were advancing in great strength on Madrid and that they had captured the castle of Chinchilla on 9 October. The Tagus 'was already fordable by individuals in many places and was likely to become so by an army'.[2] On the Burgos front the situation was more immediately serious. He had expected that, sooner or later, the Army of Portugal would attempt to relieve Burgos, but 'I had no reason to believe the enemy were so strong till I saw them. Fortunately they did not attack me: if they had, I must have been destroyed.'[3]

Around Burgos he had 35,000 men, a third of them Spaniards, to oppose a French force of 53,000.* On the Tagus, Hill had 43,000 (including 12,000 Spaniards) against 61,000. The two allied corps were 150 miles apart and it took a letter four days to travel from Wellington's headquarters to Hill's.† Either corps could be overwhelmed separately.

Wellington was not prepared to retreat all the way to Portugal unless it was unavoidable. He hoped to hold the area between the Douro and the Sierra de Guadarrama as a springboard for the cam-

---

* The Army of Portugal, now commanded by General Souham, had an effective strength of 41,000. It was reinforced by a brigade (3,400) from Bayonne, two cavalry brigades (2,300) and two incomplete infantry divisions (6,500) from the Army of the North.
† Hill's letter of '17th October, one p.m.' (mistranscribed in WD as 19 October) reached Wellington on the morning of 21 October. Some earlier letters from Hill covered the distance in 3½ days.

paign of 1813. Hill was ordered to stay on the Tagus unless 'he
should find that he could not maintain himself on it with advantage'.[4]
The northern corps was ordered to retire on Valladolid in the hope
that it could hold a line there or on the Douro. It was possible that
'the Army of Portugal will not follow us if left alone'.[5]

The retreat from Burgos began well. 'The enemy were not aware
of our movements and did not follow us till late on the 22nd.'[6] The
infantry had gained forty-eight hours' start and on the 23rd they
crossed the Pisuerga at Torquemada and took up a position on the
west bank.

The rearguard was formed by the only two brigades of cavalry
with the corps* and the two light battalions of the German Legion.
Stapleton Cotton, recovered from his Salamanca wound, was in
command. Opposed to them were nearly 6,000 French cavalry
backed by infantry.

A disaster was narrowly averted on 23 October at Venta del Pozo,
fifteen miles from Burgos. The road led across a deep, dry watercourse crossed by a narrow bridge. Anson's brigade was covering the
rear. Cotton deployed his horse artillery† to fire at the bridge and
ordered the German dragoons to charge as soon as a few French
squadrons had defiled across. Unfortunately Anson's regiments
turned the wrong way when they reached the south bank, masking
both the guns and the Germans. Before Bock's brigade could charge
the French were across in strength and there was a mêlée with both
sides hacking at each other in a stationary, confused mass. Into this
mass charged a division of French dragoons who had taken a wide
detour and crossed the watercourse by a track far on their right.
Both British brigades had to fly in disorder but they were saved by
the two battalions of the Legion who received the French cavalry in
square and inflicted 300 casualties on them. The British brigades
reformed behind them and the retreat continued in a hectic but
orderly fashion.

We had literally to fight our way for four miles; retiring, halting,
charging and again retiring. I never witnessed such a scene of

* George Anson's brigade: 11th, 12th and 16th Light Dragoons, 800 sabres. Baron
Bock's brigade: 1st and 2nd Dragoons KGL, 400 sabres.
† Bull's Troop, RHA, commanded by 2nd Captain Norman Ramsay.

anxiety, uproar and confusion. I twice thought Anson's brigade (which is weak in numbers and much exhausted by constant service) would be annihilated, and I believe we owe the preservation of that and the German heavy brigade to the admirable steadiness of Halkett's two light German battalions.* Throughout the whole of this trying occasion Cotton behaved with great coolness, judgment and gallantry. I was close to him the whole time and did not observe him for an instant disturbed or confused.[7]

That night there was also 'uproar and confusion' in the infantry.

After a most fatiguing march of seven long leagues,† we reached Torquemada late at night, the whole army being extremely fagged. Here unfortunately were numerous wine cellars which some straggling Spanish and Portuguese soldiers broke into and brought quantities of wine into the camp which they sold for next to nothing. It being midnight before the messes were cooked, the effect of the wine on the harassed, wearied and empty soldiers was instantaneous and some hundred were brutally intoxicated and utterly incapable of marching the next day.[8]

Wellington had a strong position on the rivers Carrion and Pisuerga between Palencia and Duenas. The French attacked his left and centre on 25 October. In the centre they were held by the Fifth Division but on the left the defence had been entrusted to a division of Galicians. Their commander elected to put his men into the almost unfortified town of Palencia which stands on the east, French, bank of the river. The bridge had been mined but the Spaniards fled so quickly that there was no time to fire the mine and the French dashed across mixed with the fugitives. With his position compromised, Wellington performed an intriguing and effective manoeuvre. He passed his whole army across the Pisuerga and faced the French across it with his left at Valladolid and his right, secured on a river, twenty miles upstream. Thus instead of defending the right bank facing east, as he had been on the 25th, he was defending the left bank facing west on the 27th. His new position was un-

---

* The two Light Battalions KGL were awarded the unique battle honour of 'Venta del Poza'. This honour was worn by their successor units in the Hanoverian (and subsequently Prussian) army until 1918.

† Four differing lengths of league were currently in use in the Peninsula, being respectively 2·63, 3·49, 4·00 and 4·21 English miles. The English league was 3 miles. The march on this day was 26–28 miles.

assailable but it could be outflanked. Sooner or later the French would work round his left and reach the Douro at Tordesillas or beyond.

There was now no question of holding central Spain. The Army of Portugal was too strong for him. His main concern must be to stop the French getting between his own corps and Hill's. He decided to retreat due south to Arevalo and ordered Hill to join him there.

> The enemy are infinitely superior to us in cavalry, and from what I saw today very superior in infantry. We must retire, therefore, and the Douro is no barrier. If we go your situation is very delicate, and it appears to me to be necessary that you, as well as we, should retire. I propose to remain on the Pisuerga tomorrow [28th], if I can, and as long as I can upon the Douro, and then retire upon Arevalo. God knows whether I shall be able to remain on either river, and if I cannot, your retreat should be by the valley of the Tagus; if I can, we should join [at Arevalo].[9]

There is a note of resignation, almost of despair, in this letter, a note which recurs nowhere else in Wellington's voluminous correspondence. He was tired after ten months of campaigning and too many things had gone wrong in the last two months. His temper was not improved when he found that his new Quartermaster General was writing discouraging reports on the campaign and its prospects to the Opposition newspapers.*

There was more bad news on 29 October when the French got a foothold on the south bank of the Douro at Tordesillas. Captain Guingret led fifty-five naked swimmers across the river and drove a company of Brunswickers away in disorder. The bridgehead was effectively sealed, but it was another irritating misadventure. Two days later Wellington heard that 'Buonaparte was at Moscow on 19th September. How it is to end, God knows.'[10]

Although he could not know it, the steam went out of the French advance at this time. Caffarelli, commanding the Army of the North, insisted on withdrawing most of the troops with which he had re-

---

* Colonel James Willoughby Gordon, formerly Military Secretary to the Duke of York, was appointed QMG in succession to George Murray in May 1812. He served with the army from August to December 1812 when, fortunately, he went sick. Murray returned in March 1813.

inforced Souham near Burgos. Caffarelli's responsibility was primarily on the north bank of the Ebro and there the guerrillas, with
the help of Commodore Popham, controlled almost all the countryside except for a handful of fortresses. His defection left the Army
of Portugal little bigger than Wellington's force but they still moved
steadily westward along the Douro and reached Toro before the end
of October. This put them in a position to cut in between Wellington
and Portugal. The allies must fall back south-westward and Wellington told Hill to bring his corps to Salamanca rather than Arevalo.

Hill received Wellington's order to retire from the Tagus on 30
October. In fact he had already retired his main body from the river
and was established on a strong position between Guadalajara and
the Puente Larga. He felt he was strong enough there to hold back
the combined southern armies. Soult advanced cautiously and, while
waiting for d'Erlon's column to join him, only probed Hill's outposts. Hill would have got clean away had the mine previously laid
under the Puente Larga exploded as it should have done. When it
misfired, Skerrett's brigade* had to fight a sharp rearguard action
before the engineers managed to blow two arches out of the bridge.
After that the retreat went smoothly except when 'on the night of 1st
November, we bivouacked in the park of the Escurial, where two
wild boars galloped through the lines, and caused great confusion;
a soldier of the 52nd was overturned by one of them, which bounded
over him without doing further damage'.[11] On 8 November the two
parts of the allied army were close together and ready for action in
the area Salamanca–Alba de Tormes.

King Joseph re-entered Madrid on 2 November after an absence
of twelve weeks. 'A new and hastily formed municipal body received
him and, in a greatly embarrassed speech, endeavoured to excuse the
inhabitants by pleading the disasters of the time and entreated the
royal clemency. Nor was the appeal made in vain; there were no
recriminations and no informers were listened to.'[12] Joseph and his
army did not linger in Madrid. After forty-eight hours they marched
out to the north leaving no garrison in the city. Joseph was determined to join all the available troops, the Armies of the South, the

* Previously a part of the Cadiz garrison. It consisted of 3/1st Guards and 2/47th,
2/87th and 2/95th Rifles (2 coys).

Centre and of Portugal, in an attempt to deal with Wellington's army once and for all.

At Salamanca, drawn up on the position from which he had attacked Marmont in July, Wellington was prepared to put everything to the test of battle provided that his retreat to Portugal was still open. On 15 November the French, 80,000 strong, came up to the Arapil position where Wellington had 65,000 men, British, Portuguese and Spaniards. The scene was set for a climacteric battle which would settle the fate of Spain and Portugal. To the intense disappointment of the soldiers on both sides, nothing happened.

Soult had been given temporary command of all three French armies. A council of war had agreed a plan on the previous day but, faced with his enemy, Soult behaved with what the bitterly angry Joseph described as 'extreme circumspection'.[13] Mid-day passed and only a few skirmishing shots had been exchanged. It started to rain at two o'clock and still nothing had happened. Wellington decided that he was not going to be attacked and ordered the army to start marching off towards Portugal. The rain grew heavier 'and the sky was so overcast that at four o'clock it was as dark as night'.[14] Marshal Jourdan commented, 'Thus Lord Wellington effected his retreat without even being harassed in the presence of 80,000 of France's best troops and the opportunity was lost of putting right in a single day all the misfortunes of the campaign.'[15]

Soult's failure to attack was unaccountable to the French troops.* One of their generals wrote, 'We had an army one third stronger than Wellington with a great superiority in cavalry and artillery. Every man was confident of victory. At last we had a chance to beat the English, perhaps to drive them out of the Peninsula. With everything in our favour, this splendid, decisive opportunity was allowed to slip away.'[16]

Wellington's soldiers were no better pleased. A Scottish sergeant wrote:

* King Joseph ascribed Soult's inactivity to concern for his younger brother, General Pierre Soult, whose 'incapacity' as a cavalry brigadier was notorious. Sir Charles Oman suggests that 'after Albuera, he had a wholesome dread of attacking a British army in position'. Since he did this on five occasions in the following year, this explanation seems unlikely.

I never saw the troops in such a bad humour. Retreating before the enemy at any time was a grievous business, but in such weather it was doubly so. The night was dismally dark, the cold wind blew in heavy gusts and the roads became gradually worse. Few words were spoken and, as if ashamed to complain of the hardships we suffered, execrating the retreat and blaming Lord Wellington for not having sufficient confidence in us to hazard a battle with the enemy, were the only topics discussed.[17]

The allied army lost more men on the four days that followed than it did in the storm of Badajoz. Soult's pursuit was ineffective except on the third day but the weather was a more devastating enemy than the French.

Each morning, as soon as the road was distinguishable, we were on the march, ankle deep in mud which tore the shoes from the soldiers' feet; in this manner we trudged along the whole day. One hour after nightfall we drew up under the trees, hungry and in the most miserable plight; the fires were kindled with difficulty, while roasting on one side, we were shivering and perishing on the other, the rain still pouring down unmercifully.[18]

No rations were issued. Colonel Gordon, the arrogant and incompetent Quartermaster General, had sent all supplies to the rear on the wrong road. Officers and men subsisted on handfuls of acorns. 'Let it not be supposed that these acorns were the same as we have in England: they were nearly equal to the Spanish chestnut and, in my opinion, when eaten raw, are preferable.'[19]

Three divisions were gratuitously harassed by the behaviour of their commanders. William Stewart, commanding First Division, 'and certain other generals* held a Council of War to decide whether they would obey my orders to march by a particular road. He, at the head, decided they would not; they marched by a road leading they knew not where, and when I found them in the morning they were in the utmost confusion, not knowing where to go and what to do.'[20] When Wellington was asked later what he said to the three generals, 'he replied, "Oh, by God, it was too serious to say anything." '[21]

An officer who had served in Moore's army considered that:

---

* Lord Dalhousie (Seventh Division) was certainly one of the others. The third was probably John Oswald (Fifth Division) but may have been Henry Clinton (Sixth).

In some respects the hardships were greater, for on [the retreat to Coruña] the troops were generally under cover, such as it was, during the night; but here the only resting place was a bleak swampy plain. I have seen something of Lord Wellington during these proceedings and more to admire in him than ever. His temper, naturally hasty, seemed to grow more calm as that of the weather rose, but it was a calmness that indicated elevation rather than depression of spirits.[22]

His temper was not proof against all the follies of his subordinates. 17 November was the worst day of the retreat. The Quartermaster General sent the rearguard of cavalry away to a flank without telling the infantry that there was nothing between them and the French. Consequently the Light Division was attacked before it had left its bivouac, a situation from which only its superb training and discipline saved it. Next, Edward Paget, newly returned as second-in-command of the army, was captured riding unescorted between two divisional columns.

The last straw was when in the afternoon the Light Division, commanded by Charles Alten, was moving down to cross the Huebra river at San Muñoz. Four French batteries were firing at them and they were being harassed by *voltigeurs*. William Napier wrote:

> Lord Wellington rode up and finding the division, strangely enough, formed up in squares while the French infantry skirmishers were actually infesting our flanks and rear, was very angry and reprimanded Alten, who was near, by his manner of addressing me:
> 'What the devil are you about here with your squares?'
> 'They are not my squares, they are General Alten's.'
> 'Get into column and retreat with the division.'
> 'There is General Alten, sir.'
> 'Don't reply—order the division to retreat, and, do you hear, sir?
> —cover it with four companies of the Forty Third and Riflemen.'
> I took the hint and carried the order to retreat.[23] *

The skirmish on the Huebra was the last fighting of the year. Soult broke off the pursuit and the allied army reached Ciudad

---

* It is probable that Napier exaggerates Wellington's treatment of Alten on this occasion. Napier did not like Alten but Wellington is known to have had a high opinion of him.

Rodrigo on 19 November. They were back where they had started, and the troops grumbled incessantly. They had marched hundreds of miles and routed the Army of Portugal, but they seemed to have achieved nothing. Twenty-two thousand British troops, two-fifths of the army, were sick or missing[24] and the rest 'are the funniest cripples you ever saw, in uncommon pain, our toes feeling as if they were always out of bed on a cold night, and the foot has all kind of *aitches* in it. There are no marks and we all hobble about like Grimaldi.'[25]

Tempers were not improved by a scathing letter which Wellington sent to his generals. It was modelled, consciously or not, on Moore's General Order issued at the height of the disorders on the retreat to Coruña* and was widely, but not universally, resented.

> The Peer Wellington has just issued what he calls a circular to the army,† in which he obligingly informs them that they are a parcel of the greatest knaves and the worst soldiers that he not only ever had to deal with, but worse than any army he ever *read* of. He was good enough to say that he excepted the Light Division and the Guards, but he makes no exceptions in writing.[26]

Despite immediate appearances, the benefits earned during the summer and autumn campaign of 1812 were vast and enduring. As Wellington claimed,

> In the months elapsed since January this army has sent to England little short of 20,000 prisoners and they have taken and destroyed or have themselves the use of the enemy's arsenals in Ciudad Rodrigo, Badajoz, Salamanca, Valladolid, Madrid, Astorga, Seville, the lines before Cadiz &c.: and upon the whole we have taken little short of 3,000 cannon. The siege of Cadiz has been raised and all the countries south of the Tagus have been cleared of the enemy.[27]

On the psychological side the gains were even more impressive. All Europe could see that the French kingdom of Spain was a sham. King Joseph had had to abandon his capital twice within three months. He was able to spend Christmas there but it was now dangerously near the edge of the territory he could claim to control.

---

* See p 81.
† It was not a circular to the army but a confidential letter to 'officers commanding divisions and brigades' which was leaked to the troops and the press in England.

His realm was now smaller than it had been in December 1809. The guerrillas were rampant. Northern Spain was infested with patriotic bands and Mina, the greatest of the *guerrilleros*, was levying customs tolls on imports from France. The minority of Spaniards who had attached themselves to Joseph's cause dared not move out of the protection of French bayonets.

The morale of the French had slumped. The myth of French invincibility, tarnished at Bailen, was shattered at Salamanca. Wellington had established a moral ascendancy over his opponents which was to stand him in good stead for the rest of his active career. One French general wrote privately that Salamanca had 'raised Wellington to the level of the Duke of Marlborough. Earlier we had realised his prudence, his eye for a good position, his skill in defending it. At Salamanca he showed himself a master of manoeuvre.'[28]

PART FIVE

The Liberation of Spain,
January–September 1813

CHAPTER 15

Across the Ebro

THERE was little contact between the French and British armies for six months after Wellington's return to Ciudad Rodrigo. In that time the character of the war in Europe changed. At midnight on 18 December 1812 Napoleon returned to Paris. The city had been shocked the previous day by the publication of the 29me Bulletin describing the retreat from Moscow. Napoleon said of this Bulletin, 'I have told the whole truth.'[1] This was an overstatement. He had told nothing but the truth but not the whole truth. Readers were left with the impression that although the weather had destroyed the cavalry and the dearth of draught animals had made retreat inevitable, the infantry was still substantially intact. When Napoleon reached Paris Prince Eugene and Ney were trying desperately to stem the Russian advance with 20,000 men.

A copy of the 29me Bulletin reached Madrid by way of Valencia on 6 January, seventeen days after it had been read in London.* It did not make plain to Joseph and his staff the extent of the Russian disaster. They continued to ask hopefully for reinforcements. So tight was the guerrilla hold on northern Spain that no letters from Paris reached Madrid until 16 February. The latest letter of the batch was dated 14 January. One letter opened the king's eyes to the situation in the east. It came from the ADC who had been sent to Moscow with the report of Soult's misdeeds. He had marched back with the Young Guard.

---

* Wellington received the Bulletin in Lisbon on 18 January, the mails having been delayed by adverse winds. London told him at the same time that the Russians claimed 'not less than 10,000 prisoners [and] the greater part of Napoleon's artillery'.

It is impossible to describe the distress of this army. No rations were issued for more than a month; there was nothing to eat but dead horses; even marshals often had no bread. Hundreds of men died each night in the bivouacks. At least 100,000 were lost in this way alone. I am convinced that not more than 20,000 men will have reached the Niemen. Should your Majesty ask me where the retreat will stop, I can only say that that will depend on the enemy.[2]

At the same time Napoleon's orders reached Madrid. Twenty thousand men were to be sent back to France as a cadre for the new Grande Armée on the eastern front.* 'Tell the king, in cypher, that as things stand I think he should put his headquarters at Valladolid; that he should occupy Madrid with one of his flanks; that he should use the period while the English are inactive in pacifying Navarre, Biscay and the province of Santander.'[3]

By the same mail came an order recalling Soult from Spain. Joseph had hoped that he would be recalled in disgrace but instead he was summoned to imperial headquarters to act as a possible substitute for the chief of staff, Alexandre Berthier, who was on the verge of a nervous breakdown. Soult set off accompanied by a great convoy of waggons loaded with Andalusian loot, and Joseph could at last feel that he was in full command of the armies facing Wellington. He could also feel that he had enough men to defend what was left of his kingdom. The Armies of Portugal, the Centre and the South could deploy 95,000 men† to defend the area between the Douro and the Tagus, a force more than twice as large as that which had been available for the same area in the previous summer. Although there were some Spanish troops north of the Douro and south of the Tagus, these could be watched by negligible flankguards.

Despite his eastern preoccupations, Napoleon would not leave the defence of Spain to Joseph and Jourdan. As soon as he returned to Paris he resumed his habit of giving detailed instructions to subordinate commanders in Spain. He became obsessed with the delays in communication between Bayonne and Valladolid. His Minister of War complained on 16 March that 'seventy two days have

---

* 5,000 of these came from Suchet's armies in eastern Spain, 15,000 from the armies opposed to Wellington.

† Army of the South (Gazan) 36,000, Army of the Centre (d'Erlon) 17,000, Army of Portugal (Reille) 42,000.

passed since the courier left with the emperor's orders [of 3rd January] and I have received no reply'.[4] Impatient at the delay, Napoleon ordered that the six infantry divisions of the Army of Portugal should be made available to the Army of the North to clear the road north-east of Burgos. At last Wellington earned a handsome dividend from his apparently abortive Burgos campaign. To drive him away from that city the French had been forced to collect so many men that northern Spain had reverted to the guerrillas. Now the area north of the Ebro had to be reconquered and the troops to do the job could come only from the armies facing Wellington.

On the Portuguese frontier Joseph was left with 33,000 infantry, 9,000 cavalry and 100 guns. He was unconvinced by reports from Paris that Wellington had only 30,000 British and 20,000 Portuguese. He asked Paris what he should do if the allies attacked before the six divisions returned from the north. 'Should the king, with the Armies of the South and the Centre hold the Douro and risk a battle? Should he retire on Burgos?'[5]

In Paris no one would admit that the problem existed.

> Bearing in mind the circumstances in which the enemy finds himself, there is no reason to suppose that he will take the offensive. His remoteness, his shortage of transport, his constant and timid caution in any operation out of the ordinary, all demonstrate to us that we can act as seems most suitable without worry or inconvenience.[6]

Despite his 'timid caution' Wellington was within seventy-five miles of Burgos on the day this emollient letter was written. He had marched with 52,000 British and 28,000 Portuguese. Twenty-five thousand Spaniards were co-operating with him. 'The troops,' he reported, 'are more healthy than I have ever known them.'[7]

Wellington never favoured disclosing his intentions in advance. Too often in the past had information of his situation or plans appeared in the English papers for the edification of the French. In the early summer of 1813 he indicated to the Secretary of State only that 'I propose to commence our operations by turning the enemy's position on the Douro, by passing the left of our army over that river within the Portuguese frontier. Our next operation must depend on circumstances.' His army was stronger in May 1813 than it was ever likely to be in the future and 'I cannot have a better opportunity for trying the fate of a battle which, if the enemy should be unsuccessful, must oblige him to withdraw altogether.'[8]

The idea of making the French 'withdraw altogether' from Spain had been in his mind, though not in his words, ever since he had heard of the retreat from Moscow. A month before he received the 29me Bulletin he had been guardedly optimistic. 'I propose to get in Fortune's way and we may make a lucky hit in the commencement of the campaign.'[9] After the news arrived he began to make discreet but concrete plans for clearing Spain. He asked for a siege train to be shipped to Coruña. It was not to be disembarked 'as events may render it necessary for the army to undertake one or more sieges in the north of Spain'.[10] Burgos might be regarded as one of these northern fortresses, but there were no others south of the Ebro. At the end of April, he wrote to the admiral off the coast that 'it is not impossible that we may have to communicate with the shipping in one of the ports in the north of Spain'.[11] It was most unlikely that he intended to entangle his army in the rugged mountains of the Asturias. Thus it is certain that by this time he had set his sights on Santander and beyond.

To drive the French behind the Pyrenees would need skill and good fortune. If Joseph could collect the Armies of the South, the Centre and of Portugal and reinforce them from the Army of the North he could oppose Wellington with 100,000 experienced French troops and 'the fate of a battle' would be uncertain in the extreme. Wellington's project entailed driving the French back on their reinforcements. It could succeed only if they were hustled so fast that they had no time to concentrate their armies.

Joseph and Jourdan were in a state of confusion before the campaign opened. They thought that Wellington would advance on the Ciudad Rodrigo–Salamanca road as he had done in 1812. Their plan was to collect the troops immediately available on the Douro, with their right at Toro. There they expected to be able to hold the river line until the infantry of the Army of Portugal returned from the north. This would enable them to fight with equal numbers. A mass of conflicting information reached them at Valladolid. At the end of March it seemed so certain that Wellington was marching on Madrid that reserves were moved towards the capital. In April they were assured that Rodrigo had been handed over to the Spaniards and that the Anglo-Portuguese army was massing in the Tagus valley. Three allied divisions were reported to be approaching Astorga on the north bank of the Douro on 20 May. Two days later a cavalry sweep of that area reported that it was clear of allied troops. As this last report arrived another came that the southern wing of the allied army was moving north but that Wellington was placidly reviewing troops near Rodrigo.

On 24 May General Villatte, whose division held Salamanca, asserted that the allies were marching in great strength on that city. He added that Wellington was sick and was following his army in a coach. Orders for a concentration on the Douro were issued and Villatte withdrew from Salamanca after a brisk skirmish. Three days later Joseph wrote to Clausel, who commanded the Army of the North, asking for the six divisions to be returned 'if your operations are sufficiently advanced to make this possible without compromising the outcome'.[12] This belated and tentative request reflected the pause which fell over the campaign after the loss of Salamanca. The allied advance seemed to have ground to a halt. But the French were soon disabused of this idea. On 2 June the British hussar brigade crashed into the flank of the French position on the Douro at Morales. Joseph's blocking position on the Douro had been turned before it had been fully manned.

Villatte had been right when he had reported that Wellington was marching on Salamanca. He had been wrong about his health. Nor did he appreciate the strength of the force which approached the city. There was a thick screen of cavalry, 4,000 sabres, but behind it were only 29,000 infantry of whom one-third were British.* The bulk of the Anglo-Portuguese army, 50,000 men under Thomas Graham, were on the north bank of the Douro. They had scrambled through the Portuguese province of Tras os Montes by roads the French had believed impassable. A dragoon officer wrote, 'We were two hours getting up one hill, and for three days never got the regi-

---

* Hill's column. Cavalry: British 3,111, Spanish 1,300. Infantry: British 11,310, Portuguese 10,200, Spanish 7,800.

ment out of single files, scrambling over rocks, mountains and precipices for eight hours every day.'[13] To the north of them, marching towards Benavente, were a further 12,000 Spaniards.

Graham's column* crossed the frontier from Bragança and Miranda de Douro on 26 May. Their first obstacle was the river Esla, 'about the width of the Thames at Windsor'.[14] On the last day of May the hussar brigade crossed with infantrymen clinging to their stirrups. The stream was rapid and deeper than had been expected. Chaos ensued. 'There were three regiments of cavalry and two of infantry plunging about in the river and so dark we could scarcely see each other, besides expecting every moment to receive a volley from the enemy.'[15] No volley came. The French cavalry was culpably negligent and their nearest vedette, thirty-three strong, was captured intact. Three days later the Anglo-Portuguese army was complete on the north bank of the Douro at Toro. Hill's corps had marched due north from Salamanca and crossed the river on an improvised bridge. Apart from the Spaniards at Benavente, Wellington's striking force was more than 80,000 strong.† King Joseph, who had only half that number, retreated and wrote letters of increasing desperation to Clausel, begging for the return of the borrowed infantry.

For a fortnight after the hussar action at Morales on 2 June contact between the armies was confined to two minor skirmishes. Wellington's army did not suffer a single battle casualty. In this time Joseph's army retreated 180 miles.

The French were unprepared for the scope of Wellington's manoeuvre. His 'constant and timid caution in any operation out of the ordinary' had become an article of faith in their military thinking. They expected at worst another retreat to Burgos, a pause while their reinforcements came up and a war of manoeuvre in which the allies would probably be pushed back to Rodrigo. In their high command opinions were sharply divided as to how they should proceed. The three army commanders, Gazan (South), d'Erlon (Centre) and Reille (Portugal), advocated standing for a battle on any favourable

---

* Graham's column. Cavalry: British 2,700, Portuguese 900. Infantry: British 29,000, Portuguese 17,000.

† One small Spanish infantry division was left near Salamanca. A larger division and a cavalry brigade stayed with Hill's column when it marched north to Toro.

position. Jourdan as Chief of Staff proposed an offensive to the south of Wellington's line of advance aimed at cutting him off from Portugal. Joseph had to make the decision. He maintained that Napoleon's orders 'enjoined him above all to keep open the direct communications with France'.[16] He believed there was no alternative to falling back on the road to France, gathering up the detached infantry as they went. This displeased the junior officers who were loud for a battle. 'Sarcasm and jests were showered on the prudence of those opposed to fighting. Their prudence was called by another name.'[17]

Jourdan's plan for striking at Wellington's communications was out of date. The allied base was being shifted. The long overland haul from Lisbon was to be abandoned. In future supplies were to be landed in northern Spain. On 10 June, when the army was approaching Burgos, Wellington ordered a convoy of stores to be sent to Santander. The naval officer responsible was to be told that 'if he should find Santander occupied by the enemy, I beg him to remain off the port till the operations of this army have obliged the enemy to abandon it'.[18] Such boldness disconcerted even his own staff.

> Some of my officers remonstrated with me about the imprudence of crossing the Ebro, and advised me to take up the line of that river. I asked them what they meant by taking up the line of the Ebro, a river three hundred miles long, and what good I was to do along that line? I thanked them but said to myself I preferred the Pyrenees.[19]

The French took up a series of delaying positions—on the Pisuerga, at Burgos, on the Ebro. All they saw of their enemy was a handful of cavalry, usually Spaniards. It was a demoralising experience. Gazan's ADC said to a British prisoner, 'What can have become of Lord Wellington? We are in full retreat but we are permitted to move at a leisurely pace. We are not harassed or hurried, we have not lost a single carriage. It is inexplicable to me.'[20]

What the French could not see was the allied army in three huge columns swinging round their right flank. They marched on by-roads 'over a dreary tableland, the surface of which resembled the black incrustations of lava', until on 15 June they reached 'the head of a pass descending into the valley of the Ebro. It was one of the most beautiful views I ever beheld, our admiration was, perhaps, heightened by its contrast with the dreary regions through which we had just passed. It was one of those spots where nature sometimes delights, amid the wildest scenes, to stamp her seal of loveliness. Nor was the enchantment much diminished when, on descending into the valleys, we pursued a road winding through gardens and cherry orchards, the trees of which latter, laden with ripe fruit, seemed inviting us to partake of their abundance.'[21]

The French bewilderment deepened. Their retreat had found the fortifications of Burgos only partially repaired and, although the allies did not attack the castle, French engineers demolished it. Joseph established his army to defend the line of the Ebro between Frias and Haro. Twenty miles beyond their right the allies poured across the river unopposed. Away to the north General Giron and the Spanish army of Galicia seemed to be aiming for Bilbao. 'We keep up our strength,' wrote Wellington, 'and the army is very healthy and in better order than I have ever known it. God knows how long this will last. It depends entirely on the officers.'[22]

Both sides were now deep into the area of the Army of the North but neither had any news of Clausel's movements. Wellington realised that Clausel had enough infantry to pose a serious threat to the main operation. He could cut the allied communications with both Portugal and Santander. To guard against such a move one Anglo-Portuguese division was left at Medina de Pomar, a crucial road junction. The rest of the army marched westward, aiming for Vitoria.

On his retreat Joseph had found three of the divisions of the Army of Portugal, adding 15,000 to his strength. He heard nothing from Clausel or of the 25,000 infantry which were somewhere behind him and who would give him enough men to be able to face the enemy. Messengers scoured the country searching for Clausel. That general was at Pamplona directing a sweep against some of the northern guerrillas. None of the king's letters reached him until 15 June when a batch of three arrived. He immediately called in his troops and marched to join the main army with four divisions. Like the other French commanders he failed to appreciate the scope and speed of Wellington's operation. He expected to find the king near

Burgos and went by the shortest road. When he was needed at Vitoria he was on the Ebro at Logroño.

Joseph had little idea where Wellington's army was, but he did hear of the Galicians' advance towards Bilbao. This posed a threat to his communications with France and he detached Reille with the three available divisions of the Army of Portugal to the north on 18 June. The roads by which they marched intersected those by which Wellington was moving. Two French divisions escaped after a skirmish at Osma. The third, Maucune's, was not so fortunate. It was surprised by the Light Division at San Milan. It was so badly mauled that Joseph considered it fit only for a baggage guard.

Joseph's headquarters was at Miranda de Ebro when he heard of the actions at Osma and San Milan. The Armies of the South and the Centre were still lining the river. The news showed that Wellington was aiming for their rear. Unless they retreated quickly their retreat would be cut off. They risked being pinned against the Ebro with a hostile Spain at their backs. The same British prisoner recalled that 'all the confident and matured arrangements of the French army were at once overset; hurry and confusion followed the knowledge of what had happened, and an immediate night march was the consequence. Drums beat in all directions; cavalry filed past; while the town, crowded with unwieldy ambulances containing plunder, presented a scene of strange confusion.'[23] By the evening of 19 June the whole of King Joseph's army was in the plain of Vitoria.

The French were within sixty-five miles of their own frontier. Wellington had driven them back from Salamanca at a cost of 201 casualties (killed 29, wounded 168, missing 4). He had driven them straight back on their reserves but had done it with such speed and skill that only three out of every eight of those reserves had reached the vital point when the decisive battle was fought on 21 June. It was a manoeuvre which can stand comparison with any of Napoleon's.

A horse gunner wrote on 20 June:

Since I last wrote to you, we have been marching every day, and almost every day, through such a country as few armies have ever attempted to go over, and I really believe none ever performed the

H

like and suffered less. It cannot be supposed that the march of such an army through so difficult a country, and with such despatch, could be accomplished without some privations; but they have been trifling, and they have in no way injured the health, order or equipment of the army, and as the communication is open with Santander we shall be plentifully supplied.[24]

CHAPTER 16

Vitoria

VITORIA lies in a roughly oval plain, twelve miles long and seven across at its widest. The city stands towards the eastern end of the plain. Two miles to the north the river Zadorra passes it, flowing from east to west. Six miles west of Vitoria the river makes a hairpin bend near the village of Tres Puentes. For a time it flows south-east but then, meandering, turns south-west, past the village of Nanclares, and leaves the plain through the defile of La Puebla. The hills round the plain are rugged rather than steep. Infantry could pass over them almost anywhere but guns and formed cavalry would have to keep to the tracks. Vitoria was important as a road centre. In the city the great road from Madrid to the French frontier is crossed by the road from Bilbao to Logroño and the lower Ebro valley. Other roads, most of them suitable only for ox-carts and pack mules, radiate in all directions.

Vitoria has few virtues as a defensive position. King Joseph was a military novice. Jourdan was not a brilliant general but it is inconceivable that either of them would have chosen Vitoria as the site of a battle which would decide the fate of Joseph's kingdom. A day's march to the north-east was the pass of Salinas where a smaller army than Joseph's could have defied one larger than Wellington's.

It was because Vitoria was a road centre that the French stayed there from 19 June to 21 June. It was the most convenient place for Clausel to join them. Tactically it was good for no more than a delaying action. Joseph insisted on staying there so that the lumbering convoys, replete with loot and swarming with *afrancesados*,

Vitoria

could get away to France escorted by the wreck of Maucune's division.

Jourdan spent 20 June in bed wracked with fever. His illness paralysed the French headquarters. Everyone assumed that Wellington would march round their right flank as he had done ever since they had stood on the Douro.

> The town was crowded with carriages and vehicles of all descriptions. A train of siege artillery, useless in a battle, encumbered the outskirts of the city and blocked the road. No new dispositions were made. No orders were issued. This led to the belief that all was well. About 5 p.m. the troops on the Bilbao road were attacked. The firing was sharp but ceased at nightfall. It was announced that it was a guerrilla attack. Nobody believed that. Retreat was proposed but now it was too late. The chance had gone. Our only comfort was the hope that General Clausel might join us before we were attacked. There was nothing else for us to hope. The convoy eventually set off at 2 a.m. on the 21st. They had to leave the siege guns behind as there were not enough draught horses.[1]

No one had taken the trouble to reconnoitre the road leading due east to Salvatierra which would be their only line of retreat if Wellington did swing round their right and cut the Bayonne road.[2]

The army was 60,000 strong including the enlisted Spaniards and some details of Clausel's force who had been swept up on the retreat. There were 11,000 cavalry and 138 field guns.[6/8] The main strength was deployed to cover the exit from the Puebla defile. Although only a piquet defended the defile itself, four-and-a-half divisions of the Army of the South held the first line in the plain behind. Maransin's brigade held the village of Subijana de Alava as an advanced post and almost a mile behind them three divisions blocked the gap between the hills and the river. Their left was in the hamlet of Zumelzu on the high ground; their right on a knoll in a bend of the river opposite Nanclares. Villatte's division was in reserve near Arinez.

The Army of the Centre was in second line. Both the infantry divisions were near Villatte's, in the area of, and possibly on, the isolated hill of Arinez. To their right was the hairpin bend of the Zadorra, crossed by three bridges. The river was not deep but its steep banks made it impassable for cavalry and artillery and a difficult obstacle for infantry. D'Erlon neglected the defences of this bend.

He left all the bridges standing and allocated less than 500 cavalry to guarding them.

In the original dispositions of the French army the Army of Portugal had been allocated a third-line position on a well-marked ridge near the village of Zuazo de Alava, three miles west of Vitoria. After the outburst of firing on the Bilbao road on the evening of 20 June the king ordered them to move to their right and face north with one division on either side of the river. To their right, on the eastern bank, were Casapalacios' Spaniards, reinforced by the detachments of the Army of the North. The result of this redeployment was that the Armies of the South and of Portugal were six miles apart and had their backs to each other. The only general reserve consisted of the Royal Guards, less than 3,000 strong, who were stationed on the Zuazo ridge.

Marshal Jourdan had recovered from his fever by the morning of the 21st. At dawn he set off with the king on a leisurely inspection of their position. They had no expectation of attack. By the time they reached the Zuazo ridge they had decided that it would be better if the Army of the South was pulled back to the ridge on which they stood. They sent a message to General Gazan asking him to ride back and discuss the move with them. Gazan replied that heavy columns were approaching the Puebla defile.

The French were right in thinking that Wellington was planning to turn their right flank. What they did not appreciate was that this was only part of his scheme. The allied army[5/11] was divided into four columns. One of these, 20,000 men under Thomas Graham, formed the left of the army and was marching round Monte Arrato, the block of hills which marked the north-western side of the Vitoria plain. Graham's orders were to advance down the Bilbao road towards Vitoria and to cut the main road from the city to France.

The right-hand column, 20,000 men under Rowland Hill, was given the task of forcing the Puebla defile, an operation which would certainly draw the attention of most if not all of the Army of the South. On Hill's left was the main striking force under Wellington's own control. This consisted of the Light and Fourth Divisions and 4,500 cavalry. Wellington intended moving it along the north bank of the Zadorra and putting it across the river at the bridges south of the hairpin bend, on the flank or rear of the Army of the South. The remaining, left centre, column consisted of two divisions under Lord Dalhousie. It was to advance over the western shoulder of Monte Arrato and aim for the bridge of Mendoza, east of the hairpin, acting as a link between the columns of Wellington and Graham.

If Wellington's plan worked perfectly Joseph's army would be surrounded and destroyed. Wellington, however, recognised that such a concentric manoeuvre, depending on long approach marches over difficult roads without lateral communication, was unlikely to succeed completely. He was prepared to be satisfied with routing the French army if he could not capture it entire.

Gazan had seen Hill's troops marching towards the defile. They were led by Morillo's Spanish division who turned off to their right, swarmed up the hill and drove the French piquet off the heights. The Second Division moved through the defile and started to deploy in the plain. Gazan's reaction was to send the nearest troops, Maransin's brigade from Subijana, to recapture the heights. Hill responded by sending Cadogan's brigade to reinforce Morillo. Seeing this Gazan sent his reserve division, Villatte's, to Maransin's support. Thus Gazan had detached one-third of his force to his extreme left and was much worried when another strong body of troops, Wellington's column, marched along the opposite bank of the river and halted near Nanclares.

By this time Joseph and Jourdan had galloped forward to join him on the knoll in the Nanclares bend of the river. He asked for reinforcement from d'Erlon's army but was roughly refused. 'Marshal Jourdan announced loudly and publicly that all movements against our right were feints to which no attention must be paid. If we lost the battle it would be because the heights on the left of the Zadorra remained in the hands of the enemy.'[3]

Abandoning the belief that the French right was to be turned, Jourdan became obsessed with the idea that Wellington's main blow would come from due south. He sent one of d'Erlon's divisions and some dragoons to block the road from Logroño. Nothing could have suited Wellington better.

Wellington had intended to pass the Light Division across the bridge of Villodas. This seemed likely to be a bloody operation and he was relieved when a peasant came with the news that the bridge of Tres Puentes, near the point of the hairpin, was intact and unguarded. Kempt's brigade, supported by the Fifteenth Hussars, doubled round to the bridge and crossed, installing themselves on a knoll within the bend. This irruption within their lines was ignored by the French command. 'Sir James Kempt expressed much surprise at our critical position and at our not being molested. Some French dragoons coolly and at a slow pace came to within fifty yards of us but a few shots from the Rifles caused them to decamp. As I looked over the bank I could see *El Rey* Joseph, surrounded by at least 5,000 men, within five hundred yards of us.'[4]

Meanwhile the Second Division had taken Subijana, vacated by Maransin when he moved up to the heights, without firing a shot. Two French divisions counter-attacked but their advance was tentative and they made no impression. On the heights the battle was much fiercer. Cadogan was killed and for a time his brigade was reduced to clinging to the edge of the summit. For a time the French could feel that they had stabilised the situation. Jourdan continued in his belief that the main allied thrust would come up the Logroño road.

There was a lull in the battle but this had been imposed not by the French counter-attacks but by Wellington's orders. Graham's circuitous march had taken longer than was anticipated and it was not until noon that his leading troops came within sight of the Army of Portugal on the Bilbao road. At about the same time Dalhousie's column began to appear over Monte Arrato. Hearing firing north of Vitoria, Jourdan realised that he had misread the battle. It was urgently necessary to bring Gazan's men back to Vitoria so that the wings of the French army could support each other. The Army of the South was ordered to fall back 'to a position which Marshal Jourdan would point out'.[5]

Dalhousie's leading division, the Third, crossed the river without difficulty. A feeble attempt to resist them was outflanked by Kempt's men. The Fourth Division crossed at Nanclares as Gazan withdrew and Wellington was able to deploy a line of three-and-a-half divisions,* supported by a large number of guns, between the hills and the river. On their right, Hill's corps started to march eastward south of the road with its right moving along the crest of the heights.

The heaviest fighting was to the north of Vitoria. The Army of Portugal was driven back to the riverline but the allies could not force the bridges. Only on the extreme left did they make any progress. Longa's Spaniards drove their renegade compatriots away from the bridge at Durana and cut the main road to France. They could not advance further and the Salvatierra road remained open.

The first position attacked by Wellington's line of battle was a ridge near the village of Arinez. The village was first taken by two companies of Riflemen who captured three French guns. They were driven out by two battalions of Frenchmen charging up the street in column. More Riflemen counter-attacked screening Picton's division. Riding among the greenjackets was Wellington, oblivious to the French fire, 'calling out, "That's right, my lads! Keep up a good fire." '6 Seeing the Connaught Rangers coming up behind 'in extreme disorder, I halted them and made them form under the brow of the hill. As soon as formed they advanced in good order and drove [the French] into and through Arinez.'7

The French attempted another stand on the Zuazo ridge. Their field artillery was powerful and well handled but their infantry did not have their hearts in the fight. The long retreat had demoralised them and every man could hear over his right shoulder the heavy firing as Graham tried to storm the bridge at Gamarra Mayor. If that fell they would all be prisoners. Matters were made worse by the spinelessness of Gazan. He had been told that Jourdan would show him a new position for the Army of the South. In the confusion the marshal failed to do so. Instead of choosing one of the well-marked positions on his retreat Gazan continued to fall back by divisions in succession, constantly exposing the flank of the Army of the Centre on his right. Only the Army of Portugal fought stoutly holding the line of the Zadorra until their left was threatened by Wellington's advance. Then they retired in good order, covering the retreat of their comrades, a retreat which soon became a rout.

---

* From right to left: Fourth, Light, Third and Grant's brigade of Seventh Division.

In and around Vitoria there was chaos. The streets were jammed
with carriages, waggons, guns and limbers. Into this confusion
Wellington launched the hussar brigade who swept round the north
of the city spreading consternation and panic. The drivers cut the
traces and rode off on their teams leaving the road blocked with
guns. The king narrowly escaped capture and galloped off the field
on a troop horse. Only one field gun and one howitzer accompanied
the troops on the retreat.

As the British advanced,

> every step we took proved the decided nature of the *déroute* that had
> overtaken the French army. Cannon, overturned carriages, broken
> down waggons, forsaken tumbrils, wounded soldiers, civilians,
> women, children, dead horses and mules absolutely covered the
> face of the country.[8]

> Beside the military chest, there was the baggage of King Joseph
> and his court. In fact the battle of Vitoria was to the French like salt
> on a leech's tail. The plunder of Spain was disgorged in a single
> throe.[9]

> The road to Pamplona was choked with carriages filled with im-
> ploring ladies, waggons loaded with specie, powder and ball,
> wounded soldiers, intermixed with droves of oxen, sheep, goats,
> mules, horses, asses, milch cows, *filles de chambres* and officers. In
> fact, such a jumble surely was never seen before. Our brigade
> marched past this strange scene of domestic strife in close column,
> nor did I see a soldier attempt to quit the ranks.[10]

Other brigades were not so well disciplined. An orgy of looting
took place. The hussars set an example, eagerly followed by the rag
tag and bobtail of all the armies—British, Spanish, Portuguese and
French—and by the civilians. The strongboxes of the French pay-
master were broken open and the contents vanished in a flash leaving Wellington seething with rage since he needed the money
urgently to pay the expenses of the army.

> The soldiers of the army have got among them about a million
> sterling, with the exception of about 100,000 dollars which were got
> for the military chest. The night of the battle, instead of being
> passed in getting rest and food for the pursuit of the following day,
> was passed by the soldiers in looking for plunder. The consequence
> was that they were incapable of marching and were totally knocked

up. The new regiments are, as usual, the worst of all. The Eighteenth Hussars are a disgrace to the name of soldier, in action as well as elsewhere; and I propose to draft their horses from them and send the men to England if I cannot get the better of them in any other manner.[11]

Looting was not the only reason for the failure of the pursuit. The infantry had covered twenty miles during the day and could not be expected to go further. Not all the cavalry behaved as badly as the Eighteenth but they could not operate effectively. The Salvatierra road on which the French were flying was 'so intersected with impassable ravines, ditches, etc., that our advance was broken and impeded at every step'.[12] Two French regiments, 15me Dragoons and 3me Hussars, were a strong enough rearguard to hold the width of the narrow valley in which the road ran. The French infantry got away unmolested but disorganised.

King Joseph, exhausted and dishevelled, reached Salvatierra at eleven o'clock at night. He was having supper with his staff when Jourdan arrived. 'As he entered, he said, "Well, gentlemen, you would have a battle and we seem to have lost it." Then he sat down to share our meagre meal and nothing more was said.'[13] Jourdan's baton was among the trophies left on the field. Wellington sent it to the Prince Regent who replied, 'You have sent me, among the trophies of your unrivalled fame, the staff of a French marshal, and I send you in return that of England.'[14] *

Vitoria was not a particularly large or bloody battle. The French lost 8,000 men, the allies 5,000.† King Joseph was able to reassemble his army, about 50,000 men, but with only a single howitzer,‡ on the Pyrenees where he was joined by Clausel and the garrisons of northern Spain. This brought his strength up to 79,000 infantry and cavalry.

---

* This caused some embarrassment in England, since, as the Military Secretary wrote to Wellington, 'It does not appear that there has ever been an English baton. I am therefore getting one prepared to present to each of our Marshals and if I am not interfered with from the *Fountain of Taste*, I trust it will be found an appropriate badge of command.'

† British 3,675, Portuguese 921, Spanish 562.

‡ The only field gun brought away from Vitoria was captured on 24 June.

The French kingdom of Spain was at an end. At the beginning of August Joseph's realm consisted of three beleaguered fortresses.* He was in despair and wrote to his wife, 'I do not think that affairs in Spain can be re-established except by a general peace. I am staying here because the frontier is in danger but as soon as the first wave of terror wears off and the defence is organised I shall be useless. I cannot see there is anything for me to do once the emperor has taken the appropriate steps.'[15]

The effects of Vitoria were felt far beyond Spain. The war on France's eastern front had reached a critical stage. The momentum of the Russian advance had slackened as soon as French troops had been cleared from Russian territory. In this breathing space Napoleon had created a new army, an administrative feat of genius. At the start of the campaign of 1813 he took the field with more men than the Russians and their new allies the Prussians could bring against him. He defeated them at Lützen on 2 May, recaptured Dresden and the alliance of the King of Saxony. Before the end of the month he won another victory at Bautzen.

Lützen and Bautzen were only tactical victories and achieved nothing. Napoleon's new army was cripplingly short of cavalry and his young infantry had not the stamina of their predecessors. No effective pursuit could be undertaken. Both battles were won at enormous cost to the French. At Bautzen alone Napoleon lost more men than both armies together had lost at Vitoria. The only gain was the loss of confidence among the Russian and Prussian commanders. They realised that they could not win the war unless Austria joined them. Despairingly they asked for a suspension of hostilities. Napoleon, whose situation was little better than theirs, agreed. By the Armistice of Pleischwitz, signed on 4 June,† it was agreed that fighting should cease until the end of July, a date that was later extended to 17 August.

Austria, Prussia and Russia had a low opinion of the part Britain had played in the war against Napoleon. Their experiences of co-

---

* Suchet still occupied eastern Spain north of the Ebro but this had been annexed to France in 1812 as four *départements*, Montserrat, Segre, Bouches D'Ebre and Ter.

† News of the Armistice reached Wellington from captured French newspapers on 19 June, two days before Vitoria (Frazer 154).

operating with the British army in Italy, at Cuxhaven and at the
Helder, had given them little regard for Britain's military capabili-
ties. The power of the Royal Navy was hardly considered. Britain's
value to an anti-French coalition was measured solely in terms of the
subsidies she could provide from her apparently illimitable stock of
gold. On 6 June 1813 Charles Stewart,* who was leading the British
military mission to the eastern powers, wrote to his brother, the
Foreign Secretary, 'We are not considered here (from all I see going
on). Wellington must send you a victory to bruit forth with the
Armistice.'[16]

With infinite patience Castlereagh built up a coalition of Prussia,
Russia and Sweden and cemented it with sterling. Austria continued
to haver. The Emperor Francis II was unwilling to wage war on his
son-in-law. Metternich, the chief minister, was convinced that
Napoleon must be overthrown but unwilling to commit his country
until victory was certain. From London the Prime Minister wrote to
Wellington, 'If Austria would declare war, we might really hope to
put an end to the tyranny which has been so long oppressing the
world; but on this event no reliance can, I fear, be placed.'[17]

Vitoria and the liberation of Spain could not have been better
timed. The news reached London on 3 July and 'every precaution
was taken to transmit the Gazette in French, Dutch and German to
the different parts of the coast, beside a messenger being sent to
Stralsund† and to the headquarters of the Russian and Prussian
armies'.[18] The news reached the Austrian court in the middle of the
night. Metternich was woken by a colleague who burst into his
bedroom crying, 'Le roi Joseph est f—— en Espagne!' Mobilisation
was ordered immediately and Austria declared war on France on 12
August. Count Nugent took a copy of Wellington's dispatch to
Francis II who 'received it with the greatest joy' and sent a message
to Wellington that 'he would be happy to give you the command of
the army if you could come here, and the Emperor of Russia said
the same thing'.[19]

---

* He had been Wellington's Adjutant General until April 1812.
† This was for the information of the Prince Royal of Sweden, formerly Marshal
Bernadotte. He was Joseph Bonaparte's brother-in-law and by 1813 was a leading
member of the coalition against Napoleon.

Napoleon received an incomplete account of Vitoria at Dresden on 1 July. He immediately wrote to Joseph:

> I have decided it would be proper to nominate Marshal Soult as my lieutenant general and commander in chief of all my armies in Spain and in the Pyrenees. You will hand over command to him. You will put your Guard and the armed Spaniards under the Marshal's orders. It is my wish that you do not interfere with the affairs of my armies.[20]

The king was to retire to some suitable country house, preferably within Spain although if necessary he might go as far into France as Bayonne. The Minister of Police was instructed that 'if the king comes to Paris you must arrest him'.[21] To the government and the army Joseph was to be the scapegoat.

> It is all his fault [wrote the Emperor]. The English accounts show how stupidly the army was commanded. Of course the king is not a soldier but he is responsible for his vices and the greatest fault is to follow a profession one does not understand. If there was one man lacking in the army it was a general. If there was one man too many it was the king.[22]

The Emperor's brother could not be publicly disgraced, and for a time the French newspapers ignored the whole affair. Nearly six weeks after Vitoria Napoleon was prepared to issue only a guarded statement to the press.

> It would be advisable to let the public know about affairs in Spain. Nothing must be said of Vitoria and the king. The first notice in *Le Moniteur* should read, 'His Majesty has appointed the Duke of Dalmatia [Soult] as lieutenant general commanding his armies in Spain. The marshal assumed command on 12th July and immediately made dispositions for marching against the English who are besieging Pamplona and San Sebastian.'[23]

CHAPTER 17

San Sebastian and the Pyrenees

SOULT took over as commander-in-chief on 12 July. His first act was to sweep away the forlorn titles of the Armies of the North, South, Centre and Portugal and combine all the troops into a single Army of Spain. Apart from essential garrisons he had 72,000 infantry and 7,000 cavalry. The broken country of the Pyrenees made the latter almost useless. The arsenal at Bayonne produced 140 field guns and the horses to draw them were procured from the southern *départements*. He organised the infantry into three corps, which a whim of the Emperor's insisted on calling 'lieutenancies', and a large, amorphous Reserve.[6/9]

Napoleon's orders required him to 're-establish my affairs in Spain and to preserve Pamplona and San Sebastian'.[1] Both fortresses had been under siege since the end of June and the experience of Ciudad Rodrigo and Badajoz showed the French that Wellington was capable of taking a fortress with astonishing speed. In the fortnight after his arrival Soult performed a remarkable feat in changing an army which was demoralised and lacking artillery, discipline and rations into a formidable force which could fight the allies on equal terms. Indiscipline and hatred of service in Spain could not be quickly eradicated but in late July the Army of Spain gave Wellington the most dangerous week of his whole command in the Peninsula.

Wellington wrote that 'I think that I can hold the Pyrenees as easily as I can Portugal',[2] but the line of the Pyrenees could not be secure while San Sebastian and Pamplona were held against him. Pamplona commanded two of the three roads from France into

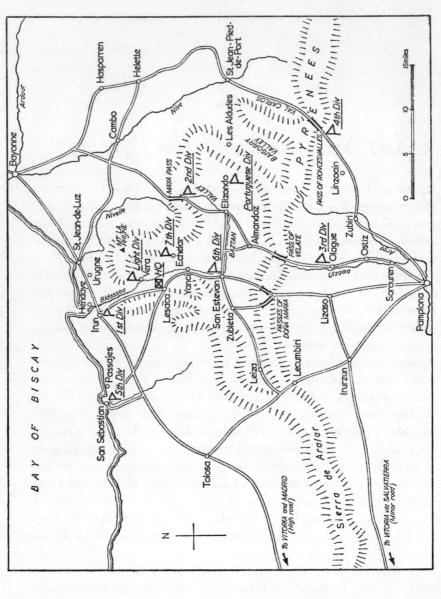

Pyrenees – position of Allied divisions on 25 July 1813

Spain. San Sebastian was dangerously near the third and possessed a fine port which was needed for supplies from Britain which, until it was captured, had to be unloaded at the sheltered but difficult small harbour at Passajes. Having only one siege train, Wellington decided to use it against San Sebastian. Pamplona was blockaded by Spanish troops. Starvation was the only possible counter weapon.

Wellington's main problem was the disposition of his covering force. It had to cover two sieges forty miles apart and separated by the rugged Sierra de Aralar, the range which joins the Pyrenees to the Cantabrian mountains of northern Spain. The passes across this Sierra were few and rough so that the siege of Pamplona and the divisions covering it were almost isolated from the rest of the army. Reinforcement of this end of the front must be a lengthy business. The only consolation was that the front line position on the Pass of Roncesvalles was immensely strong by nature.

Sixty-two thousand infantry and artillery* were available for the covering force. Covering Pamplona was Lowry Cole with the re-inforced Fourth Division at Roncesvalles. To support them was Picton's Third which was stationed well to the rear at Olague, where the main pass over the Sierra de Aralar debouches into the lower ground round Pamplona. North of the Sierra was Hill's corps (Second and Portuguese Divisions) in the Baztan valley guarding the Maya pass and the smaller passes to the right of it. The coastal plain, immediately covering the siege of San Sebastian, was en-trusted to a Spanish force supported by the First Division. Head-quarters was at Lesaca between the Baztan and coastal sectors and close by were two divisions, Seventh and Light, which could be used as reserves. 'The truth is,' wrote Wellington, 'that having two objects in hand, viz. the siege of San Sebastian and the blockade of Pamplona, we are not so strong as we ought to be.'[3] It was clear that Soult could bring overwhelming strength at any single point. What remained to be seen was whether Wellington could move his reserves quickly enough to stop the French relieving one or both of the fortresses.

Wellington expected that Soult would strike first for San Seba-

---

* The cavalry was stationed well to the rear at Vitoria except for two brigades of light dragoons which were needed forward to keep up the lateral communications.

stian. The town seemed ripe to be taken whereas Pamplona was known to have supplies for some weeks to come. Spies reported that materials for two pontoon bridges were stored near the lower Bidassoa and although they also told of a concentration of French troops on the inland sector, this could well be a feint. 'It would appear that he entertains serious designs to draw our attention from the side of Irun, and then attempt to pass the river.'[4]

Soult had decided to strike for Pamplona. Small boats brought out regular reports from San Sebastian and the governor assured him that the place was in no immediate danger. From Pamplona he had heard nothing. He had intended to have all three corps concentrated and ready to attack on 24 July. Difficulties in providing four days' rations for 53,000 men caused the attack to be postponed for twenty-four hours. By coincidence Thomas Graham, commanding on the allied left, intended to storm San Sebastian on the 25th.

That morning Wellington was at his headquarters at Lesaca. He was noticed as being 'very anxious' about the storm.

> He came out to the churchyard, where we were listening, about eight o'clock, to judge from the noise of the guns whether our batteries had ceased and what the firing was. He appeared to wish to leave it to Graham, and not directly to interfere. At eleven, however, Colonel Burgh came over with the account of our attempt having failed. Lord Wellington has ordered his horse and is going over immediately.[5]

Soon after he had left Lesaca, firing was heard there from the allied right. In the middle of the afternoon a message arrived to say that the French had attacked at the Maya but had been beaten off. Firing was still audible and Murray, the Quartermaster-General, put the two reserve divisions on immediate readiness to move. He could do no more in Wellington's absence without more definite information.

Wellington returned about 9 pm to be greeted by a message from Lowry Cole. This had been written at noon and reported that he had been attacked at Roncesvalles but that he had held his ground. Wellington continued to believe that both these attacks on his right were feints. At 10 pm he wrote: 'It is impossible to judge of Soult's plan yet. One can hardly believe that with 30,000 men he proposes to force himself through the passes of the mountains. The remainder of his force, one would think, must come into operation on some other point, either tomorrow or the day after.'[6] Even if the attacks on the right were Soult's main effort, there was no reason to believe that the positions at Maya and Roncesvalles could not be held until reinforcements arrived.

Soult had indeed decided to 'force himself through the passes of the mountains' not with 30,000 men but with 60,000. D'Erlon's corps was to force the Maya pass and then seize the Col de Velate, the main pass over the Sierra de Aralar and Wellington's best road for passing reinforcements to his right. Simultaneously, the corps of Clausel and Reille were to fight their way through Roncesvalles and march on Pamplona. The French could be assured of great numerical superiority in both attacks but speed was essential. It was recognised that no food could be obtained from the country and if the four days' rations issued before the attack started did not last long enough to get the troops to Pamplona the army would have to retreat to France or starve.

At Maya the defence was mismanaged. William Stewart was in immediate charge of the pass with two British brigades of Second Division.* He 'decided that the enemy would not attack him: and he sent half the troops a league to the rear and ordered the whole to cook, and went himself to Elizondo',[7] nearly ten miles in the rear.

The commander of the outlying piquet reported that he had seen 'a group of horses and a column of troops pass along the face of a distant hill at dawn and disappear. A deputy quarter-master general came up soon after; rode a little in front, said there was, indeed, a small column discernible but it was only a change of bivouac or some trifling movement of no consequence. The light companies were ordered up by this officer as a measure of precaution: a weak and insufficient one. In less than two hours my piquet and the light companies were heavily engaged. It was a surprise, and it was not a surprise.'[8] The signal guns were fired and in the camps below the

---

* These were the 1st and 3rd brigades of Second Division (see Order of Battle for Vitoria on p 382). The 1st brigade was commanded at Maya by Lieut-Col John Cameron and the 3rd by Maj-Gen William Pringle.

pass the two brigades fell in 'and got away up hill as fast as we could (the men never went on parade at any time but in heavy marching order, just as if they were never going to return to the same spot); but the pass up was narrow, steep and tiresome, the loads heavy, and the men blown. We laboured on but all too late—our comrades were *all* killed wounded or prisoners. The enemy had full possession of the ground; some ten thousand men were there.'[9]

All morning the two brigades fought to regain the crest, but there were only 4,000 of them and d'Erlon had 20,000, although the narrowness of the pass made it impossible for the French to deploy their full strength. When Stewart returned from his ride early in the afternoon losses had been heavy on both sides. He ordered the survivors to take a position immediately below the crest, but they were attacked in overwhelming force. They must have been swept away in rout, but Barnes' brigade of Seventh Division had marched to their assistance by a lateral track and charged in unexpectedly on the French flank, causing a temporary panic. The situation was saved, but Stewart's brigades had suffered 1,347 casualties. Hill ordered a retreat to Elizondo at nightfall.

At Roncesvalles Cole had 11,000 men.* He defended his position successfully all day with only moderate loss. Late in the afternoon a thick mist rolled up and Cole 'determined to retire from the pass, which it was evident could not be maintained against the very great superiority of the force opposed to me, amounting to from 30,000 to 35,000 men'.[10] He was worried by the sound of firing behind his right flank caused by a demonstration by National Guards. In fact his force could have held the pass for a long time and his orders, several times repeated, were to hold his ground 'to the utmost'.[11] Cole was a man of outstanding bravery but found responsibility intolerable. Wellington did not blame him for retiring when he judged it right to do so but did find fault with his failure to pass information. 'General Cole never told me exactly how far he found it necessary to give way, or let me know by what a superior force he was pressed, and that he intended giving way, or my arrangements

---

* Cole's force at Roncesvalles consisted of Fourth Division (as at Vitoria except that Maj-Gen Robert Ross commanded 2nd Brigade), Byng's brigade of Second Division and Morillo's Spanish Division.

would have been quite different; and the French might have been stopped sooner than they were.'[12]

With no message from Cole dated later than noon on 25 July, Wellington spent most of the 26th arranging for troops to meet d'Erlon's column coming down the Baztan, believing this to be the main French thrust. 'I suspected that all Soult's plan was merely by manoeuvres to get me out of the hills and I expected him to turn round short towards San Sebastian.'[13] By noon the situation around Elizondo was secure, and since there was still no news from Cole he decided to ride over the Col de Velate and see for himself. He ordered one division, the Sixth, to follow.

At 8 pm, when he was nearing the crest of the pass, he received a letter from Cole. It was written from a point ten miles in rear of Roncesvalles and was defeatist in tone. Although he was retreating down a valley abounding in good defensive positions, Cole spoke of retreating to Pamplona and expressed the intention 'to take the road to Vitoria, if obliged to fall back farther than Pamplona'.[14]

Wellington's only consolation was that Picton, who was senior to Cole, should by this time have joined his own division to the Fourth. No one could imagine Picton shirking a fight, but to make certain a letter was sent pointing out 'to you how necessary it is that the advance of the enemy should be checked'.[15] This letter arrived too late. Picton had already met Cole and taken counsel from his junior's fears. He ordered the whole force, 17,000 men, to retreat on Pamplona.

The 26th July was a bad day for Soult. He achieved almost nothing. D'Erlon had been severely shaken by his success the day before at the Maya. He had lost about 2,000 men in forcing the pass and Barnes' surprise attack had given him an obsession about the safety of his right flank. He spent most of the 26th sending out cautious reconnaissances and the head of his corps had advanced only six miles when it bivouacked for the night. At Roncesvalles things went little better. The mist persisted and Cole's departure was not discovered until dawn. Clausel's corps was sent in pursuit but did not come up with the allied rearguard until 4 pm. At nightfall his leading units had got no further than Linzoain, fifteen miles from Pamplona. Reille's corps had the worst day and achieved least. Soult decided to send them towards the Col de Velate by a goat track. Led by Foy's division, the corps set out in single file in the mist. They had local guides but they, being Basques, had no common language with the general. After blundering about on the mountains for several hours the corps found its way back to the main Pamplona road and took its place behind Clausel's column. Half the four days' rations issued had been eaten. Time was running out.

As Wellington rode down towards Olague in the dawn he heard stories that Picton and Cole had retired to Pamplona. It was not until 10 am when he was within seven miles of the fortress that he learned from a cavalry brigadier that Picton had taken up a defensive position at Sorauren, just in front of the blockade line. There was no news about the position of the French advanced guard.

As a position to cover the blockade of Pamplona Sorauren was excellent, but it had one serious drawback. The quickest road by which reinforcements could arrive led to a crossroads in front of the left flank of the position. Once the French closed up to the ridge, allied reinforcements would have to come by the roundabout route through Lizaso. It was urgent for Wellington to divert the Sixth Division to this new road. Then he must buy time for them to arrive.

Murray was left at Ostiz to redirect the troops as they came up. Wellington with Lord Fitzroy Somerset* rode down to Sorauren bridge. As they approached, French cavalry came in sight. Sitting on the parapet of the bridge, Wellington wrote a short note to Murray and sent it off with Somerset.

> It was rather alarming, certainly, and it was a close run thing. People were saying to me all the time, 'The French are coming! The French are coming!' I looked pretty sharp after them, however, every now and then until I had completed my orders and then set off and I saw them just near one end of the village as I went out at the other.[16]

The position at Sorauren, although shorter and less high, is almost as strong as the ridge at Busaco. It was occupied by Cole with

---

* His Military Secretary who later became Lord Raglan, Commander-in-Chief in the Crimea.

13,000 men.* Picton's division was on the right on a lower ridge, two miles further back, guarding the outer flank. Clausel urged Soult to attack at once with the 15,000 men already available. Soult hesitated. Reille's corps would be available by evening but the following day would be the last for which rations were available. He had no news of d'Erlon's progress. As the marshal debated with himself there was a stir on the Sorauren ridge. A single horseman on a panting horse rode up the left flank of the ridge from the village below.

> One of Campbell's Portuguese battalions first descried him and raised a joyful cry; then the shrill clamour, caught up by the next regiments, soon swelled as it ran along the line into that stern appalling shout which the British soldier is wont to give on the edge of battle. Suddenly, he stopped at a conspicuous point, for he desired both armies should know he was there.[17]

An officer recalled that Wellington was 'wearing his grey frock coat, buttoned close up to the chin, with his little cocked hat, covered with oil skin, without a feather. I cannot adequately express the sense of confidence and assurance that was revived by his presence in the midst of a single division of his army; cheers were vehemently raised along the whole line.'[18]

Soult's mind was made up. He called for his mid-day meal and afterwards refreshed himself with a short sleep. 'Meanwhile Clausel was leaning against an oak tree beating his forehead with rage and muttering, "Who could go to sleep at a moment like this?"'[19] Later in the day, when Reille's divisions were beginning to arrive, Soult authorised two probing attacks. They achieved nothing. The main attack was set for 1 pm on the following day. Wellington had won twenty-four hours by his calculatedly theatrical appearance. The day ended with a storm. 'The thunder and lightning were appalling and the rain came down like a cataract. Though there was no shelter the order was "No greatcoats or blankets to be loosed"; consequently we were miserably wet and cold and passed a sad night among the grass.'[20]

---

* The troops he had commanded at Roncesvalles and Campbell's brigade from the Portuguese Division which had retreated diagonally from Hill's corps.

The Sixth Division was in line on Cole's left long before the French launched their attack on the 28th. Soult still had an advantage in numbers but this was not enough to compensate for the strength of the allied position. In two places the French gained a foothold on the crest by driving back Spanish or Portuguese units but, wrote Wellington, 'I ordered the Twenty Seventh and Forty Eighth regiments to charge, first that body of the enemy which had established themselves on the height, and next, those on the left. Both attacks succeeded and the enemy were driven down with immense loss.'[21] 'I never saw such fighting as we have had here. The battle was fair bludgeon work.'[22]

The allies lost 2,652 men at Sorauren. Soult admitted to 1,800 casualties, but he was notorious for understating his losses.* His position was unenviable. His troops were at the end of their rations. Nothing was to be had from the country in his rear. There was no hope of breaking through Wellington's position which was being entrenched and reinforced. His last news from d'Erlon, dated early on the 27th, was that he had reached Elizondo but was faced with superior forces.

As it happened, these superior forces withdrew from d'Erlon's front. Wellington had ordered Hill to close in to the right. By the night of 28 July Hill's corps was around Lizaso, and next morning Soult's light cavalry met patrols sent out by d'Erlon at Ostiz. This offered Soult a solution to his dilemma. His pride would not allow him to retreat by the way he had come, but contact with his third corps made it possible for him to move his army to its right, use d'Erlon as an advanced guard and return to France by the Bidassoa valley. He announced that he was moving to relieve San Sebastian but he can scarcely have believed this a possibility. His only chance of escape lay in doing something so improbable that Wellington could not guess what he intended.

The first task was to withdraw the army from the position facing Sorauren on to the Ostiz road. This entailed marching across Wellington's front which had been extended on the 29th by the addition of Seventh Division on the left. Soult ordered this difficult

---

* The losses at Sorauren reported to Soult by Clausel and Reille amounted to more than 3,000, and even these were probably incomplete.

operation to be performed during the night of 29–30 July. The summer night was too short. At dawn the allies could see three divisions straggling across the hillside within cannon-shot. A bombardment was immediately opened. Soon the allied line moved forward. There was a fierce fight around Sorauren village where a gallant French rearguard strove to cover the retreat of their comrades. Foy's division on the left of the French line had no chance of following the rest of the army. Foy wrote, 'We were not looking for a fight and we were in close formation under the enemy's guns.' When Wellington's right wing swept forward, Foy gave orders for a retreat on Roncesvalles. As he went he gathered up units and stragglers from the rest of the army. Although his own division comprised less than 6,000 men, 'we made up a corps of 10 or 12,000 men collected confusedly from Reille's corps with parts of Clausel's; half the soldiers were straggling and were concerned only with their own safety; many were wounded. It was very hot; the soldiers were exhausted, demoralised, frightened. Two strong enemy columns followed us.'[23]

At the front of the French column d'Erlon managed to drive Hill back a short distance, thus clearing the flank of Soult's retreat. Wellington assumed that the French would fall back by the Maya pass and directed his pursuit accordingly. Soult's determination to go by the gorge of the Bidassoa saved his army but nearly destroyed it. Everything depended on whether the bridge of Yanci could be seized intact and held open while the long column passed over it. It was defended by a single Spanish unit, the 2nd Regiment of the Asturias, which put up a determined defence. Unfortunately it was not reinforced by other units of Longa's division which held the riverline to their left. They stopped the head of Soult's column for two hours but were eventually driven away by an attack by five battalions from d'Erlon's corps. The road to Echelar was open and the leading French divisions poured up it in confusion.

Even now the troubles of the French were not over. The Light Division had been at Leiza that morning, thirty miles away. At 1 am they were ordered to march to the Bidassoa and head the enemy off. Inevitably they failed. The leading brigade arrived in time to see the French rearguard marching through the gorge.

We overlooked the enemy at a stone's throw and from the edge of a tremendous precipice. The river separated us, but the French were wedged in a narrow road with inaccessible rocks on one side and the river on the other. Confusion impossible to describe followed; the wounded were thrown down in the rush and trampled upon; the cavalry drew their swords and endeavoured to charge up the pass of Echelar (the only opening on their right flank) but the infantry beat them back and several of them, horses and all, were precipitated into the river. At length they got a battalion up behind a stone wall, from whose fire we received some damage, consequently those poor fellows who had afterwards to pass were not so much exposed.[24]

Soult's army was back on French soil by 2 August. He had relieved neither of the fortresses and he had not defeated the allied army, although he had inflicted almost 7,000 casualties on them. His own losses were more than 13,000 of whom 1,300 were killed and 2,700 captured. His most serious loss was among the officers. Of 1,318 infantry officers who embarked on the short campaign, 423 were casualties. Morale among the troops dropped sharply and desertion became a serious problem.

Wellington was tempted to pursue the French into their own country on the heels of Soult's retreat. There was little that could have been done to stop him. But he resisted the temptation. Pamplona and San Sebastian were still unsubdued in his rear. More serious was the lack of news from eastern Europe. 'I entertain no doubt that I could enter France tomorrow and establish the army on the Adour, but I could go no further certainly. If peace should be made by the Powers of the North I must necessarily retire into Spain and the retreat, however short, must be difficult, on account of the hostility and the warlike disposition of the inhabitants.'[25] If Russia and Prussia made peace the whole might of France could be turned towards Spain. If that happened a retreat to Portugal would be necessary.

In fact, the eastern allies had no intention of making peace. The armistice of Pleischwitz ended on 17 August, and five days earlier Austria declared war on France. Wellington did not learn this news

until 11 September when he read it in captured French newspapers.*
Meanwhile he continued the siege of San Sebastian.

'The town stands at the foot of a promontory washed by the sea,
approach being over a low sandy isthmus occupied by one front of
fortification.'[26] It was obvious that a direct assault along the isthmus
would be immensely costly. The nearest thing to a weak point in the
defences appeared to be the eastern corner of this landward face
where it joins the east wall. Along the east front of the town the
walls are washed by the river Urumea which 'for two hours before
and after low water is so shallow as to be fordable and, for the same
period, a considerable space becomes dry on the left bank of the
river by which troops can march from the isthmus along the foot of
the sea scarp wall of the town'.[27] The plan was that the south-
eastern corner of the defences should be breached by batteries
established on the sandhills on the east bank of the Urumea and at
the landward end of the isthmus which had been cleared of sub-
sidiary French fortifications during the abortive July siege.

San Sebastian was an immensely difficult place to besiege, and the
sea which washed its walls and made the project so complicated for
the Engineers could not be used as an asset in blockading the town.
The Royal Navy was badly overstrained. This was due in part to the
demands of the American war but also to the tendency of the captains of men-of-war to indulge in 'tearing themselves to pieces in
long and distant voyages'[28] in search of prize money. The result was
that there were not enough ships on the Spanish station to enforce an
effective blockade and the French were able, at night, to keep the
town supplied and to evacuate their wounded.

The batteries were completed by the night of 25 August and next
morning 'they opened with a general salvo with fifty-seven pieces of
ordnance, viz. forty-two on the right and fifteen on the isthmus'.[29]
The bombardment continued for five days, six more guns being
added to the batteries. Under its fire trenches were dug forward up
the isthmus to give a covered approach for the assaulting infantry.

The assault was ordered for 11 am on 31 August. The attack had

---

* The news reached London on 27 August. Elaborate arrangements had been made to
pass the information quickly to Wellington, but the winds in the Channel were per-
sistently adverse.

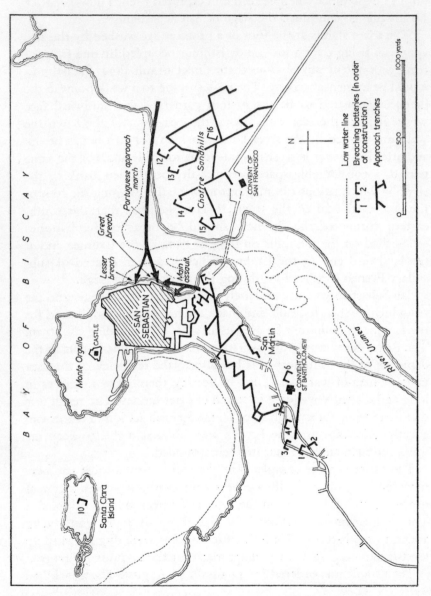

San Sebastian

to be made in broad daylight as the approach could be made only when the tide was falling. At that moment a thousand men from the Fifth Division poured from the head of the trenches. They had only 180 yards to cover to the foot of the breach. This they did with small loss although the garrison fired two mines as they approached. They dashed up the rubble of masonry to the summit of the breach 'but for a long space of time the moment of arriving on the summit was that of certain death; fresh troops pressed forward as fast as they filed out of the trenches and so severe was the loss that a staff officer had to be sent with directions to have the dead and dying removed from the *débouches*, which were absolutely choked up, so as to prevent the passage of the troops'.[30] There was no way of getting into the town from the top of the breach. 'The rampart along the interior of the breach was retained by a wall from 15 to 25 feet in depth, at the foot of which was arranged every nature of defensive obstacle. Further, this descent and the summit of the breach were closely exposed to a well covered fire of musketry from loopholes formed in the walls of the ruined buildings at the back of the breach.'[31]

There was deadlock. From the sandhills across the river watchers could see the storming party shrinking. 'The men hung on to the breach like bees, quite firm, but unable to advance.'[32] To reinforce the Fifth Division Graham ordered forward a party of 750 volunteers from the rest of the army.* Their leader wrote that 'on reaching the breach I found that the men of the Fifth Division were making no progress but rather were crouching under cover of the fallen; we tried to rouse them and seeing a little to my right some men making head, we moved towards them'.[33] They made little progress. At the same time a brigade of Portuguese ran across the river from the sandhills and assaulted a secondary breach in the wall on the river front. They made no progress.

Two hours after the first men had dashed from the trenches the stormers had still got no further than the crest of the breach. 'Every-

---

* Wellington had been dissatisfied, perhaps unjustly, with the performance of the Fifth Division at the earlier assault on 25 July. He called for volunteers from the First, Fourth and Light Divisions 'to show the Fifth Division how to mount a breach'. Not unnaturally, the volunteers were unwelcome to the Fifth.

thing that the most determined bravery could attempt was repeatedly tried in vain by the troops. No man outlived the attempt to gain the ridge.'[34] Watching the storm from the sandhills, General Graham was in a quandary. Despite his sixty-five years he was, said Napier, 'a man to have put himself at the head of the last company and die sword in hand upon the breach rather than sustain a second defeat'.[35] To send more men up the breach seemed certain to cause more casualties without breaking through. Instead he decided on an original and apparently reckless expedient.

> In the almost desperate state of the attack, after consulting with Colonel Dickson, commanding the artillery, I ventured to order the guns to be turned against the curtain [wall]. A heavy fire of artillery was directed against it; passing a few feet only over the heads of our troops on the breach, and was kept up with a precision of practice beyond all example.[36]

On the slope of the breach there was a moment of consternation 'and a cry arose to come away as our own batteries had opened on us'.[37]

> The state of stupefaction did not last long with the British troops. As the smoke and dust of the ruins cleared away, they beheld before them a space empty of defenders and they instantly rushed forward to occupy it. Uttering an appalling shout, the troops sprang over the dilapidated parapet and the rampart was their own. To reach the streets they were obliged to leap about fifteen feet or to make their way through the burning houses which joined the wall. Both courses were adopted. The French fought with desperate courage; they were literally driven from house to house, and street to street, nor was it till a late hour in the evening that all opposition on their part ceased.[38]

San Sebastian had cost the allies 3,700 casualties, 2,376 of them on 31 August. The town was sacked more comprehensively than Badajoz and the disorder was worse since many houses were on fire before the assault was launched. It had been a town of 10,000 inhabitants. Five days after the storm an officer wrote that 'with the exception of ten or twelve fortunate buildings there is nothing left of San Sebastian but the walls of its houses, and they are falling every instant'.[39]

Soult made a last effort to save San Sebastian on the day it fell.* He sent forward seven divisions against the heights of San Marcial, a sector held by Spanish troops. Twice the French scaled the heights and twice the Spaniards drove them back to the bank of the Bidassoa. Disheartened by their July failure, the French fought with less determination than at any other time in the Peninsular War. The Spaniards, on the other hand, fought better than they had done at any battle since Bailen despite the fact that for several days they had 'eaten only half or two thirds of their ration of bread and eight ounces of rice',[40] owing to the neglect of the Spanish commissaries and government.

The French repulse at San Marcial almost had a disastrous sequel. In the middle of the afternoon a blinding storm of rain fell and continued well into the night. The morning's attack had been launched across the fords of the Bidassoa, but by the time the rearguard of Clausel's corps came to cross it the river was nowhere less than six feet deep. General Vandermaesen, the senior officer on the south bank, had more than 10,000 men with him† and it was certain that they would be overwhelmed if they had not crossed the Bidassoa before daylight. His only hope was to lead them upstream to the bridge at Vera and force a crossing.

The action at Vera in the small hours of 1 September 1813 was a tragic waste of opportunity from the allied point of view. Ten thousand Frenchmen, a fifth of Soult's striking force, were cut off by an impassable river. Their loss would have crippled the French army in the Pyrenees. They escaped through the stupidity of one general.

The bridge at Vera was narrow, 'not wide enough for more than three or four to pass abreast',[41] and fifty yards long. At the northern end were some loop-holed houses held by seventy men of the Ninety Fifth under Captain Daniel Cadoux who had posted two sentries at the bridge. A mile from the bridge was the camp of Skerrett's brigade of the Light Division. Skerrett, 'an individual brave to rash-

---

* The remnants of the French garrison took refuge in the castle at the tip of the isthmus when the town fell. After a bombardment they surrendered on 5 September.
† The whole of his own division and a brigade each from the divisions of Taupin and Darmagnac.

ness but, at the head of troops, the most undecided, timid and vascillating creature I ever met with',[42] had been urged by his staff to reinforce Cadoux but had declined to do so.

At 2 am 'the enemy's column approached very quietly and then made a rush; but the rain having wet the priming of the sentries' rifles, they could not get them to go off to give the alarm, and were in a moment driven from their post. The French then, seeing that they had effected a passage, set up a shout and rushed towards the houses where Cadoux's people were, who turned out at once.'[43] The French could not break through. They were in overwhelming numbers but they had little or no firepower. The rain soaked the powder in the flashpans of their muskets and made them useless. The seventy Riflemen firing from the cover of the houses had no such trouble. Again and again the French charged across the bridge but were brought to a halt suffering dreadful casualties. Vandermaesen himself was killed.

Far from sending support, Skerrett ordered Cadoux to retire. Cadoux refused to obey. He was confident that he could hold his post and three times counter-attacked with half his force to clear the bridge. Another order to retire reached him from Skerrett. Reluctantly he prepared to obey, remarking that 'but few of the party would reach the camp'. By this time dawn was breaking. So far the Riflemen had suffered no casualties except the two sentries. In daylight and with the rain clearing they were terribly vulnerable. As they emerged from their cover they were assailed by the fire of massed muskets and artillery. Cadoux and sixteen men were killed. All the other officers and forty-three men were wounded. The enemy crossed without opposition, leaving the bridge 'choked with dead, many of his men were drowned, and all his guns were left in the river'.[44]

General Skerrett returned to England soon afterwards on sick leave, 'a step he had much desired, as his father was just dead and he was heir to an immense property'.[45] He was to die a hero's death the following year at Bergen op Zoom but that could not compensate for the 10,000 Frenchmen who got away at Vera through his obstinacy.

Page 265 'Siege and Capture of Tarragona by the French Army, 29 May 1811', artist unknown

Page 266 (*above*) 'Private,
Thirteenth Light Dragoons
1812', by Charles Hamilton
Smith;
(*left*) engraving after Meyer
of Marshal Marmont, Duke
of Ragusa, by J. N. Joly.

CHAPTER 18

British Operations on the East Coast of Spain, 1812–1813

THE French attempt to subjugate Catalonia, Aragon and Valencia was carried on in isolation from the rest of the Peninsular War. Ever since the French had occupied Barcelona in 1808 it had been difficult for the French commanders there to communicate with Madrid. Letters usually had to go by way of France. Napoleon was anxious to encourage this isolation since he intended to annex to France all Spain north of the Ebro. In 1810 he forbade his generals in Aragon and Catalonia to make reports to King Joseph. Marshal Augereau was told 'that he commands the Army of Catalonia and will receive orders only from me. He should establish a provincial administration and, instead of the Spanish ensign, should fly only the French and Catalan flags. The king and his ministers have nothing to do with Catalonia.'[1] In 1812 Catalonia and Aragon were converted into four French *départements** and the generals there were not included in Joseph's responsibilities when he was made Commander-in-Chief. Circumstances drove the king to the east coast in the late summer of 1812 but he lost touch with affairs there as soon as he returned to Madrid. In June 1813 he was writing, 'As for Aragon, I know nothing of what happens there. I never receive a report from the generals there. I do not even know their names.'[2]

In the same way the Spanish forces in those provinces paid little attention to the Junta and Regency in Cadiz but pursued the war in their own way. It was an effective way. The Spanish armies there

---

* See first footnote on p 244 above.

I

showed even more resilience than those in the rest of the kingdom. Occasionally they won a minor victory. The provisioning of Barcelona was a constant preoccupation of the French commanders and the city was usually more or less under siege. The guerrillas of Catalonia were as formidable as any in Spain and even William Napier, no admirer of Spaniards, admitted that 'their courage was higher, their patriotism purer and their efforts more sustained than those of the rest'.[3] They gave constant employment to large numbers of French troops. Despite substantial withdrawals for the Russian campaign there were still 76,000 men on the muster rolls of the French armies on the east coast of whom more than 60,000 were *présents sous armes*.*

The French commander in the east was Louis Gabriel Suchet, Duke of Albufera, who had won his marshal's baton by taking Tarragona. Napoleon regarded him as one of the best of his commanders and remarked in 1812 that 'if I had two more generals like him to lead my troops in Spain the war would be over'.[4] Unlike most of his colleagues, he tried to introduce a measure of justice into his dealings with the Spaniards and succeeded in pacifying such parts of his area as were consistently under French control. He resembled his colleagues in being extremely reluctant to co-operate with other French armies and although Joseph regarded him as a personal friend Suchet never willingly contributed a single battalion to help the king in his adversity. But Wellington could never afford to forget the possibility that he might send troops into the centre of Spain either voluntarily or on orders from Paris. The intervention of 20,000 of Suchet's troops in the campaigns of Salamanca or Vitoria would have swung the balance decidedly to the French side. Suchet, however, controlled a long coastline on the Mediterranean which was exposed to raids from the dominant British fleet and Wellington was insistent that such raids should be backed by British troops from the garrison of Sicily.

Sicily had had a British garrison since Nelson's day. In 1810 they had repelled a half-hearted French invasion but since that time their

---

* Army of Catalonia (Gen Charles Decaen) 29,462 effective all ranks. Army of Aragon and Valencia (Marshal Suchet) 32,018 effective all ranks. (Return of 15 October 1812.)

dangers had come more from the deviousness of Queen Maria Carolina, sister to Marie Antoinette. Wellington felt that some of the dozen British battalions on the island could be usefully employed in keeping Suchet's attention fixed on his own zone of occupation. The government in London had approved the idea but in sending orders to carry it into effect they had felt bound to leave a measure of discretion to the commander on the spot.

Unfortunately the commander on the spot was deficient in discretion. Lord William Bentinck, a man of every natural advantage, had most of the virtues but no understanding of what was practicable. 'He is,' wrote Greville, 'not right headed and has committed some great blunder or other in every public situation in which he has been placed.'[5] While in Sicily he was consumed by two ambitions—to establish parliamentary democracy in Palermo and to liberate Italy and the Dalmatian coast with his handful of British troops.

Before launching the Salamanca campaign Wellington asked Bentinck to land a force near either Barcelona or Tarragona in the third week of June. Lord William immediately agreed to send 10,000 men.[6] A month later, in March, he changed his mind and decided to use the troops for an invasion of Italy. Urgent representations from London and from Wellington persuaded him to return to the original plan and on 7 June he embarked 8,000 men under General Maitland with orders to sail to Minorca. (The remainder of the troops were sent to Montenegro.) On 9 June he cancelled Maitland's orders, only to reinstate them on 28 June.

Having met headwinds, Maitland did not reach the coast of Spain until 31 July, having first picked up 6,000 Spanish troops from Minorca. The troops he brought from Sicily included five British and KGL battalions. He rightly considered that an attack on Barcelona was too bold an enterprise for his force and first touched shore at Palamos, sixty-five miles north-east of the city where he consulted several Spanish commanders. Wellington had suggested Tarragona as an alternative target for the expedition since it was known to be poorly fortified and lightly garrisoned. Maitland, however, decided that it would be too much for him and, on the excuse that the Catalan generals gave him conflicting information, decided to land at Alicante, 250 miles down the coast from Tarragona where he would cause no trouble to the French. The Catalans were justifiably angry and Suchet was much relieved.

The expedition stayed at Alicante in complete inactivity until the spring of 1813. Its main occupations were building unnecessary fortifications and changing its commander. Maitland's health gave way in September and he was succeeded by General John Mackenzie who lasted until 20 November when he was succeeded by William Clinton* who commanded for two weeks before handing over to James Campbell. In February Sir John Murray took command.

Murray was one of the most unsatisfactory British generals in a period when there were many unsatisfactory British generals. He had served in India where his alternations of torpor and feverish activity had greatly embarrassed the young Arthur Wellesley with whom he was supposed to be co-operating. He had commanded a brigade in Portugal in 1809 but had obtained permission to leave the country lest he be required to serve under Beresford who was his junior in British rank but his senior in his position of Marshal of Portugal. Wellington said of him that 'I entertain a very high opinion of [his] talents; but he always appeared to me to want what is better than abilities, viz. sound sense. There is always some mistaken principle in what he does.'[7]

In Sicily Bentinck continued on his vacillating course. At one time he proposed to withdraw the whole Alicante force in order to invade Italy in company with 15,000 hypothetical Russians. During the winter he borrowed 2,000 men for an abortive raid on Tuscany. Despite his vagaries the force was reinforced until by the time Murray took command the contingent from Sicily amounted to about 10,000 men, although some units were of most dubious reliability. With them, and under Murray's command, were two Spanish divisions, 8,000 men, and the possibility of help from the Spanish regular troops in Murcia.[5/10]

On 13 April 1813 this rather miscellaneous force defeated a corps led by Suchet at Castalla in a battle which did more credit to the staunchness of the British infantry than to Murray's generalship. Soon afterwards he was ordered by Wellington to take the bulk of

---

* William Clinton was the brother of Henry Clinton who commanded Wellington's Sixth Division at Salamanca.

his force by sea to capture Tarragona, a move designed to coincide with the opening of the main campaign of 1813 and to stop Suchet intervening in central Spain.

The naval commander of the expedition was Rear-Admiral Sir Ben Hallowell, an enthusiastic advocate of landing soldiers on enemy coasts. He put Murray and 16,000 men ashore at Salou Bay, six miles south of Tarragona, on 2 June. With them was landed the siege train with which Wellington had taken Badajoz. They were greeted on landing by the Spanish general Copons who brought with him an infantry division of more than 7,000 men and a handful of cavalry. The whole force made up 24,000 men of whom half were Spanish. There were 3,000 Italians and Sicilians and the remainder were British or Germans in British pay. Copons reported that there were no French field forces in the vicinity.

The fortifications of Tarragona were extensive and had not been repaired since Suchet stormed the town in 1811. General Bertoletti, who commanded the garrison, had only 1,600 men, half of whom were Italians. He decided to abandon the outer walls and to concentrate his men in the old town, perched on a cliff above the sea. He left company-strength garrisons in two small detached works, the Bastion of San Carlos and Fort Royal. Neither of these works was in good condition and they could have been stormed out of hand. Murray, however, developed a cautious streak and decided that they must be reduced separately in formal sieges. Three batteries were established against Fort Royal and by 7 June it was completely disabled. Murray nevertheless postponed the assault until 11 June. There was no confirmed information of French moves to relieve the place. Copons' division covered the approaches from Barcelona while a British detachment held a fort in the pass of Balaguer which effectively blocked the road to the south.

Rumours of French movements abounded and Murray allowed them to drive him into a state bordering on panic. On 7 June he wrote to Wellington:

> I am much afraid we have undertaken more than we are able to perform, but to execute your lordship's orders I will persevere as long as prudence will permit. I have as yet no perfect information of Suchet's movements but there are reports, and if they prove true, I

am to be attacked by a force so immeasurably superior, without the
hopes or chance of a retreat in case of misfortune. I calculate that
Suchet can bring into the field 24,000 or 25,000 without difficulty;
and my force, supposing the Spaniards really have what they say
they have, will not exceed, of all sorts, 19,000 of which I must leave
at least 4,000 to cover our guns and mask the garrison.[8]

This was the language of despair. He had understated his own army
by 5,000 men and he knew, since Wellington had spelt it out for
him before he sailed from Alicante, that it was impossible for Suchet
to collect a field force of 24,000 men. On 9 June he gave secret orders
for re-embarkation.

Murray might have been less despondent if he could have known
the confusion into which his landing had thrown the French.
Suchet had been at Valencia, a hundred miles from Tarragona, when
he saw the vast convoy sail northward along the coast. He could have
no idea of their destination. He scraped together a corps of 8,000
men and started to march northward. He also sent orders to General
Decaen, commanding in Catalonia, to meet him at Reus, ten miles
inland from Tarragona, with all his disposable troops. Decaen believed that any allied landing would be between Barcelona and the
French frontier. He was confirmed in this belief when a party of
Royal Marines made a landing at Rosas Bay, near the frontier, on
8 June. Reluctantly he dispatched General Maurice Mathieu with
6,000 men to try to join Suchet at Reus. Since Murray commanded
the only road between the two French forces no further orders from
Suchet reached either Decaen or Mathieu.

Thus the threat which so terrified Murray consisted only of
14,000 Frenchmen advancing in two bodies from opposite directions
and out of touch with each other. Even this threat did not last long.
Suchet heard that the Spanish Army of Murcia was advancing on
Valencia and turned back. Mathieu reached Copons' outposts, heard
the strength of the allied force from peasants and started to march
back to Barcelona.

Murray rode out to see Copons on the morning of 11 June. Reports were coming in that Mathieu's division was approaching, but
Copons had a strong position and was confident of being able to
hold it. Murray promised to reinforce him with six British battalions

and all the allied cavalry. They parted in great amity when Murray rode back to Tarragona to supervise the storm of Fort Royal.

As soon as he reached the siege lines Murray was greeted by a new batch of Spanish rumours saying that both Suchet and Mathieu were pressing their advances. Without hesitation Murray cancelled the assault and gave orders for all the stores to be embarked. He sent a message to Copons telling him that he was 'under the necessity of withdrawing part of his besieging apparatus'. Nevertheless he repeated his promise to send the six battalions and the cavalry to the Spaniard's support.[9] Next he saw Admiral Hallowell. By this time it was midnight and the admiral was furiously angry at Murray's decision. It was some time before he could be induced to agree to load the stores. Finally the general called for the commander of his artillery and ordered him to have the siege guns brought down to the beach immediately. The gunner pointed out that this could not be done in less than thirty hours as fire from the fortress would make work impossible in daylight. Reluctantly Murray agreed to postpone embarkation for twenty-four hours.

The next day was one of confusion and fraying tempers. Some guns were available for immediate embarkation and the sailors started getting them aboard. Murray then changed his mind and sent to the beach an order that the cavalry should be embarked first. The cavalry were five miles away with Copons. The chief staff officer, General Donkin, was on the beach and told the sailors that only men were to be embarked. He insisted that a gun which was already hoisted should be lowered back on to the sand. Hallowell then arrived. Donkin told him that apart from men only a few staff horses were to be embarked 'as it was Sir John Murray's wish to indulge the general officers by allowing them to take on board one favourite horse each, if it could be done'.[10] He added that the guns were to be spiked and the carriages burned.

Hallowell retorted by telling the sailors to accept no orders from army officers and stormed away to see Murray.

I informed him of the disgraceful manner in which they were going on on the beach. I warned him of the disgrace we were bringing on the British character by such conduct. I intreated him, if he was determined on raising the siege, to do it in a soldierlike manner, and I pledged myself, if he would allow the guns to remain until night, that I would take everything off. Sir John Murray denied giving directions to spike the guns.[11]

Murray had probably lost track of the directions he had given. One of his divisional commanders complained that between dawn and 1.30 pm he had received six sets of contradictory orders. At noon, however, Murray finally made up his mind. A report reached him that 5,000 or 6,000 Frenchmen were approaching Copons' position. Immediate orders were given for the army to embark. Anything which could not be put on board during the day was to be left behind. Copons learned of this decision when the allied cavalry which held part of his front line trotted quietly away to the rear. Late that evening he received a note from Murray advising him to escape to the mountains.

During the night all the Anglo-Sicilian troops embarked, but naval working parties stayed on the beach most of the next day salvaging stores which the soldiers had abandoned. The French garrison was too exhausted and astonished to intervene. The two relieving columns were in retreat. In the abandoned siege lines lay eighteen heavy guns, spiked and dismounted. They were the guns with which Wellington had battered his way into Ciudad Rodrigo and Badajoz.

Murray's spirits revived abruptly as soon as he was on board HMS *Malta*. He decided to land the whole force at Balaguer, twenty miles to the south, where his detachment still occupied the fort blocking the pass. The long-suffering sailors put most of the soldiers ashore there on 15 June while Murray had a field day of indecision. The admiral commented that 'the debarkation and the re-embarkation continually going on was enough to confound any operation in the world. Every mast-head was covered with his signals and four fast-moving gigs were hardly sufficient to convey his orders.'[12]

Late in the day the general had a new idea. He proposed to Hallowell that 5,000 men should be re-embarked and landed close to Tarragona, hoping to take the garrison by surprise. The admiral 'gave it as my opinion that, as he had not felt himself equal to such an enterprise when he was there with his whole force and his batteries erected, I did not think him equal to it now with 5,000 men'.[13]

As soon as the allies had sailed from Tarragona Bertoletti sent a messenger to Mathieu who turned about once more and reached the fortress by a forced march on 16 June. Hearing that Murray was at Balaguer, French patrols were sent out to discover his strength. The sight of French cavalry threw Murray back to despondency. He sent a frantic message to Copons for help and the Spaniard was forgiving enough to turn back from his mountain retreat. Then Murray decided that it would be better to re-embark his force but omitted to inform Copons that he was doing so. Scarcely were the troops once more on board than the main Mediterranean fleet appeared over the horizon. The flagship flew a signal telling that Lord William Bentinck was on board. With more enthusiasm than tact Hallowell replied, 'We are all delighted.'

Bentinck took over command and shipped the army back to Alicante. The operation had cost 15 killed, 82 wounded and 5 missing.

Murray was ordered to be court-martialled but the court did not meet until the war was over in 1814. He was acquitted on all charges except that of abandoning his guns without due cause, 'such conduct being detrimental to the service'. He was sentenced to be admonished since the court believed that his fault 'proceeded from a mere error of judgment'. He chose to regard this as an honourable acquittal and petitioned the Prince Regent for the Order of the Bath 'to cancel former injuries'. He was unsuccessful.*

---

* He later received the Guelphic order of Hanover. This order was not highly regarded in England and it is said that Wellington, when told by William IV that he had 'Guelphed', some notable, replied, 'Serve him damned well right.'

PART SIX

The Invasion of France, October 1813–April 1814

CHAPTER 19

Across the Pyrenees

VITORIA had played its part in consolidating and heartening the alliance against Napoleon in the east. The eastern allies expected Wellington to continue to press Napoleon's southern flank. They were vociferously backed by the British press. Wellington was reluctant to invade southern France until the situation in the east was clearer. He had no confidence in the tactics of Austria, Prussia and Russia in their German campaign. He complained that he 'would not march even a corporal's guard upon such a system'.[1] It was far from impossible that Napoleon would win a great victory in Germany after which he could dictate peace in the east. If that happened the position of the Anglo-Portuguese army would be very dangerous if it had thrust deep into France. In mid-September news reached Wellington of a French victory at Dresden (26–27 August). This information came from French sources and did not add that lack of cavalry prevented Napoleon taking advantage of his success. Nor was it clear that in the same week as Dresden was fought subordinate French commanders had been defeated at Grossbeeren, Kulm, Dennewitz and on the Katzbach. Wellington's informants could not be aware that this week of fighting had cost France 100,000 men and 300 guns. Nevertheless Wellington was acutely aware of his obligations to the eastern allies. Although Pamplona was still unsubdued in his rear, 'I think I ought and will bend to the views of the allies, if it can be done with safety to the army notwithstanding I should prefer to turn my attention to Catalonia.'[2]

He could not overlook the possibility of an attack on his open right flank by Suchet's troops. As usual, the Anglo-Sicilian corps on

the east coast was causing him concern. William Bentinck had retained the command for only ten weeks. In that period Suchet had
withdrawn from the Ebro valley. Bentinck had followed him and
had succeeded in getting his advanced guard sharply defeated on the
heights of Ordal (13 September). Lord William immediately returned
to Sicily leaving the command in the hands of William Clinton of
whom he wrote that his 'diffidence makes him unfit for command;
his fear of responsibility, and the uneasiness he suffers under it,
would, I am sure, in a very short time, ruin his constitution'.[3]

The operation Wellington had in mind was the crossing of the
lower Bidassoa. There would be great prestige in being the first
allied army established on French soil, but more important there
would be solid tactical advantages. 'The heights on the right of the
Bidassoa command such a view of us that we must have them, and
the sooner the better.'[4] He had intended to secure them as soon as
San Sebastian surrendered. Unfortunately the bungling of an
Engineer officer delayed the arrival of the pontoon bridges for some
weeks.

Soult's position was not unlike that which Wellington had held
before the battles of the Pyrenees in late July. It was naturally strong
but the country was broken and lateral communication was made
difficult by two mountain massifs which broke up his thirty-mile
front. If the front was to be held in strength there could not be
enough reserves behind each sector to seal off a local breakthrough.
His right was on the sea and his left at St-Jean-Pied-de-Port. Between
these points were Mont Larroun and Pic Monderrain, both serious
obstacles. The marshal would have preferred to shorten his line by
retreating to a shorter and more convenient position. He would
require permission from the Emperor to abandon French territory
unnecessarily and his application to do so was one of the many
letters dealing with the Spanish war which Napoleon failed to
answer. Meanwhile the Minister of War received so many com-
plaints of the conduct of the troops on their native soil that he
instructed Soult to take his stand as near to the frontier as possible.

The security of the frontier line depended on Soult's ability to
guess Wellington's plan of attack. He divided the front into three
sectors, each under a corps commander, realising that each sector

must be defended out of its own resources. The left seemed to be the most vulnerable. Here the allies held the crestline of the mountains and the passes of Maya and Roncesvalles. Soult based his defence on the belief that Wellington would make his main attack over the Maya and try to drive down the valley of the river Nivelle to St-Jean-de-Luz. D'Erlon's corps was stationed on the left and was reinforced to four divisions. His left was at St-Jean-Pied-de-Port, which had its own garrison, and his right on the Nivelle near Ainhoa.

The defence of the Nivelle valley was shared with the three divisions of Clausel's corps whose left was in touch with d'Erlon's right on the river. Clausel's sector included the mountainous mass of Mont Larroun and its under-features. One division covered its western and southern approaches while the other two were deployed on the eastern slopes down to the Nivelle.

Reille's corps, reduced to two divisions, held the seaward sector with their left at the point where the Bidassoa ceased to form the Franco-Spanish frontier. The only bridge in this sector had been at Béhobie but it had been destroyed by the French in their retreat at the end of June. The only known fords were upstream of the Île de la Conference, below Béhobie, and the bulk of Reille's forward troops were stationed to guard them.

Behind the front, armed camps were being built astride the Nivelle at Bordagain and Serres. The Reserve division, reduced to 8,000 men in order to bring the three corps up to strength after the Pyrenean battles, was stationed at Serres and Ascain, astride the Nivelle valley close to St-Jean-de-Luz. In that position they could form a second line of defence against a thrust down the Nivelle valley or send troops to assist Reille on the French right. In all, Soult had 61,000 infantry and artillery to man his line.* The cavalry once more had no part to play in the forthcoming battles.

---

* The French order of battle was basically the same as that given (p 393) for the battle of the Pyrenees. The corps were composed as follows:

D'Erlon's Corps: Divisions of Foy, Darmagnac, Abbé and Darricau. 19,244 all ranks.
Clausel's Corps: Divisions of Conroux, Maransin and Taupin. 15,315 all ranks.
Reille's Corps: Divisions of Maucune and Boyer. 10,551 all ranks.
Reserve (Villatte) 8,530.
Artillery, Engineers, etc, 8,530 all ranks.

Bidassoa and Nivelle

Wellington's Anglo-Portuguese army amounted to 64,000 infantry and artillery but he had 25,000 Spaniards available for field operations. These he was reluctant to use for an invasion of France since they were 'neither fed nor paid, and ... must plunder [and] will raise the country against us'.[5] Some of these he stationed at the pass of Roncesvalles and the remainder he allocated to other inhospitable sectors where the opportunities for looting were limited.

The allies lost no opportunity of confirming Soult in his belief that their attack would come through the Maya. Wellington showed himself in that sector and on 1 October a Portuguese brigade made a reconnaissance in strength there and returned with 70 French prisoners and 2,000 sheep. On the morning of 7 October Soult, who had spent the night at Espelette, was inspecting the fortifications his troops were busily building in his eastern sector. He saw the Sixth Division, led by its Portuguese brigade, advance purposefully from the Maya. The Portuguese stormed the ironworks at Urdax and pushed on beyond. D'Erlon's reserve divisions were called forward but Soult noticed that the redcoats did not come on with the same impetuosity as their allies.* He realised that he was watching a feint attack and galloped off towards the sea. He reached Reille's headquarters at Urrugne at 1 pm and found the battle over.

Soult and Reille had considered the Bidassoa estuary below the Île de la Conference to be the safest sector in the front. The river widened to a thousand yards. At high water it was twenty feet deep. What no French commander discovered was that the tidefall was sixteen feet at certain times. Basque fishermen had shown allied intelligence officers a number of fords. The tides were at their lowest on 7 October.

There was heavy rain on the evening of 6 October. A young lieutenant wrote that 'the lightning was more vivid than any which I have ever seen and peals of thunder, echoed back as they were by the rocks and mountains around, sounded more like one continual rending of the elements, than intermittent discharges of an electric cloud'.[6] The rain stopped by midnight but the sky was still overcast

---

* The Portuguese were carried away by their enthusiasm. Their commander was reprimanded for 'getting into unnecessary scrapes. He had lost 150 men for nothing and in disobedience to orders'.

and there was 'a sharp hoar frost'.[7] The Fifth Division marched in silence down the slopes into the 'meadow ground below Fuenter-rabia. On the Spanish side of the river was erected a broad and pretty high wall of turf with a ditch behind it; we moved in silence till we reached the wall and concealed ourselves in the ditch, while our pioneers with the greatest possible silence cut several large openings through which we might pass. The storm died away, the moon had set and the night was unusually dark.'[8]

Across the river from the Fifth Division was the little town of Hendaye. On their right was the First Division and two independent brigades who were concealed in the foothills where the battle of San Marcial had been fought. They were to cross by the fords on either side of the burned bridge of Béhobie. Three Spanish brigades were to ford the river on their right. Five field batteries and three 18-pounder siege guns were in position to support them and there were enough pontoons to build three bridges. Twenty-four thousand men were ready to attack. Across the river was a single French division of 4,000 men strung out along a front of four miles. Reille's reserve division was stationed at Urrugne, four miles behind. Most of its soldiers were even further in rear, toiling at the earthworks of the camp of Bordagain.

At 7.25 am the tide was almost at its lowest and the order was given for the Fifth Division to advance. 'We rushed out at the openings made by the pioneers and dashed into the water. It was middle deep, so that the men had to hold up their arms and ammuni-tion. Our plunge into the water was echoed by the fire of the French sentries who, having fired, retreated with the utmost rapidity.'[9] Hendaye was over-run. Its garrison was only forty men and the Fifth advanced up the slopes behind with only a scattering of skirmishing fire. One brigade pushed straight ahead and two swung south to aid the attack of the troops on their right.*

At 8 am a rocket was fired from the church tower of Fuenterrabia as a signal for the attack of the First Division† and the Spaniards.

---

* Fifth Division was composed as at Vitoria (see p 384) but it was commanded by Andrew Hay. Hay's brigade was commanded by Col Greville.
† Since Vitoria First Division had been increased by another brigade consisting of 1 and 3/1st Guards and a company of 5/60th commanded by Col Peregrine Maitland. With

Where the German Legion crossed the river it was so rapid 'that we were constrained to take each other by the arm, holding our swords and muskets in the air, the water being up to the arm pits and knee deep in mud'.[10] From the far bank the French opened a sharp fire but a subaltern admitted that 'the water was so exceedingly cold and strong that I was insensible to the splashing of musketry around my chest'.[11] The allied numbers were so overwhelming that the defenders, with the Fifth Division pressing on their right, had no chance of holding the heights overlooking the river. On the right of First Division the Spaniards swarmed up the steep wooded slopes and held Mont Calvaire by 11 o'clock. Meanwhile the British had seized the Croix des Bouquets and with the whole line of the ridge in his hands Wellington halted the advance, calling back some light troops who were skirmishing around Urrugne where French reinforcements were beginning to arrive.

The whole operation had gone smoothly and cost the allies only 400 casualties. The French had been taken by surprise. During the night their sentries had reported sounds of movement from the south bank but these reports had been relayed in a leisurely fashion* and it was ten minutes to eight before they reached Reille. By that time it was too late to take effective action.

There was more serious fighting in the centre where the Light Division was set to capture the outer defences of Mont Larroun with the help of Longa's Spaniards. On their right two Andalusian divisions attempted the peak of Larroun itself. The Light attacked up two spurs while Longa's men linked them across the re-entrant. On the right-hand spur Kempt's brigade had more trouble with the country than from the French. 'The obstacles on each side of the way rendered the mountain fearfully difficult of ascent; and it was so intersected with rocks, trees, brushwood and briar that our hands and limbs were pierced with thorns and the trousers were literally torn from our legs.'[12]

The other brigade, now under John Colborne, had a more difficult

---

the First Division were Bradford's Portuguese Brigade and a new British brigade commanded by Maj-Gen Lord Aylmer and consisting of 76th, 2/84th and 85th.

* Soult blamed Maucune, whose division held the riverline, for the surprise and sent him away from the army. Maucune was a brave man but an unlucky commander. His division was dispersed at Salamanca, at San Milan and at Sorauren.

task. The spur it had to attack was crowned by a stone-built redoubt known as La Bayonette. Colborne sent out a thick screen of Riflemen but the French, taking them for Portuguese, attacked them downhill and drove them back. The French success did not last many minutes. The redcoats of the Fifty Second emerged from the trees below and Colborne led them uphill to the charge before the French had time to reform. They drove them back to their redoubt, and 'to our astonishment the enemy did not defend their well-constructed work as determinedly as we had anticipated. Although they stood behind their parapets until we were almost in the act of leaping on them, they then gave way and we were almost mixed together, till they precipitated themselves into a ravine and fled.'[13]

The Andalusians failed to take Larroun although they attacked repeatedly, as Wellington acknowledged, 'in as good order and with as much spirit as any that I have seen made by any troops'.[14] Next day, however, the French evacuated the summit where they were in danger of being encircled.

The crossing of the Bidassoa and the taking of Mont Larroun cost the allies 1,600 men. Wellington's aim had been limited to establishing his army on French soil and to acquiring a jumping-off ground for a further attack. This he was determined not to undertake until he had more heartening news from eastern Europe and until Pamplona surrendered, which it eventually did on 30 October.

Wellington's immediate pre-occupation was to stop his men from looting. Hardly had the action on 7 October finished than he 'saw many men coming in drunk and loaded with plunder. If we were five times stronger than we are we could not venture to enter France if we cannot prevent our soldiers from plundering.'[15] He issued a strongly worded General Order and several officers whose men had conspicuously misbehaved were sent back to England 'that their names may be brought under the attention of the Prince Regent'.[16] Much, though by no means all, of the trouble was caused by the Spaniards who were shamefully neglected by their government. Wellington could hardly find it in his heart to blame them for their looting and violence.

> They are in so miserable a state that it is really hardly fair to expect that they will refrain from plundering a beautiful country which they

enter as conquerors; particularly adverting to the miseries which
their own country has suffered from their invaders. However, our
success and everything depends upon our moderation and justice
and upon the good conduct and discipline of our troops.[17]

I do not mind commanding a large or small army but, large or
small, it must obey me and, above all, it must not plunder.[18]

Soult was having his own troubles with plunderers. Looting had
become an ingrained habit with his troops and they declared that it
was better for Frenchmen to be plundered by their own troops than
by foreigners. Fights between villagers and soldiers became daily
occurrences. Soult did his best to stop the pillage. Many soldiers
were hanged and a captain of the 45me, a Chevalier of the Legion of
Honour, was shot for encouraging his troops to loot a village and
for manhandling a gendarme who tried to interfere. Letters of
complaint poured into Paris from *préfets* and mayors until the
Minister of War ordered the marshal to take the offensive and get his
army back on to Spanish soil.

Soult refused to obey. 'If I was checked I should have no alternative to retreating beyond the Nive and the Adour.'[19] He set his
troops to entrenching their positions and to putting a good face on
his defeat on the Bidassoa. 'I gained a great advantage in losing the
heights on the Bidassoa for it would have been almost impossible to
supply the troops there once winter comes and if the enemy occupies
them in the rainy season we will soon be seen to have gained more
than we have lost.'[20] His troops did not take so hopeful a view. An
ADC to the Minister of War reported that 'the army could not
have less confidence in itself. It is distressing to see everyone convinced that we are going to be beaten.'[21] General Villatte, commanding the Reserve, commented that 'with troops like these we can
expect only disgrace'.[22]

Soult was fortifying a naturally strong position in the hope that he
could make it so strong that 'the enemy will have to give up the idea
of attacking it'.[23] His right rested on the sea in front of St-Jean-de-
Luz which had permanent fortifications. The town was covered by
the entrenchments of Bordagain and there were outlying strong-
points in the villages of Urrugne and Soccori. Wherever possible the
land between these fortifications had been flooded. To the south-east

of the town, Ascain was held as a bridgehead across the river from
the entrenchments of Serres. The bridgehead on the south bank was
essential since the line there swung sharply south-east to its most
formidable sector. This had as its main bastion the northern part of
the Larroun massif, a long rocky ridge, a thousand feet lower than
the main peak and separated from it by a sharp dip. This ridge was
known as Petit Larroun* and was crowned by three stone-built
redoubts. From there a series of redoubts sited in depth carried the
line on to the Nivelle at Amotz. There were two large redoubts south
of this line covering the village of Sare which was also fortified.
Beyond the river a line of redoubts along the Harismendia ridge
prolonged the front to the massif of Mont Monderrain which both
sides considered as impassable country. Beyond that was St-Jean-
Pied-de-Port to which Soult allotted not only one of his divisions but
a brigade he had acquired, without Suchet's consent, from the Army
of Catalonia. This was a more than generous defence force for his
inland flank and left him with only 52,000 infantry for the rest of the
front.

Having misread Wellington's intentions in October Soult convinced himself that the next attack would also fall in the seaward
sector. He transferred one division from d'Erlon's corps to Reille's
so that, including all but three battalions of his reserve, he had 23,000
men between the sea and the western slopes of Larroun. Clausel
had 15,000 men between Larroun (inclusive) and the Nivelle while
d'Erlon had only 11,000 between the river and Mont Monderrain.

Wellington knew that he must get his army out of the mountains
before winter set in in earnest. Snow fell at Roncesvalles and the
Thirty Fourth 'were frequently dug out of our tents of a morning by
the pioneers'.[24]

> [Even on the lower slopes] it was certainly beginning to be exceed-
> ingly cold, with frequent storms of hail and rain. Our tents, from the
> tremendous gusts of wind which suddenly and frequently assailed
> them, were torn and often rendered useless. The French officers
> would call out to us and say, 'You cannot remain in these bleak
> mountains much longer. We suppose you will retire into Spain for

---

* On modern maps it is shown as Mont Alchangue and Petit Larroun is marked as
being another feature, south of the main peak.

the winter.' Our answer was, 'Very likely we may, if we are so ordered.'[25]

Nobody, least of all Wellington, believed that they would retire into Spain. Watching the French digging their works, he remarked, 'Those fellows think themselves invulnerable, but I shall beat them out, and with ease. They have not men to man the works and lines they occupy. I can pour a greater force on certain points than they can concentrate to resist me.'[26] He planned to attack at dawn on 8 November but, as a brigadier wrote on the previous day, 'the weather is so bad and the mountain streams so swelled that it is absolutely necessary to postpone the intended attack till there is a change for the better'.[27] The new date fixed was 10 November and meanwhile good news came from Germany. On the 9th an officer wrote home:

> We have great news from the French side, which is believed by every one here, and by the French army we are told; namely that Bonaparte is beaten back to the Rhine, with the loss of three divisions cut off by blowing up a bridge too soon. This puts our party in great spirits for tomorrow and will, I hope, damp the French if believed by them, as deserters report it to be. I dined with Lord Wellington, and staid there till near ten. He was all gaiety and spirits; and only said on leaving the room, 'Remember! at four in the morning.'[28]

The news was true. On 16–18 October Napoleon had been defeated at Leipzig with the loss of 100,000 men and 300 guns.

Wellington's plan was the one with which Soult had credited him in the previous month. He aimed to drive down the Nivelle valley with three divisions on each side of the river and seize the high ground north and south of St-Pée. The French position was to be swung back as if it was a door, and to make success certain the Light Division and the Spaniards were to break the hinge. They were to take the Petit Larroun and then advance north-east taking in flank the troops and fortifications pressed by the main assault. So that Soult should not be disabused of his illusion that his right was in danger, John Hope* with 20,000 men was to demonstrate in front of St-Jean-de-Luz.[5/12]

---

* Lieut-Gen Sir John Hope succeeded Thomas Graham as second-in-command of the army in October. Graham had been forced to return to England by eye trouble.

As soon as it was dark on 9 November the troops started moving silently into their positions. A full moon came up at midnight and 'it was the most beautiful moonlight morning; and so clear that it was difficult to say at what moment the night ended and daylight began'.[29] At first light the batteries opened in the coastal sector and Hope's corps advanced against the fortified villages of Urrugne and Socorri.

> The houses and barricades of Urrugne were thronged with de-fenders, who saluted us as we approached with a sharp discharge of musketry, which, however, was more harmless than might have been expected. On our part we had no time for firing but rushed on to the charge, whilst the 9 pounders cleared the barricade with grape and cannister. In two minutes we had reached its base; in an in-stant more we were on top of it. The enemy, panic-struck at the celerity of our movements, abandoned their defences and fled. As soon as we had cleared the place of its defenders, we set about entrenching ourselves. For this purpose we tore up the barricade erected by the French, consisting of casks filled with earth, manure and rubbish and rolled them down to the opposite end of the town. We found in the village a good store of brown bread and several casks of brandy. The latter were instantly knocked on the head and the spirits poured out into the street as the only means of hindering our men from getting drunk and saving ourselves from a defeat.[30]

As Hope's corps advanced, three mountain guns were fired from the summit of Larroun as a starting signal for the rest of the army. Immediately a swarm of Riflemen and *caçadores* dashed out from hiding-places on the face of the mountain and into the saddle be-tween the main peak and the Petit Larroun. Behind them came the formed battalions of light infantry. One made straight for the forti-fications on Petit Larroun; the other swung round the flank and made for the Mouiz redoubt which commanded the retreat of the garrison of the ridge. The direct attack was made by the Forty Third under William Napier. Their objective was three stone 'castles' and they could be approached only through a single narrow cleft, 'for in the other parts the rocks were 200 feet high'. As they doubled through the cleft the French kept up a heavy fire on them but, wrote Napier, 'when the men had recovered wind I advanced against the first castle: the enemy fled with the exception of an officer and two men; but aided by my own men I scaled the wall. We put the two men to flight and took the officer, for he fought to the last, standing on the wall and throwing heavy stones at me. One I parried with my sword but I received a contusion on my thigh from another.'[31]

The French fought badly despite their strong position. They were disheartened by the sight of the Fifty Second moving to cut off their retreat. Another officer wrote that 'the rapidity of the attack was such that in less than half an hour the enemy were driven off the hill and the redoubt was in our possession. Our division reformed columns of attack on La Petit Larroun, whence we could now clearly see the whole chain of entrenchments filled with French, the redoubts bristling with cannon, and everything ready for our reception.'[32]

On the right of the Light Division three divisions under Beresford were attacking two of Clausel's divisions. Their first objective was the village of Sare which was covered by two redoubts, the Ste-Barbe and the Grenade. Eighteen guns opened against the Ste-Barbe at a range of 400 yards and after an hour's firing the French,

> seeing that our columns of infantry approached on all sides, abandoned the redoubt, made with every care having a deep ditch, an abattis in front with *trous de loup*. The [Grenade] redoubt against which we rapidly advanced our guns cost only a quarter of an hour, the enemy abandoning it with discreditable precipitation. By this time, though the ground was most difficult, the infantry were advancing with great celerity. One of those bursts of cheering which electrify one now indicated the presence of Lord Wellington. We advanced through rugged roads and up and down heights more than difficult to the village of Sare [where] the affair was checked for some time. The enemy, as if ashamed of having too hastily given up his front line, rushed from his second but on seeing our troops advancing, retired after some skirmishing to the redoubts and heights of his second line, from which he cannonaded us with great spirit.[33]

The village of Sare cost the allies a sharp struggle but it fell when it was encircled by Giron's Spaniards and the Seventh Division while the Fourth attacked it in front. At the same time the Third Division stormed into Amotz. The French fell back to the high ground and the redoubts south-west of St-Pée. They were taken in flank by the Light Division plunging down from Petit Larroun. By noon all the redoubts were in allied hands and Clausel's staff were desperately trying to rally the corps on the north bank of the river. They failed, and Clausel in disgust wrote that evening to the governor of Bayonne, 'Be so good as to arrest and put in the citadel all officers and soldiers of [my corps] who arrive unwounded at Bayonne. They are cowards who shun glory and who are content with dishonour. I beg you to excuse no one.'[34]

East of the Nivelle Hill's three divisions advanced in echelon, left in front, against the Harismendia ridge. As the allies approached the French put down a heavy cannonade and 'the hill with which we were faced was the steepest I ever climbed. The ground over which we had to pass had been intersected for months with incessant labour and French resource; every five yards exposed us to a new cross fire and deep cuts, which furnished graves for many a gallant soldier. The brambles all through were so high and thickly interwoven and the inequalities of the ground were so great as to prevent those not ten yards asunder from seeing each other.'[35]

The redoubts on top of the ridge were taken with little trouble. One of them, armed with two large ship's carronades, fell to

Lieut. Col. Leith, 31st Regiment, Lieut. Col. Norton, 66th and Ensign Dunne, 66th, at the head of a few men. Indeed the three officers carried it themselves, for they cleared the ditch with a running leap and dropped down among the garrison before a man could enter to assist them. As they leaped in, the [French] artillery officer and most of his men jumped out, but not without impunity for Leith, a Hercules in figure and strength, knocked the red-headed officer with a brickbat; but his cap saved his skull, and he managed to scramble up and get away. His sergeant, a formidable looking person and 'bearded like the pard', was not so lucky; he dislocated his shoulder in the leap and was taken prisoner.[36]

Soult, once again, played no part in the battle. He spent the morning in front of St-Jean-de-Luz waiting for Hope's demonstration to turn into a serious attack. It was not until well into the afternoon that he rode across to Serres to give orders to his reserve. By that time it was too late to do anything but retreat. The allies were across the river at St-Pée. Delay would mean that the French right wing would be cut off. St-Jean was evacuated that night and Soult fell back to a position covering Bayonne. He left 69 guns and 1,250 prisoners in allied hands, the total casualties being 4,444.

Wellington's army lost 2,625 men, an astonishingly low figure for forcing so strong a position. No one was more astonished than Soult. 'Before the attack I would not have believed that General Clausel's divisions could have been driven from their positions behind Sare and on the Petit Larroun. Such happenings are beyond the laws of probability. Their capture should have cost the enemy 25,000 men.'[37] Wellington's superiority in numbers, about four to three in infantry, was not enough to offset the strength of the French position. The battle was a triumph of generalship, and many years later when Wellington was asked which of his battles was best planned and executed he replied, 'Well, I think the battle of the Nivelle was my best work.'[38]

The sequel was unhappy. The Spaniards had fought their way into the more populous parts of France and immediately took to looting. A staff officer reached his allotted quarter in Sare on the night of the battle and found that 'the Spaniards were in possession and firing, plunder and confusion were all around'.[39] This was the thing Wellington had feared most, the one event which could bring his campaign to a halt. He could not afford to raise the civilian population against him. Rather than take the risk he sent the Spanish army back to its own country, retaining only Morillo's division which was fed and paid from British sources. To the Spanish commander he wrote: 'I have not come to France to plunder. I have not had thousands of officers and soldiers killed and wounded so that the survivors might pillage the French. On the contrary, my duty, and the duty of all of us, is to stop pillage, especially as we intend to support our troops from the resources of the country.'[40]

CHAPTER 20

Nive

THE last months of 1813 were a desperate time for the French Empire. On the eastern front the remnant of the second Grande Armée, 56,000 men,* were trying to hold off five times their number on the line of the Rhine. Wellington's army had broken into southern France. Napoleon returned to Paris to begin once more the task of creating an army. Inevitably his thoughts turned to the 80,000 veterans still in the 'Armies of Spain'.† The war could still be won if they could be disentangled from the south and brought to the eastern front. He had tried to annex Spain in 1808 by legalistic manoeuvring. He now tried to extricate himself by the same means.

For five years Prince Ferdinand had been under house arrest at Valençay, Talleyrand's country house in central France. Napoleon had never acknowledged him as anything more than Prince of the Asturias. To the people of Spain he was Ferdinand VII, King of Spain and the Indies. On 17 November 1813 the Prince-King received a visit from Count La Forest who was still accredited as Napoleon's ambassador to King Joseph. He brought a letter from Napoleon accusing England of

> fomenting anarchy, Jacobitism and the annihilation of both monarchy and aristocracy in order to establish a republic in Spain. I cannot [continued Napoleon] be indifferent to the ruin of a nation so close to my frontier and with which I have so many maritime interests in common. I therefore wish to remove all pretexts for English intervention and to re-establish the bonds of friendship and

---

* Apart from 100,000 French troops isolated in various German garrisons.
† Soult had 72,000 men in and around Bayonne. Suchet had 46,000 in Catalonia. About one-third of both forces was made up of newly raised conscripts.

good neighbourliness which have so long existed between the two nations.[1]

The Emperor proposed that Ferdinand should return to Spain as king, giving an undertaking that he would expel the British from his realm. On his side Napoleon would withdraw all French troops from Spain and repatriate 100,000 Spanish prisoners of war. As an inducement Ferdinand was offered Joseph's fourteen-year-old daughter Zenaïde as a bride. After some haggling about money Ferdinand accepted the bargain but declined Zenaïde.

It seems incredible that a man of Napoleon's acumen should have placed any faith in the word of a man so shifty and worthless as Ferdinand. It is even more remarkable that he should have been able to convince himself that the Spanish people would allow their king to keep so discreditable a promise. Ferdinand had even undertaken to pardon all Spaniards who had supported King Joseph and to confirm them in their titles and in the estates they had acquired from their 'rebel' compatriots. Such collaborators were being executed, with or without trial, whenever loyal Spaniards could lay hands on them. It seems that Napoleon did manage to deceive himself that the arrangement would work. He wrote in confidence to his minister in Italy that, 'I have come to an arrangement with the Spaniards which leaves me free to use my troops in Aragon, Catalonia and at Bayonne.'[2] Early in the New Year he began to withdraw troops from both Soult and Suchet on the grounds that they would no longer have Spanish troops opposed to them.

Meanwhile Soult had a much better chance of ending the Spanish entanglement. Ferdinand never intended to keep his word. Soult was presented with the opportunity of inflicting a defeat which could have crippled Wellington's army.

The position the allies had won in France was a cul-de-sac. On their left was the sea, on their right the broad river Nive. At the apex of the triangle formed by these two barriers was the fortress of Bayonne and the river Adour.

The city defences of Bayonne were too antiquated to be formidable but ever since Vitoria intensive work had been done to create an outer line of defences on the two sectors south of the Adour. On the short front between that river and the Nive, the *front de Mous-*

Nive and St Pierre

serolles, and on the longer face south of the city, the *front d'Espagne,* extensive earthworks had been constructed. Wherever possible they were covered by inundations. The field army held an outpost line well to the south of the fortifications and large gangs of enforced labourers continued to pile up earthworks. With the French still on the line Barroilhet–Bassussary, Wellington's view of the fortifications was very incomplete but it was sufficient for him to decide that 'it was impossible to attack the enemy in this position as long as they remained in force in it without the certainty of great loss, at the same time that success was not very probable'.[3]

The alternative was to cross the Nive. The east bank was held by the French as far south as Cambo from where they communicated by a chain of cavalry units with an isolated brigade of infantry* at St-Jean-Pied-de-Port. Their guard on the east bank was not a strong one; it was not intended to be a serious deterrent to an allied crossing. Soult understood Wellington's dilemma and realised that sooner or later part of the allied army must be put across the Nive. Nothing could suit the French better. The fortifications of Bayonne were proof against anything but a formal siege. They could be left in the charge of the regular garrison while the whole of the field force could be used against either isolated part of the allied army. Soult would have the opportunity of destroying Wellington's army in detail while it was astride the river.

To increase Soult's chance of success, his army was now equal to Wellington's in numbers. Since Wellington had sent the Spaniards back to Spain he had only 63,500 infantry.† Soult had 54,500 infantry in his field force‡ but could now count in his fighting strength the 8,000 men of the Bayonne garrison.

After some postponements due to rain the allied right under Hill crossed the Nive between Cambo and Ustaritz on 9 December. 'There was a good deal of skirmishing and some partial contests for

---

* This was General Paris' brigade, 3,500 strong, which had become detached from Suchet's army and which Soult would not release.

† 36,000 British, 23,000 Portuguese, 4,500 Spaniards (Morillo's division).

‡ Including Paris' brigade. The field army now consisted of only eight divisions and the Reserve. Taupin's division was broken up after Nivelle, the units being distributed to the other divisions. Taupin took over Conroux's division, Conroux having been killed.

particular points, but nothing serious.'⁴ Before dark Hill's men had their left flank at Villefranque. Their casualties had been less than 300.

Simultaneously the troops on the west bank made a reconnaissance in force up to the Bayonne fortifications and to the Adour estuary below the city. There was a sharp skirmish round the château of Anglet where 'a numerous party of French staff officers fled precipitately. They had evidently been surprised as the intruders found an excellent *déjeuner à la fourchette* prepared. Chickens, cutlets and other delicacies were pounced upon with no gentle avidity by the hungry soldiers; nor could the strict orders issued by Lord Wellington prevent the transfer from the table to the pocket of every silver spoon and fork within reach.'⁵ During the afternoon the troops fell back until the forward posts were on the line Barroilhet–Bassussary–Urdains, level with those of Hill on the other bank.*

This was the chance for which Soult had been waiting. That night he wrote to Paris that 'the enemy army is divided on the two banks of the Nive. Their general has lost his numerical advantage by extending himself in this way and I intend to attack him in the false position he has taken up.'⁶ Bayonne could be left to the care of its garrison. He could strike with 50,000 men on either side of the river. There were bridges within his fortifications by which he could transfer troops from side to side in safety. The allies were dependent on a repaired bridge and a pontoon bridge at Ustaritz, four miles behind the front. Work on a forward pontoon bridge near Villefranque could not start until 10 December.

Soult decided to launch his attack from the *front d'Espagne*. A breakthrough here would threaten Wellington's communications with the sea and might isolate Hill's corps on the far bank of the Nive. The country on both sides was blind and all the minor roads were ankle-deep in mud, but on the western sector the main Bayonne–St-Jean-de-Luz road was in passable condition and would be a useful artery to support the exploitation of success. The ground

---

* East Bank: Second, Third, Sixth, Portuguese and Morillo's divisions. West Bank: First, Fifth and Light Divisions. One brigade of Seventh. Independent brigades of Aylmer, Bradford and A. Campbell (commanded at the Nivelle by Wilson). Reserve: Fourth Division and two brigades of Seventh.

Page 299   Engraving of Marshal Soult, Duke of Dalmatia, by
Henri Grévedon

Page 300 (*above*) 'Storming of the Ciudad Rodrigo by the Light Division on the Night of 19 January 1812. . . . The Forlorn Hope Led by Capt Gurwood', by J. H. Clark and H. Merke after a sketch by an officer; (*below*) 'Badajoz, on the Guadiana, as Approached From Albuquerque and Elvas 1812', by H. Merke after Henry Smith

on this front was 'extraordinarily difficult even for single horsemen
in moving through the country and the numerous enclosures and
copses denied any distinct view'.[7] This, however, was a disadvantage
common to both armies. French information about allied dispositions was good although they believed that five Anglo-Portuguese
divisions, instead of four, were on the east bank.

Although the allied position had a front of three miles it was so
intersected with ravines that only three lines of attack were available. The most easterly of these, the road that runs along the Nive,
was impracticable as it had to cross the Urdains stream where the
bridge was closely defended by a brigade of Seventh Division. In
the centre was the road Bassussary–Arcangues which was defended
by the Light Division. On the west the main road between Anglet
and Bidart was confined between two lakes, the Lac de Mouriscot
and the Etang de Brindos. At the southern exit of this defile was the
hamlet of Barroilhet of which the principal building was the house
of the mayor of Biarritz, then a negligible fishing port. This part of
the front was Hope's responsibility.

Soult had difficulty in deciding how to allocate his divisions between these two lines of attack. In his first orders he nominated six
divisions to the central attack and only two to the western. Later he
switched one division from centre to west. Villatte's reserve and a
division of dragoons waited within the Bayonne defences to support
whichever attack needed help and to exploit success. Four of the
divisions were tired, having skirmished with Hill on the previous
day and marched through Bayonne during the night. The other four,
which were to lead the attacks, were ordered to move into position
silently, to keep under cover and to make the initial assault with the
bayonet alone.

Wellington was not expecting this massive offensive so soon. He
spent the night of 9–10 December on the east bank, intending to
supervise a further advance by Hill's corps with the aim of establishing their right flank on the Adour north of Vieux Mouguerre, where
they could command the river with a battery, 'by which operation
the enemy, already distressed for provisions, would lose the means
of communication with the interior afforded by that river and become still more distressed'.[8] The French who had opposed Hill on

K

the 9th left their campfires blazing when they retreated into Bayonne and it was not until well after dawn that the British outposts realised that the enemy had decamped.

On the west bank no attack was anticipated. Wellington had given orders for Barroilhet and Bassussary to be fortified but not a sod had been turned by the morning of the 10th. Hope felt so secure that he had left Barroilhet to the care of his two independent Portuguese brigades. Fifth Division was stationed three miles in rear at Bidart while First Division and Aylmer's brigade had been withdrawn seven miles to billets in St-Jean-de-Luz.

The Light Division had its forward posts in front of Bassussary. Its main body was in Arcangues, but one brigade was under orders to retire to Arbonne. At dawn on 10 December Lieutenant Cooke, Forty Third, was in charge of the piquets on a spur running north from Bassussary. His French opposite numbers were 'within one hundred yards, loitering about as usual, without any outward display of anything going on, or any signs indicating they were about to assume offensive operations'. At 8 am his brigadier, Kempt, his commanding officer, William Napier, and their staffs came up to his piquet house.

> They all entered into an indifferent conversation, without contemplating that an attack was meditated by the enemy. Major Napier remarked that he thought the French loiterers seemed very busy, which induced us to approach the window, which commanded a full view of the enemy's piquet house, and having looked at them for some time without seeing the cause of the alarm, some of the party burst into a loud laugh and declared it was only Napier's fancy; but he still persisted and would not give up his point, saying he had seen them very often before, in a like manner, walking off by ones and twos, to assemble at given points, before making some rapid and simultaneous assault; and sure enough before the expiration of half an hour these one and twos increased considerably all along the hedges.

Kempt was still sceptical but was persuaded to alert the brigade and to reinforce the piquet. He and Napier rode off to give the orders.
Left alone, Cooke made a tour of his sentries, when one of them,

> stationed on the most rising ground turned his back on the French and beckoned me. On my reaching his post, he informed me that he

had seen a mountain gun brought on a mule's back and placed
behind a bush. In a few minutes, Marshal Soult with about forty
staff officers came to within point blank range of my piquet to
reconnoitre the ground. During this interval I fancied I heard a
buzz of voices behind a small hillock and, on climbing a fruit tree,
I could just descry the enemy lying down in readiness to pounce
upon us.

Cooke dashed off a message to the general and returned to his
observation.

I saw some French soldiers, headed by an officer, issue from the
hedges and move round our right flank, within one hundred yards.
The officer naturally thought we should fire at him. Therefore to
feign indifference, he placed his telescope to his eye, looked carelessly about in all directions, and made a bow to us. The French,
witnessing our civility to their small party, were not to be outdone
in *politesse* and called out to our sentinels to retire in French and
Spanish.*
   At half past nine a.m., the enemy's skirmishers came forward in a
careless fashion, talking to each other, and good naturedly allowed
our sentinels to retire without firing at them.

Cooke had been ordered not to open fire 'until the very last
moment' and waited until the French were only twenty yards from
a barrier his men had built across the road. Then he called:

'Now, fire away!' The first discharge did great execution. The
enemy then debouched from behind the thickets in crowds; our
flanks were turned right and left, and the brisk French *voltigeurs*
rushed impetuously forward, covered by two mountain guns, their
trumpets blowing, and shouting 'En avant, en avant, Francais!
Vive l'Empereur!'[9]

The Light Division's outposts retreated with small loss except on
the extreme right where fifty men were trapped and captured. The
main body of the division was drawn up to receive the enemy on the
ridge of Arcangues. This was 1,000 yards wide and was crowned by

---

This courtesy between the outposts was one of the more civilised features of the
Peninsular War and was always observed between the French and the Anglo-Portuguese armies (the Spaniards did not subscribe). Wellington remarked, 'I always encouraged this; the killing of a poor fellow of a vedette or carrying off a post could not
influence the battle and I always when I was going to attack sent to tell them to get out
of the way' (Croker i 433).

a château and a church, both ready-made fortifications, and flanked by marshy re-entrants. Held by 4,000 men supported by two mountain guns, it was a position which could not be taken without heavy loss, if indeed it could be forced at all. The French made one unenthusiastic attack which was beaten off with ease and settled down to a prolonged bombardment with twelve guns, 'firing within about a thousand yards, which knocked about the tombstones during the greater part of the day. The walls of the church were cannon proof.'[10]

Soult rode away to stimulate his right-hand attack. He had heard from deserters that the allied reserves were stationed far to the rear and was disappointed that this had not been the case at Arcangues. At Barroilhet, his information was correct. The piquet line between the lakes was surprised and more than 200 men captured. A Portuguese brigade checked the French advance beside the Mouriscot lake but French dragoons charged some unprepared Portuguese infantry and broke them. The defence force fell back to the Mayor's house at Barroilhet and for some hours there was desperate fighting around the buildings. Allied reinforcements dribbled in from their quarters at Bidart and Guéthary but they were always greatly outnumbered. Reille had started the day with three divisions. When Soult saw that the attack at Arcangues was grinding to a halt he diverted a division from there to strengthen Reille and also sent Villatte's Reserve to his support. The enclosed ground hampered the French greatly but they 'pushed our troops a good deal and we began to give way in disorder. To add to the perplexity of the moment the Fifth Division, having been separated during the night, and the ammunition not being forthcoming, had hardly a round left. There was nothing to do but hold our ground as well as we could till more troops and ammunition should arrive. In this situation, ebbing and flowing, repulsing the enemy and being ourselves forced back, we continued until about two o'clock.'[11]

Everything depended on the time it took the First Division and Aylmer's brigade to march up from St-Jean-de-Luz. No one had anticipated fighting that day. The troops had marched twenty miles the previous day and were tired. The general impression was that the army was going into winter quarters and that the campaign would not be resumed until the spring dried out the roads. Even the sounof firing to the north did not stir any excitement. The chaplain at headquarters was writing a letter and, hearing 'a heavy cannonade', told his correspondent 'the weather is so wet that I have not thought it worthwhile to go and see the fight'.[12] No one seems to have taken any more notice.

At eleven o'clock an ADC dashed into the town from Barroilhet and a few minutes afterwards the bugles sounded for the troops to get under arms.

> We had not proceeded above a mile when indications of what was going on in front began to present themselves, in the form of baggage, mules and horses pouring in all haste and confusion to the rear; whilst a wounded man or two dragged himself in the same direction, and gave, as the wounded invariably do, the most alarming account of the state of affairs. 'Push on! Push on! for God's sake,' said one poor fellow who had been shot through the head and was lying across a horse. 'Push on or it will all be over!' Of course we quickened our pace with infinite good will.[13]

They had ten miles to cover and it was two o'clock before the first to arrive, Aylmer's brigade, reached the ridge behind Barroilhet and saw 'a very magnificent, as well as gratifying, spectacle. The merest handful of British troops were opposing themselves, in the most determined manner, to a mass of men, so dense and so extended, as to cover the whole of the main road as far as the eye could reach. Our people were, it is true, giving way. But no sooner had the head of our column shown itself than their confidence completely returned and they renewed their struggle with increased alacrity.'[14] The French attack faltered and their advanced troops were withdrawn to regroup.

Soult made one further attack. His men forced their way up to the walls of the Mayor's house and nearly surrounded it. John Hope, who was observing the battle from an upstairs window, had to run to his horse and gallop away while his staff slashed at the *voltigeurs* with their sabres. The general was wounded in the leg and his clothes and hat shot through in several places. The sight of the First Division approaching checked the French advance and a report from his right that the British were massing behind the Urdains stream induced Soult to order a retreat. He left his advanced posts on the ground occupied that morning by the allied piquets.

10 December was an unsatisfactory day for both sides. Each army lost about 1,600 men.* Soult had had an opportunity that was never likely to recur. If all had gone well he could have maimed Wellington's army and given himself the chance to destroy it before the New Year. He failed because he could not decide to strike a hammer blow at one point and had dispersed his superiority in two attacks. His errors were compounded by his subordinates who fought without determination. Clausel in particular directed the attack on Arcangues in a way that could only be described as timid. The troops, taking their cue from the generals, attacked without the *élan* which had marked their assaults at Vimeiro, Talavera, Busaco and as late as Sorauren.

On the allied side, Wellington and Hope were both surprised. The weight and timing of the French attack had caught them on the wrong foot. Hope had some excuse since he was new to the theatre. Wellington, wrote Napier, was from 'a long course of victory somewhat negligent of his own security'.[15] If his orders to entrench the key points of Bassussary and Arcangues had been promptly obeyed the situation would have been much less dangerous, but it is hard to acquit him of having failed to check on Hope's dispositions instead of spending the night with the dependable Hill. Hill, he said, 'had invariably done well, always exactly obeyed my orders and executed them successfully'.[16] Hill was known to be trustworthy. Hope was an unknown quantity, although his determination extracted him from the mess into which his lack of foresight had landed him. In the event it was the staunchness of the troops, British and Portuguese, which defeated the French, and Wellington remarked later, 'I will tell you the difference between Soult and me: when he gets into a difficulty, his troops don't get him out of it; mine always do.'[17]

That night Soult suffered a further loss to his army. Three German battalions, who had fought with the French in Spain since 1808, marched into the British lines and asked to be repatriated. Their sovereign prince, the Grand Duke of Nassau, had been liberated by the eastern allies and contrived to send a message to their commanding officer, Colonel Krüse, ordering him to change sides. Another

---

* The allied total included 500 prisoners, the largest total ever lost by the Anglo-Portuguese army in a single day under Wellington's command.

German battalion failed to get away and was disarmed by Soult. The total loss to the French was about 2,000 men.

There were constant minor actions around Barroilhet on 11 and 12 December. Each side feared that the other was meditating a major attack, whereas neither wished for more than minor adjustments of the outpost line. The fighting was to the advantage of the French. They suffered fewer casualties and kept the allied attention and reserves concentrated on the west bank of the Nive. The allied position was, however, strengthened by the completion of a pontoon bridge at Villefranque constructed of 'seventeen country boats'.[18]

On the night of 12 December the new bridge was washed away by the flooding river. Hill, with the Second and Portuguese Divisions, 14,000 men and 10 guns, was out of reach of immediate support. The heavy skirmishing of the last two days had persuaded Wellington to keep two reserve divisions near the western end of the Villefranque bridge, within four miles' march of Hill's line, but with the bridge gone they could cross only at Ustaritz with a march three times as long.

As the water was rising and sweeping the 'seventeen country boats' downstream towards Bayonne, Soult's field force was crossing the river to St-Pierre d'Irube at the foot of the position held by Hill's corps. At about 8 am four French divisions with two more in support started to attack uphill. There were three infantrymen attacking for every one of the defenders and twenty-two guns against ten.

Hill was fortunate in that 'our front was necessarily confined, extending (at about a league from Bayonne which was in full view) from Petit Mouguerre on our right to a swamp near the Nive on our left'.[19] Soult's startline was even shorter and the French had trouble and delay in deploying from the two bridges and the narrow *Front de Mousserolles*. For several hours the battle swung in the balance. The French had an uncovenanted advantage when two British lieutenant-colonels, Nathaniel Peacocke of the Seventy First and William Bunbury of the Buffs, lost their nerve and left the field, Bunbury taking his battalion with him. Hill fed his few reserves into the battle with skill and spirit. Each French attack was met and, by a narrow margin, held. Detached companies held on in isolation until relieved by such driblets of reinforcement as could be spared. 'Dead or alive,' said

Hill, 'we must hold our ground.' Colonel Brown turned to his battalion, the North Gloucesters, and shouted, ' "There they come, my boys; if you don't kill them they'll kill you. Fire away!" This was the longest address he ever made to his men; he never had but one book, and that was the Army List.'[20]

> Positions were taken and retaken at the point of the bayonet. The Ninety Second, under the gallant veteran Cameron, was at one time nearly overwhelmed by the force of numbers, and obliged to give way; but it was only for a moment. Reforming their skeleton ranks they returned to the charge with bagpipes playing and colours flying, led on by their colonel, sword in hand, over the bodies of their slain comrades. With a shout that rose above the shrill tones of the pipes the veterans charged, in two ranks deep, the mass before them, and regained the ground they had lost. At every point the enemy gave way.[21]

Soult ordered another attack but the brigade which was to lead it had already suffered much from artillery fire. The battalions were disordered by fugitives and wounded men pouring through their ranks. They refused to advance. The first of the allied reserve divisions reached the ground but they were no longer needed. The battle was won. Riding up to the corps commander Wellington took his hand and said, ' "Hill, the day's your own." Our men threw up their caps and gave one long thrilling cheer, that echoed down the valleys amongst the retiring foe.'[22]

The battle of St-Pierre was, according to a gunner who was present, 'a murderous day. The main road in places was literally running in blood.'[23] Hill's corps lost 1,750 men and the French almost twice as many. In all, the four-day battle of the Nive cost the allies 5,000 casualties and the French 1,000 more, apart from the 2,000 Germans who changed sides. It had been Soult's last chance. Wellington had broken out of his cul-de-sac and the marshal was now faced with the impossible task of defending open country with an inferior and increasingly despondent army. For the next nine weeks weather alone halted the allied advance.

Page 309 'Battle of Salamanca', engraving by J. T. Whitmore after Campion

The capture of Sir Edward Paget on the retreat from Burgos, 1812, by M. Dubourg after

CHAPTER 21

The Occupation of Gascony

A week after the battle of St-Pierre, an artillery officer wrote, 'The rains have returned, the country is almost impassable and we have had a good deal of lightning.' Three days later he added, 'A stormy day, the rains have carried away all our bridges over the Nive.'[1] The eastern allies urged Wellington to keep up his pressure on Soult, but he wrote:

> I beg you will assure the Russian ambassador that there is nothing I can do with the force under my command that I will not do. In military operations there are some things which cannot be done; one of these is to move troops during or immediately after a heavy fall of rain. I should be guilty of a useless waste of men if I were to attempt an operation during the violent falls of rain which we have here. Our operations, then, must necessarily be slow but they shall not be discontinued.[2]

Until mid-February the campaign stagnated, both sides putting their troops in billets. There had often been long pauses during the campaigns in Portugal and Spain, but this was the first time such a pause had occurred with the outposts in close touch with each other. Relations across no-man's-land became friendly. British and French cavalry colonels arranged for the horses of their regiments to be watered at the same spot at different times. A major 'riding a troublesome horse got close to a French sentinel. The latter called out several times and ordered him off. The horse still plunging on, and the officer apparently not understanding the man, the French sentry turned the horse the other way by the bridle and sent him back.'[3] French officers bartered brandy for tea. They 'kindly proffered their services in sending into Bayonne for anything for us that we required. I got a piece of cloth to make up a new Sunday pair of inexpressibles, very much required.'⁴

Behind the allied line the French civilians were finding themselves better treated by their enemies than they had been by their own troops. No units had to be detached to guard the allied communications. 'We now go about the roads here as safely as in Spain; the only marauders indeed are the followers of our own army and runaway Spaniards and muleteers.'⁵ 'What do you think,' asked Wellington of an officer who had served earlier on his staff, 'of the French people running into our posts for protection from the French posts, with their bundles on their heads and their *beds*, as you will recollect to have seen the people of Portugal and Spain?'⁶

This was discouraging to Soult who was vainly trying to stir up a guerrilla against the allies, but he had more pressing worries. The eastern allies had crossed the Rhine on New Year's Day. By the middle of January they had reached Nancy. The Austrians occupied Switzerland. Napoleon was defending the whole length of France's eastern frontier with 85,000 men against 180,000. He knew that only desperate measures could save his empire. Planning an attack on St-Dizier, he ordered, 'Requisition at Vitry 2 to 300,000 bottles of wine and brandy, to be issued to the army today and tomorrow. If there is only champagne, take it all the same.'⁷ Even 300,000 bottles of champagne among a corps of 30,000 men was not enough to stem the tide. More troops were essential. Soult was ordered to send eastwards two infantry divisions and half his cavalry. Suchet had to contribute 10,000 men. Around Bayonne only 60,000 men with 77 field guns were left.⁶/¹⁰

Soult asked the Emperor for new orders. They were a long time in coming. Meanwhile he strove to contain Wellington on a line anchored at the ends by the fortresses of Bayonne and St-Jean-Pied-de-Port. He expected the allies to undertake the siege of Bayonne by passing one or two corps across the Adour above the fortress. To meet such a move he stationed three of his divisions on the north bank of the river between Bayonne and Port de Lanne. Four more were on the south bank at right angles to the Adour with their left flank at Hellette. Their front was covered by the river Joyeuse. From

Hellette the cavalry continued the line to St-Jean, which was beset by Mina's guerrilla now designated as a regular Spanish brigade. With his headquarters at Peyrehorade, Soult intended to attack Wellington's flank as he attempted the crossing of the Adour.

Once more Soult had misread his enemy's intention. Bayonne with its port would have been valuable to Wellington, but it could be taken quickly only by using the whole allied army. He preferred to invest it with a single corps and conduct a leisurely siege while fighting Soult in open country with the rest of the army. He was convinced that crossing the Adour above the city would be a difficult and dangerous operation. The siege was to be conducted by Hope's corps reinforced by as many Spaniards as were needed. The other two corps were to draw Soult away from Bayonne. The British cavalry were ordered up from their billets at Vitoria. The light brigades were at the front when the campaign opened, the heavy a few weeks later.

The rain continued into February. On 4 February a staff officer wrote, 'Still rain, rain, rain, all night. All yesterday, all the night before, and still continuing.' A week later he could say, 'we have had three days' fine weather now together and this last is absolutely warm; thermometer in my room, window open and no fire, 58° in the sun'.[8] The weather stayed bright and on 14 February Wellington's move started. Hill's corps* marched eastward from Urrcarray towards Harispe's division at Hellette. Harispe fell back towards St-Palais and the line of the river Bidouse. Simultaneously Picton's division on Hill's left moved on Bonloc. Villatte, who held that town, realised that Harispe's retreat had uncovered his flank and fell back to the Bidouse without fighting. On Hill's right Morillo's Spaniards made their way through the foothills of the Pyrenees.

Next day Hill's advanced guard came up with Harispe at Garris, a little short of St-Palais. The French had a good position on a long ridge and Harispe decided to make a stand although he had the single bridge over the Bidouse in his rear. Pringle's brigade, leading Hill's

---

* Hill's corps consisted, as usual, of the Second and Portuguese Divisions and Morillo's Spaniards. With them was Fane's cavalry brigade (13th and 14th Lt Dgns). In the early stages the Third Division was also under Hill's command, giving him a strength of about 20,000.

column, probed the French defences but did not press their advance. It was late in the day and all ranks 'were looking forward to the repose of the bivouack when an aide-de-camp at full speed quickly delivered an order from Lord Wellington, pointing to the enemy's position—"Take the hill before dark!" The effect was electrical. The men responded by the loud, deep animating cheer. The words were then given—"Fix bayonets! Shoulder arms! Double quick!" and the next instant the brigade in close column plunged into the ravine.'⁹ Wellington was determined that the enemy should have no time to settle themselves on the line of the Bidouse and hurled at them the first troops available. He was amply justified. Pringle's two battalions* reached the crest of the ridge, and although they were strongly counter-attacked they held their foothold. Meanwhile Morillo's Spaniards were aiming to cut in between the river and Garris and the Portuguese Division began to close in on the bridge. Harispe hurriedly ordered a retreat which turned into a rout. Having lost 300 killed and wounded, the division poured over the bridge in confusion leaving 200 prisoners on the west bank. Harispe could not halt them at St-Palais and was able to reform the division only at Dornezain. The French line on the Bidouse had proved as ineffective as that on the Joyeuse. Hill's corps was delayed on the river only by the difficulties in crossing an inexpertly blown bridge.

When Soult heard on the morning of the 16th that St-Palais was lost he ordered a retreat to the line Peyrehorade–Sauveterre–Navarrenx, the line of the lower Saison and the Gave d'Oleron. At the same time he called for two of the three divisions which he had stationed on the north bank of the Adour. This would give him seven divisions, 32,000 infantry and 3,800 cavalry, to oppose Wellington's western drive.

On the same day, 16 February, Wellington ordered Beresford's corps† to advance on Hill's left, aiming for the Bidouse at Bidache. The allied striking force was made up to 42,000 infantry and 3,000

* Pringle had only two battalions (1/28th and 2/34th) and his Rifle company, about 950 rank and file. 1/39th was absent collecting new clothing at St Jean-de-Luz.

† Beresford's corps consisted of the Fourth, Sixth, Seventh and Light Divisions with the light cavalry brigades of Lord Edward Somerset (7th, 10th and 15th Hussars) and Hussey Vivian (18th Hussars and 1st Hussars KGL). The strength was 23,000 infantry and 2,400 cavalry.

cavalry. Behind them Soult had left Abbé's division, bringing the garrison of Bayonne up to 14,000, more than he could afford to spare from the operating army.

Soult had his seven divisions in position on his new line by 18 February. He held a bridgehead on the south bank at Hastingues which Beresford's cavalry reconnoitred that day while Hill probed at Sauveterre. That evening the weather broke. 'Very cold and rainy, changing into sleet and snow.'[10] The allied advance halted for four days and all troops not in contact with the enemy were billeted in houses. It was a necessary precaution. The long campaign had played havoc with their clothing. An observer said of the Fifty Seventh that 'the men are absolutely in rags and tatters, here and there there are five or six inches of bare thigh or arm visible through the patches; some have had only linen pantaloons all the winter through.'[11] *

Wellington did not wish to hurry Soult at this stage. He was anxious that the French move away from Bayonne should be completed. Then he intended to return to St-Jean-de-Luz to check the arrangements for his next venture. He rode there through the snow on 19 February but was back at his headquarters at Garris by the night of the 21st.

Six years earlier, when he had been defending Oporto, Soult had been convinced that Wellesley would try to turn the river line by a seaborne hook across the mouth of the Douro. He neglected to guard the river above the city and was surprised by an attack on that side. A memory of this mistake may have been in his mind when he gave his orders for the defence of Bayonne in 1814. Abbé's division, the only field formation available, was disposed upstream from the city. No guard was set below Bayonne. It is hard to blame the marshal for this omission. The estuary of the Adour beyond the reach of the guns of the fortress is at least 300 yards across and has a tidal rise and fall of 14 feet. With the right of the allied army committed to a campaign which entailed the frequent crossing of rivers

---

* New clothing was issued to regiments at the beginning of each year. During this part of the campaign battalions were being sent down to St-Jean-de-Luz in rotation to be reclothed.

and *gaves*, it seemed impossible that Wellington could summon up enough pontoons to bridge such a formidable river.

Wellington had no intention of relying on pontoons. Instead he hired at the ports along the coast forty-eight small-decked vessels known as *chasse-marées*,* which were to be brought into position by sailing them into the mouth of the Adour. 'There were put on board each, 28 three inch planks 12 feet in length, one piece of timber 10 inches square, having five grooves in its upper surface, 2 hand-saws, 2 axes and two skeins of Hambro' line.'[12] The five grooves were to accommodate 13-inch cables, 'supplied by the Admiral or purchased in St-Jean-de-Luz', which were to carry the planking of the bridge. At the near end of the bridge an elaborate frame of balks of timber with blocks and tackles to adjust the length of the cables to the rise and fall of the tide was to be built. At the far end the cables were to be secured by attaching 'an 18 pounder iron gun to the end of each and raising the gun over the embankment wall of the river, which was fourteen feet in height next the water; and then lowering it down ten feet (the depth of the wall towards the land) into a marsh where it would bury itself'. Two men of the Royal Sappers and Miners were embarked in each *chasse-marée* 'for the purpose of cutting away the waste boards to render the deck level and also to spike down the timber prepared with grooves to receive the cables'. They were then to lay the three-inch planks across the cables, securing them with the Hambro' line, to form a roadway. It was an improvisation of genius but, considering that there could be no reconnaissance of the further bank, its employment was a most daring operation.

Wellington had hoped to be present to supervise the crossing but, he wrote on 20 February, 'the weather is so unfavourable that it is impossible to attempt this operation at the present moment and I leave it to Lieut-General Sir John Hope to cross the Adour whenever the weather will permit'.[13] It was not until the afternoon of the 22nd that the fleet of *chasse-marées* could put to sea. That night the First Division with some pontoons and heavy artillery moved up to a covered position near the estuary. At dawn next day Hope sent

---

* The *chasse-marées* were between 53 and 40 feet long, from 30 to 50 tons burden. The cost of their hire was '£123. 8s. 6d. per day besides the expense of 200 rations issued to the crews'.

some of the other formations of his corps to conduct a noisy demonstration against the southern defences of Bayonne, and the First Division reached the estuary at a point two-and-a-half miles below the fortress. The heavy guns drove away the corvette *Sapho* and some French gunboats which were on the Adour below Bayonne. By the end of the morning there was no sign of the *chasse-marées*. A change in the wind had blown them all out to sea.

Hope had only five pontoons and four jolly-boats but he decided that it would be better to risk a crossing with these inadequate means than to sacrifice surprise. On the far bank there was only a weak French piquet which was easily scared away by artillery. Fifty men crossed in the jolly-boats taking with them a hawser. The pontoons, lashed together as rafts, were then hauled to and fro across the river loaded with men. It was a slow business, especially as the tide began to flow strongly during the afternoon. Only six companies of the Guards and two of the Sixtieth were across with a troop of Congreve rockets when, towards dusk, the French showed some signs of interest. Two weak battalions, about 700 men, advanced towards the bridgehead from Bayonne. 'They came on with apparent spirit, but after having a few rockets fired at them hastily retired, not having more than twenty men killed and wounded, of whom several fell by the rockets; one rocket having killed one man and wounded four others seemed the signal for retiring, which they did precipitately.'[14] The crossing continued all night by the light of the moon and huge bonfires lit on either bank.

It was not until the afternoon of 24 February that the wind

set direct on the land, driving a heavy sea before it. Immediately the flotilla, led by an English gunboat, ran for the mouth of the river. A high surf on the bar and the uncertainty of hitting a shifting channel dismayed the native crews of the *chasse-marées*, but stimulated to the performance of their duty by the officers and sappers most of them ventured on and 34 entered the river without accident. One grounded on the bar, one was driven on shore and 12 returned to St.-Jean-de-Luz. A sloop was driven ashore, and also one of the gun boats, and went to pieces. The *chasse-marées*, immediately on reaching the spot selected for the bridge, were anchored head and stern in a masterly manner by the navy, the cables stretched across the river, the planking fastened to them, and

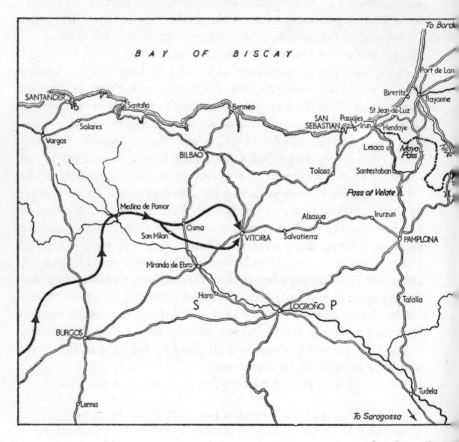

Southern Fran

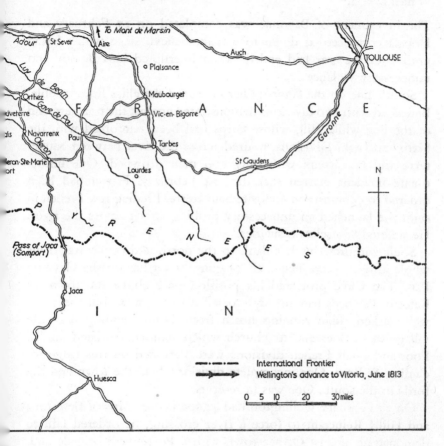

Adour St Sever Aire To Mont de Marsin

Luy de Béarn Plaisance Auch TOULOUSE

Orthez Gave de Pau Maubourget F R A N C E Garonne

uveterre Vic-en-Bigorre

dis Navarrenx Pau Oloron Tarbes

eron-Ste-Marie St Gaudens

ort Lourdes N

P Y R E N E E S

Pass of Jaca (Somport)

Jaca I N

Huesca

International Frontier

Wellington's advance to Vitoria, June 1813

0 5 10 20 30 miles

hern Spain

every other arrangement carried into effect with such assiduity (the sappers working throughout the night), that by noon on the following day the bridge was reported passable and many troops filed over it.[15]

The investment of Bayonne was completed on 27 February and Hope's corps settled down to a make-believe siege which lasted until after the war had ended, when it erupted into bloody and unnecessary violence.

Soult's line on the Gave d'Oleron caused the allies little trouble. Beresford with two divisions demonstrated against the northern end of the line while Hill, whose corps had been reinforced with the Sixth and Light Divisions, poured across the river between Sauveterre and Navarrenx with only two men drowned. One unfortunate incident marred that day, 24 February. Picton had been ordered to demonstrate opposite Sauveterre. Finding few French in sight, he launched an unnecessary probing attack across the river. He suffered 80 useless casualties.

Soult withdrew his left flank to the north and concentrated his whole army, 36,000 men with 48 guns, at Orthez on the Gave de Pau. The Gave protected his position only above the town, as Beresford's corps had already crossed it to the west, but there is a well-marked ridge running north from Orthez ending near the village of St-Boes and its church which stand on isolated knolls. Four-and-a-half French divisions were stationed on this ridge including St-Boes. One incomplete division* held the town and the fords to the south. One was in reserve.

On 27 February Wellington had 44,000 in the corps of Beresford and Hill.† Reluctant to force a river crossing, he ordered Hill to demonstrate against Orthez town with a Portuguese brigade and, with two divisions, to be ready 'to effect the passage of the river near Orthez as soon as he could'.[16] At the other end of Soult's line Beresford was to attack St-Boes with the Fourth Division supported by the Seventh. On their right the Third followed by the Sixth was

---

* This was Harispe's 8th Division which, unlike the others, had three brigades. One brigade was on the ridge. The other two were on the left but they were as strong as most of the other French divisions.
† Morillo's division had been detached to besiege Navarrenx and five British battalions were absent collecting their new clothing.

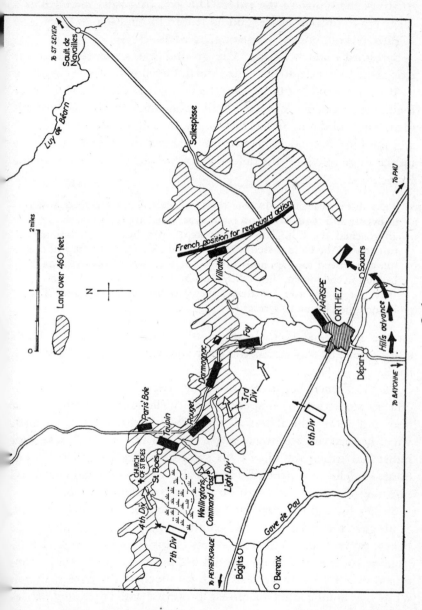

To ST SEVER

Sault de Navailles

Luy de Béarn

Sallespisse

French position for rearguard action

Villatte

2 miles

Land over 460 feet

N

Foy

Darmagnac

Rouget

3rd Div

Paris Bde

Taupin

CHURCH OF ST BOES

St Boes

Light Div

Wellington's Command Post

4th Div

7th Div

To PEYREHORADE

Bagits

Berenx

Gave de Pau

6th Div

Départ

To BAYONNE

HARISPE

ORTHEZ

So_ars

Hills advance

To PAU

Orthez

to attack the centre of the ridge. This was originally intended as a diversion to prevent Soult sending troops to reinforce St-Boes. The Light Division, only 3,500 strong, acted as reserve.

Beresford's attack failed. 'The ground was so narrow that the troops could not deploy.'[17] The Fourth Division took the church of St-Boes but could not break into the village. A counter-attack drove them back from the church. Wellington immediately changed his plan. The Third and Sixth Divisions were told to press their attack and the Fifty Second Regiment was ordered to advance diagonally up the ridge to cut off the defenders of St-Boes from the rest of the French line.

> They did it beautifully [wrote their colonel]. They marched down as evenly and regularly as on parade, accelerating their march as we approached the hill. The French kept up a heavy fire, but for-tunately all the balls passed over our heads. I rode to the top of the hill and waved my cap, and though the men were over their knees in mud in the marsh, they trotted up in the finest order. As soon as they got to the top I ordered them to halt and open fire. The French then began to retreat.[18]

At the same time Picton's division reached the crest and Hill's corps forced its way across the river and started to turn the French flank.

As the French began to give way, Alava, the Spanish liaison officer, was struck by a spent bullet. Wellington was laughing at him 'and telling him it was all nonsense and that he was not hurt, when he received a blow, a worse one, on the hip'.[19] A case shot bullet had struck the hilt of his sword, driving it against his hip bone. He fell to the ground. He was able to remount and continued directing the battle although he was in considerable pain.

Seeing his right giving way and his left being turned by Hill, Soult gave the order to retire behind the next riverline, the Luy de Béarn, twelve miles in his rear. Many of his conscripts were already running for it as fast as they could go, but the veteran troops con-tinued to put up a strong resistance for much of the retreat. Picton wrote that Soult started his retreat 'protected with large solid masses of infantry, successively taking up the most advantageous ground that offered; and the retreat was for some time made with great order and regularity; but as the evening approached, the disorder gradually increased'.[20]

The French were uncomfortably aware that behind them was the single bridge at Sault de Navailles, and the closer they got to it the more men left the columns and made the best way they could to the rear. The three British cavalry brigades were forward but the ground was, as a French historian described it, 'un terrain de steeple-chase',[21] and only the Seventh Hussars were able to make an effective charge, taking 200 prisoners. By nightfall Soult's army was across the Luy and in temporary safety. It had lost 4,000 men of whom 1,350 were left as prisoners of war. Many more deserted. The Anglo-Portuguese loss was less than 2,200.

Soult realised it was useless to defend the Luy de Béarn with his defeated and demoralised army. He hurried them northward to the Adour at St-Sever. There he had to choose between defending Bordeaux and defending Toulouse. He could not attempt to do both. Bordeaux was the third city of France and its port would be invaluable to Wellington. Militarily it was in a desert. Round it stretched the sandy, barren Landes where no army could hope to feed itself. His supply problem was becoming acute. His two main forward supply bases, Mont de Marsan and Dax, were hopelessly vulnerable. Food could be obtained only further inland. 'Failing positive orders to the contrary, I shall not fall back towards Bordeaux, where I should be in difficulties with the Garonne behind me. I should have to leave the whole of the south of the Empire open to the enemy. I shall manoeuvre in the direction of Toulouse.'[22]

Wellington's aim was to destroy Soult's army, but he could not afford to neglect Bordeaux. Apart from its port facilities it was a moral prize of great value and a centre of anti-Bonapartist feeling. He detached Beresford with the Seventh Division, supported by the Fourth, and some cavalry to occupy the city. To make up the numbers of his field force he called forward his heavy cavalry and, with some trepidation, 8,000 Spanish infantry. This could be done only if he paid and supplied them. 'I undertake,' he wrote to their commander, 'to give them pay as for the other troops of the army and to give them rations. Please make available such supplies as you have in your depots and I will credit them to the account of the

Spanish government. This can be arranged officially.'[23] It was not Soult's army that he feared at this stage, but a persistent rumour came to him that Suchet had sent 10,000 men to help his brother marshal. Beresford occupied Bordeaux amid the acclamations of the inhabitants on 12 March. He left the Seventh Division in the city and brought the Fourth Division back to the main army.

Wellington manoeuvred the French out of Aire in a messy little skirmish on 2 March, whereupon Soult fell back to the east bank of the Adour (which here runs from south to north) around Maubourget and Plaisance. Here, to his surprise, the marshal found himself left in peace for ten days. The pause occurred because Wellington, between detaching Beresford to Bordeaux and the arrival of the Spanish reinforcements, had only 29,000 infantry and cavalry in hand, a smaller force than Soult's army.

During the pause the orders Soult had requested from the Emperor arrived. Like most of Napoleon's orders for the Peninsular army, they were unequivocal but too late to be obeyed.

> Tell the Duke of Dalmatia that he should keep in close touch with Bayonne but that he should resume the offensive by falling on one of the enemy's flanks even if he can only do so with 20,000 men. He must seize his opportunity boldly and he will win the upper hand over the allies. He has enough talent to understand what I mean.[24]

Soult assured Paris that he intended to take the offensive but restricted his movements to a cautious probing of Wellington's right. Seeing that the allies were ready to fight in a good position, he retreated to Tarbes on 17 March.* By that time his momentary advantage had evaporated. The Spaniards had come into line, the heavy cavalry brigades were close behind, and on 19 March the Fourth Division was back with Wellington.

A day earlier the allied army moved forward in three columns. Wellington hoped that the flanking divisions would be able to encircle Soult's rear.

We attacked the enemy's rearguard at Vic Bigorre on the 19th and

---

* On 17/18 March French cavalry made a showy demonstration against the allied rear areas. Captain Daunia with 100 troopers rode round the southern flank and captured 100 prisoners near St-Sever. It was a bold and brilliantly executed raid but, since it was the only one of its kind, it achieved very little.

we had a partial affair with their whole army at Tarbes on the 20th and were very near to catching them in a terrible situation. We have since followed them but their troops have marched with such celerity that, apart from the advanced guard of cavalry who attacked them at St. Gaudens, our troops have never been able to come up with them.[25]

Having escaped from the trap which Wellington had set for him, Soult entered one of his own devising. He put the whole of his field army into Toulouse. His troops had shown themselves unable to cope with their enemy in open country. As a last resort he packed them into a city with permanent fortifications.

CHAPTER 22

Victory

THE advanced guard of the eastern allied armies entered Paris on 31 March 1814. They were applauded as liberators. There were shouts of 'Down with Bonaparte' and 'No conscription', but there was no enthusiasm for any form of alternative government. Napoleon, who was planning a flank attack to the east of the capital, was astonished when he heard that the city had fallen. He hurried to Fontainebleau with 60,000 men, determined to retake his capital. He outlined his plan to Marshals Berthier, Ney, Macdonald and Oudinot. Ney told him bluntly that the army would not march. Raising his voice, the Emperor declared, 'The army will obey me.' 'The army,' replied Ney, 'will obey its generals.' That evening Napoleon abdicated in favour of his son. He was too late. Marmont had conducted an epic defence of Paris against great odds. On 4 April he and his corps surrendered. The allies thereupon insisted on an unconditional abdication. Napoleon consented at 6 am on 6 April. Later that day the Senate voted that 'The French people freely call to the throne of France Louis-Stanislas-Xavier, brother to the last king.'

At midnight on 7 April 'Colonel Cooke, of the service of his Britannic Majesty, and Colonel St Simon of the French service' rode out of Paris on the Bordeaux road. They carried the proclamation of the end of the war, but they did not reach Wellington until 12 April.

The allied cavalry had come within sight of Toulouse on 26 March. The weather was abominable and Wellington's first problem was to cross the river Garonne. Toulouse stands on the east bank of that

Page 327 'Storming the Town and Castle of San Sebastian in Spain. Sept 1813', by Clark and Dubourg after a drawing by an officer

Page 328 (*above*) 'Ford across the Bidassoa at Endarlacha 5 Miles above Irun'; (*below*) 'Bridge of Boats across the Adour below Bayonne'. Both from *Campaign in the Western Pyrenees and the South of France*, R. Batty, 1823

considerable river. On the west was only the fortified suburb of St-
Cyprien. Toulouse, wrote the Quartermaster-General, 'is quite unassailable in that direction'.[1] The easiest line of attack against Toulouse is from the south, but there were not enough pontoons with
the army to cross both the Garonne and, as would be necessary on
the south, its tributary the Arriège. A bridging site had to be found
north of the city. This would bring the allies up against the water
defences of Toulouse. Two miles east of the city the little river Ers
runs parallel to the Garonne. Round the north and east faces of the
city walls runs the Languedoc canal. Between the Ers and the canal
is a long ridge, the Heights of Calvinet (Mont Rave), which domi-
nates the defences. Soult had fortified the Heights with redoubts and
devoted most of his infantry strength to their defence.

Wellington's pontoon bridge was put across the Garonne eleven
miles downstream from Toulouse on 4 April at the top of the
corridor between the Garonne and the Ers. By nightfall three infantry divisions, two cavalry brigades and two batteries were on the
east bank. 'The enemy's cavalry retired and we expected every
moment that their troops would appear to oppose the passage. But
not a man showed himself. The river is exceedingly rapid and we had
our fears for the bridge which, in despite of four stays made fast to
trees on the sides of the river, soon assumed a circular shape.'[2]

Next day the fears were justified. The bridge broke and could not
be re-established until the 8th. For three days 19,000 men were
isolated on the far bank, but Soult did not move a man against them.
British light cavalry were able to push southward astride the Ers and
on 8 April captured intact the bridge over that river at Croix
d'Orade, north-east of Toulouse. This was done in a neat charge by
the Eighteenth Hussars, a manoeuvre which went some way to
redeeming the reputation they had lost at Vitoria.

The attack on Toulouse, more the assault of a fortress than a
battle, was fixed for 10 April, Easter Sunday. On the west bank Hill
with two divisions was to 'threaten the suburb [of St-Cyprien] as
circumstances admit of, in order to draw a part of the attention and
force of the enemy to that side'.[3] The rest of the army was on the east
bank. The aim was to seize the Heights of Calvinet, but they were so
strongly held that a single attack on the northern end, the only part

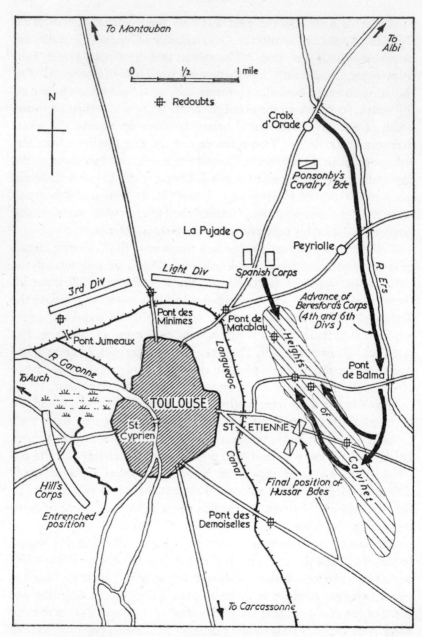

Toulouse

immediately accessible, could not hope to succeed. They would also
have to be assaulted on their long eastern face and to do this 'it was
necessary to march between Mont Calvinet and the river Ers, the
distance not being greater from the works upon the summit anywhere than 2,000 yards, diminishing to 1,000 yards, and in some
places to 500 yards. The distance to be marched was not less than 2
miles under the fire of the enemy's position.'[4]

This dangerous but unavoidable manoeuvre was entrusted to
Beresford with the Fourth and Sixth Divisions. Five hussar regiments covered his outer flank. A simultaneous attack on the northern
end of the ridge was to be made by Freyre's two Spanish divisions
who were to advance from Croix d'Orade 'formed in two lines with
a reserve and will attack at the same time as they see the Fourth and
Sixth Divisions on the left make their attack'.[5] On the right of the
Spaniards were the Light and Third Divisions which had the dual
task of containing the French bridgeheads north of Toulouse and of
acting as a reserve. Two brigades of heavy cavalry were also available in the latter rôle. The force on the east bank was 36,000 strong
and Hill had 12,600 on the other side of the river.

Soult had stationed one division in St-Cyprien and another on the
canal north of the city. Travot's division of newly raised conscripts
held the city walls. This left four divisions for the defences beyond
the canal. One of these, Darmagnac's, held the gap between the
canal and the northern end of the heights, and two more, those of
Harispe and Villatte, were on the Heights themselves with Taupin's
division in reserve. Pierre Soult's cavalry covered the eastern and
southern approaches. The French force was 42,000 strong[6/11] and
was very powerfully supplied with artillery, as there were about
forty heavy guns mounted on the walls and in the redoubts in addition to the field batteries.

Hill's threat on the west bank began at dawn. He made no assault
on the main fortifications but engaged in house-to-house fighting on
the fringes of the town. 'As the enemy retired or were driven back
they fired the houses they left to arrest our progress. We found in
many houses the furniture piled up in the rooms ready for the torch.
The streets were barricaded and cannon planted at every entrance,
pounding away at the first blink of a red coat; but our men dashed

on through fire and smoke, and carried on the work surely and gradually.'[6] The fighting in St-Cyprien was lively but not very dangerous. There were less than 80 casualties, but across the river to the north things were more serious. Picton had been ordered to make feints against the fortified bridgehead at Pont Jumeaux. Having cleared some outworks with ease, he tried to storm the redoubt north of the river. He was beaten off with 400 casualties.

Beresford's march across the face of the Heights took much longer than was expected. The advance was across ploughed fields and the men were ankle-deep in mud. It was so difficult to move the divisional batteries that Beresford ordered them to be unlimbered opposite the north-eastern end of the ridge to give covering fire while the infantry trudged on southward.

Seeing the batteries come into action, Freyre assumed that Beresford was beginning his attack and ordered the Spanish divisions forward. On their right the Light Division watched with some trepidation.

> Although full half a mile from the enemy they started in double quick time. 'This' we said, 'won't last long.' They, however, drove the French from some entrenchments on the side of the hill, and continued to ascend till they reached a high-road which, being cut out of the side of the hill, afforded them shelter from the fire of the enemy. Here they came to a halt; and not all the endeavours of their officers, many of whom set a gallant example, could make them move a step further. The French after a little time sent down a strong body of *voltigeurs*, who, firing right among the Spaniards, sent them headlong down the hill. Our division immediately formed line and the Spaniards rallied in our rear.[7]

Meanwhile Beresford's corps was having trouble in deploying. Between their line of advance and their objective were a wet ditch and a marshy meadow.

> We ran along the bank until we came to a place where we could leap the ditch and formed on the swampy ground beyond it. We had scarcely formed when a strong column of the enemy, with drums beating a march, descended the hill in our front, and thinking from the nature of the ground we should neither be able to advance or retreat, rushed down confident of success. For us to retire would have been scarcely practicable; the bank from which we had leaped

down was too high in several places to leap back from such uncertain footing, for we were sinking to the ankles, and sometimes deeper at every step; to advance was the only alternative. The light companies of the division were by this time in our front and without any hesitation dashed forward; we followed fast and the opposing column reascended the hill.[8]

As the Sixth Division with the Fourth on their left mounted the ridge, Freyre again led his Spaniards up the northern end. They attacked with great gallantry but were again repulsed. 'In a moment Lord Wellington galloped to the spot, and by his personal exertions rallied them. A squadron or two of British heavy dragoons sent to the rear of the routed Spaniards rallied them by striking them with the flats of their swords.'[9] Wellington remarked to his Adjutant-General, ' "There I am, with nothing between me and the enemy!" Pakenham said, "Well, I suppose you'll order up the Light Division now," and he replied, "I'll be *hanged* if I do." '[10]

There was no need to bring up more troops. Beresford's divisions had gained the summit of the ridge and after a pause while the guns were dragged up with infinite toil, they started to clear the crest moving northward. They captured two redoubts, only to lose them to a counter-attack. The Fourth Division had to be brought through the Sixth before the centre of the heights could be consolidated. Only Great Redoubt at the northern end remained to be captured, and before an attack against it could be mounted, Soult withdrew his troops into the inner defences of the city. Toulouse would become untenable as soon as the 18-pounders of Wellington's artillery reserve could be dragged up the Heights of Calvinet.

It had been a bloody battle. The allied army had suffered 4,500 casualties. Two thousand of these were among Freyre's Spaniards, one man in four. One thousand five hundred came from the Sixth Division which had gone into action 5,693 strong. Soult admitted 3,236 casualties. For once he does not seem to have understated his loss.*

---

* For the last three months of the war Soult was taking every opportunity to convince Paris that his army was even smaller than it was. Faced with a task he believed to be hopeless, his aim seemed to be to show that it was a command no longer worthy of a Marshal of the Empire. It may have been for this reason that he left Abbé's division at Bayonne, a move which is otherwise inexplicable.

Soult had no doubt about his next move. On the day after the battle he reported:

> I shall stay in my position today and we will defend ourselves if we are attacked. We are greatly in need of supplies before we can march but I think we shall have to leave Toulouse tonight and manoeuvre in open country. I shall probably aim at joining my troops to those of Marshal Suchet.[11]

At 9 pm that evening the French evacuated the city, taking the southerly road towards Carcassonne. They left in Toulouse 1,600 wounded men including three generals. General Taupin had died before they left. The municipal authorities lost no time in inviting Wellington to enter the town.

At 11 o'clock on 12 April one of the British staff

> arrived at the fortified entrance and found, instead of the enemy behind the works, the *maire* of the town among all the officers of the *garde urbaine*, a considerable number of national guard officers, deserters &c., about two hundred smart but awkward men of the city guard and a band of music, all wearing the white cockade, and a great crowd of citizens besides, all waiting to receive Lord Wellington. Unluckily he went in at another entrance and passed on, almost unknown.[12]

Wellington was changing for dinner at five o'clock when Lieutenant-Colonel Frederick Ponsonby, Twelfth Light Dragoons, came to his room having ridden post from Bordeaux.

> He found Wellington pulling on his boots, in his shirt. 'I have extraordinary news for you!'
> 'Ay, I thought so. I knew we should have peace; I've long expected it.'
> 'No; Napoleon has abdicated.'
> 'How, abdicated? Ay, 'tis time indeed. You don't say so, upon my honour. Hurrah!' said Wellington, turning round on his heel and snapping his fingers.[13]

Three hours later Cooke and St-Simon rode in with the despatches from Paris. They were sent on to Soult with a note from Wellington saying that 'the news they carry seems to me to give grounds for hope that peace will be established between France and the allied powers'.[14] Soult queried the authenticity of the messengers and their despatches and it was not until 17 April that an armistice was agreed.

There was one final burst of fighting. Hope's siege of Bayonne had been leisurely to the point of apathy. On 10 April, almost six weeks after the fortress had been invested, he was writing that siege operations might start in a fortnight's time. So far nothing had occurred but an occasional exchange of long-range fire. Thouvenot, the governor, had been as inactive as Hope. He knew of Napoleon's abdication by 12 April although he had not been officially notified. He determined to make a sortie, although he had done no such thing since the allies had crossed the Adour. At 3 am on 14 April, a dark and moonless night, he attacked with 6,000 men. It was a pointless operation which cost the British 838 and the French 905 casualties. No ground was gained and Thouvenot's only trophy was Sir John Hope who had been wounded and captured in the darkness. Bayonne surrendered on 27 April.

General Order   Toulouse, 21 April 1814.
Upon congratulating the army upon the prospect of an honourable termination of their labours, the Commander of the Forces avails himself of the opportunity of returning the General Officers, Officers and troops his best thanks for their uniform discipline and gallantry in the field and for their conciliating conduct towards the inhabitants of the country which, almost in equal degree with their discipline and gallantry in the field, have produced the fortunate circumstances that now hold forth to the world the prospect of genuine and permanent peace.

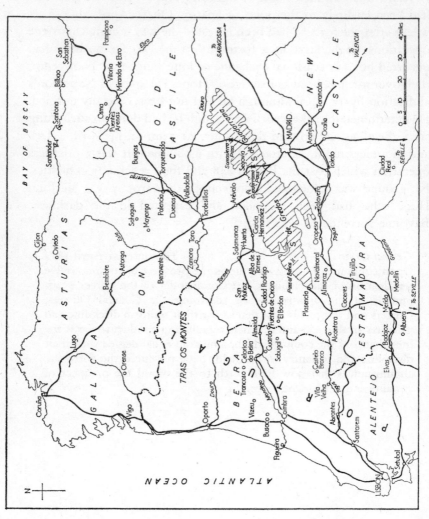

Northwest Spain and Northern Portugal

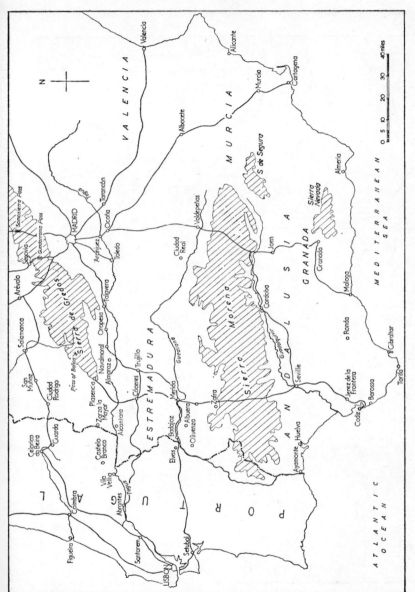

Southern Spain

L

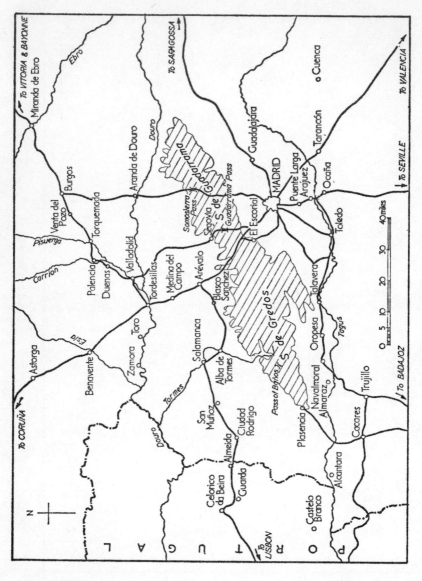

The Burgos Campaign, 1812

Appendices

Biographical Notes

To avoid an even larger proliferation of footnotes in the text, these notes are intended to supplement easily accessible information either on persons mentioned in the text or on those whose letters, diaries or memoirs are quoted in the body of the book. Established figures in world history (eg Napoleon and Wellington) are omitted except where the appointments they held at particular times during the war are significant.

ALAVA, Miguel de (1771–1843). Probably the only man who fought at both Trafalgar and Waterloo. At Trafalgar he was a midshipman in the Spanish navy; at Waterloo he was Spanish ambassador to the exiled Louis XVIII. From 1811 to 1814 he was a major-general and Spanish liaison officer at Wellington's headquarters.

ALTEN, Charles, Baron von (1764–1840). Colonel in the Hanoverian army when the country was overrun in 1803, when he joined the King's German Legion in England. Maj-gen in British army 1810. Commanded Light Division 1812–14 and a division at Waterloo. Wellington called him 'the best of the Hanoverians'. Later field-marshal of the Hanoverian army. Should be distinguished from his elder brother Victor, an unsatisfactory cavalry brigadier.

AUGEREAU, Pierre François Charles (1757–1816). Son of a Parisian stonemason. Enlisted in royal army and, after killing an officer, fled and enlisted in the Russian, and subsequently the Prussian, armies. Elected to command a revolutionary battalion in 1792. Divisional commander in Army of Italy 1796. Marshal of the Empire 1804. Duke of Castiglione

1808. Commanded VII Corps and was Governor of Catalonia 1809–10. Fought in Russian campaign of 1812 and campaign of 1813–14.

BAIRD, David (1757–1829). As captain 71st Foot captured by Hyder Ali and imprisoned in Seringapatam 1781–4. Stormed Seringapatam 1799. Led force from Red Sea to Cairo in Egyptian campaign of 1801–2. Captured Cape of Good Hope 1805. Second-in-command to Moore at Coruña where he lost an arm. Baronet 1810.

BALLASTEROS, Francisco (1770–1832). Commanded a Spanish division which consistently harassed French in Andalusia 1810–12. Attempted *coup d'état* against Regency as protest against Wellington's appointment as commander of all the Spanish armies 1812. Exiled. Pardoned at end of war but subsequently rebelled against Ferdinand VII.

BATHURST, Henry, 3rd Earl (1762–1834). Secretary of State for War and the Colonies 1812–27.

BECKWITH, Sydney (1772–1831). Served at Copenhagen with Nelson and in Hanover. As lieut-col 95th Rifles commanded a brigade in the Light Division 1810–11. Took part in American war of 1812. Wounded at Waterloo. C-in-C Bombay 1829.

BELL, George (1794–1877). Ensign 34th Foot 1811, lieut 1814. Served in Peninsula 1811–14. Commanded a brigade in the Crimean War.

BENTINCK, Lord William (1774–1839). Second son of 3rd Duke of Portland. Served in Netherlands and with Suvarov in Switzerland. Recalled from India after mutiny at Vellore (1807). Commanded brigade at Coruña. C-in-C Sicily 1811–15. Governor-General of India 1833–5.

BERESFORD, William Carr (1768–1854). Natural son of 1st Marquess of Waterford. Maj-gen 1805. Served Peninsula 1808–14. Commanded Portuguese army with rank of marshal 1809–22. Conde de Trancoso, in Portuguese peerage, 1810. Baron (UK) 1814, Viscount 1823. 'The ablest man I have yet seen with this army' (Wellington in 1812).

BERTHIER, Louis Alexandre (1753–1815). Son of a surveying engineer. Fought with French engineers in American War of Independence. Maj-gen of National Guards at Versailles during Revolution. Chief of staff to Napoleon 1796–1814. Marshal of the Empire 1804. Prince of Neufchâtel (1806) and of Wagram (1809). Fell to his death from a balcony in Bamberg on 1 June 1815. The circumstances of his death have never been adequately explained.

BESSIÈRES, Jean Baptiste (1766–1813). A barber who enlisted in the Royal Guard of Louis XVI. Captain of cavalry after Revolution, later commanded Imperial Guard. Marshal of the Empire 1804. Duke of Istria 1808. Corps commander in Army of Spain 1808–9. Withdrawn to command cavalry corps in Austria 1809. Returned to Spain to command Army of the North in 1811. Commanded Imperial Guard in Moscow campaign. Killed at Lützen.

BLAKE, Joachim (1759–1827). Spanish general of Irish ancestry. Renowned in Spain as he had won one battle and lost only fifteen. Captured with his army at Valencia, January 1812. Beresford remarked that 'I think it would be impossible to act with him for long.'

BLAKENEY, Robert (1789–1858). Ensign 28th Foot 1804, lieut 1805. Served at Copenhagen, at Coruña and on Walcheren expedition. Returned to Peninsula 1810. Promoted captain 36th Foot for his conduct at Arroyo dos Molinos.

BRISCALL, Rev Samuel (1778–1848). Fellow of Brasenose College, Oxford. Chaplain at headquarters in the Peninsula. 'An excellent young man' (Wellington).

BURGH, Ulysses (1788–1863). As captain 92nd Foot was ADC to Wellington, 1809–14. Carried victory despatches for Busaco (brevet major) and capture of Madrid (brevet lieut-col). ADC to Wellington at Waterloo as capt and lieut-col 1st Guards. Succeeded as 2nd Baron Downes in 1826.

BURGOYNE, John Fox (1782–1871). Natural son of Gen John Burgoyne (who surrendered at Saratoga). Captain Royal Engineers 1809. Served throughout Peninsular War. Engineering adviser to Lord Raglan in Crimea. Field-marshal 1868.

BURRARD, Harry (1755–1813). Fought in American War of Independence and in Flanders. Taken prisoner in raiding operation against Bruges canal in 1798; exchanged. Served at the Helder and at Copenhagen. Appointed second-in-command in Portugal 1808. One of his sons died as ADC to Moore at Coruña, another as a volunteer in the breach at San Sebastian.

CADOGAN, the Hon Henry (1780–1813). Seventh son of 1st Earl Cadogan. His sister married Wellington's brother Henry but eloped with Lord Paget (qv). Cadogan fought a duel with Paget in which neither was hurt. He commanded the 71st Foot in the Peninsula and was killed, commanding a brigade, at Vitoria.

CAFFARELLI, Louis Marc (1766–1849). Commanded the Army of the North, May 1812–January 1813. Detested by Marmont. Thiébault called him 'a brainless peacock'.

CANNING, George (1770–1827). Foreign Secretary 1807–9 when he fought a duel with Castlereagh (qv), and again 1822–7. Prime Minister 1827. Wellington considered him 'a man of imagination, always in a delusion, who never saw things as they were'.

CASTAÑOS, Xavier. As Captain General of Andalusia defeated Dupont at Bailen in 1808. Subsequently a member of the Spanish Council of Regency for a short time.

CASTLEREAGH, Robert Stewart, Lord (1769–1822). Eldest son of 1st Marquess of Londonderry (whom he succeeded in 1821). Chief Secretary for Ireland, 1799. Secretary for War and the Colonies, 1805 and 1807–9, when he fought a duel with Canning (qv). Foreign Secretary 1812–22. Committed suicide.

CAULAINCOURT, Louis de (1772–1827). Successively Napoleon's ambassador to the Tsar, Foreign Minister and Master of the Horse. Napoleon trusted his disinterestedness and used him as a confidant. Created Duke of Vicenza.

CLARKE, Henri Jacques Guillaume (1776–1818). Napoleon's Minister of War. Created Duke of Feltre. Acted as Minister of War to Louis XVIII during Waterloo campaign. Napoleon in 1814 described him as 'nothing but a head book-keeper become vain'.

CLAUSEL (or CLAUZEL), Bertrand (1772–1842). Divisional commander in Army of Portugal 1810. Succeeded to command of that army when Marmont and Bonet were wounded at Salamanca. Superseded but transferred to command of Army of the North which he led from January to July 1813. Lieutenant of the Left under Soult 1813–14. Commanded 'Corps of the Western Pyrenees' during the Hundred Days. Subsequently Governor of Algeria and Marshal of France.

CLINTON, Henry (1771–1829). Younger son of Gen Sir Henry Clinton, British c-in-c in American War of Independence. Military Attaché to Russian army at Austerlitz. Commanded Wellington's Sixth Division 1812–14 and Second Division at Waterloo.

CLINTON, William (1769–1846). Elder brother of Henry Clinton. Twice commanded Anglo-Sicilian corps on east coast of Spain with extreme trepidation. Led British expedition to Lisbon 1826.

COLBORNE, John (1778–1863). Military Secretary to Moore at Coruña, at whose dying wish he was made a lieutenant-colonel. Commanded 66th Foot 1809–11, and 52nd Foot 1811–15. Played leading part at Waterloo. Lieut-Governor of Upper Canada and suppressed rebellion of 1838. Created Baron Seaton 1839. C-in-C Ireland 1855–60. Field-marshal 1860. Step-uncle to Charlotte Yonge.

COLE, the Hon Galbraith Lowry (1772–1842). Second son of 1st Earl of Enniskillen. MP for Fermanagh 1803–23. Commissioned 1787. Fought at Maida 1806. Maj-gen 1808. Commanded Fourth Division 1810–14 except when wounded at Albuera and Salamanca. Wellington said that 'Cole gives the best dinners going'.

COOKE, Henry Frederick (1784–1837). Staff officer in Peninsula 1809–12. As capt and lieut-col Coldstream Guards attached to staff of Sir Charles Stewart, Military Commissioner to Eastern Allies 1813–14.

COOKE, John Henry (?–1867). Ensign 43rd Foot 1809, lieut 1810. Served at Walcheren, in Peninsula 1811–14, and at New Orleans.

COSTELLO, Edward (1788–1869). Enlisted in Dublin Militia 1806. Volunteered for 95th Rifles 1808. Served in Peninsula 1809–14. Sergeant by 1814. Wounded at Waterloo. Invalided out 1818. Captain in British Legion serving in Carlist Wars 1835–7. Yeoman Warder 1838–69.

COTTON, Sir Charles, 5th Bart (1753–1812). Midshipman in Royal Navy 1772. Served in American War of Independence. Vice-admiral 1802. Commanded squadron off Tagus 1807–8. Commanded Channel Fleet 1812.

COTTON, Stapleton (1773–1865). (No relation to Sir Charles.) After service in Flanders, the Cape and India, he commanded Wellington's cavalry 1810–14 except after being seriously wounded at Salamanca. MP for Newark 1806–14. Created Baron Combermere 1814 and Viscount 1827 after taking the great Indian fortress of Bhurtpore. Field-marshal 1855. He was a great dandy and his abilities have been under-rated by historians. Wellington said that 'I do not know where we should find an officer that would command our cavalry in this country half as well as he does [but] not exactly the person I should select to command the army.'

CRAUFURD, Robert (1764–1812). Served in India, Ireland, Germany and Buenos Aires. Commanded Light Brigade and Light Division 1809–12. His 'Standing Orders for the Light Division' were a model for the army for decades to come. Killed in the breach at Ciudad Rodrigo.

CUESTA, Gregorio Garçia (1740–1812). Decrepit Spanish general to whom Napoleon offered the Viceroyalty of Mexico. Cuesta refused on grounds of health and became Captain General of Estremadura. Defeated by Victor at Medellin (1809) and later co-operated, up to a point, with Wellington at Talavera. Soon afterwards was incapacitated by a heart attack. 'Cuesta is too old and has not the talents to conduct in due order the great and confused affairs of a battle' (Wellington).

DALRYMPLE, Hew (1759–1830). Served one campaign in Flanders 1793. Governor of Guernsey 1796–1801. Lieut-Governor of Gibraltar 1806–8. Commanded army in Portugal 1808 but recalled after signing Convention of Cintra. Baronet 1815.

DECAEN, Charles Mathieu Isidore (1769–1832). Fought in Army of the Rhine and in La Vendée. Governor of Mauritius 1804–10 and of Catalonia 1811–14.

D'ERLON, Jean-Baptiste Drouet, Count (1765–1844). Fought at Jena and Friedland. Commanded IX Corps in Army of Portugal and later under Soult. Commanded Armies of Portugal and Centre alternately 1812–13. Lieutenant of the Centre 1813–14. Corps commander at Waterloo. Subsequently Governor of Algeria and Marshal of France. 'A mixture of inadequacy and kindness' (Thiébault).

DE ESPAÑA, Carlos (1775–1839). French *emigré*, Charles d'Espagne, who joined Spanish army after French Revolution. Divisional commander 1810–14. Governor of Madrid 1812. Murdered during Carlist wars.

DICKSON, Alexander (1777–1840). Captain Royal Artillery, lieut-col Portuguese Artillery. Supervised artillery at sieges of Ciudad Rodrigo and Badajoz. Wellington gave him command of the allied artillery although several of his seniors in British rank were available.

DONKIN, Rufane Shaw (1773–1841). Commanded brigade at Talavera and was QMG to Anglo-Sicilian corps on east coast of Spain. Founded Port Elizabeth in South Africa. FRS.

DORSENNE, Jean-Marie (?–1812). Lieut-col of Grenadiers of Imperial Guard at Austerlitz. Commanded Imperial Guard at Essling. Military

Governor of Burgos 1810–11. Commanded Army of the North 1811–12. Died of a trepanning operation in Paris 1812. A brave man but Thiébault did not much exaggerate when he called him 'an incompetent mountebank'.

DUPONT, Pierre (1765–1840). A distinguished soldier of the Revolutionary wars. Napoleon imprisoned him for surrendering to the Spaniards at Bailen. Louis XVIII pardoned him and, tactlessly, made him Minister of War.

D'URBAN, Benjamin (1777–1849). Commissioned 1793. Brevet lieut-col 1805. Served in Peninsula from 1808. QMG to Portuguese army 1809–18 except when commanding a Portuguese cavalry brigade in 1812. Governor of Cape of Good Hope 1842–7. Occupied Natal and gave his name to its capital.

ELLEY, John (?–1839). Enlisted as a trooper in Royal Horse Guards. Promoted to quartermaster and, subsequently, cornet. Lieut-col RHG 1806. Assistant Adjutant General to the cavalry in the Peninsula 1809–14 and at Waterloo. Colonel 1813, KCB 1815, lieut-gen 1837.

ERSKINE, Sir William, 1st Bart (1769–1813). Distinguished himself as captain 15th Lt Dgns at Villiers-en-Couche 1793, and was made a baronet for his gallantry. MP for Fifeshire 1796 and 1802–5. Committed suicide in Lisbon 1813. Wellington said that 'it is impossible to trust to his judgement in any critical case'.

FOY, Maximilien Sebastien (1775–1825). 2nd lieut Artillery 1792, colonel 1801. Served throughout Peninsular War. Brigadier-general 1808. Sent to Paris by Massena with his report from before the Lines of Torres Vedras. Napoleon made him *général de division* on arrival. Wounded at Orthez. Commanded division at Waterloo where he was again wounded. Wrote history of Peninsular War (incomplete) and valuable series of letters.

FRAZER, Simon Augustus (1776–1835). Commanded artillery at Buenos Aires (where Dickson (qv) served under him). Commanded Horse Artillery in Peninsula (1812–14) and at Waterloo. FRS 1816.

GAZAN, Honoré Theophile Maxime, Count (1765–?). Commanded division in Army of the South 1810 and became chief of staff to Soult. Succeeded to command of that army in 1813. Chief of staff to Soult 1813–14.

GLEIG, George Robert (1796–1886). Lieut in 85th Foot when that regiment was reconstituted in 1813. Served at Bidassoa, Nivelle, Bayonne and

New Orleans. Took Holy Orders in 1820 and became Chaplain General to the Forces in 1844. Not a charitably minded cleric.

GODOY, Manuel de (1767–1851). A young officer in the Spanish Royal Guard who became Chief Minister. Created Prince of the Peace after negotiating treaty with France. Lived in exile in Italy and France 1808–51.

GOMM, William (1784–1875). Staff officer in Fifth Division. Served in Peninsula 1808–14 and at Waterloo. Subsequently C-in-C India and a field-marshal.

GORDON, James Willoughby (1773–1851). Commissioned 1783. Served at Toulon, in Canada and the West Indies. Lieut-col 1801. Military Secretary to Commanders-in-Chief 1804–12. Appointed Quartermaster General in Peninsula 1812. Showed himself incompetent and disloyal and was replaced early in 1813. To be distinguished from the Hon Alexander Gordon (1786–1815), one of Wellington's ADCs.

GRAHAM, Thomas (1748–1843). Scottish landowner and cricketer who raised 90th Foot at his own expense to avenge insult to his wife's corpse from a French revolutionary mob. Fought at Toulon and with Austrian army in Italy. ADC to Moore at Coruña. Commanded at Cadiz 1810–11. Second-in-command to Wellington 1811–12 and 1812–13. Invalided home with defective eyesight. Commanded British army in Netherlands 1814. Created Baron Lynedoch 1814. Founded United Services Club.

GRATTAN, William (?1792–?1853). Ensign 88th Foot 1809, lieut 1812. Served in Peninsula 1809–13.

GURWOOD, John (1788–1845). Ensign 52nd Foot 1808, lieut 1809. Led Forlorn Hope at Ciudad Rodrigo and received governor's sword. As a reward he was promoted captain in Royal Africa Corps. Brigade major to Household Cavalry at Waterloo. Edited Wellington's Despatches.

HALLOWELL, Benjamin (1760–1834). Born in Canada. Captain RN at Battle of the Nile. Rear-admiral 1811. Commanded Home Fleet 1816–24.

HARDINGE, Henry (1785–1856). Served in Peninsula 1808–14. On Moore's staff at Coruña. DQMG Portuguese army 1809–14. Commanded Portuguese brigade in 1814. Wellington's liaison officer with Blücher in 1815. Lost hand at Ligny. Governor-General of India 1844–7. Created Lord Hardinge of Lahore 1846. Commander-in-Chief of the army 1852–5. Field-marshal 1855.

HAY, Andrew (1762–1814). Commanded 3/1st Foot at Coruña. Maj-gen 1811. Commanded brigade in Fifth Division 1810–14, taking over the division when Leith was incapacitated by one of his frequent wounds. Killed in the sortie from Bayonne. One of his fellow brigadiers commented that Hay 'is a fool and I verily believe, with many others on my side, an arrant coward. He is a plundering paltry old wretch.'

HILL, Rowland (1772–1842). Commissioned 1790. Served Toulon, Egypt, Ireland and Hanover. Maj-gen 1805. Divisional and corps commander in Peninsula 1808–14. Commanded corps at Waterloo. Commander-in-Chief of the army 1828–39. Created Baron Hill 1814, Viscount 1842. Wellington said: 'The best of Hill is that I always know where to find him.'

HOPE, the Hon John (1765–1823). Second son of 2nd Earl of Hopetoun. Served in West Indies, Egypt. Commanded division at Coruña and supervised embarkation after death of Moore and wounding of Baird. Second-in-command of Peninsular army 1813–14. Captured during Bayonne sortie. Created Baron Niddry 1814. Succeeded as 4th Earl of Hopetoun 1816. To be distinguished from Maj-Gen John Hope (1765–1836), a distant cousin who commanded Seventh Division in 1812.

JONES, John Thomas (1783–1843). Royal Engineer. Present at Maida 1806. Served in Peninsula 1808–14. Largely responsible for construction of Lines of Torres Vedras. Wounded at Burgos 1812. Wrote a history of the Peninsular War and a journal of the sieges in Spain.

JOURDAN, Jean Baptiste (1762–1833). Son of a doctor. Enlisted in royal army and served in American War of Independence. Subsequently travelled in haberdashery. Elected to command a battalion during Revolution. Divisional commander in 1793 and led Army of Sambre et Meuse to victory over the Austrians at Fleurus 1794. Marshal of the Empire 1804 but received no imperial title as he was on bad terms with Napoleon. Chief of staff to King Joseph 1809 and 1812–13.

JUNOT, Androche (1771–1813). ADC to Napoleon at Toulon and in Army of Italy. Commanded a division in Egyptian expedition. Governor of Paris 1807–8. Occupied Lisbon 1808 and created Duke of Abrantes. Corps commander in Army of Portugal (1810–11) and in Moscow campaign. Committed suicide.

KELLERMANN, François Etienne, Count of Valmy (1770–1825). Son of Marshal Kellermann, Duke of Valmy (whom he succeeded in 1820). Distinguished himself commanding a cavalry brigade at Marengo.

Served in Peninsula 1807–11. Commanded cavalry corps in campaign of 1813–14 and at Waterloo.

KINCAID, John (1787–1862). 2nd lieut 95th Rifles 1809, lieut 1811. Adjutant at Waterloo. Inspector of Prisons and Factories for Scotland 1850.

LARPENT, Francis Seymour (1776–1845). Fellow of St John's College, Cambridge, 1799. Barrister. Judge Advocate General in Peninsula 1812–14.

LEITH, James (1763–1816). Commissioned 1780, maj-gen 1808. Commanded 5th Division in Peninsula 1810–13 except when disabled by wounds at Salamanca and San Sebastian.

LEITH HAY, Andrew (1785–1862). ADC to his uncle, James Leith (qv) 1808–13. Captured 1813 but exchanged on day before Vitoria. MP for Elgin 1832–8 and 1841–7. Published *Castellated Architecture of Perthshire*.

LE MARCHANT, John Gaspard (1766–1812). Commissioned 1781. Devised 'Sword Exercises for Cavalry'. First Lieutenant-Governor of Royal Military College 1800–11. Maj-gen 1811. Killed at Salamanca 1812.

LIVERPOOL, Robert Banks Jenkinson, 2nd Earl of (1770–1828). MP 1790–1803. Foreign Secretary 1801–3. Created Lord Hawkesbury. Home Secretary 1804–6 and 1807–9. Succeeded to earldom 1808. Secretary for War and the Colonies 1809–12. Prime Minister 1812–27.

LONG, Robert Ballard (1771–1825). Lieut-col 15th Hussars, maj-gen 1811. A fretful and incompetent cavalry brigadier. Sent home by Wellington in 1813.

MCGRIGOR, James (1771–1858). Regimental Surgeon 88th Foot 1793–1802 in Flanders, West Indies, India and Egypt. Inspector General of Hospitals 1809. Head of medical staff in Peninsula 1811–14. Director-General of Army Medical Department 1815–51. Knighted 1814, FRS 1815, bart 1830.

MARMONT, Auguste Frédéric Louis de (1774–1852). Artillery officer. ADC to Bonaparte in Army of Italy. Reorganised French artillery 1800–2. Governor of Dalmatia and Illyria 1805–11. Duke of Ragusa 1808. Marshal of the Empire 1809. Commanded Army of Portugal 1811–12. Severely wounded at Salamanca.

MASSENA, André (1758–1817). Son of a merchant in Nice. Served in ranks of Régiment Royal-Italien 1775–89. Rejoined army after Revolution. Brigadier 1793. Corps commander in Army of Italy. Distinguished himself by his defence of Switzerland (1799) and Genoa (1800). Marshal of the Empire 1804. Conquered Naples 1806. Duke of Rivoli 1808. Created Prince of Essling for his part in the Austrian campaign of 1809. Commanded Army of Portugal 1810–11. Military Governor of Toulon 1813–15. Wellington said that of all his opponents Massena was 'the most dangerous and difficult to deal with'.

MINA, Francisco Epoz y (1784–1836). Navarrese guerrilla who was made maj-gen in regular army in 1813. Besieged and took Jaca in 1814. Subsequently prominent as a Carlist general.

MIOT, André François, Count of Melito (1762–1841). Close friend of Joseph Bonaparte (who created him Count of Melito in the peerage of Naples). Master of the Household to Joseph while King of Spain.

MOORE, John (1761–1809). Son of an Edinburgh doctor. Commissioned 1776. MP Selkirk Burghs 1784–90. Served American War of Independence, Corsica, West Indies, Irish Rebellion, Helder Expedition, Egypt (1801). Lt-gen 1805. Died of wounds at Coruña, January 1809.

MURAT, Joachim (1767–1815). Son of land agent to Talleyrand family. Cavalry officer. Procured guns with which Bonaparte's 'whiff of grape shot' was administered. ADC to Bonaparte in Army of Egypt. Married Caroline Bonaparte and commanded Napoleon's cavalry. Marshal of the Empire 1804. Grand Duke of Berg and Cleves 1807. Grand Admiral of France. King of Naples 1808–15. Took part in Russian campaign but abandoned the army after Napoleon had left him in command. Arranged with Austrians to retain Naples after Napoleon's first abdication but led a Neapolitan army against them during the Hundred Days. Shot in 1815, for his part in the murder of the Duke of Enghien in 1804. 'He is a brave man,' said Napoleon, 'but he has no head.'

MURRAY, George (1772–1846). QMG in the Peninsula under Burrard, Dalrymple, Moore and Wellington except when posted to Ireland for a period in 1812. Subsequently C-in-C Ireland 1825–8 and Secretary for War and the Colonies 1828–30. Edited Marlborough's despatches.

MURRAY, John (1768–1827). QMG in India 1801–5. Commanded a brigade in Portugal 1809. Succeeded as 8th Bart in 1811. Commanded Anglo-Sicilian corps on east coast of Spain 1813. Court-martialled for his conduct before Tarragona.

NAPIER, Charles (1782–1853). Son of Col George Napier and Lady Sarah, *née* Lennox. Commanded 50th Foot at Coruña where he was wounded and captured. Exchanged 1810 and present at Busaco as a volunteer. As maj-gen conquered Sind in 1843.

NAPIER, George (1784–1855). Brother to above. Served in Peninsula as capt 52nd Foot (becoming brevet lieut-col). Governor of Cape of Good Hope 1837–43.

NAPIER, William (1785–1860). Brother to above. Served in Peninsula as capt, later major (brevet lieut-col), 43rd Foot. Governor of Guernsey 1842–7. Wrote *History of the War in the Peninsula and South of France*.

NEY, Michel (1769–1815). Son of a cooper. Hussar trooper before Revolution. Cavalry captain in Army of Sambre et Meuse. Marshal of the Empire 1804. Distinguished himself at Ulm. Created Duke of Elchingen 1808. Commanded Corps in Peninsula 1809–11. Sent back to France by Massena for insubordination. Created Prince of the Moskova for his gallantry in charge of the rearguard on retreat from Moscow. Commanded left wing in Waterloo campaign. Shot for treachery by Louis XVIII. Napoleon called him 'Le brave des braves'.

PAGET, the Hon Edward (1775–1849). Fourth son of 1st Earl of Uxbridge. Commanded the Reserve in Coruña campaign. Second-in-command of Peninsular army for four days in 1809, when he lost his arm at Oporto, and for five weeks in 1812, until captured at San Muñoz. C-in-C India 1820–4.

PAGET, Henry, Lord (1768–1854). Eldest son of 1st Earl of Uxbridge (whom he succeeded in 1812). Commanded Moore's cavalry in Coruña campaign and a division at Walcheren. Second-in-command and cavalry commander at Waterloo where he lost a leg. Created Marquess of Anglesey 1815. Lord Lieutenant of Ireland 1828–9 and 1830–3. Field-marshal 1846.

PAKENHAM, the Hon Edward (1778–1815). Second son of 2nd Baron Longford and brother to Catherine, Duchess of Wellington. Deputy Adjutant General in the Peninsula 1810–12. Commanded Third Division at Salamanca and Sixth Division for two periods in 1813. Adjutant General 1813–14. Killed in action at New Orleans Jan 1815. Wellington said of him, 'He may not be the brightest genius but he is one of the best we have.'

PERCEVAL, Spencer (1762–1812). Barrister. Attorney-General 1802.

Chancellor of the Exchequer 1807. Prime Minister 1809 until assassinated in 1812.

PICTON, Thomas (1758–1815). Commissioned 1772, maj-gen 1808. Commanded Third Division in Peninsula 1810–14 with two short breaks. Wounded at Badajoz and Quatre Bras. Killed at Waterloo. Wellington said of him that he was 'as rough a foul-mouthed devil as ever lived, but he always behaved extremely well; no man could do better in the various services I assigned to him'.

PONSONBY, the Hon Frederick (1783–1837). Second son of 3rd Lord Bessborough. Commanded 23rd Lt Dgns at Talavera and 12th Lt Dgns 1811–14. Severely wounded at Waterloo. Subsequently Governor of Malta.

POPHAM, Home Riggs (1762–1820). Midshipman RN 1778. Post captain 1795. Commanded naval forces at capture of Cape of Good Hope 1806. Reprimanded by court-martial for unauthorised attack on Buenos Aires 1806. Commanded naval squadron off north coast of Spain 1812–13. C-in-C Jamaica 1817–20.

PORTLAND, William Henry Cavendish Bentinck, 3rd Duke of (1738–1801). Prime Minister 1783. Home Secretary 1794–1801. Prime Minister 1807–9. Father of Lord William Bentinck (qv).

REILLE, Honoré Charles (1775–1860). Served in Army of Italy. Commanded division of Imperial Guard at Wagram (1809), temporary Army of the Ebro (1811) and corps under Suchet in 1812. Commanded Army of Portugal 1813. Lieutenant of the Right 1813–14. Commander of II Corps at Quatre Bras and Waterloo. Subsequently Marshal of France.

REYNIER, Ebenezer (1771–1814). Commanded a division in Joseph's kingdom of Naples and was defeated at Maida by Sir John Stuart in 1806. Corps commander in Army of Portugal 1810–11. Led a Saxon corps in Russian campaign of 1812. Captured at Leipzig.

ROSS, Hew Dalrymple (1779–1868). Nephew of Sir Hew Dalrymple (qv). Commanded A Troop (the Chestnut Troop), Royal Horse Artillery, in the Peninsula (1809–14) and at Waterloo. Field-marshal 1868.

ROSS-LEWIN, Henry (1778–?). Ensign 32nd Foot 1795, captain 1804 (brevet major 1814). Served in West Indies, Irish Rebellion, Copenhagen, Peninsula (1808–14) and Waterloo.

SEBASTIANI, Horace (1772–1851). Commanded IV Corps in Spain 1809–11. Commanded cavalry corps in eastern campaigns of 1812 and 1813–14. Subsequently Marshal of France and Minister of Foreign Affairs.

SHERBROOKE, John Coape (1764–1830). Served as regimental officer under Wellesley in 33rd Foot in Flanders and India. Second-in-command of Peninsular army 1809–10. Governor of Nova Scotia 1811–16. Governor-General of Canada 1816–18.

SHERER, Moyle (or Mogh) (1789–1869). Lieut 34th Foot 1807, captain 1812. Served in Peninsula from 1809 until taken prisoner at Maya Pass 1813.

SIMMONS, George (1785–1858). A former medical student and Asst Surgeon, Royal South Lincs Militia. 2nd lieut 95th Rifles 1809, lieut 1811. Served in Peninsula 1809–14. Severely wounded at Waterloo.

SMITH, Harry (1787–1860). Son of a Cambridgeshire surgeon. 2nd lieut 95th Rifles 1805, captain 1812. Served in Peninsula 1809–14. Brought home despatches announcing the capture of Washington DC. Adjutant-General in India 1842–6. KCB 1844. Won the battle of Aliwal in Sikh war. Governor of Cape of Good Hope 1847–50. Married in April 1812 Juana Maria de los Dolores de Leon, a refugee from the sack of Badajoz. The towns of Harrismith and Ladysmith in Natal are named after them.

SOMERSET, Lord Fitzroy (1788–1855). Seventh son of 5th Duke of Beaufort. ADC to Wellington 1808–10. Military Secretary to Wellington 1810–18 and 1827–52. Lost arm at Waterloo. Married Wellington's niece, Emily Wellesley Pole. Created Baron Raglan 1852. Master General of the Ordnance 1852–4. Commanded British army in the Crimea 1854–5. William Napier said that he 'is as good as he is clever and nearly as clever as Lord Wellington himself'.

SOULT, Nicholas Jean-de-Dieu (1769–1851). Son of a country notary. Enlisted in royal army. Second-in-command to Massena in Switzerland and at Genoa. Marshal of the Empire 1804. Duke of Dalmatia 1808. Distinguished himself at Austerlitz. Corps commander in Spain 1808–9. Chief of staff to King Joseph 1809–10. Commanded Army of the South 1810–12 and Army of Spain 1813–14. Minister of War under Louis XVIII 1814–15. Chief of staff to Napoleon during Waterloo campaign. Minister of War to Louis Philippe 1830–2. Prime Minister 1832–4. Ambassador Extraordinary to Coronation of Queen Victoria 1838. 'The only military brain in Spain' (Napoleon). 'Unrivalled as a strategist but timid in action' (Wellington). His brother Pierre commanded a cavalry brigade with consistent incompetence.

SPENCER, Brent (1760–1828). Commissioned 1778. Served in West Indies, Netherlands and Egypt. Second-in-command to Wellington 1808 and 1810–11. 'He was exceedingly puzzle headed. He would talk of the Thames for the Tagus' (Wellington).

STEWART, the Hon Charles (1778–1854). Half-brother to Castlereagh (whom he succeeded as 3rd Marquess of Londonderry in 1822). Lieut-col 5th Dragoons which were disbanded for sedition in 1797, 18th Hussars (1799–1813). Commanded cavalry brigade in Coruña campaign. Adjutant-General in the Peninsula 1809–12. Minister to Prussia 1813 and Military Commissioner to the eastern allies 1813–14. Created Lord Stewart 1814. Ambassador to Vienna 1814–22. Wrote a history of the Peninsular War. Wellington remarked that he 'should be sorry to see a large body of cavalry exposed to his guidance in the field against the enemy'.

STEWART, the Hon William (1774–1827). Fourth son of 7th Earl of Galway. MP 1795–1816. Commissioned 1786. First lieut-col of the Rifle Corps (later 95th Rifles) 1800. Commanded divisions in the Peninsula 1811–14. 'It is necessary that Stewart should be under the particular charge of somebody' (Wellington).

STURGEON, Henry (1781–1814). Lieut-col Royal Staff Corps. An engineer of extreme ingenuity. Repaired the Roman bridge at Alcantara and designed the bridge across the Adour. Killed in action at Vic Bigorre 19 March 1814.

SUCHET, Louis Gabriel (1772–1826). Son of a silk merchant. Commanded a division in the defence of Genoa under Massena 1800. Commanded a corps in Spain and subsequently the Armies of Aragon and Catalonia. Marshal of the Empire and Duke of Albufera 1811. Commanded Army of Italy during Hundred Days. Napoleon said, 'If I had two more generals like him to lead my troops in Spain the war would be over.'

SURTEES, William (1781–1830). Enlisted in Northumberland Militia 1795. Transferred to 56th Foot 1797. Discharged 1802 but re-enlisted in 95th Rifles. Corporal 1802, sergeant 1803, quartermaster-sergeant 1809, quartermaster 1809.

TRANT, Nicholas (1769–1839). Captain in Royal Staff Corps who was attached to the Portuguese army in which he became a brigadier. Governor of Coimbra after he recaptured the city in 1810. Wellington described him as 'a very good officer, but a drunken dog as ever lived'.

VICTOR, Claud Perrin (1766–1841). Drummer in pre-revolutionary army. Served with Bonaparte at Toulon. Marshal of the Empire 1807. Duke of Belluno 1808. Commanded I Corps in Spain 1808–11. Fought in eastern campaigns of 1812 and 1813–14. Loyal to Louis XVIII during Hundred Days and subsequently Minister of War.

WARRE, William (1784–1853). A son of the great port family. Served in Peninsula 1808–12. ADC to Beresford 1809–13. DQMG at Cape of Good Hope 1813–21.

WHINYATES, Edward Charles (1782–1865). 2nd captain of D Troop RHA at Busaco and Albuera, captain 1813. Commanded Rocket Troop at Waterloo. Director-General of Artillery 1852.

APPENDIX 2

British Regiments of Cavalry and Infantry Which Took Part in the Peninsular War

Only regiments appearing in the Army List are mentioned. Improvised units (eg the Anglo-Italian Levy) are omitted.

Dates of landing and re-embarkation refer only to the metropolitan territory of Spain or Portugal. Units in garrison at Gibraltar are shown only where they landed/re-embarked in such territory.

Units are shown as having been engaged in an action only if they were sufficiently involved to have suffered casualties. This is not necessarily the case when official Battle Honours were awarded.

In addition to those actions for which official Honours were granted a number of other engagements have been included. Some (eg Douro and Bidassoa) were unaccountably omitted from the official list, others (eg Burgos) because they ended in failure.

Units serving other than with the main army under Moore or Wellington (including the detached corps in Estremadura) are shown as follows:

    (C)   Garrison of Cadiz

(CT) Garrison of Cartagena
(E)   Corps on east coast of Spain (mainly from Sicily)
(G)   Garrison of Gibraltar

The actions included are indicated by the following abbreviations:

ADM	Arroyo dos Molinos, 28 October 1811
ALB	Albuera, 16 May 1811
ALM	Bridge at Almaraz, 18 May 1812
BAD (1)	Badajoz, May–June 1811
BAD (2)	Badajoz, 6 April 1812
BAR	Barossa, 5 March 1811
BAY	Sortie from Bayonne, 14 April 1814
BEN	Benevente, 1 January 1809
BID	Forcing of the Bidassoa, 7 October 1813
BUR	Burgos, September–October 1812
BUS	Busaco, 27 September 1810
CAS	Castalla, 13 April 1813
CIU	Ciudad Rodrigo, 19 January 1812
COR	Retreat to and battle of Coruña, January 1809
DOU	Forcing of the Douro (Oporto), 12 May 1809
ELB	El Bodon and Carpio, 25 September 1811
FDO	Fuentes de Oñoro, 3–5 May 1811
FUE	Fuengirola, 13 October 1810
GCH	Garçia Hernandez, 23 July 1812
MAG	Maguilla, 11 June 1812
MAY	Maya Pass, 25 July 1813
NLE	Nivelle, 10 November 1813
NVE	Nive, 9–12 December 1813 (excluding St-Pierre)
ORD	Ordal and Villafranca, 12–13 September 1813
ORT	Orthez, 27 February 1814
PYR	Pyrenees, 25 July–2 August 1813 (excluding MAY, RON and SOR)
ROL	Roliça, 17 August 1808
RON	Roncesvalles Pass, 25 July 1813
SAB	Sabugal, 3 April 1811
SAH	Sahagun, 21 December 1808
SAL	Salamanca, 22 July 1812
SAN	San Sebastian, 25 July and 31 August 1813
SOR	Sorauren, 28 and 30 July 1813
STP	St-Pierre, 13 December 1813
TAL	Talavera, 27–28 July 1809
TAR	Tarragona, June 1813
TFA	Defence of Tarifa, December 1811–January 1812

TOU	Toulouse, 10 April 1814
USA	Usagre, 25 May 1811
VDP	Venta del Poza, 23 October 181?
VIM	Vimeiro, 21 August 1808
VIT	Vitoria, 21 June 1813

CAVALRY

Household Cavalry	*Date landed*	*Date re-embarked*	*Principal actions in which engaged*
1st Life Guards (2 sqns)	Jan 1813	End of war	VIT, TOU
2nd Life Guards (2 sqns)	Jan 1813	End of war	VIT, TOU
Royal Horse Guards (2 sqns)	Jan 1813	End of war	VIT, TOU

Cavalry of the Line

3rd (Prince of Wales's) Dragoon Guards	May 1809	End of war	TAL, ALB, USA, VIT
4th (Royal Irish) Dragoon Guards	Aug 1811	Apr 1813	—
5th (Princess Charlotte of Wales's) Dragoon Guards	Sep 1811	End of war	SAL, VIT, TOU
1st (Royal) Dragoons	Oct 1809	End of war	FDO, ELB, MAG, VIT
3rd (King's Own) Dragoons	Aug 1811	End of war	MAG, SAL, VIT, TOU
4th (Queen's Own) Dragoons	May 1809	End of war	TAL, ALB, USA, SAL, VIT, TOU
7th (Queen's Own) Light Dragoons (Hussars)	(i) Nov 1808	Jan 1809	SAH, BEN
	(ii) Sep 1813	End of war	ORT
9th Light Dragoons	Jul 1811	Mar 1813	ADM
10th (Prince of Wales's Own Royal) Light Dragoons (Hussars)	(i) Nov 1808	Jan 1809	SAH, BEN
	(ii) Apr 1813	End of war	VIT, ORT, TOU
11th Light Dragoons	Jun 1811	Mar 1813	ELB
12th (Prince of Wales's) Light Dragoons	Jun 1811	End of war	SAL, VIT, NLE, NVE
13th Light Dragoons	Apr 1810	End of war	ALB, USA, NLE, ORT
14th (Duchess of York's Own) Light Dragoons	Nov 1808	End of war	DOU, TAL, FDO, ELB, SAL, PYR, NVE, ORT
15th (King's) Light Dragoons (Hussars)	(i) Nov 1808	Jan 1809	SAH
	(ii) Apr 1813	End of war	VIT, ORT, TOU
16th (Queen's) Light Dragoons	Apr 1809	End of war	DOU, TAL, FDO, ELB, VIT
18th Light Dragoons (Hussars)	(i) Sep 1808	Jan 1809	SAH, BEN
	(ii) Apr 1813	End of war	VIT, TOU
20th Light Dragoons	(i) Aug 1808	Jul 1809	VIM, DOU
	(ii) Aug 1812	End of war	(E) CAS, ORD
23rd Light Dragoons	Jun 1809	Nov 1809	TAL

Foreign Corps	*Date landed*	*Date re-embarked*	*Principal actions in which engaged*
1st Dragoons KGL	Jan 1812	End of war	GCH
2nd Dragoons KGL	Jan 1812	End of war	GCH
1st Hussars KGL	May 1809	End of war	TAL, FDO, ELB, SAL, TOU
2nd Hussars KGL	Apr 1811	End of war	(C) BAR, ADM
3rd Hussars KGL	Sep 1808	Jan 1809	SAH, BEN
Duke of Brunswick Oels' Hussars	Aug 1812	End of war	(E) ORD

INFANTRY

Brigade of Guards

1st Foot Guards, 1st Bn	(i) Oct 1808	Jan 1809	COR
	(ii) Oct 1812	End of war	NLE, NVE, BAY
2nd Bn	(i) Oct 1808	Jan 1809	COR
	(ii) Apr 1810	Nov(?) 1811	(C) BAR
3rd Bn	Nov(?) 1811	End of war	(C) until Oct 1812 NLE, NVE, BAY
Coldstream Guards, 1st Bn	Mar 1809	End of war	DOU, TAL, FDO, SAL, BUR, BID, NLE, NVE, BAY
2nd Bn (2 coys)	Apr 1810	Nov(?) 1811	(C) BAR
3rd Foot Guards, 1st Bn	Mar 1809	End of war	DOU, TAL, FDO, SAL, BUR, BID, NLE, NVE, BAY
2nd Bn (3 coys)	Apr 1810	Nov(?) 1811	(C) BAR

Infantry of the Line

1st (Royal Scots), 3rd Bn	(i) Oct 1808	Jan 1809	COR
	(ii) Apr 1810	End of war	FDO, SAL, VIT, SAN, BID, NLE, NVE, BAY
2nd (Queen's)	(i) Aug 1808	Jan 1809	VIM, COR
	(ii) Mar 1811	End of war	SAL
(with 2/53rd as 2nd Provisional Bn)			VIT, RON, SOR, NLE, TOU
3rd (East Kent) (Buffs), 1st Bn	Aug 1808	End of war	DOU, TAL, ALB, VIT, RON, SOR, NLE, STP, ORT
4th (King's Own), 1st Bn	(i) Aug 1808	Jan 1809	COR
	(ii) Nov 1810	End of war	BAD (2), SAL, VIT, SAN, BID, NLE, NVE
5th (Northumberland), 1st Bn	(i) Aug 1808	Jan 1812	ROL, VIM, COR
	(ii) May 1812	End of war	SAL, VIT, NLE, ORT, TOU
2nd Bn	Dec 1809	Oct 1812	BUS, FDO, ELB, CIU, BAD (2), SAL

	Date *landed*	*Date* *re-embarked*	*Principal actions* *in which engaged*
6th (1st Warwicks), 1st Bn	(i) Aug 1808	Jan 1809	ROL, VIM, COR
	(ii) Nov 1812	End of war	NLE, MAY, SOR, ORT
7th (Royal Fuzileers), 1st Bn	Jul 1810	End of war	BUS, ALB, BAD (2), SAL, VIT, NLE, ORT, TOU
2nd Bn	Apr 1809	Jun 1811	DOU, TAL, ALB
9th (East Norfolk), 1st Bn	(i) Aug 1808	Jan 1809	ROL, VIM, COR
	(ii) Mar 1810	End of war	BUS, FDO, BAD (2), SAL, VIT, SAN, BID, NLE, NVE, BAY
2nd Bn	(i) Aug 1808	Jun 1809	VIM, COR, DOU
	(ii) Feb 1811	Mar 1811	(G) BAR (2 coys)
10th (North Lincolnshire), 1st Bn	Aug 1812	End of war	(E) CAS, TAR, ORD
2nd Bn	Dec 1812	Apr 1813	(E) (1 coy) CAS
11th (North Devon), 1st Bn	Aug 1809	End of war	SAL, SOR, NLE, TOU
2nd Bn	Oct 1811	Sep 1812	TFA (2 coys)
14th (Buckinghamshire), 1st Bn	Oct 1808	Jan 1809	COR
20th (East Devon)	(i) Aug 1808	Jan 1809	VIM, COR
	(ii) Dec 1812	End of war	VIT, RON, SOR, NLE, ORT, TOU
21st (R. North British Fuzileers), 1st Bn	Dec 1812	Apr 1813	(E) (1 coy) CAS
23rd (Royal Welsh Fuzileers), 1st Bn	Nov 1810	Apr 1813	ALB, BAD (2), SAL, VIT, RON, SOR, NLE, ORT, TOU
2nd Bn	Oct 1808	Jan 1809	COR
24th (Warwickshire), 2nd Bn	Apr 1809	End of War	TAL, BUS, FDO, SAL, BUR
(with 2/58th as 3rd Provisional Bn)			SOR, PYR, NLE, ORT
26th (Cameronian), 1st Bn	Oct 1808	Jan 1809	COR
27th (Inniskilling), 1st Bn	Nov 1812	End of war	(E) CAS, TAR, ORD,
2nd Bn	Dec 1812	End of war	(E) CAS, TAR, ORD
3rd Bn	Nov 1808	End of war	ALB (1 coy), BAD (2), SAL, VIT, RON, SOR, NLE, ORT, TOU
28th (North Gloucestershire), 1st Bn	(i) Aug 1808	Jan 1809	COR
	(ii) Feb 1811	Mar 1811	(G) BAR
	(iii) Jul 1811	End of war	ADM, VIT, MAY, NLE, STP, TOU
2nd Bn	Sep 1809	Aug 1811	ALB
29th (Worcestershire)	Aug 1808	Oct 1811	ROL, VIM, DOU, TAL, ALB
30th (Cambridgeshire), 2nd Bn	Oct 1810	May 1813	FDO, BAD (2), SAL
31st (Huntingdonshire) 1st Bn	Dec 1812	Apr 1813	(E) (1 coy) CAS
2nd Bn	Nov 1808	End of war	TAL, ALB

	Date landed	Date re-embarked	Principal actions in which engaged
(with 2/66th as 1st Provisional Bn)			VIT, RON, SOR, NLE, STP
32nd (Cornwall), 1st Bn	(i) Aug 1808	Jan 1809	ROL, VIM, COR
	(ii) Jul 1811	End of war	SAL, SOR, NLE, TOU
34th (Cumberland), 2nd Bn	Jul 1809	End of war	ALB, ADM, ALM, VIT, MAY, NLE, STP, TOU
36th (Herefordshire), 1st Bn	(i) Aug 1808	Jan 1809	ROL, VIM, COR
	(ii) Mar 1811	End of war	SAL, SOR, NLE, TOU
38th (1st Staffordshire), 1st Bn	(i) Aug 1808	Jan 1809	ROL, VIM, COR
	(ii) Jun 1812	End of war	SAL, VIT, SAN, BID, NLE, NVE
2nd Bn	Apr 1810	Dec 1812	BUS, BAD (2), SAL
39th (Dorsetshire), 2nd Bn	Jul 1809	End of war	ALB, ADM, ALM, VIT, MAY, NLE, STP, TOU
40th (2nd Somerset), 1st Bn	Aug 1808	End of war	ROL, VIM, TAL, BUS, ALB (1 coy), BAD (2), SAL, VIT, RON, SOR, NLE, ORT, TOU
42nd (Royal Highland), 1st Bn	(i) Sep 1808	Jan 1809	COR
	(ii) Mar 1812	End of war	SAL, BUR, SOR, NLE, ORT, TOU
2nd Bn	Jul 1809	May 1812	BUS, FDO
43rd (Monmouthshire) Light Infantry, 1st Bn	(i) Oct 1808	Jan 1809	
	(ii) Jun 1809	End of war	BUS, SAB, FDO, CIU, BAD (2), SAL, VIT, PYR, BID, NLE, NVE
2nd Bn	Aug 1808	Jan 1809	VIM, COR
44th (East Essex), 1st Bn	Jul(?) 1813	End of war	(E) —
2nd Bn	Oct 1810	May 1813	FDO, BAD (2), SAL
45th (Nottinghamshire), 1st Bn	Aug 1808	End of war	ROL, VIM, TAL, BUS, SAB, CIU, BAD (2), SAL, VIT, SOR, NLE, ORT, TOU
47th (Lancashire), 2nd Bn	May(?) 1810	End of war	(C) until Sep 12, BAR (2 coys), TFA, VIT, SAN, BID, NLE, NVE, BAY
48th (Northamptonshire), 1st Bn	Jun 1809	End of war	TAL, ALB, BAD (2), SAL, VIT, RON, SOR, NLE, ORT, TOU
2nd Bn	Apr 1809	Jun 1811	DOU, TAL, ALB

	Date landed	Date re-embarked	Principal actions in which engaged
50th (West Kent), 1st Bn	(i) Aug 1808	Jan 1809	ROL, VIM, COR
	(ii) Sep 1810	End of war	FDO, ADM, ALM, VIT, MAY, STP, ORT, TOU
51st (2nd West Riding) Light Infantry	(i) Oct 1808	Jan 1809	COR
	(ii) Feb 1811	End of war	FDO, BAD (1), SAL, VIT, SOR, NLE
52nd (Oxfordshire) Light Infantry, 1st Bn	(i) Aug 1808	Jan 1809	COR
	(ii) Jun 1809	End of war	BUS, SAB, FDO, CIU, BAD (2), SAL, VIT, BID, NLE, NVE, ORT, TOU
2nd Bn	(i) Aug 1808	Jan 1809	VIM
	(ii) Mar 1811	Feb 1812	FDO, CIU
53rd (Shropshire), 2nd Bn (with 2nd as 2nd Provisional Bn)	Apr 1809	End of war	DOU, TAL, SAL VIT, RON, SOR, NLE, TOU
57th (West Middlesex), 1st Bn	Oct 1809	End of war	ALB, VIT, RON, NLE, STP
58th (Rutlandshire), 1st Bn	Aug 1812	End of war	(E) CAS, TAR
2nd Bn (with 2/24th as 3rd Provisional Bn)	Jun 1809	End of war	SAL, BUR SOR, PYR, NLE
59th (2nd Nottinghamshire), 2nd Bn	(i) Oct 1808	Jan 1809	COR
	(ii) Sep 1812	Mar 1813	(C) —
	(iii) Apr 1813	End of war	VIT, SAN, BID, NLE, NVE
60th (Royal Americans), 5th Bn	Aug 1808	End of war	ROL, VIM, DOU, TAL, BUS, SAB, FDO, ELB, ADM, CIU, BAD (2), ALM, SAL, BUR, VIT, MAY, RON, SOR, BID, NLE, NVE, STP, ORT, TOU, BAY
8th Bn*	Nov 1813	End of war	(C) —
61st (South Gloucestershire), 1st Bn	Jun 1809	End of war	TAL, SAL, SOR, NLE, ORT, TOU
62nd (Wiltshire) 1st Bn	Dec 1812	Apr 1813	(E) (1 coy) CAS
2nd Bn	Oct 1813	End of war	NVE
66th (Berkshire), 2nd Bn (with 2/31st as 1st Provisional Bn)	Apr 1809	End of war	DOU, TAL, ALB VIT, RON, SOR, NLE, STP
67th (South Hants), 1st Bn	Dec 1812	Mar 1813	(E) (1 coy) —
2nd Bn	(i) Dec 1810	Jan 1812	(C) BAR

* This unit existed from 1811 but until November 1813 was known as the 'Battalion of German Deserters'.

	Date landed	Date re-embarked	Principal actions in which engaged
	(ii) Jan 1812	May 1813	(CT) —
	(iii) May 1813	End of war	(E) TAR
68th (Durham) Light Infantry	Jul 1811	End of war	SAL, VIT, SOR, NLE
71st (Highland) Light Infantry, 1st Bn	(i) Aug 1808	Jan 1809	ROL, VIM, COR
	(ii) Sep 1810	End of war	FDO, ADM, ALM, VIT, MAY, STP, ORT, TOU
74th (Highland)	Feb 1810	End of war	BUS, FDO, CIU, BAD (2), SAL, VIT, SOR, NLE, ORT, TOU
75th (Highland)	Dec 1812	Apr 1813	(E) (1 coy) CAS
76th	(i) Oct 1808	Jan 1809	COR
	(ii) Jul 1813	End of war	NLE, NVE
77th (East Middlesex)	Jul 1811	End of war	ELB, CIU, BAD (2)
79th (Cameron Highlanders), 1st Bn	(i) Aug 1808	Jan 1809	COR
	(ii) Feb 1810	Sep 1810	(C) —
	(iii) Sep 1810	End of war	FDO, SAL, BUR, SOR, NLE, TOU
81st, 1st Bn	Aug 1812	End of war	(E) CAS, TAR, ORD
2nd Bn	Oct 1808	Jan 1809	COR
82nd (Prince of Wales's Volunteers), 1st Bn	(i) Aug 1808	Jan 1809	ROL, VIM, COR
	(ii) Oct 1810	Oct 1810	(G) FUE
	(iii) Dec 1811	Jan 1812	(G), TFA (2 coys)
	(iv) Jun 1812	End of war	VIT, MAY, SOR, NLE
2nd Bn	Feb 1811	Mar 1811	(G) BAR (2 coys)
83rd, 2nd Bn	Apr 1809	End of war	DOU, TAL, BUS, SAB, FDO, ELB, CIU, BAD (2), SAL, VIT, NLE, ORT, TOU
84th (York & Lancaster), 2nd Bn	Jul 1813	End of war	NLE, NVE
85th (Bucks Volunteers)	(i) Mar 1811	Oct 1811	FDO, BAD (1)
	(ii) Jul 1813	End of war	NLE, NVE
87th (Prince of Wales's Own Irish), 2nd Bn	Apr 1809	End of war	TAL (C) 10 Feb– 12 Sep, BAR, TFA, VIT, NLE, ORT, TOU
88th (Connaught Rangers), 1st Bn	Feb 1809	End of war	TAL, BUS, SAB, FDO, ELB, CIU, BAD (1), SAL, VIT, SOR, NLE, ORT, TOU
2nd Bn	Sep 1810	Jul 1811	FDO
89th, 2nd Bn	Oct 1810	Oct 1810	(G) FUE (4 coys)

	Date landed	Date re-embarked	Principal actions in which engaged
91st, 1st Bn	(i) Aug 1808	Jan 1809	ROL, VIM, COR
	(ii) Oct 1812	End of war	SOR, NLE, ORT, TOU
92nd, 1st Bn	(i) Aug 1808	Jan 1809	COR
	(ii) Oct 1810	End of war	FDO, ADM, ALM, VIT, MAY, STP, ORT
94th (Connaught Rangers)	Feb 1810	End of war	(C) Feb–Sep 1810, SAB, FDO, ELB, CIU, BAD (2), SAL, VIT, NLE, ORT, TOU
95th (Riflemen), 1st Bn	(i) Aug 1808	Jan 1809	VIM (2 coys), COR (5 coys)
	(ii) Jun 1809	End of war	BUS, SAB, FDO, CIU, BAD (2), SAL, VIT, PYR, BID, NLE, NVE, TOU
2nd Bn	(i) Aug 1808	Jan 1809	(4 coys) ROL, VIM
	(ii) Mar 1811	End of war	(C) BAR (2 coys), TFA (1 coy), CIU, BAD (2) (2 coys), FDO (1 coy), SAL (4 coys), (6 coys) VIT, BID, NLE, NVE
3rd Bn	Jun 1810	End of war	(C) BAR (2 coys), (1 coy) FDO, (5 coys) CIU, BAD (2), VIT, PYR, BID, NLE, NVE, TOU
97th (Queen's Own)	Aug 1808	Oct 1811	VIM, DOU, TAL, ALB (1 coy)

Note on British Infantry. The territorial and other titles given are those shown in the Army List of 1814. Where no battalion number(s) are given against a regiment it is a single battalion unit.

Foreign corps

	Date landed	Date re-embarked	Principal actions
1st Bn Light Infantry KGL	(i) Aug 1808	Jan 1809	—
	(ii) Mar 1811	End of war	ALB, SAL, VDP, VIT, BID, NLE, NVE, BAY
2nd Bn Light Infantry KGL	(i) Aug 1808	Jan 1809	—
	(ii) Mar 1811	End of war	ALB, SAL, VDP, VIT, BID, NLE, NVE, BAY
1st Line Bn KGL	Aug 1808	End of war	DOU, TAL, BUS, FDO, SAL, BUR, BID, NLE, NVE, BAY

	Date landed	Date re-embarked	Principal actions in which engaged
2nd Line Bn KGL	Aug 1808	End of war	DOU, TAL, BUS, FDO, SAL, BUR, BID, NLE, NVE, BAY
3rd Line Bn KGL	Dec 1812	Apr 1813	(E) (2 coys) CAS
4th Line Bn KGL	Aug 1812	End of war	(E) CAS, TAR, ORD
5th Line Bn KGL	Aug 1808	End of war	DOU, TAL, BUS, FDO, SAL, BUR, BID, NLE, NVE, BAY
6th Line Bn KGL	Aug 1812	Apr 1813	(E) CAS
7th Line Bn KGL	Aug 1808	July 1811	DOU, TAL, BUS, FDO
8th Line Bn KGL	Dec 1812	Apr 1813	(E) CAS (1 coy)
Duke of Brunswick Oels' Light Infantry	Nov 1810	End of war	FDO, BAD (2), SAL, VIT, RON, MAY, SOR, SAN, BID, NLE, NVE, ORT
Roll's Regiment [Swiss]	Aug 1812	End of war	(E) (3 coys) CAS, TAR, ORD
Dillon's Regiment [Italian]	Aug 1812	End of war	(E) (5 coys) CAS, TAR
Watteville's Regiment [Swiss]	Oct 1811	Apr 1813	(C), (CT) —
Chasseurs Britanniques [French]	Jan 1811	End of war	FDO, BAD (1), SAL, VIT, SOR

Note on foreign corps. The nationalities shown against the last four regiments are those from which the units were originally recruited. As the war progressed each of them became diluted with deserters and enlisted prisoners from the French army, most of them Germans and Italians but including many other nationalities.

APPENDIX 3

Staff of the British Army in the Peninsular, 1808–1814

MILITARY DEPARTMENTS

Quartermaster-General
August 1808
  Lieut-Col James Bathurst, 60th Foot
August 1808–January 1809
  Capt and Lieut-Col George Murray, 3rd Guards

April 1809–December 1811
  Col George Murray, 3rd Guards (Brig-Gen 1811)
December 1811–August 1812
  Lieut-Col William Howe de Lancey, QMG's Dept (acting)
August–December 1812
  Col James Willoughby Gordon, Royal Africa Corps
December 1812–March 1813
  Lieut-Col W. H. de Lancey (acting)
March 1813–April 1814
  Maj-Gen George Murray, 3rd Guards

Adjutant-General
August 1808
  Lieut-Col John Goulston Tucker, 72nd Foot
August 1808–January 1809
  Col Henry Clinton, 1st Guards
April 1809–April 1812
  Brig-Gen the Hon Charles Stewart, 18th Light Dragoons. (Absent from army for two months in the winter of 1809–10 and for six months in 1810–11. Col Pakenham deputised in these periods.)
April–August 1812
  Col Lord Aylmer, Coldstream Guards (acting)
August 1812–January 1813
  Lieut-Col John Waters, Portuguese Staff (acting)
January–July 1813
  Col Lord Aylmer (acting)
July 1813–April 1814
  Maj-Gen the Hon Edward Pakenham, 6th West India Regiment

Military Secretary
August 1808
  Lieut-Col Henry Torrens, 89th Foot
August–October 1808
  Capt Adolphus Dalrymple, 18th Light Dragoons
October 1808–January 1809
  Major John Colborne, 20th Foot
April 1809–December 1810
  Lieut-Col James Bathurst, 60th Foot
December 1810–April 1814
  Capt Lord Fitzroy Somerset, 43rd Foot (Brevet major 1811, brevet lieut-col 1812)

ORDNANCE CORPS

Commander, Royal Artillery
August 1808
  Lieut-Col William Robe, RA
August 1808–January 1809
  Col John Harding, RA
April 1809–July 1811
  Brig-Gen Edward Howarth, RA
July–December 1811
  Lieut-Col Hoylett Framingham, RA
December 1811–March 1812
  Maj-Gen William Borthwick, RA
March–August 1812
  Lieut-Col Hoylett Framingham, RA
August–October 1812
  Lieut-Col William Robe, RA
October–December 1812
  Lieut-Col Charles Waller, RA
December 1812–May 1813
  Lieut-Col George Bulteel Fisher, RA
May 1813–April 1814
  Brevet Lieut-Col Alexander Dickson, RA

Commanders, Royal Engineers
August 1808
  Capt Howard Elphinstone, RE
August 1808–June 1812
  Brevet Major Richard Fletcher, RE (Lieut-Col, June 1809)
June 1812–April 1813
  Brevet Lieut-Col John Fox Burgoyne, RE (acting)
April–August 1813
  Lieut-Col Sir Richard Fletcher, Bart, RE
September–October 1813
  Brevet Lieut-Col John Fox Burgoyne, RE (acting)
October 1813–April 1814
  Lieut-Col Howard Elphinstone, RE

CIVIL DEPARTMENTS

Commissary-General
August 1808
  Dep Com-Gen James Pipon
August 1808–January 1809
  Com-Gen Robert Hugh Kennedy
April 1809–June 1810
  Com-Gen John Murray
June 1810–December 1811
  Com-Gen Robert Hugh Kennedy
December 1811–October 1812
  Com-Gen John Bissett
October 1812–December 1813
  Com-Gen Robert Hugh Kennedy
December 1813–March 1814
  Com-Gen Charles Dalrymple
March–April 1814
  Com-Gen Sir Robert Hugh Kennedy

Chief of the Medical Department
August 1808
  Inspector of Hospitals R. W. Shapter
August 1808–January 1809
  Inspector of Hospitals James Franck, MD
April–August 1809
  Deputy Inspector of Hospitals William Ferguson
August 1809–January 1812
  Inspector of Hospitals James Franck, MD
January 1812–April 1814
  Inspector of Hospitals James McGrigor, MD

Judge Advocate
August 1808–October 1812
  None
October 1812–April 1814
  DJAG Francis Seymour Larpent, Barrister at Law

Senior Chaplain
August 1808
  None
August 1808–Jan 1809
  Rev H. J. Symons

April 1809–March 1810
  Rev John Owens
March–September 1810
  Vacant
September 1810–April 1814
  Rev Samuel Briscall (who was absent, sick, from November 1811 to
  June 1813, no deputy being nominated)

Camp Commandant at Headquarters
May 1809–April 1814
  Major Colin Campbell, 70th Foot (Brevet Lieut-Col September 1811)

APPENDIX 4

Commanders of the French Armies in Spain

NORTHERN AND WESTERN SPAIN

Army of Portugal (formerly II, VI and VIII Corps)
May 1810–May 1811
  Marshal André Massena, Prince of Essling, Duke of Rivoli
May 1811–July 1812
  Marshal Auguste Frédéric Marmont, Duke of Ragusa
July–September 1812
  General Baron Bertrand Clausel
September–November 1812
  General Joseph Souham
November 1812–January 1813
  Jean-Baptiste Drouet, Count d'Erlon
January–July 1813
  General Count Honoré Reille

Army of the South (formerly I, IV and V Corps)
July 1810–March 1813
  Marshal Jean-de-Dieu Soult, Duke of Dalmatia
January–July 1813
  General Honoré Gazan

Army of the North
January–July 1811
  Marshal Jean-Baptiste Bessières, Duke of Istria
M

July 1811–May 1812
  General Count Jean-Marie Dorsenne
May 1812–January 1813
  General Louis Marc Caffarelli
January–July 1813
  General Baron Bertrand Clausel

Army of the Centre
October 1810–January 1813
  Joseph Napoleon, King of Spain
January–July 1813
  General Jean-Baptiste Drouet, Count d'Erlon

In July 1813 the four armies above were combined into the Army of Spain under Marshal Soult. In 1814 this army was sometimes called the Army of the Pyrenees.

EASTERN SPAIN

Army of Catalonia (formerly VII Corps)
February–May 1810
  Marshal Pierre François Augereau, Duke of Castiglione
May 1810–October 1811
  Marshal Etienne Macdonald, Duke of Tarantum
October 1811–January 1814
  General Charles Decaen

Army of Aragon (formerly III Corps)
February 1810–April 1814
  General Louis Gabriel Suchet, who in June 1811 became Marshal Duke of Albufera

The Army of Valencia was an offshoot of the Army of Aragon and was also commanded by Marshal Suchet, who superintended in addition the Army of Catalonia.

APPENDIX 5

Orders of Battle of the British Army at the Principal Battles

1   *Order of Battle of the British Army at Vimeiro, 21 August 1808*
Commander of the Forces: Lieut-Gen the Hon Sir Arthur Wellesley

	Rank and file
1st Brigade (Maj-Gen Rowland Hill)	2,658
1/5th, 1/9th, 1/38th Foot	
2nd Brigade (Maj-Gen Ronald Craufurd Fergusson)	2,449
1/36th, 1/40th, 1/71st Foot	
3rd Brigade (Brig-Gen Miles Nightingall)	1,520
29th, 1/82nd Foot	
4th Brigade (Brig-Gen Barnard Foord Bowes)	1,813
1/6th, 1/32nd Foot	
5th Brigade (Brig-Gen Catlin Crauford)	1,832
1/45th, 1/91st Foot	
6th Brigade (Brig-Gen Henry Fane)	2,005
1/50th, 5/60th Foot, 2/95th Rifles (4 coys)	
7th Brigade (Brig-Gen Robert Anstruther)	2,703
2/9th, 2/43rd, 2/52nd, 97th Foot	
8th Brigade (Brig-Gen Wroth Palmer Acland)	1,332
2nd, 20th (7½ coys) Foot, 1/95th Rifles (2 coys)	
20th Light Dragoons (3 sqns)	240
Artillery (Lieut-Col William Robe RA)	226
Batteries of Carthew, Morrison and Raynsford,	
Royal Artillery	
Sappers and miners*	15

2   *Order of Battle of the British Army, December 1808–January 1809*
Commander of the Forces: Lieut-Gen Sir John Moore

	Strength on *19 December 1880*
Cavalry (Lieut-Gen Lord Paget)	
1st Brigade (Brig-Gen John Slade)	1,538
7th, 10th, 15th Light Dragoons (Hussars)	
2nd Brigade (Brig-Gen the Hon Charles Stewart)	912
18th Light Dragoons (Hussars), 3rd Light	
Dragoons KGL	
Infantry	
1st Division (Lieut-Gen Sir David Baird)	
1st Brigade (Maj-Gen Henry Warde)	2,357
1 & 2/1st Guards	
2nd Brigade (Maj-Gen Lord William Bentinck)	2,428
1/4th, 1/42nd, 1/50th Foot	

---

* Owing to a quirk of British military organisation, the engineering services of the British army were organised by two separate bodies with a horizontal demarcation line between them. Thus the officers belonged to the Royal Engineers while sergeants and below served in the Royal Military Artificers.

Strength on 19 Dec 1808

3rd Brigade (Maj-Gen Coote Manningham)   1,957
  3/1st, 1/26th, 2/81st Foot
2nd Division (Lieut-Gen the Hon John Hope)
1st Brigade (Maj-Gen James Leith)   1,727
  51st, 2/59th, 2/76th Foot
2nd Brigade (Maj-Gen Rowland Hill)   2,755
  2nd, 1/5th, 2/14th, 1/32nd Foot
3rd Brigade (Brig-Gen Catlin Craufurd)   2,360
  1/36th, 1/71st, 1/92nd Foot
3rd Division (Lieut-Gen Alexander Mackenzie Fraser)
1st Brigade (Maj-Gen William Carr Beresford)   2,297
  1/6th, 1/9th, 2/23rd, 2/43rd Foot
2nd Brigade (Brig-Gen Henry Fane)   2,473
  1/38th, 1/79th, 1/82nd Foot
Reserve Division (Maj-Gen the Hon Edward Paget)
1st Brigade (Brig-Gen Robert Anstruther, who
    died 15 January 1809; Lieut-Col Robert Ross)   2,147
  20th, 1/52nd Foot, 1/95th Rifles
2nd Brigade (Brig-Gen Moore Disney)   1,548
  1/28th, 1/91st Foot
Flank Brigades (detached to Vigo on 31 December)
1st Flank Brigade (Col Robert Craufurd)   1,900
  1/43rd, 2/52nd Foot, 2/95th Rifles
2nd Flank Brigade (Brig-Gen Charles, Baron Alten)   1,658
  1st and 2nd Light Bns KGL
Artillery (Col John Harding)   1,297
Troops of Downman and Evelegh, RHA
Batteries of Bean, Bandreth, Carthew, Crawford,
  Drummond, Raynsford, Wall and Wilmot, RA
Engineers, staff corps etc   137

3 *Order of Battle of the Anglo-Portuguese Army, 6 May 1809*
Commander of the Forces: Lieut-Gen Sir Arthur Wellesley

Main Army   *Rank and file**
Cavalry (Maj-Gen Stapleton Cotton)   1,463
  14th Light Dragoons (less 1 sqn), 16th Light
  Dragoons, 20th Light Dragoons (2 sqns), 3rd Light
  Dragoons KGL (1 sqn)
Infantry
1st Brigade (Brig-Gen H. F. Campbell)   2,292
  1/Coldstream Guards, 1/3rd Guards, Coy 5/60th Foot

---

* No returns are available for the Portuguese units. The battalions seem to have been 500–600 strong.

	Rank and file
2nd Brigade (Brig-Gen Alexander Campbell)	1,206
2/7th, 2/53rd, Coy 5/60th Foot, 1/10th Portuguese Line	
3rd Brigade (Brig-Gen John Sontag)	1,307
2nd Bn of detachments,* 97th Regt, Coy 5/60th Foot, 2/16th Portuguese Line	
4th Brigade (Maj-Gen Rowland Hill)	2,007
1/3rd, 2/48th, 2/66th, Coy 5/60th Foot	
5th Brigade (Brig-Gen Alan Cameron)	1,316
2/9th, 2/83rd, Coy 5/60th Foot, 2/10th Portuguese Line	
6th Brigade (Brig-Gen Richard Stewart)	1,290
29th Foot, 1st Bn of detachments,* 1/16th Portuguese Line	
7th Brigade (Maj-Gen John Murray)	2,913
1st, 2nd, 5th, 7th Line KGL, Dets 1 & 2 Light Bns KGL	
Artillery (Col E. Howorth)	1,249
Batteries of Sillery and Lawson, RA	
Batteries of Tieling and Heise, KGA	
Flanking Column (Marshal William Carr Beresford)	
Cavalry	
14th Light Dragoons (1 sqn),† 1st Portuguese Dragoons	
Infantry	
British brigade (Maj-Gen Christopher Tilson)	1,439
2/87th, 1/88th, 5/60th (5 coys) Foot	
Portuguese brigade	
2/1st, 1 & 2/7th, 1 & 2/19th Portuguese Line	
Artillery	
2 Portuguese batteries	
Column at Abrantes (*watching Spanish frontier*)	
Cavalry	
British Brigade (Brig-Gen Henry Fane)	1,304
3rd Dragoon Guards, 4th Dragoons	
Portuguese Brigade	
3rd & 4th Portuguese Dragoons (5 sqns together)	
Infantry	
British Brigade (Maj-Gen Alex Randoll Mackenzie)	2,709
2/24th, 3/27th, 2/31st, 1/45th Foot	

---

* The two battalions of detachments were made up of men who had not marched
o Spain with Moore's army.
† Numbers returned with Cotton's brigade above.

Rank and file

Portuguese Brigade
  1/1st, 1 & 2/3rd, 1 & 2/4th, 1 & 2/13th, 1 & 2/15th
    Portuguese Line, 1st, 4th & 5th Caçadores

Artillery
May's Battery, RA   315
2 Portuguese batteries

4 *Order of Battle of the British Army at Talavera de la Reina,*
27–28 July 1809
Commander of the Forces: Lieut-Gen Sir Arthur Wellesley
Cavalry (Lieut-Gen William Payne)   *Rank and file*
1st Brigade (Brig-Gen Henry Fane)   1,069
  3rd Dragoon Guards, 4th Dragoons
2nd Brigade (Maj-Gen Stapleton Cotton)   1,189
  14th & 16th Light Dragoons
3rd Brigade (Brig-Gen George Anson)   910
  23rd Light Dragoons, 1st Hussars KGL

Infantry
1st Division (Maj-Gen (local Lieut-Gen) John Coape
  Sherbrooke)
1st Brigade (Brig-Gen Henry Frederick Campbell)   2,045
  1/Coldstream & 1/3rd Guards, Coy 5/60th Foot
2nd Brigade (Brig-Gen Alan Cameron)   1,364
  1/61st, 2/83rd, Coy 5/60th Foot
3rd Brigade (Brig-Gen Ernst, Baron Langwerth)   1,388
  1st & 2nd Linc Bns KGL, Dets 1 & 2 Light Bns KGL
4th Brigade (Brig-Gen Sigismund, Baron Löw)   1,167
  5th & 7th Line Bns KGL
2nd Division (Maj-Gen Rowland Hill)
1st Brigade (Maj-Gen Christopher Tilson)   1,871
  1/3rd, 2/48th, 2/66th, Coy 5/60th Foot
2nd Brigade (Brig-Gen Richard Stewart)   2,014
  29th, 1/48th Foot, 1st Bn Detachments
3rd Division (Maj-Gen Alexander Randoll Mackenzie)
1st Brigade (Maj-Gen Alexander Randoll Mackenzie)   2,276
  2/24th, 2/31st, 1/45th Foot
2nd Brigade (Col Rufane Shaw Donkin)   1,471
  2/87th, 1/88th, 5/60th (5 coys) Foot
4th Division (Brig-Gen Alexander Campbell)
1st Brigade (Brig-Gen Alexander Campbell)   1,032
  2/7th, 2/53rd, Coy 5/60th Foot

Rank and file

2nd Brigade (Col James Kemmis)   1,928
   1/40th, 97th Foot, 2nd Bn Detachments, Coy 5/60th
    Foot
Artillery (Brig-Gen Edward Howorth), 30 guns   1,011
Batteries of Lawson, Sillery and Elliot, RA
Batteries of Rettberg and Heise, KGA

5 *Order of Battle of the Anglo-Portuguese Army at Busaco,*
27 September 1810
Commander of the Forces: Lieut-Gen Viscount Wellington
Commanding the Portuguese troops: Marshal William Carr Beresford
Cavalry   *All ranks*
4th Dragoons (2 sqns)   210
Infantry
1st Division (Maj-Gen (local Lieut-Gen) Brent Spencer)
1st Brigade (Col the Hon Edward Stopford)   1,684
   1/Coldstream & 1/3rd Guards, Coy 5/60th Foot
2nd Brigade (Lieut-Col Lord Blantyre)   1,516
   2/24th, 2/42nd, 1/61st, Coy 5/60th Foot
3rd Brigade (Maj-Gen Sigismund, Baron Löw)   2,061
   1st, 2nd, 5th, 7th Line Bns KGL, Dets Light Bns
    KGL
4th Brigade (Col the Hon Edward Pakenham)   1,792
   1/7th, 1/79th
2nd Division (Maj-Gen Rowland Hill)
1st Brigade (Maj-Gen the Hon William Stewart)   2,247
   1/3rd, 2/31st, 2/48th, 2/66th, Coy 5/60th Foot
2nd Brigade (Col William Inglis)   1,818
   29th, 1/48th, 1/57th Foot
3rd Brigade (Brig-Gen Catlin Craufurd)   1,672
   2/28th, 2/34th, 2/39th Foot
3rd Division (Maj-Gen Thomas Picton)
1st Brigade (Col Henry Mackinnon)   1,808
   1/45th, 1/74th, 1/88th Foot
2nd Brigade (Maj-Gen Stafford Lightburne)   1,160
   2/5th, 2/83rd, 3 coys 5/60th Foot
Portuguese Brigade (Col Champlemond)   1,775
   1 & 2/9th, 1/21st Portuguese Line
4th Division (Maj-Gen the Hon Lowry Cole)
1st Brigade (Brig-Gen Alexander Campbell)   2,109
   2/7th, 1/11th, 2/53rd, Coy 5/60th Foot
2nd Brigade (Col James Kemmis)   2,448
   3/27th, 1/40th, 97th Foot

	All ranks
Portuguese Brigade (Col Richard Collins)	2,843
1 & 2/11th, 1 & 2/23rd Portuguese Line	
5th Division (Maj-Gen James Leith)	
British Brigade (Lt-Col James Stevenson Barnes)	1,879
1/3rd, 1/9th, 2/38th Foot	
Portuguese Brigade (Col William Frederick Spry)	2,619
1 & 2/3rd, 1 & 2/15th Portuguese Line, Thomar Militia	
Loyal Lusitanian Legion (2 bns)	1,646
1 & 2/8th Portuguese Line (2 bns)	1,161
Light Division (Brig-Gen Robert Craufurd)	
1st Brigade (Lieut-Col Sydney Beckwith)	1,896
1/43rd Foot, 1/95th Rifles (4 coys), 3rd Caçadores	
2nd Brigade (Lieut-Col Robert Barclay)	1,891
1/52nd Foot, 1/95th Rifles (4 coys), 1st Caçadores	
Portuguese Division (Maj-Gen John Hamilton)	
1st Brigade (Brig-Gen Archibald Campbell)	2,250
1 & 2/4th, 1 & 2/10th Portuguese Line	
2nd Brigade (Brig-Gen A. Luiz Fonseca)	2,690
1 & 2/2nd, 1 & 2/14th Portuguese Line	
Independent Portuguese Brigades	
1st Brigade (Brig-Gen Denis Pack)	2,769
1 & 2/1st, 1 & 2/16th Portuguese Line, 4th Caçadores	
5th Brigade (Brig-Gen Alexander Campbell)	3,249
1 & 2/6th, 1 & 2/18th Portuguese Line, 6th Caçadores	
6th Brigade (Brig-Gen Francis John Coleman)	2,345
1 & 2/7th, 1 & 2/19th Portuguese Line, 2nd Caçadores	
Artillery (Brig-Gen Edward Howorth), 60 guns	2,230
Troops of Ross and Bull, RHA	
Batteries of Thompson and Lawson, RA	
Batteries of Von Rettberg and Cleeves, KGA	
Batteries of de Rozierres, da Cunha Preto, da Silva and Freira, Portuguese Artillery	

6 *Order of Battle of the Anglo-Portuguese corps at Barossa, 5 March 1811*
GOC: Lieut-Gen Thomas Graham

	Rank and file
Cavalry (Maj Augustus Frederick, Baron von Bussche)	193
2nd Hussars KGL (2 sqns)	
Infantry	
1st Brigade (Brig-Gen William Thomas Dilkes)	1,311
2/1st Guards, 2/Coldstream Guards (2 coys), 2/3rd Guards (3 coys), 3/95th Rifles (2 coys)	

	Rank and file
2nd Brigade (Col William Wheatley)	1,605
1/28th (8 coys), 2/67th, 2/87th Foot	
Gibraltar Flank Bn (Lieut-Col J. F. Brown)	514
Grenadier and Light coys of 1/9th, 1/28th, 2/82nd Foot	
Cadiz Light Bn (Lieut-Col Andrew Barnard)	615
2/47th Foot (2 coys), 3/9th Rifles (4 coys)	
Portuguese Flank Bn (Lieut-Col Richard Bushe)	316
Grenadier and Light coys of 1 & 2/20th Portuguese Line	

Note. After the confusion of Graham's counter-march the companies of Coldstreams became attached to Wheatley's brigade and 5 coys of 2/67th to Dilkes'.

Artillery (Maj Alexander Duncan), 10 guns	342
Batteries of Hughes and Shenley, RA	

7   *Order of Battle of the Anglo-Portuguese Army at Fuentes de Oñoro, 3–5 May 1811*

Commander of the Forces: Lieut-Gen Viscount Wellington

	All ranks
Cavalry (Maj-Gen Stapleton Cotton)	
1st Brigade (Maj-Gen John Slade)	766
1st Dragoons, 14th Light Dragoons	
2nd Brigade (Lieut-Col Frederick von Arentschildt)	776
16th Light Dragoons, 1st Hussars KGL	
Portuguese Brigade (Brig-Gen Count Barbacena)	312
4th & 10th Portuguese Dragoons	
Infantry	
1st Division (Maj-Gen Miles Nightingall, vice Lieut-Gen Brent Spencer commanding 1st & 3rd Divisions)	
1st Brigade (Col the Hon Edward Stopford)	1,943
1/Coldstream & 1/3rd Guards, Coy 5/60th Foot	
2nd Brigade (Lieut-Col Lord Blantyre)	1,774
2/24th, 2/42nd, 1/79th, Coy 5/60th Foot	
3rd Brigade (Maj-Gen Kenneth Alexander Howard)	1,934
1/50th, 1/71st, 1/92nd Foot, Coy 3/95th Rifles	
4th Brigade (Maj-Gen Sigismund, Baron Löw)	1,914
1st, 2nd, 5th & 7th Line Bns KGL, Dets Light Bns KGL	
3rd Division (Maj-Gen Thomas Picton)	
1st Brigade (Col Henry Mackinnon)	1,863
1/45th, 1/74th, 1/88th, 3 coys 5/60th Foot	
2nd Brigade (Maj-Gen Hon Charles Colville)	1,967
2/5th, 2/83rd, 2/88th, 94th Foot	
Portuguese Brigade (Col Manley Power)	1,650
1 & 2/9th, 1 & 2/21st Portuguese Line	

All ranks

5th Division (Maj-Gen Sir William Erskine, Bart)
1st Brigade (Col Andrew Hay)   1,770
   3/1st, 1/9th, 2/38th Foot, Coy Brunswick Oels
2nd Brigade (Maj-Gen James Dunlop)   1,624
   1/4th, 2/30th, 2/44th Foot, Coy Brunswick Oels
Portuguese Brigade (Brig-Gen William Frederick Spry)   1,764
   1 & 2/3rd, 1 & 2/15th Portuguese Line, 8th Caçadores
6th Division (Maj-Gen Alexander Campbell)
1st Brigade (Col Richard Hulse)   2,041
   1/11th, 2/53rd, 1/61st, Coy 5/60th Foot
2nd Brigade (Col Robert Burne)   514
   1/36th (2nd Foot detached at blockade of Almeida)
Portuguese Brigade (Brig-Gen Frederick, Baron Eben)
   1 & 2/8th, 1 & 2/12th Portuguese Line   2,137
7th Division (Maj-Gen William Houston)
1st Brigade (Maj-Gen John Sontag)   2,409
   51st, 85th Foot, Chasseurs Britanniques, Brunswick
     Oels LI (8 coys)
Portuguese Brigade (Brig-Gen John Doyle)   2,181
   1 & 2/7th, 1 & 2/19th Portuguese Line, 2nd Caçadores
Light Division (Brig-Gen Robert Craufurd)
1st Brigade (Lieut-Col Sydney Beckwith)   1,631
   1/43rd Foot, 1/95th Rifles (4 coys), 2/95th Rifles (1
     coy), 3rd Caçadores
2nd Brigade (Col George Drummond)   2,184
   1 & 2/52nd Foot, 1/95th Rifles (4 coys), 1st Caçadores
Independent Portuguese Brigade (Col Charles Ashworth)   2,539
   1 & 2/6th, 1 & 2/18th Portuguese Line, 6th Caçadores
Artillery (Brig-Gen Edward Howorth), 48 guns   987
Troops of Ross and Bull, RHA
Batteries of Lawson and Thompson, RA
Portuguese Batteries of Von Arentschild (2), Da Cunha
   and Rozierres

8 *Order of Battle of the Allied Armies at Albuera, 16 May 1811*
Commander-in-Chief: Marshal William Carr Beresford

All ranks

Anglo-Portuguese Corps
Cavalry (Maj-Gen the Hon William Lumley)
Heavy Brigade (Col the Hon George de Grey)   761
   3rd Dragoon Guards, 4th Dragoons
Unbrigaded   403
   13th Light Dragoons

	All ranks
Portuguese Brigade (Col Loftus Otway)	849
1st & 7th Portuguese Dragoons, 1 sqn each of 5th & 8th Portuguese Dragoons	

Infantry
2nd Division (Maj-Gen the Hon William Stewart)

1st Brigade (Lieut-Col John Colborne)	2,066
1/3rd, 2/31st, 2/48th, 2/66th Foot	
2nd Brigade (Maj-Gen Daniel Hoghton)	1,651
29th, 1/48th, 1/57th Foot	
3rd Brigade (Lieut-Col the Hon Alexander Abercromby)	1,597
2/28th, 2/34th, 2/39th Foot	
3 coys 5/60th	146

4th Division (Maj-Gen the Hon Lowry Cole)

1st Brigade (Lieut-Col Sir William Myers, Bart)	2,015
1/7th, 2/7th, 1/23rd Foot	
Portuguese Brigade (Brig-Gen William Harvey)	2,297
1 & 2/2nd, 1 & 2/14th Portuguese Line, 1/Loyal Lusitanian Legion	
Detached Light Companies of 2/27th, 1/40th, 97th	165

Portuguese Division (Maj-Gen John Hamilton)

1st Brigade (Brig-Gen Archibald Campbell)	2,390
1 & 2/4th, 1 & 2/10th Portuguese Line	
2nd Brigade (Brig-Gen A. Luiz Fonseca)	2,429
1 & 2/2nd, 1 & 2/14th Portuguese Line	

Independent Brigades

German Brigade (Maj-Gen Charles, Baron von Alten)	1,098
1 & 2 Light bns KGL	
Portuguese Brigade (Col Richard Collins)	1,385
1 & 2/5th Portuguese Line, 5th Caçadores (drawn from garrison of Elvas)	
Artillery (Maj Alexander Dickson)	766

Lefebure's Troop, RHA
Hawker's Battery, RA
Cleeve's and Braun's batteries, KGA
Braun's and Arriaga's batteries, Portuguese Artillery
Spanish Army
Commander-in-Chief: Capt-Gen Joachim Blake
Cavalry

Brigades of Loy and Penne Villemur	1,905

Infantry

Vanguard Division (Lardizabal)	2,398
3rd Division (Ballasteros)	3,525
4th Division (Zayas)	4,882

	All ranks
Estremaduran Brigade (Carlos de España)	1,778
Artillery (Col José de Miranda), 2 batteries	165

9   *Order of Battle of the Allied Army at Salamanca, 22 July 1812*
Commander of the Forces: Lieut-Gen (local General) the Earl of
Wellington

All ranks

Cavalry (Lieut-Gen Sir Stapleton Cotton, Bart)

1st Brigade (Maj-Gen John Gaspard Le Marchant) — 1,022
   5th Dragoon Guards, 3rd & 4th Dragoons

2nd Brigade (Maj-Gen George Anson) — 1,004
   11th, 12th, 16th Light Dragoons

3rd Brigade (Maj-Gen Victor von Alten) — 746
   14th Light Dragoons, 1st Hussars KGL

4th Brigade (Maj-Gen George, Baron Bock) — 771
   1st & 2nd Dragoons KGL

Portuguese Brigade (Brig-Gen Benjamin D'Urban) — 482
   1st & 11th Portuguese Dragoons (12th Dragoons
     escorting the baggage)

Infantry

1st Division (Maj-Gen Henry Frederick Campbell)

1st Brigade (Col the Hon Thomas Fermor) — 1,972
   1/Coldstream & 1/3rd Guards, Coy 5/60th Foot

2nd Brigade (Maj-Gen William Wheatley) — 2,628
   2/24th, 1/42nd, 2/58th, 1/79th, Coy 5/60th Foot

3rd Brigade (Maj-Gen Sigismund, Baron Löw) — 1,628
   1st, 2nd & 5th Line Bns KGL

3rd Division (Col (local Maj-Gen) the Hon Edward
   Pakenham)

1st Brigade (Lieut-Col Alexander Wallace) — 1,803
   1/45th, 74th, 1/88th, 3 coys 5/60th Foot

2nd Brigade (Lieut-Col James Campbell) — 1,777
   1/5th, 2/5th, 2/83rd, 94th Foot

Portuguese Brigade (Col Manley Power) — 2,197
   1 & 2/9th, 1 & 2/21st Portuguese Line, 12th Caçadores

4th Division (Maj-Gen (local Lieut-Gen) the Hon Lowry
   Cole

1st Brigade (Maj-Gen William Anson) — 1,216
   3/27th, 1/40th, Coy 5/60th Foot

2nd Brigade (Lieut-Col Henry Watson Ellis) — 1,421
   1/7th, 1/23rd, 1/48th Foot, Coy Brunswick Oels

Portuguese Brigade (Col George Stubbs) — 2,554
   1 & 2/11th, 1 & 2/23rd Portuguese Line, 7th Caçadores

All ranks

5th Division (Maj-Gen (local Lieut-Gen) James Leith
1st Brigade (Lieut-Col the Hon Charles Greville)   2,606
   3/1st, 1/9th, 1 & 2/38th Foot, Coy Brunswick Oels
2nd Brigade (Maj-Gen William Pringle)   1,780
   1 & 2/4th, 2/30th, 2/44th Foot, Coy Brunswick Oels
Portuguese Brigade (Brig-Gen William Frederick Spry)   2,305
   1 & 2/3rd, 1 & 2/15th Portuguese Line, 8th Caçadores
6th Division (Maj-Gen Henry Clinton)
1st Brigade (Maj-Gen Richard Hulse)   1,464
   1/11th, 2/53rd, 1/61st, Coy 5/60th Foot
2nd Brigade (Col Samuel Venables Hinde)   1,436
   2nd, 1/32nd, 1/36th Foot
Portuguese Brigade (Brig-Gen Conde de Rezende)   2,631
   1 & 2/8th, 1 & 2/12th Portuguese Line, 9th Caçadores
7th Division (Maj-Gen John Hope)
1st Brigade (Col Colin Halkett)   1,569
   1st & 2nd Light Bns KGL, Brunswick Oels (7 coys)
2nd Brigade (Maj-Gen J. H. C. von Bernewitz)   1,358
   51st, 68th Foot, Chasseurs Britanniques
Portuguese Brigade (Col Richard Collins)   2,168
   1 & 2/7th, 1 & 2/19th Portuguese Line, 2nd Caçadores
Light Division (Maj-Gen Charles, Baron von Alten)
1st Brigade (Lieut-Col Andrew Barnard)   1,674
   1/43rd Foot, 2/95th Rifles (4 coys), 3/95th Rifles (5
   coys), 3rd Caçadores
2nd Brigade (Maj-Gen John Ormesby Vandeleur)   1,874
   1/52nd Foot, 1/95th Rifles (8 coys), 1st Caçadores
Independent Brigades
1st Brigade (Brig-Gen Denis Pack)   2,605
   1 & 2/1st, 1 & 2/16th Portuguese Line, 4th Caçadores
2nd Brigade (Brig-Gen Thomas Bradford)   1,894
   1 & 2/13th, 1 & 2/14th Portuguese Line, 5th Caçadores
Spanish Division (Maj-Gen Don Carlos de España)   3,360
   2/Princesa, Tiradores de Castilla, 2/Jaen, 3/1st Seville,
   Caçadores de Castilla
Artillery (Lieut-Col Hoylet Framingham), 54 guns   1,300
Troops of Ross, Bull and Macdonald, RHA
Batteries of Lawson, Gardiner, Greene, Douglas and
   May, RA
Arriaga's Battery, Portuguese Artillery
Engineers, staff corps and waggon train   246

10   *Order of Battle of the Anglo-Sicilian Army at Alicante, April 1813*
General Officer Commanding: Lieut-Gen Sir John Murray, Bart
Cavalry
20th Light Dragoons (2 sqns), Brunswick Hussars (1 sqn)
1st Sicilian Cavalry
Infantry
1/10th, 1 & 2/27th, 1/58th, 1/81st Foot, 4th & 6th Line bns KGL
Lt Coys, 3rd & 8th Line Bns KGL, De Roll's (3 coys), Dillon's (5 coys)
Calabrese Free Corps, 1st & 2nd Anglo-Italian Levy
Estero Regiment (2 bns) (Sicilian)
Artillery
Batteries of Holcombe, Thompson and Williamson, RA
Maximiano's battery, Portuguese Artillery
Garzia's battery, Sicilian Artillery

11   *Order of Battle of the Allied Army at Vitoria, 21 June 1813*
Commander of the Forces: Lieut-Gen (local Gen) The Marquess of
    Wellington, Duke of Ciudad Rodrigo (Spain) and Vitoria (Portugal)

	All ranks Return of 25 May 1813
RIGHT COLUMN (Lieut-Gen Sir Rowland Hill)	
Cavalry	
1st Brigade (Maj-Gen Victor, Baron Alten)	1,005
14th Light Dragoons, 1st Hussars KGL	
2nd Brigade (Maj-Gen Henry Fane)	842
3rd Dragoon Guards, 1st Dragoons	
Infantry	
2nd Division (Lieut-Gen the Hon William Stewart)	
1st Brigade (Col the Hon Henry Cadogan)	2,777
1/50th, 1/71st, 1/92nd, Coy 5/60th Foot	
2nd Brigade (Maj-Gen John Byng)	2,465
1/3rd, 1/57th Foot, 1st Provisional Bn (2/31st & 2/66th), Coy 5/60th Foot	
3rd Brigade (Col the Hon Richard O'Callaghan)	2,530
1/28th, 2/34th, 1/39th, Coy 5/60th Foot	
Portuguese Brigade (Brig-Gen Charles Ashworth)	3,062
1 & 2/6th, 1 & 2/18th Portuguese Line, 6th Caçadores	
Portuguese Division (Maj-Gen Francisco Silveira, Conde de Amaranthe)	
1st Brigade (Brig-Gen Hippolita da Costa)	2,492
1 & 2/2nd, 1 & 2/14th Portuguese Line	
2nd Brigade (Brig-Gen Archibald Campbell)	2,795
1 & 2/4th, 1 & 2/10th Portuguese Line, 10th Caçadores	

	All ranks
Spanish Division (Maj-Gen Pablo Morillo)	4,551
Artillery (Maj Joseph Carncross)	*
Beane's Troop, Royal Horse Artillery	
Maxwell's Battery, RA	
2 Portuguese Batteries under Maj Tulloh	

RIGHT CENTRE COLUMN (Marquess of Wellington)
Cavalry

1st Brigade (Lieut-Col Sir Robert Hill)	870
1st & 2nd Life Guards, Royal Horse Guards (2 sqns each)	
2nd Brigade (Col Colquhoun Grant)	1,624
10th, 15th, 18th Light Dragoons (Hussars)	
3rd Brigade (Maj-Gen the Hon William Ponsonby)	1,238
5th Dragoon Guards, 3rd & 4th Dragoons	
Portuguese Brigade (Brig-Gen Benjamin D'Urban)	685
1st, 11th, 12th Portuguese Dragoons	

Infantry
4th Division (Lieut-Gen the Hon Sir Lowry Cole)

1st Brigade (Maj-Gen William Anson)	2,395
3/27th, 1/40th, 1/48th Foot, 2nd Provisional Bn (2nd & 2/53rd), Coy 5/60th	
2nd Brigade (Maj-Gen John Byne Skerrett)	2,049
1/7th, 20th, 1/23rd, Coy Brunswick Oels	
Portuguese Brigade (Col George Stubbs)	2,842
1 & 2/11th Foot, 1 & 2/23rd Portuguese Line, 7th Caçadores	

Light Division (Maj-Gen Charles, Baron von Alten)

1st Brigade (Maj-Gen James Kempt)	2,597
1/43rd Foot, 1/95th Rifles (8 coys), 3/95th Rifles (5 coys), 3rd Caçadores	
2nd Brigade (Maj-Gen John Ormesby Vandeleur)	2,887
1/52nd Foot, 2/95th Rifles (6 coys), 17th Portuguese Line, 1st Caçadores	
Artillery (Maj Augustus Simon Frazer)	*
Troops of Ross, Gardiner, and Ramsay, RHA	
Sympher's battery, KGA	

LEFT CENTRE COLUMN (Lieut-Gen the Earl of Dalhousie)
Infantry
Third Division (Lieut-Gen Sir Thomas Picton)

---

* Numbers given under Army Troops.

	All ranks
1st Brigade (Maj-Gen Thomas Brisbane)	2,723
1/45th, 74th, 1/88th, 3 coys 5/60th Foot	
2nd Brigade (Maj-Gen the Hon Charles Colville)	2,272
1/5th, 2/83rd, 2/87th, 94th Foot	
Portuguese Brigade (Maj-Gen Manley Power)	2,460
1 & 2/9th, 1 & 2/21st Portuguese Line, 11th Caçadores	

Seventh Division (Lord Dalhousie)

1st Brigade (Maj-Gen Edward Barnes)	2,322
1/6th Foot, 3rd Provisional Bn (2/24th & 2/58th), Brunswick Oels (7 coys)	
2nd Brigade (Col William Grant)	2,538
51st, 68th, 1/82nd Foot, Chasseurs Britanniques	
Portuguese Brigade (Maj-Gen Francisco Le Cor)	2,437
1 & 2/7th, 1 & 2/19th Portuguese Line, 2nd Caçadores	

Artillery (Maj Richard Buckner)   *
Batteries of Cairnes and Douglas, RA

LEFT COLUMN (Lieut-Gen Sir Thomas Graham)

Cavalry

1st Brigade (Maj-Gen George Anson)	819
12th & 16th Light Dragoons	
2nd Brigade (Maj-Gen George, Baron Bock)	632
1st & 2nd Dragoons KGL	

Infantry

1st Division (Maj-Gen Kenneth Alexander Howard)

1st Brigade (Maj-Gen the Hon Edward Stopford)	1,728
1/Coldstream, 1/3rd Guards, Coy 5/60th Foot	
2nd Brigade (Col Colin Halkett)	3,126
1st, 2nd & 5th Line, 1st & 2nd Light Bns KGL	

5th Division (Maj-Gen John Oswald)

1st Brigade (Maj-Gen Andrew Hay)	2,292
3/1st, 1/9th, 1/38th Foot, Coy Brunswick Oels	
2nd Brigade (Maj-Gen Frederick P. Robinson)	2,061
1/4th, 2/47th, 2/59th Foot, Coy Brunswick Oels	
Portuguese Brigade (Brig-Gen Frederick William Spry)	2,372
1 & 2/3rd, 1 & 2/15th Portuguese Line, 8th Caçadores	

Independent Portuguese Brigades

1st Brigade (Maj-Gen Denis Pack)	2,297
1 & 2/1st, 1 & 2/16th Portuguese Line, 4th Caçadores	
2nd Brigade (Maj-Gen Thomas Bradford)	2,392
1 & 2/13th, 1 & 2/24th Portuguese Line, 5th Caçadores	
Spanish Division (Col Francisco Longa), 5 bns	3,130

---

* Numbers given under Army Troops.

All ranks

Artillery
Batteries of Dubordieu and Lawson, RA   *
ARMY TROOPS
Artillery (Lieut-Col Alexander Dickson)   4,307†
Reserve Artillery (Lieut-Col Julius Hartmann)
   Webber Smith's troop, RHA
   Parker's battery, RA
   Arriaga's battery, Portuguese Artillery
Engineers, staff corps, waggon train, etc   892

12   *Order of Battle of the Allied Army at the Nivelle, 10 November 1813*
Commander of the Forces: Field Marshal the Marquess of Wellington
All ranks

LEFT CORPS (Lieut-Gen the Hon Sir John Hope)
Infantry
1st Division (Maj-Gen Kenneth Alexander Howard)
1st Brigade (Col Peregrine Maitland)   1,680‡
   1 & 3/1st Guards, Coy 5/60th Foot
2nd Brigade (Maj-Gen the Hon Edward Stopford)   2,042‡
   As at Vitoria
3rd Brigade (Maj-Gen Heinrich von Hinüber)   3,176
   As at Vitoria
Fifth Division (Maj-Gen Andrew Hay)
1st Brigade (Col the Hon Charles Greville)   1,456
   As at Vitoria less coy Brunswick Oels
2nd Brigade (Maj-Gen Frederick P. Robinson)   1,332
   As at Vitoria, less Brunswick Oels
Portuguese Brigade (Brig-Gen Luiz de Regoa)   1,765
   As at Vitoria
Independent Brigades
British Brigade (Maj-Gen Lord Aylmer)   1,816
   76th, 2/84th, 85th Foot
Portuguese Brigade (Brig-Gen John Wilson)   2,185
   As at Vitoria when commanded by Pack
Spanish Troops (Gen Don Manuel Freyre)
3rd Division (Maj-Gen Del Barco), 8 bns   5,830
4th Division (Maj-Gen Barcena), 6 bns   4,154
Artillery
Troops of Webber, Smith and Ramsay, RHA

---

* Numbers given under Army Troops.
† Including units in the four columns and train personnel.
‡ The figures for all the companies of 5/60th are included with the headquarters companies in 3rd Division.

All ranks

Batteries of Carmichael, Mosse, Greene, Michell and
  Morrison, RA

Arriaga's Battery, Portuguese Artillery

1 Spanish bty

LEFT CENTRE CORPS (Maj-Gen Charles, Baron Alten)

Light Division (Baron Alten)

1st Brigade (Maj-Gen James Kempt)   2,416
  As at Vitoria

2nd Brigade (Lieut-Col John Colborne)   2,554
  As at Vitoria

Spanish Troops

6th Galician Division (Brig-Gen Francisco Longa), 5 bns   2,607

Army of Reserve of Andalusia (Gen Pedro Giron)

1st Division (Maj-Gen Virues), 6 bns   4,123

2nd Division (Maj-Gen La Torre), 6 bns   3,530

Artillery

Portuguese Mountain Battery

Independent Brigade

Portuguese Brigade (Maj-Gen Thomas Bradford)   1,614
  As at Vitoria

RIGHT CENTRE CORPS (Marshal Sir William
  Beresford)

Third Division (Maj-Gen the Hon Charles Colville)

1st Brigade (Maj-Gen Thomas Brisbane)   2,684*
  As at Vitoria

2nd Brigade (Col John Keane)   2,347
  As at Vitoria

Portuguese Brigade (Maj-Gen Manley Power)   2,303
  As at Vitoria

Fourth Division (Lieut-Gen the Hon Sir Lowry Cole)

1st Brigade (Maj-Gen William Anson)   2,167
  As at Vitoria

2nd Brigade (Maj-Gen Robert Ross)   1,799
  As at Vitoria, less Brunswick Oels

Portuguese Brigade (Brig-Gen José Vasconcellos)   2,419
  As at Vitoria

Seventh Division (Maj-Gen Carlos Le Cor)

1st Brigade (Maj-Gen Edward Barnes)   1,915
  As at Vitoria

2nd Brigade (Maj-Gen William Inglis)   1,827
  As at Vitoria + 3 coys Brunswick Oels

---

* Including detached coys 5/60th.

All ranks

Portuguese Brigade (Col John Milley Doyle)   2,326
  As at Vitoria
Artillery (Lieut-Col Augustus Frazer)
Ross' Troop, RHA
Douglas' Battery, RA
Sympher's Battery, KGA
RIGHT CORPS (Lieut-Gen Sir Rowland Hill)
Second Division (Lieut-Gen the Hon Sir William Stewart)
1st Brigade (Maj-Gen George Townshend Walker)   1,644
  As at Vitoria
2nd Brigade (Maj-Gen John Byng)   2,183
  As at Vitoria
3rd Brigade (Maj-Gen William Pringle)   1,937
  As at Vitoria
Portuguese Brigade (Brig-Gen Charles Ashworth)   2,713
  As at Vitoria
Sixth Division (Lieut-Gen Sir Henry Clinton)
1st Brigade (Maj-Gen Denis Pack)   2,161
  1/42nd, 1/79th, 1/91st Foot
2nd Brigade (Maj-Gen John Lambert)   2,490
  1/11th, 1/32nd, 1/39th, 1/61st Foot
Portuguese Brigade (Col James Douglas)   2,067
  As at Salamanca
Portuguese Division (Lieut-Gen Sir John Hamilton)
1st Brigade (Brig-Gen Hippolita Da Costa)   2,558
  As at Vitoria
2nd Brigade (Brig-Gen John Buchan)   2,391
  As at Vitoria
Artillery (Lieut-Col Alexander Tulloh)
Batteries of Cunha Preto and Judice, Portuguese
  Artillery
Mountain Battery of Lieut W. L. Robe, RA (with Portu-
  guese gunners and British drivers)
Spanish Troops (under Hill's orders but operating in-
  dependently beyond the flank of the corps)
1st Galician Division (Maj-Gen Pablo Morillo), 6 bns   4,924

Note. The allied cavalry was quartered in the rear except for the 13th
Light Dragoons which accompanied Hope's corps and had one man
wounded.

APPENDIX 6

Outlines of the Organisation of the French Army at Various Periods of the War

1   *The French Army at Vimeiro, 21 August 1808*
Commander-in-Chief: General Androche Junot, Duke of Abrantes

	All ranks
1st Division (Delaborde)	5,000
Brigades of Brennier and Thomieres	
2nd Division (Loison)	4,000
Brigades of Solignac and Charlot	
Reserve of Grenadiers (Kellermann)	2,100
4 bns	
Cavalry (Margaron)	1,900
4 regts	
Artillery, engineers, etc	700

Note. These French strengths have to be based on a return more than four weeks old and can only be approximate. The figures are likely to be under-estimates rather than over-estimates.

2   *The French Army at Coruña, 16 January 1809*
Commander-in-Chief: Nicholas Soult, Marshal, Duke of Dalmatia
1st Division (Merle), 13 bns
    Brigades of Reynaud, Sarrut and Thomieres
2nd Division (Mermet), 12 bns
    Brigades of Gaulois, Jardon and Lefebvre
3rd Division (Delaborde), 10 bns
    Brigades of Foy and Arnaud
Cavalry
1st Division (Lorge), 4 regts
2nd Division (La Houssaye), 4 regts
Artillery, 20 guns

Note. Delaborde's division had belonged to Junot's VIII Corps and was allocated to Soult to compensate for his division left at Santander. Nine battalions which had been with Junot in Portugal before the Convention of Cintra fought with Soult at Coruña.

The strength of Soult's army at Coruña has been the subject of much dispute, some French authorities putting it as low as 13,000. The most reliable French sources suggest that the actual numbers were:

	All ranks
Infantry	11,928
Cavalry	3,298
Artillery	930

16,156

The British strength at the battle is almost more difficult to determine since there are no returns between that of mid-December and the disembarkation return (which is incomplete) made in England. It is a reasonable estimate that about 15,000 British troops fought at Coruña. All of these except the crews of nine guns were infantry. Soult's small superiority in strength was, therefore, composed of cavalrymen who were not of much use in the circumstances. He had a great superiority in artillery both in numbers (20–9) and in weight of metal.

3   *The French Army at Talavera de la Reina, 27–28 July 1809*
Commander-in-Chief: Prince Joseph Napoleon, King of Spain
Chief of Staff: Marshal Jean-Baptiste Jourdan

	All ranks
I Corps (Marshal Victor, Duke of Belluno)	
1st Division (Ruffin), 9 bns	5,286
2nd Division (Lapisse), 12 bns	6,862
3rd Division (Villatte), 12 bns	6,135
Cavalry Brigade (Beaumont), 2 regts	980
IV Corps (Gen Horace Sebastiani)	
1st Division (Sebastiani), 12 bns	8,118
2nd Division (Valence), 2 bns	1,600
3rd Division (Leval), 9 bns	4,537
Cavalry Brigade (Merlin), 4 regts	1,188
Madrid Division (Gen Dessolles)	5,737
Royal Guard, 6 line bns, 2 sqns cavalry	
Reserve of Cavalry	
1st Dragoon Division (Latour-Maubourg), 6 regts	3,279
2nd Dragoon Division (Milhaud), 7 regts	2,356
Artillery (Gen Sénarmont), 80 guns	
Numbers included in divisional totals	

4   *The Army of Portugal, 15 September 1810*
Commander-in-Chief: André Massena, Marshal of the Empire, Prince of Essling, Duke of Rivoli

	All ranks
II Corps (Gen Jean Louis Ebenezer Reynier)	
1 Division (Merle), 12 bns	6,589
2 Division (Heudelet), 14 bns	8,087

All ranks
Cavalry Brigade (P. Soult), 4 regts   1,397
Artillery, engineers, staff, etc   1,645
VI Corps (Marshal Ney, Duke of Elchingen)
1st Division (Marchand), 11 bns   6,671
2nd Division (Mermet), 11 bns   7,616
3rd Division (Loison), 12 bns   6,826
Cavalry Brigade (Lamotte), 2 regts   1,680
Artillery, engineers, staff, etc   1,513
VIII Corps (Gen Androche Junot)
1st Division (Clausel), 11 bns   6,794
2nd Division (Solignac), 12 bns   7,226
Cavalry Brigade (Ste-Croix), 2 sqns each of 6 regts   1,863
Artillery, engineers, staff, etc   1,056
Reserve of Cavalry (Montbrun), 5 regts   3,479
Reserve artillery, engineers, staff, gendarmerie, etc   2,608

5   *The French Army at Fuentes de Oñoro, 3–5 May 1811*
Army of Portugal

All ranks
Commander-in-Chief: André Massena, Marshal, Prince of Essling, Duke
    of Rivoli
II Corps (Gen Jean Louis Ebenezer Reynier)
1st Division (Merle), 9 bns   4,891
2nd Division (Heudelet), 12 bns   5,491
Cavalry Brigade (P. Soult), 3 regts   682
VI Corps (Gen Louis Henri Loison)
1st Division (Marchand), 12 bns   5,872
2nd Division (Mermet), 12 bns   6,702
3rd Division (Ferey), 10 bns   4,232
Cavalry Brigade (Lamotte), 2 regts   334
VIII Corps (Gen Androche Junot, Duke of Abrantes)
2nd Division (Solignac), 10 bns   4,714
(1st Division and cavalry absent on lines of communication)
IX Corps (Gen Count Drouet d'Erlon)
1st Division (Claparéde), 9 bns   4,716
2nd Division (Conroux), 9 bns   5,588
Cavalry Brigade (Fournier), 3 regts   794
Reserve of Cavalry (Montbrun), 6 regts   1,187
Artillery (Eblé), 40 guns   430
Engineers, staff, train, etc   900 (?)
Army of the North
Commander-in-Chief: Jean Baptiste Bessières, Marshal Duke of Istria
Light Cavalry of the Imperial Guard (Lepic)   881

	All ranks
Light Cavalry Brigade (Wathier), 4 regts	784
Artillery, 6 guns	73

6 *The French Army at Albuera, 16 May 1811*

Commander-in-Chief: Nicholas Soult, Marshal, Duke of Dalmatia

	All ranks
Cavalry (Gen Marie-Charles, Comte de Latour Maubourg)	
1st Brigade (Briche), 3 regts	823
2nd Brigade (Bron), 3 regts	1,093
3rd Brigade (Bouvier des Ecats), 3 regts	879
3 regts unbrigaded	1,217
Infantry	
1st Division (Girard), 9 bns	4,234
2nd Division (Gazan), 8 bns	4,203
Werls'é Brigade, 9 bns	5,621
Godinot's Brigade, 6 bns	3,928
Reserve of Grenadiers, 11 coys	1,033
Artillery (Gen Ruty), 48 guns	1,233
Engineers and train	

Note. Characteristically, Soult in his report gave his strength as 18,000 men.

7 *The Army of Portugal, July 1812*

Commander-in-Chief: Auguste Frédéric Marmont, Marshal, Duke of Ragusa

	All ranks *(return of 15 July 1812)*
Cavalry	
Light Cavalry Division (Curto), 18 sqns	1,879
Heavy Cavalry Division (Boyer), 8 sqns	1,500
Infantry	
1st Division (Foy), 8 bns	4,933
2nd Division (Clausel), 10 bns	6,336
3rd Division (Ferey), 9 bns	5,382
4th Division (Sarrut), 9 bns	5,002
5th Division (Maucune), 9 bns	5,030
6th Division (Brennier), 8¼ bns	4,315
7th Division (Thomières), 8 bns	4,335
8th Division (Bonet), 12 bns	6,411
Artillery (Tirlet), 78 guns	3,347
Engineers, gendarmerie, train, staff, etc	1,306

8 *The French Army at Vitoria, 21 June 1813*
Commander-in-Chief: Prince Joseph Napoleon, King of Spain
Chief of Staff: Marshal Jean Baptiste Jourdan

	All ranks *(return of 29 May* *1813)*
Army of the South (Gen Honoré Gazan)	
Cavalry	
1st Division (P. Soult), 4 regts	1,502
2nd Division (Tilly), 6 regts	1,929
3rd Division (Digeon), 4 regts	1,692
Infantry	
1st Division (Leval)	4,678
3rd Division (Villatte)	5,692
4th Division (Conroux)	6,396
6th Division (Daricau)	5,693
Maransin's Brigade	2,937
Artillery (including artillery train, pontonniers)	1,510
Engineers, gendarmerie, train, staff, etc	915
Army of the Centre (Gen Count Drouet d'Erlon)	
Cavalry	
1st Division (Treillard), 4 regts	1,038
2nd Division (Avy), 2 regts	474
Infantry	
1st Division (Darmagnac)	4,472
2nd Division (Cassagne) (on loan from Army of South)	5,209
Artillery (including artillery train)	501
Engineers, etc	329
Army of Portugal (Gen Honoré Reille)	
Cavalry	
1st Division (Mermet), 5 regts	1,801
2nd Division (Boyer), 4 regts	1,471
Infantry	
4th Division (Sarrut) including divisional artillery	4,802
6th Division (Lamartinière) including divisional artillery	6,535
Reserve artillery, engineers, etc	2,455
Army of the North	
Details (bn infantry, troop cavalry, section of guns)	800 approx
King Joseph's Spanish Army	
Guard (French troops in Spanish service) (Guy)	
Infantry	2,380 estimated
Cavalry	425 estimated

	All ranks *(return of 29 May* *1813)*
Troops of the Line (Casapalacios)	
Infantry	2,070 estimated
Cavalry	670 estimated
Artillery	98 estimated

9   *The Army of Spain as reorganised, July 1813*
Commander-in-Chief: Marshal Soult, Duke of Dalmatia
Chief of Staff: General Honoré Gazan

	All ranks
Lieutenancy of the Left (Gen Bertrand Clausel)	
4th Division (Conroux), 9 bns	7,056
5th Division (Vandermaesen), 7 bns	4,181
8th Division (Taupin), 9 bns	5,981
Lieutenancy of the Centre (Gen Count Drouet d'Erlon)	
2nd Division (Darmagnac), 8 bns	6,961
3rd Division (Abbé), 9 bns	8,030
6th Division (Maransin), 7 bns	5,966
Lieutenancy of the Right (Gen Honoré Reille)	
1st Division (Foy), 9 bns	5,922
7th Division (Maucune), 7 bns	4,186
9th Division (Lamartinière), 10 bns	7,127
Reserve (Villatte)	
French troops in 2 brigades, 17 bns	9,102
Foreign troops (German, Italian, Spanish), 10 bns	4,583
Spanish Royal Guards (French), 6 bns	2,019
Gendarmerie and embodied National Guards	1,550
Cavalry	
3 regts of Chasseurs à cheval attached to lieutenancies	808
14 regts in 2 divisions (P. Soult and Treillard)	6,239
Artillery, engineers, train, etc	9,000

10   *The Army of Spain as reorganised in late January 1814*
Commander-in-Chief: Marshal Soult, Duke of Dalmatia

	All ranks
1st Division (Foy)	4,600
2nd Division (Darmagnac)	5,500
3rd Division (Abbé)	5,300
4th Division (Taupin, vice Conroux, killed)	5,600
5th Division (Maransin, later Rouget)	5,000
6th Division (Villatte, vice Daricau)	5,200
8th Division (Harispe)	6,600

	All ranks
Cavalry (P. Soult)	3,800
Artillery, engineers, etc	7,300
Garrison of Bayonne	8,800
Garrison of St-Jean-Pied-de-Port	2,400

Note. 7th and 9th Divisions with Treillard's dragoons had been sent to the eastern front. 8th Division had been disbanded after Nivelle but was reconstructed from Paris' brigade from the Army of Catalonia and the two French brigades from Villatte's Reserve which was disbanded when its German brigade changed sides and the Italian brigade was sent to reinforce the French Army of Italy. The Spanish brigade had disintegrated.

11 *The French Army at Toulouse, 10 April 1814*
Commander-in-Chief: Marshal Soult, Duke of Dalmatia

	All ranks
1st Division (Daricau, vice Foy, wounded at Orthez)	3,839
2nd Division (Darmagnac)	5,022
4th Division (Taupin)	5,455
5th Division (Maransin)	3,717
6th Division (Villatte)	4,609
8th Division (Harispe)	5,084
Reserve Division of conscripts (Travot)	7,267
Cavalry (P. Soult)	2,700
Artillery	3,603
Engineers, gendarmerie, etc	747

Note. One of the three brigades of 8th division had been broken up and the units distributed as reinforcements to the other formations.

References

Note: For abbreviations found in these references, the Bibliography should be consulted. In addition, the following are used:

H. Wellesley = Lord Wellington's brother Henry
JN = Joseph Napoleon, King of Spain
Ld Wellesley = Lord Wellington's brother Richard
N = Napoleon I, Emperor of the French
W = Arthur Wellesley, Lord Wellington
W. Wellesley Pole = Lord Wellington's brother William

1 *Napoleon's Europe, 1807 (pp 21–6)*
 1 Lefebvre i 163
 2 Bourrienne 112
 3 Champagny. Quoted in Lefebvre ii 8
 4 RG 235
 5 Quoted in Lefebvre ii 8
 6 Greville. Quoted in RG 247

2 *Arms and the Men (pp 27–41)*
 1 Müffling 214
 2 Larpent 76
 3 WD v 11 and 15. W to Ld Wellesley, 8 August 1809
 4 NC xviii 14462 and 14469. N to Dejean, 11 and 13 November 1808
 5 Ward 82
 6 WD viii 409. Memorandum for the Commissary General, 20 November 1811
 7 WD viii 414. W to Bissett, 21 November 1811
 8 WD ix 297. W to Bathurst, 21 July 1812
 9 Marmont iv 341. Marmont to Berthier, 26 February 1812
 10 WD vii 434. W to Chapman, 8 April 1811
 11 Stanhope 109

12 WD xi 314. W to Bathurst, 22 November 1813
13 Larpent 355
14 Neale. Letter of 22 August 1808
15 Smith 39
16 Guthrie, *Treatise on Gunshot wounds* (1820)
17 Henry i 73
18 Celer et Audax 160
19 Cooper 160
20 WD xi 141. W to Bathurst, 24 September 1813
21 Cooper 21
22 WD vii 195. W to Ld Wellesley, 26 January 1811
23 SD x 219. W to Bathurst, 4 May 1815
24 Stanhope 18
25 WD vi 576. W to Torrens, 2 November 1810
26 Stepney 18
27 WD xi 303. W to Bathurst, 21 November 1813
28 —— 413.   „   1 January 1814
29 —— 306.   „   21 November 1813
30 Dumouriez. Quoted in *Campaigns in Spain and Portugal* (1812) i 407
31 WD iv 303. W to Beresford, 6 May 1809
32 Larpent 196
33 SD vi 373. Ld Wellesley to W, 19 September 1809
34 WD vii 25. W to H. Wellesley, 2 December 1810
35 WD v 335. W to Frere, 6 December 1809
36 Stanhope 9
37 Chad 2

3   *Napoleonic Aggression* (*pp 45–55*)
 1 Thiébault ii 196
 2 ——   199
 3 LIN i 136. N to Junot, 7 January 1808
 4 Jourdan 9
 5 Beauharnais to Talleyrand, 12 July 1807. Quoted in GG i 89
 6 Ibid
 7 Caulaincourt 1812 569
 8 NC xvi 13632. N to Murat,   9 March 1808
 9 ——   13652.   „   14 March 1808
10 ——   13696.   „   29 March 1808
11 MM ii 215–16
12 Roederer 234
13 MM ii 170
14 Gourgaud 130
15 Bourrienne 113
16 Caulaincourt 1812 31

17 Murat to N, 18 May. Quoted in Oman i 62
18 MM ii 231
19 JN iv 339. JN to N, 10 July 1808
20 —— 343.   „   12 July 1808
21 —— 371.   „   19 July 1808
22 MM ii 253
23 JN iv 375. J to JN, 20 July 1808
24 MM ii 274
25 NC xvii 14192. N to Savary, 13 July 1808
26 JN iv 381. JN to N, 24 July 1808
27 —— 385.   „   26 July 1808
28 —— 386.   „   27 July 1808
29 —— 389.   „   28 July 1808
30 NC xvii 14184. N to JN, 12 July 1808
31 JN iv 373. N to JN, 21 July 1808
32 NC xvii 14242. N to Clarke, 3 August 1809
33 JN iv 425. N to JN, 16 August 1808
34 NC xvii 14378. N to JN, 13 October 1808
35 MM ii 274

4   *British Intervention* (*pp 56–71*)
1   SD vi 80. Undated memorandum from W
2   Elers 7
3   Rose, *William Pitt and the Great War with France* (1911), 556
4   Croker ii 342
5   *Morning Chronicle*, 16 June 1808
6   Dalrymple 233. Collingwood to Dalrymple, 23 June 1808
7   WD iv 55. W to Castlereagh, 1 August 1808
8   SD vi 95. W to Richmond, 1 August 1808
9   Hussar i 248
10 WD iv 72. W to Castlereagh, 8 August 1808
11 Cox Diary. Quoted in WV i 145
12 Warre 25
13 WD iv 103. W to Castlereagh, 18 August 1808
14 Cintra 162. Burrard's evidence
15 Croker ii 122
16 Cammisc 6. W to W. Wellesley Pole, 22 August 1808
17 Hussar i 265
18 Thiébault ii 208–9
19 Croker ii 122
20 Hussar i 267
21 Warre 32
22 Cintra 197. Torrens' evidence
23 —— 165. Burrard's evidence

24 Sherer 43
25 Hulot. Quoted in Oman i 267
26 Cintra 104. W's evidence
27 SD vi 123. W to Castlereagh, 23 August 1808
28 ——— 132. W to Richmond, 9 September 1808
29 Cintra 19. Dalrymple's evidence
30 *Morning Chronicle,* 7 September 1808
31 ———   21 September 1808
32 Cintra 231

5   *Napoleon and Sir John Moore* (*72–87*)
 1 NC xviii 14413
 2 Moore's Diary ii 272
 3 Moore Appendix 16. Moore to Castlereagh, 9 October 1808
 4 Moore's Diary ii 155
 5 Colborne 109
 6 ———   265
 7 Moore 104. Moore to Frere, 27 November 1808
 8 ——— 114. Moore to Hope, 28 November 1808
 9 Moore's Diary 283
10 Moore Appendix 91. Moore to Castlereagh, 12 December 1808
11 ——— Appendix 89.   „   10 December 1808
12 ——— 148. Moore to Baird, 5 December 1808
13 ——— 196. Moore to Frere, 12 December 1808
14 Gordon 101
15 Graham 292
16 *Madrid Gazette,* 12 December 1808
17 NC xviii 14620. N to JN, 27 December 1808
18 ———   14606. N to Josephine, 22 December 1808
19 TS 53
20 Harris 75
21 Patterson i 281
22 Gordon 154–66
23 Verner 15
24 Moore 316
25 Neale 322. Letter of January 1809
26 NC xviii 14640. N to JN, 2 January 1809
27 ———   14692. N to Clarke, 13 January 1809
28 Harris 105
29 Moore 135. Moore to Castlereagh, 13 January 1809
30 Colborne 100
31 Hall ii 327–35
32 C. Napier i 94–5
33 Blakeney 121

34 Moore 359. Harding's narrative
35 Smith 17
36 Moore 132. Moore to Castlereagh, 13 January 1809

6 *The Second French Invasion of Portugal* (*pp 88–98*)
 1 NC xviii 14731. N to Jerome, 16 January 1809
 2 LIN i 390. N to Caulaincourt, 7 January 1809
 3 Jourdan 170
 4 NC xviii 14469. N to Dejean, 13 November 1808
 5 LIN i 397. N to Caulaincourt, 14 January 1809
 6 Jourdan 170
 7 NC xviii 14684. N to JN, 11 January 1809
 8 Jourdan 170
 9 Malmesbury ii 405
10 Castlereagh vii 44
11 SD vii 39. Beresford to W, 4 January 1811
12 Beresford to Lady Anne Beresford, 23 April 1809
13 D'Urban. Quoted in Oman iii 173
14 Warre 78. Letter of 6 September 1809
15 WD iv 303. W to Beresford, 6 May 1809
16 —— 269. W to Castlereagh, 24 April 1809
17 Londonderry 276
18 Foy 80
19 Cooper 8
20 Leslie 114
21 Hawker. Quoted in Oman ii 341
22 WD iv 343. W to Castlereagh, 18 May 1809
23 —— 349. W to Frere, 20 May 1809

7 *Talavera and Ocaña* (*pp 101–16*)
 1 WD iv 374. W to Villiers, 31 May 1809
 2 Hill 106. Letter of 25 July 1809
 3 WD iv 414. W to Castlereagh, 11 June 1809
 4 —— 413. W to Villiers, 11 June 1809
 5 —— 473. W to Huskisson, 28 June 1809
 6 JN vi 270. JN to N, 9 July 1809
 7 NC xix 15340. N to Clarke, 12 June 1809
 8 JN vi 278. Jourdan to Soult, 22 July 1809
 9 WD iv 553. W to Castlereagh, 1 August 1809
10 —— 527. W to Frere, 24 July 1809
11 Asst Surgeon Brooke. MS letter of 22 August 1809
12 Munster 210
13 Hill 112. Memorandum of 1827
14 ——109. Letter of 30 July 1809

15 Leith Hay i 149
16 ———   152
17 Jourdan 258–9
18 Cooper 21–2
19 Stanhope 190
20 Munster in PS i 145–6
21 Leith Hay i 159–60
22 Beamish i 213. Narrative of Capt von Linsingen
23 Bessborough 188. F. Ponsonby's letter of 3 September 1809
24 JN vi 284. JN to N, 29 July 1809
25 Simmons 22. Diary for 30 July 1809
26 Burgoyne i 50
27 WD iv 430. W to Castlereagh, 17 June 1809
28 Leach 93
29 SD vi 364. Gauntlett to Sherbrooke, 15 September 1809
30 WD iv 524. W to Frere, 25 July 1809
31 WD v 94. W to Beresford, 30 August 1809
32 ———   403. W to Villiers, 2 January 1810
33 SD vi 343. W to Burghersh, 1 September 1809
34 WD v 108. W to Ld Wellesley, 1 September 1809
35 ———   150. W to Roche, 14 September 1809
36 ———   335. W to Frere, 6 December 1809
37 SD xiii 376. W to Richmond, 28 November 1809
38 WD v 235. W to Fletcher, 20 October 1809

8 *Andalusia and the Siege of Cadiz* (*pp 117–29*)

1   JN vii 107. JN to N, 3 December 1809
2   NC xviii 14684. N to JN, 11 January 1809
3   JN vii 199. Soult to Berthier, 11 January 1810
4   ———   238. JN to N, 27 January 1810
5   MM ii 385
6   MM ii 387
7   JN vii 249. JN to N, 2 February 1810
8   ———   259.   „   18 February 1810
9   Fée 135
10 Swabey 174. Diary for 26 May 1813
11 Quoted in Brett James 200
12 Blakeney 187
13 Barnard. Letter of 8 March 1811. JAHR No 191, p 134
14 Gough i 53
15 WD vii 396. W to Graham, 25 March 1811
16 JN vii 306. JN to N, 8 August 1810
17 Bigarré 280
18 NC xx 16192. N to Berthier 31 January 1810

19 —— 16031
20 WD iv 261. Memorandum on Defence of Portugal, 7 December 1809
21 NC xx 16504. N to Berthier, 27 May 1810

9 *The Third French Invasion of Portugal* (*pp 130–48*)
1 Hulot. Reminiscences 303. Quoted in Oman iii 208
2 W to C. Stewart, 28 February 1810. Quoted in Maxwell i 186
3 NC xx 16519. N to Berthier, 29 May 1810
4 WD vi 189. W to Craufurd, 12 June 1810
5 Picton i 273
6 C. Napier i 138. Journal for 24 July 1810
7 WD vi 454. W to C. Stuart, 18 September 1810
8 —— 461. Massena to Berthier, 22 September 1810
9 —— 460. W to Cotton, 21 September 1810
10 Whinyates. Letter of 20 October 1810
11 Grattan 33
12 —— 35–40
13 Foy 104
14 G. Napier 124
15 Whinyates. Letters of 20 October 1810 and 2 September 1811
16 SD vi 607. W to W. Wellesley Pole, 4 October 1810
17 Schaumann 255
18 Kincaid 17
19 Massena to Berthier, 22 November 1810. Quoted in Foy 343
20 SD vi 612. W to Arbuthnot, 5 October 1810
21 Stanhope MS. Quoted in Fortescue vii 547
22 NC xx 16732. Berthier to Massena, 29 July 1810
23 NC xxi 17131. N to Berthier, 14 November 1810
24 JN vii 449. Soult to Berthier, 22 January 1811
25 Pakenham. Letter of 20 March 1811
26 WD vii 503. W to Beresford, 24 April 1811
27 Records of 43 LI 146. Account of Hopkins
28 Random Shots 167
29 Sergeant 126
30 Ross. Letter of 8 April 1811
31 Random Shots 169
32 Picton ii 8
33 Grattan 62
34 WD vii 445. W to Liverpool, 9 April 1811

10 *The Watershed* (*pp 149–70*)
1 Stanhope 163
2 WD vii 515. W to Liverpool, 1 May 1811

N

3　Marbot ii 457
4　Larpent 65
5　Simmons 169
6　RUSIJ 1912–13, 'Peninsular Recollections of Cornet Hall'
7　Simmons 169
8　Napier iii 153
9　Simmons 181
10　Grattan 67
11　Ibid
12　Ibid
13　Costello 69
14　SD vii 176. W to W. Wellesley Pole
15　Larpent 65
16　WD vii 565. W to Liverpool, 5 May 1811
17　SD vii 123. W to W. Wellesley Pole, 15 May 1811
18　WD vii 490. Memorandum for Beresford, 23 April 1811
19　SD vii 126. Beresford to W, 15 May 1811
20　D'Urban to Taylor. Quoted in Oman iv 372
21　Napier iii 164
22　SD xiii 651. Soult to Berthier, 21 May 1811
23　Strictures 227
24　Napier vi 314. Note by Hardinge
25　SD vii 494. W to Torrens, 6 December 1812
26　Colborne 159. Account by Clarke (66th Foot)
27　Leslie 222
28　PS ii 358
29　PS ii 327
30　SD xiii 651. Soult to Berthier, 21 May 1811
31　Croker iii 275
32　SD xiii 651. Soult to Berthier, 21 May 1811
33　Cooper 64
34　Napier iii 170
35　Blakeney (2/7th Foot). Quoted in Oman iv 392
36　Napier iii 170
37　Cooper 65
38　PS ii 359
39　SD xiii 653. Soult to Berthier, 21 May 1811
40　Return given in Oman iv 635
41　SD vii 135. W to Cooke, 23 May 1811
42　SD xiii 659. Bessières to Berthier, 6 June 1811
43　NC xxii 17752. N to Berthier, 27 May 1811
44　———　17813. Speech of 16 June 1811
45　MM ii 511
46　WD vii 622. W to H. Wellesley, 29 May 1811

47 SD vii 176. W to W. Wellesley Pole, 2 July 1811
48 WD viii 94. W to Liverpool, 11 July 1811

11 *The Fortresses* (*173–87*)
 1 WD viii 118. W to Liverpool, 18 July 1811
 2 ——   121. Memorandum for Cols Framingham and Fletcher, 19 July 1811
 3 ——   232. W to Liverpool, 27 August 1811
 4 ——   258.   „   4 September 1811
 5 Grattan 116
 6 Graham 599. Letter of 1 October 1811
 7 SD vii 228. W to Liverpool, 9 October 1811
 8 Berthier to Marmont, 18 September 1811. Quoted in Oman iv 590
 9 WD viii 482. W to Hill, 24 December 1811
10 ——   519. Memorandum of Operations in 1811, 28 December 1811
11 Grattan 134
12 Jones Sieges i 96
13 Marmont iv 272. Berthier to Marmont, 13 December 1811
14 ——   286. Dorsenne to Marmont, 5 January 1812
15 SD xiv 9. Marmont to Berthier, 18 January 1812
16 Grattan 142
17 Costello 76
18 G. Napier 181
19 Grattan 166
20 NC xxiii 18496. Berthier to Marmont, 11 February 1812
21 Marmont iv 341 and 345. Marmont to Berthier, 26 February 1812
22 ——   335. Berthier to Marmont, 21 February 1812
23 JN viii 353. Soult to Berthier, 8 September 1812
24 Burgoyne i 135
25 Cooke i 144
26 Simmons 228
27 Smith 64
28 Simmons 229
29 Kincaid 133
30 McGrigor 272–3
31 Asst Engineer 46
32 Leith Hay i 296
33 Henry i 64
34 Napier iv 450, Account of Lieut E. P. Hopkins, 4th Foot
35 Bell i 123
36 Napier iv 123
37 W to Liverpool, 6 April 1812. Quoted in Oman v 255

12 *Salamanca (pp 188–205)*
1   SD vii 338. W to H. Wellesley, 28 May 1812
2   MM i 187
3   NC xxiii 18583. N to Berthier, 16 March 1812
4   Jourdan 395. Clarke to Berthier, 9 May 1812
5   Rapp 145
6   Jourdan 392. Memorandum of 28 May 1812
7   JN ix 34. Deprez to JN, 13 June 1812
8   WD ix 170. W to Liverpool, 26 May 1812
9   Ibid
10 WD ix 236. W to Graham, 14 June 1812
11 ——— 284. W to Bathurst, 14 June 1812
12 Marmont iv 122. Jourdan to Marmont, 30 June 1812
13 Napier iv 256
14 Simmons 241
15 WD ix 296. W to Bathurst, 21 June 1812
16 Marmont iv 136. Marmont to Berthier, 31 July 1812
17 Foy 173
18 WD ix 297. W to Bathurst, 21 July 1812
19 Croker ii 120. Alava's account
20 Grattan 242
21 Leith Hay ii 55
22 Grattan 245
23 Leith Hay ii 57
24 Napier iv 270
25 Bragge 64
26 Ross Lewin ii 25
27 WN i 101 and Napier iv 299
28 Ross 31
29 WD ix 310. W to Graham, 25 July 1812
30 SD vii 401. Liverpool to W, 19 August 1812
31 ——— 422. Sydenham to H. Wellesley, 12 September 1812

13 *Madrid and Burgos (pp 206–12)*
1   Leveson Gore ii 455. Letter of Lt-Col the Hon F. Ponsonby
2   Gomm 281
3   SD vii 384. W to Malcolm, 17 August 1812
4   WD ix 370. W to Bathurst, 18 August 1812
5   JN ix 64. Clausel to Clarke, 29 July 1812
6   ——— 58. Marmont to JN, 25 July 1812
7   ——— 55. Clausel to JN, 25 July 1812
8   ——— 60. JN to Soult, 29 July 1812
9   ——— 65. Soult to JN, 12 August 1812
10 Hugo ii 97

11 SD vii 477. W to E. Cooke, 25 November 1812
12 DMSS 742. Robe to Dickson, 18 September 1812
13 Ellesmere 146
14 WD ix 443. W to Bathurst, 21 September 1812
15 ——— 469. W to Hill, 5 October 1812
16 JN ix 68. Soult to Clarke, 12 August 1812
17 ——— 86. JN to N, 9 September 1812
18 Jourdan 436
19 SD vii 477. W to E. Cooke, 25 November 1812
20 Ellesmere 143
21 JN ix 94. N to Clarke, 19 October 1812

14 *Retreat lo Portugal* (*213–22*)
 1 WD ix 526. W to Bathurst, 31 October 1812
 2 ——— 514.   „   26 October 1812
 3 SD vii 438. W to E. Cooke, 25 November 1812
 4 WD ix 514. W to Bathurst, 26 October 1812
 5 ——— 512. W to Hill, 22 October 1812
 6 ——— 515. W to Bathurst, 26 October 1812
 7 SD vii 464. Sydenham to H. Wellesley, 26 October 1812
 8 Malmesbury ii 326. Bowles' letter of 8 December 1812
 9 WD ix 518. W to Hill, 27 October 1812
10 ——— 530. W to H. Wellesley, 1 November 1812
11 Cooke i 228
12 MM ii 575
13 JN ix 119. JN to Clarke, 28 November 1812
14 Ibid
15 Jourdan 444
16 Foy 142
17 Donaldson 181
18 Cooke i 233
19 Bunbury 167
20 SD vii 494. W to Torrens, 6 December 1812
21 Greville iv 142
22 Gomm 290. Letter of 20 November 1812
23 WN i 111
24 Return of 29 Nov 1812
25 WN i 123. Letter of 1 December 1812
26 WN i 124
27 WD ix 573. W to Liverpool, 23 Nov 1812
28 Foy 178

15 *Across the Ebro* (*225–34*)
 1 Hortense II 152

2 JN ix 180. Deprez to JN, 3 January 1813
3 NC xxiv 19411. N to Clarke, 3 January 1813
4 JN ix 220. Clarke to JN, 16 March 1813
5 —— 274. Jourdan to Clarke, 16 May 1813
6 —— 290. Clarke to Jourdan, 7 July 1813
7 WD x 400. W to Bathurst, 25 May 1813
8 —— 372.   ,,   11 May 1813
9 WD ix 617. W to Beresford, 10 December 1812
10 WD x 104. W to Bathurst, 10 February 1813
11 —— 334. W to Martin, 28 April 1813
12 JN ix 280. JN to Clausel, 27 May 1813
13 Bragge 98. Letter of 23 May 1813
14 Larpent 129. Letter of 3 June 1813
15 Wheeler 112. Letter of 1 June 1813
16 Jourdan 466
17 MM ii 598
18 WD x 429. W to Bourke, 10 June 1813
19 Croker ii 308
20 Leith Hay ii 176
21 Blakiston ii 193
22 WD x 436. W to Bathurst, 13 June 1813
23 Leith Hay ii 178
24 Ross 39. Letter of 20 June 1813

16 *Vitoria (235–46)*
1 MM ii 598
2 Ibid
3 SD xiv 238. Gazan's report
4 Cooke i 263
5 SD xiv 238. Gazan's report
6 Costello 126
7 WD x 530. W to Picton, 16 July 1813
8 Leith Hay ii 203
9 Blakiston ii 216
10 Cooke i 272
11 WD x 473. W to Bathurst, 29 June 1813
12 Long 275. Letter of 23 June 1813
13 MM ii 610
14 WD x 532. Prince Regent to W, 3 July 1813
15 JN ix 343. JN to Julie, 1 July 1813
16 Castlereagh ix 22. C. Stewart's letter of 6 June 1813
17 SD viii 50. Liverpool to W, 3 July 1813
18 —— 64.   ,,   7 July 1813
19 —— 132. Nugent to W, 27 July 1813

20 LIN ii 254. N to JN, 1 July 1813
21 ——— 272. N to Savary, 20 July 1813
22 ——— 271. N to Cambacères, 20 July 1813
23 ——— 277. N to Clarke, 1 August 1813

17 *San Sebastian and the Pyrenees* (*pp 247–64*)
1 NC xxv 20208. N to Soult, 1 July 1813
2 WD x 524. W to Bathurst, 2 July 1813
3 ——— 527. W to Hill, 14 July 1813
4 ——— 563. W to Graham, 24 July 1813, '¼ before 12 a.m.'
5 Larpent 200. Letter of 25 July 1813
6 WD x 566. W to Graham, 25 July 1813
7 ——— 596. W to Bathurst, 4 August 1813
8 Sherer 351
9 Bell i 103
10 SD viii 127. Cole to W, 27 July 1813
11 ——— 114. Murray to Cole, 24 July 1813
12 Larpent 242, Letter of 24 August 1813
13 Ibid
14 SD viii 125. Cole to Murray, 26 July 1813 (misdated as 27 July)
15 SD xiv 259. Murray to Picton, 26 July 1813
16 Larpent 242. Letter of 24 August 1813
17 Napier v 227
18 Smyth 396. Bainbrigge's account
19 Lemonnier-Delafosse. Quoted in Oman iv 663
20 Cooper 98
21 WD x 582. W to Bathurst, 1 August 1813
22 ——— 602. W to Bentinck, 5 August 1813
23 Foy 224
24 Cooke i 317
25 WD x 614. W to Bathurst, 8 August 1813
26 Jones History ii 169
27 Jones Sieges ii 17
28 SD viii 147. Melville to W, 28 July 1813
29 Jones Sieges ii 59
30 Leith Memoir 141
31 Jones Sieges ii 75
32 DMSS 997. Dickson to Macleod, 1 September 1813
33 WN i 267. Account of Col Hunt
34 WD xi 62. Graham to W, 1 September 1813
35 Napier v 275
36 WD xi 63. Graham to W, 1 September 1813
37 WN i 267. Account of Col Hunt
38 Gleig 55

39 Gomm 319. Letter of 5 September 1813
40 SD viii 22. Freyre to W, 2 September 1813
41 Frazer 278. Letter of 3 October 1813
42 Bunbury 116
43 Surtees 236
44 Smith 123
45 Ibid

18 *British Operations on the East Coast of Spain, 1812–1813*
(*pp 267–75*)
  1   NC xx 16275. N to Clarke, 21 February 1810
  2   JN ix 285. JN to Clarke, 5 June 1813
  3   Napier i 57
  4   Bigarré 293
  5   Greville iii 346
  6   SD vii 296. Bentinck to W, 23 February 1812
  7   WD x 616. W to Torrens, 8 August 1813
  8   SD vii 467. J. Murray to W, 7 June 1813
  9   J. Murray to Copons, 11 June 1813. Quoted in Fortescue ix 60
 10   Murray Court Martial 78
 11   Ibid
 12   Ibid 556
 13   Ibid 554

19 *Across the Pyrenees (pp 279–93)*
  1   WD x 639. W to Bathurst, 14 August 1813
  2   WD xi 124.   „   19 September 1813
  3   SD viii 219. Bentinck to W, 1 September 1813
  4   WD xi 161. W to Graham, 5 October 1813
  5   ——— 124. W to Bathurst, 19 September 1813
  6   Gleig 94
  7   Wheatley 3
  8   Malcolm. Quoted in Beatson 73
  9   Ibid
 10   Wheatley 4
 11   Ibid
 12   Cooke ii 25
 13   Smith 134
 14   WD xi 178. W to Bathurst, 9 October 1813
 15   ——— 170. W to Hope, 8 October 1813
 16   ——— 170. GO of 8 October 1813
 17   ——— 306. W to Bathurst, 21 November 1813
 18   Stepney 76
 19   Soult to Clarke, 18 October 1813. Quoted in VdeB i 516

20 Soult to Clarke, 26 October 1813. Quoted in VdeB i 516
21 Balthazar to Clarke, 8 October 1813. Quoted in VdeB i 512
22 Villatte to Thouvenot, 7 October 1813. Quoted in VdeB 520
23 Soult to Clarke, 25 October 1813. Quoted in VdeB 332
24 Bell i 118
25 Simmons 319
26 Smith 142
27 D'Urban 312
28 Larpent 296. Letter of 9 Nov 1813
29 Batty. Quoted in Beatson 143
30 Gleig 126
31 WN i 132
32 Leach 347
33 Frazer 335. Letter of 11 November 1813
34 Clausel to Thouvenot, 10 November 1813. Quoted in VdeB i 566
35 Blakeney 318
36 Henry i 178
37 Soult to Clarke, 19 November 1813. Quoted in Beatson 182
38 Bunbury. Quoted in Beatson 173
39 Larpent 229. Letter of 12 November 1813
40 WD xi 287. W to Freyre, 14 November 1813

20 *Nive* (*pp 294–308*)
 1 N to Ferdinand, 12 November 1813. Quoted in VdeB ii 17
 2 NC xxv 21039. N to Melzi, 25 December 1813
 3 WD xi 365. W to Bathurst, 14 December 1813
 4 Frazer 358. Letter of 10 December 1813
 5 Henegan ii 172
 6 Soult to Clarke, 9 December 1813. Quoted in VdeB ii 163
 7 Napier v 394
 8 WD ix 365. W to Bathurst, 14 December 1813
 9 Cooke ii 60–3
10 —— 64
11 Frazer 360. Letter of 10 December 1813
12 Briscall MS. Letter of 10 December 1813
13 Gleig 172
14 Ibid
15 Napier v 394
16 Greville iv 39
17 Stepney 102
18 Frazer 371. Letter of 14 December 1813, 4 am
19 Ibid
20 Bell i 137

21 Henegan ii 174
22 Bell i 137
23 Frazer 370–4. Letter of 14 December 1813, 4 am and 2 pm

21 *The Occupation of Gascony* (*pp 311–25*)
1 Frazer 377–8. Letters of 20 and 23 December 1813
2 WD xi 384. W to Bathurst, 21 December 1813
3 Larpent 343. Letter of 4 January 1814
4 Bell i 142
5 Larpent 333. Letter of 21 December 1813
6 SD viii 510. W to Burghersh, 14 January 1814
7 NC xxv 21135. N to Berthier, 26 January 1814
8 Larpent 381. Letter of 4 February 1814
9 PS ii 155
10 Simmons 336. Diary for 18 February 1814
11 Larpent 398. Letter of 19 February 1814
12 Jones Sieges ii 114
13 WD xi 523. W to Bathurst, 20 February 1814
14 Frazer 415. Letter of 26 February 1814
15 Jones Sieges ii 415
16 SD viii 600. 'Memorandum on the movement of the troops on 27th March'
17 WD xi 536. W to Bathurst, 1 March 1814
18 Colborne 202
19 Larpent 422 and 425. Letters of 5 and 7 March 1814
20 Picton ii 273. Letter of 4 March 1814
21 VdeB ii 243
22 Soult to Clarke, 4 March 1814. Quoted in VdeB ii 384
23 WD xi 519. W to Freyre, 17 February 1814
24 NC xxv 21365. N to Clarke, 25 February 1814
25 WD xi 606 and 604. W to Hope, 26 March 1814, and to Bathurst, 25 March 1814

22 *Victory* (*pp 326–35*)
1 SD viii 744. Memorandum by Maj-Gen G. Murray
2 Frazer 452. Letter of 5 April 1814, 6 am
3 SD viii 726. W to Hill, 9 April 1814
4 —— 756. Memorandum by W, May 1838
5 —— 736. W to Freyre, 10 April 1814
6 Bell i 165
7 Blakiston ii 359
8 Anton 278
9 Frazer 472. Letter of 13 April 1814
10 Colborne 205

11 SD xiv 468. Soult to Clarke, 11 April 1814
12 Larpent 485. Letter of 13 April 1814
13 Hobhouse ii 190
14 WD xi 631. W to Soult, 12 April 1814

Bibliography

Anton. Anton, James. *Retrospect of a Military Life* (1841)

Asst Engineer. Macarthy, J. *Recollections of the Storming of the Castle of Badajoz* (1836)

Batty. Batty, Robert. *Campaigns in the Western Pyrenees and the South of France* (1823)

Beamish. Beamish, N. Ludlow. *History of the King's German Legion*, 2 vols (1832)

Beatson. Beatson, F. C. *Wellington: the Bidassoa and Nivelle* (1931)

Bell. Bell, George. *Rough Notes of an Old Soldier*, 2 vols (1867)

Bessborough. Bessborough, Earl of, and Oglander, A. (eds). *Lady Bessborough and Her Family Circle* (1940)

Bigarré. *Mémoires du Général Auguste Bigarré, Aide-de-Camp du Roi Joseph* (nd)

Blakeney. Sturgis, J. (ed). *A Boy in the Peninsular War: The Services, Adventures and Experiences of Robert Blakeney* (1899)

Blakiston. Blakiston, John. *Twelve Years Military Adventure*, 2 vols (1840)

Bourrienne. Sanderson, E. (ed and trans). *Memoirs of Napoleon Bonaparte* (1904)

Bragge. Cassels, S. A. C. (ed). *Peninsular Portrait: The Letters of Captain William Bragge* (1963)

Brett James. Brett James, Antony. *General Graham* (1959)

Bunbury. Bunbury, Thomas. *Reminiscences of a Veteran* (1861)

Burgoyne. Wrottesly, George (ed). *The Life and Correspondence of Field Marshal Sir John Burgoyne*, 2 vols (1873)

Cammisc. Webster, Sir Charles (ed). 'Some Letters of the Duke of Wellington to His brother William Wellesley Pole', *Camden Miscellany*, xviii (1948)

Castlereagh. Londonderry, Marquess of (ed). *Correspondence of Viscount Castlereagh* (1851)

Caulaincourt 1812. Hanoteau, J. (ed). *Memoirs of Général de Caulaincourt 1812-1813*, trans Hamish Miles (1935)

Caulaincourt 1814. Hanoteau, J. (ed). *Memoirs of Général de Caulaincourt 1814*, trans George Libraire (1938)

Celer et Audax. Rigaud, Gibbes. *A Sketch of the Services of the 5th Battalion, 60th Regiment (Rifles)* (1879)

Chad. Wellington, 7th Duke of (ed). *The Conversations of the 1st Duke o, Wellington with George William Chad* (1956)

Cintra. *Proceedings upon the Inquiry Relative to the Armistice and Convention Made and Concluded in Portugal in August 1808* (1809)

C. Napier. Napier, William (ed). *Life and Opinions of General Sir Charles Fox Napier*, 4 vols (1857)

Colborne. Smith, C. G. Moore. *Life of Sir John Colborne, Lord Seton* (1903)

Cooke. Cooke, John. *Memoir of the Late War*, 2 vols (1831)

Cooper. Cooper, John Spencer. *Rough Notes of Seven Campaigns*, 2nd ed (1884)

Costello. Costello, Edward. *Adventures of a Soldier*, ed Antony Brett James (1967)

Croker. Jennings, L. W. (ed). *The Croker Papers*, 3 vols (1884)

Dalrymple. Dalrymple, J. A. (ed). *Memoir Written by General Sir Hew Dalrymple Bt* (1830)

DMSS. Leslie, J. H. (ed). *The Dickson Manuscripts. Series C* (1908–9)

Donaldson. Donaldson, Joseph. *Recollections of the Eventful Life of a Soldier*, new ed (1841)

D'Urban. Rousseau, I. J. (ed). *Peninsular Journal of Major-General Sir Benjamin D'Urban* (1830)

Elers. Monson, Lord, and Leveson Gower, George (eds). *Memoirs of George Elers* (1903)

Ellesmere. Ellesmere, Francis, 1st Earl of. *Personal Reminiscences of the Duke of Wellington*, ed Alice, Countess of Suffolk (1904)

Fée. Fée, A. L. A. *Souvenir de la Guerre d'Espagne* (1856)

Fortescue. Fortescue, Sir John. *A History of the British Army*, vols 6–10 (1910–20)

Foy. Girod de l'Ain, M. (ed). *Vie Militaire du Général Foy* (1900)

Frazer. Sabine, E. (ed). *Letters of Sir Augustus Frazer* (1859)

GG. Grandmaison, Geoffroy de. *L'Espagne et Napoléon*, 3 vols (1908–31)

Gleig. Gleig, G. R. *The Subaltern* (1825), ed Ian Robertson (nd)

G. Napier. Napier, W. C. E. (ed). *Early Military Life of Sir George Napier*, 2nd ed (1886)

Gomm. Gomm, F. C. Carr (ed). *Journals of Field Marshal Sir William Gomm* (1881)

Gordon. Wyllie, H. C. (ed). *A Cavalry Officer in the Corruna Campaign: The Journal of Captain Gordon* (1913)

Gough. Rait, Robert S. *Life and Campaigns of Hugh, 1st Viscount Gough*, 2 vols (1903)

Gourgaud. Gillard, Sydney (trans). *The St Helena Journal of General Baron Gourgaud* (1932)

Graham. Delavoye, Alex M. *Life of Thomas Graham, Lord Lyndoch* (1880)

Grattan. Grattan, William. *Adventures in the Connaught Rangers*, ed Sir John Fortescue (1902)

Greville. Reeve, H. (ed). *The Greville Memoirs*, new ed, 8 vols (1896)

Hall. Hall, Basil. *Fragments of Voyages and Travels* (1831)

Harris. Hibbert, Christopher (ed). *The Recollections of Rifleman Harris* (1970)

Henegan. Henegan, Richard. *Seven Years Campaigning*, 2 vols (1846)

Henry. Henry, Walter. *Events of a Military Life*, 2nd ed (1843)

Hill. Sidney, Edward. *Life of Lord Hill* (1845)

Hobhouse. Hobhouse, John Cam. *Recollections of a Long Life*, ed Lady Dorchester, 2 vols (1909)

Hortense. Hanoteau, J. (ed). *Mémoires de la Reine Hortense*, 3 vols (1927)

Hugo. *Mémoires du Général J. L. S. Hugo* (1823)

Hussar. Gleig, G. R. (ed). *The Hussar: The Story of Sergeant Norbert Landsheit* (1837)

JAHR. *Journal of the Society for Army Historical Research*

JN. Ducasse, A. (ed). *Mémoires et Correspondance Politiques et Militaires du Roi Joseph*, 10 vols (1854)

Jones History. Jones, John T. *Account of the War in Spain, Portugal and the South of France*, 2 vols (1821)

Jones Sieges. Jones, John T. *Journal of the Sieges Carried Out by the Army under the Duke of Wellington*, 3rd ed, 3 vols (1846)

Jourdan. Grouchy, Vicomte de (ed). *Mémoires Militaires du Maréchal Jourdan* (1899)

Kincaid. Kincaid, John. *Adventures in the Rifle Brigade* (1830)

Larpent. Larpent, Sir G. (ed). *Private Journal of Judge Advocate Larpent*, 3rd ed (1851)

Leach. Leach, Jonathan. *Rough Notes of the Life of an Old Soldier* (1831)

Lefebvre. Lefebvre, George. *Napoleon*, trans H. J. Stockhold, 2 vols (1969)

Leith Hay. Leith Hay, Andrew. *A Narrative of the Peninsular War*, 2 vols (1834)

Leith Memoir. Leith Hay, Andrew. *Memoirs of the late Lieutenant-General Sir James Leith* (1818)

Leslie. *Military Journal of Colonel Leslie of Balquhain* (1887)

Leveson Gower. Castalia, Countess Granville (ed). *Lord Granville Leveson Gower: Private Correspondence*, 2 vols (1916)

LIN. Lecestre, L. (ed). *Lettres Inédites de Napoleon 1er*, 2 vols (1897)

Londonderry. Stewart, Charles, 3rd Marquess of Londonderry. *Narrative of the Peninsular War 1808-13*, 2nd ed (1828)

Long. McGuffie, T. H. (ed). *Peninsular Cavalry General: The Correspondence of Robert Ballard Long* (1951)

McGrigor. *The Autobiography and Services of Sir James McGrigor* (1861)

Malmesbury. Malmesbury, 3rd Earl of (ed). *Letters of the 1st Earl of Malmesbury, His Family and Friends*, 2 vols (1870)

Marbot. *Mémoires du Général Baron de Marbot*, 3 vols (1892)

Marmont. *Mémoires du Maréchal Marmont, Duc de Raguse*, 5 vols (1857)

Maxwell. Maxwell, Sir Herbert. *Life of Wellington*, 2 vols (1907)

MM. Fleischmann (ed). *Memoirs of Count Miot de Melito*, trans Hoey and Lillie, 2 vols (1881)

Moore. Moore, James. *Narrative of the Campaigns of the British Army in Spain Commanded by Sir John Moore* (1809)

Moore Diary. Maurice, Sir J. F. (ed). *The Diary of Sir John Moore*, 2 vols (1904)

Müffling. Müffling, F. C. E. *Passages from My Life*, trans P. Yorke (1853)

Munster. Munster, Earl of. *Account of the British Campaign of 1809 in Portugal and Spain* (1831)

Murray Court Martial. *The Trial of Lieutenant-General Sir John Murray Bt, by a Court Martial Held at Winchester* (1815)

Napier. Napier, William. *History of the War in the Peninsula and South of France*, cabinet ed, 6 vols (1852)

NC. *Correspondance de Napoleon Ier*, 32 vols (1854–69)

Neale. Neale, Adam, MD. *Letters from Portugal and Spain* (1809)

Oman. Oman, Sir Charles. *History of the Peninsular War*, 7 vols (1902–30)

Pakenham. Longford, Lord (ed). *The Pakenham Letters 1800–1815* (1914)

Patterson. Patterson, John. *Camp and Quarters*, 2 vols (1840)

Picton. Robinson, H. B. *Memoirs of Lieutenant General Sir Thomas Picton*, 2 vols (1835)

PS. Maxwell, W. H. (ed). *Peninsular Sketches by Actors on the Scene*, 2 vols (1845)

Random Shots. Kincaid, John. *Random Shots of a Rifleman*, 2nd ed (1847)

Rapp. *Mémoires du Général Rapp* (1823)

Records of 43 LI. Levinge, R. G. A. *Records of the 43rd (Monmouthshire) Light Infantry* (1868)

RG. Glover, Richard. 'The French Fleet 1807–13. Britain's Problem and Madison's Opportunity', *Journal of Modern History*, vol 39, no 3

Roederer. Vitras, M. (ed). *Autour de Bonaparte: Journal du Comte P. L. Roederer* (1909)

Ross. *Memoir of Sir Hew Dalrymple Ross* (1871)

Ross Lewin. Ross Lewin, H. *Life of a Soldier*, 3 vols (1834)

RUSIJ. *Journal of the Royal United Service Institution*

Schaumann. Schaumann, A. E. F. *On the Road with Wellington*, trans A. M. Ludovic (1924)

SD. Wellington, 2nd Duke of (ed). *Supplementary Despatches and Memoranda of Field Marshal the Duke of Wellington*, 14 vols (1858–72)

Sergeant. *Memoirs of a Sergeant, Late in the 43rd Light Infantry Regiment* (1835)

Sherer. Sherer, G. Moyle. *Recollections of the Peninsula* (1823)

Simmons. Verner, Willoughby (ed). *A British Rifleman: Journals and Correspondence of Major George Simmons* (1899)

Smith. Smith, C. G. Moore (ed). *The Autobiography of Sir Harry Smith* (1901)

Smyth. Smyth, B. *History of the XX Regiment* (1889)

Stanhope. Stanhope, Earl of. *Notes of Conversations with the Duke of Wellington* (1889)

Stepney. Stepney, Stepney Cowell. *Leaves from the Diary of an Officer of the Guards* (1854)

Strictures. Anon. *Strictures on Parts of Colonel Napier's 3rd Volume*, 2nd ed (1835)

Surtees. Surtees, William. *Twenty-Five Years in the Rifle Brigade* (1833)

Swabey. Swabey, William. *Diary of Campaigns in the Peninsula*, ed F. A. Whinyates (1895)

Thiébault. Butler, A. J. (trans). *Memoirs of Baron Thiébault* (1896)

TS. *Journal of TS of the 71st Highland Light Infantry* (1828)

VdeB. La Blanche, Vidal de. *L'Evacuation de l'Espagne et l'Invasion dans le Midi*, 2 vols (1914)

Verner. *Reminiscences of William Verner, 7th Hussars*, Special Publication no 8, Society for Army Historical Research (1965)

Ward. Ward, S. G. P. *Wellington's Headquarters* (1957)

Warre. Warre, William. *Letters from the Peninsula 1808–12*, ed E. Warre (1909)

WD. Gurwood, J. (ed). *The Despatches of Field Marshal the Duke of Wellington*, 12 vols (1834–9)

Wheatley. Hibbert, Christopher (ed). *The Wheatley Diaries* (1964)

Wheeler. Hart, B. H. Liddell (ed). *The Letters of Private Wheeler* (1951)

Whinyates. Whinyates, F. T. (ed). *The Whinyates Family Record*, 2 vols (1894–6)

WN. Bruce, H. A. (ed). *Life of General Sir William Napier*, 2 vols (1864)

WV. Verner, Willoughby. *History and Campaigns of the Rifle Brigade*, 2 vols (1912–19)

Index

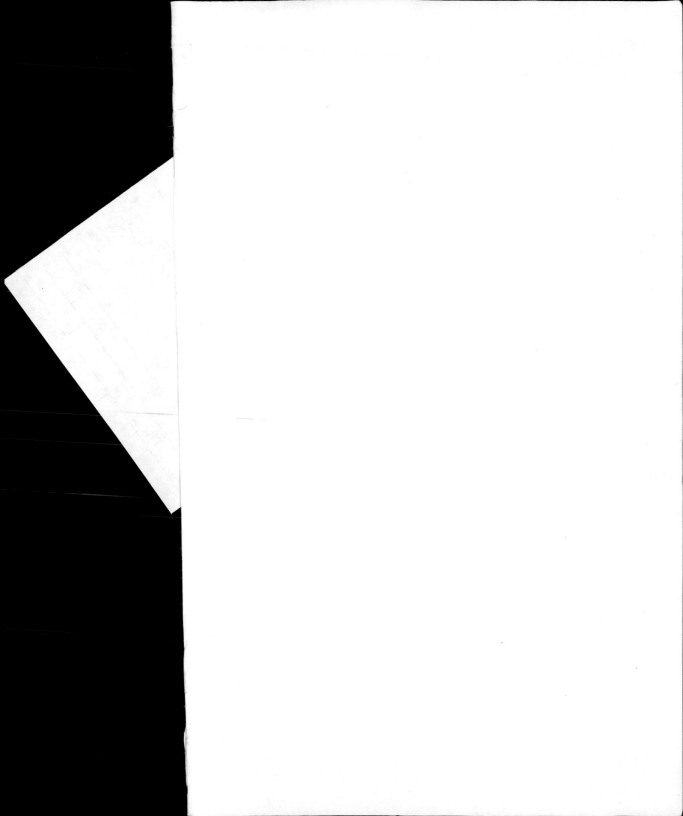

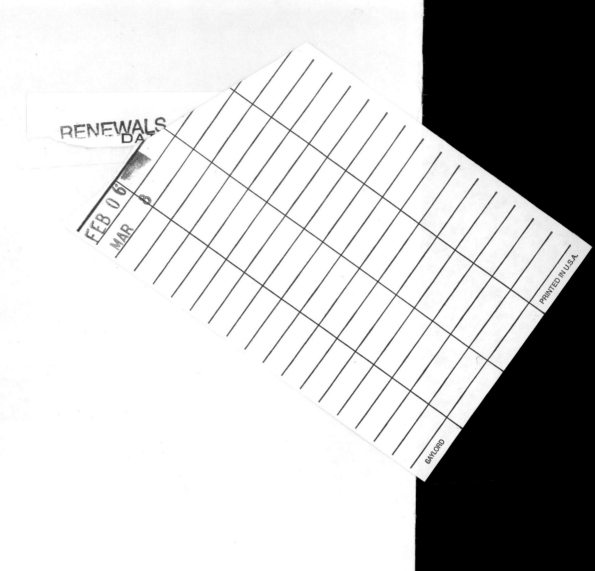

GAYLORD

PRINTED IN U.S.A.